Marching Masters

A NATION DIVIDED:
STUDIES IN THE CIVIL WAR ERA

Orville Vernon Burton and
Elizabeth R. Varon, Editors

MARCHING MASTERS
Slavery, Race, and the Confederate Army during the Civil War

∴

COLIN EDWARD WOODWARD

∴

UNIVERSITY OF VIRGINIA PRESS
CHARLOTTESVILLE AND LONDON

University of Virginia Press
© 2014 by the Rector and Visitors of the University of Virginia
All rights reserved
Printed in the United States of America on acid-free paper

First published 2014
First paperback edition published 2023
ISBN 978-0-8139-4984-0 (paper)

1 3 5 7 9 8 6 4 2

The Library of Congress has cataloged the hardcover edition as follows:

Woodward, Colin Edward, 1975–
Marching masters : slavery, race, and the Confederate army
during the Civil War / Colin Edward Woodward.
pages cm. — (A nation divided : studies in the Civil War era)
Includes bibliographical references and index.
ISBN 978-0-8139-3541-6 (cloth : alk. paper) — ISBN 978-0-8139-3542-3 (e-book)
1. Soldiers—Confederate States of America—Attitudes. 2. Confederate States of America—Military policy. 3. Confederate States of America. Army—Military life. 4. United States—History—Civil War, 1861–1865—African Americans. 5. United States—History—Civil War, 1861–1865—Participation, African American. 6. United States—History—Civil War, 1861–1865—Social aspects. 7. Slavery—Southern States—History—19th century. I. Title.
E607.W66 2014
973.7'42—dc23

2013029859

To my parents

Contents

Acknowledgments ix

Introduction 1

1 • "The Question of Slavery": Confederate Soldiers and the Southern Cause, 1861–1862 11

2 • Planters and Yeomen, Officers and Privates: Race, Class, and Confederate Soldiers 31

3 • The Greatest of Masters: The Confederate Army and the Impressment of Black Labor 55

4 • "Send Me the Negro Boy": Confederate Soldiers and the Need for Slaves in Camp 80

5 • "We Crushed Their Freedom": Emancipation and the Problem of Slave Loyalty 104

6 • On Battlefields and in Prisons: Confederate Soldiers Confront Black Union Troops 130

7 • Free to Fight: The Confederate Army and the Use of Slaves as Soldiers 155

8 • Relics of the Antebellum Era: Confederate Soldiers and the Postwar World 180

Conclusion: "Republics Have Proverbially Short Memories" 203

Notes 211
Bibliography 245
Index 275

Acknowledgments

The writer must write alone but he nevertheless accumulates many debts. This book began in late 2000 as a dissertation at Louisiana State University. At LSU, I want to thank my advisor, Charles Royster, who took me on as a graduate student and nearly saw my dissertation to its conclusion. Illness in the spring of 2005 prevented him from attending my doctoral defense, and I want to thank Bill Cooper not only for seeing the project to its end, but for providing me with valuable advice on proceeding from dissertation to book.

At LSU, Gaines Foster always found the time to provide me with help and advice. I also must thank Mark Thompson and David Culbert for serving on my dissertation committee and giving me valuable feedback. The history department, furthermore, provided me not only with six years of graduate assistantship funding, but also a T. Harry Williams fellowship, which gave me much-needed time to complete the dissertation.

The archivists at Hill Memorial Library saw a lot of me while I was at LSU. Their help, especially that of Mark Martin, was much appreciated during frequent trips to the research room. Rand Dotson at LSU Press took an early interest in my book and assured it was in much better condition than when I first showed him the manuscript. David Gauthier and Keith Finley were good friends during the dissertation process and continued to be so after graduation. Keith read the manuscript in its entirety and gave me compliments at a time when the book project seemed stalled.

The Virginia Historical Society helped me in many ways. A Mellon research grant enabled me to conduct my first archival research outside of Louisiana. The grant gave me access to the VHS's wonderful resources and exceptional staff, and it brought me to Richmond, which I fell in love with instantly. Living in the former Confederate capital helped me better understand the war. Trips to the Byrd, Deep Groove Records, and Scuffletown Park, furthermore, were inspiring.

The VHS employed me as an archivist while I was revising the manu-

ACKNOWLEDGMENTS

script. Nelson Lankford was kind enough to read several chapters of my book and provide feedback and encouragement. A VHS staff fellowship, furthermore, enabled me to visit the archives at Chapel Hill in 2009.

In 2008, I was honored that Duke University awarded me a two-week John Hope Franklin research stipend. My days in Durham allowed me to add much-needed literary color and geographic diversity to my group of Confederate soldiers.

One of my greatest debts is to Aaron Sheehan-Dean, formerly an acquisitions editor at the University of Virginia Press. Back in 2008, I opened my e-mail one morning to find him asking about whether I was interested in sending him my book manuscript. Eventually, I did. And he, more than anyone, is responsible for this book becoming part of the Nation Divided series.

At UVA Press, I wish to thank my editors, Dick Holway and Morgan Myers, for their time and patience, as well as the other staff who contributed. I am also indebted to the outside reviewers who read and commented on the manuscript and recommended it for publication. My copy editor, too, Ruth Steinberg, deserves many thanks.

My greatest debt of all is to my wife, who has been extremely supportive throughout the writing of this book. She endured my many hours of solitary research and slogging through revisions. Her love has made me much stronger than I was before this project began. She also gave me a daughter, who has made my life even better.

This book is dedicated to my parents, who assured that I put a high value on writing, thinking, and the truth.

INTRODUCTION

James Paul Verdery of the Forty-Eighth Georgia Infantry got into position. It was about eight o'clock in the morning on 30 July 1864. He and the rest of the men in Mahone's division could barely load their rifles before the Union forces stormed over their breastworks. The Federals kept charging, but Verdery and his comrades would not retreat in the face of the attacking "Niggers." "As fast as they came over the Bayonet was plunged through their hearts & the muzzle of our guns was put on their temple & their brains blown out," Verdery wrote his sister, describing the infamous Battle of the Crater. Using explosives placed far below the Confederate trenches, Northern forces blew a hole in the Rebel lines 170 feet long, 60 feet wide, and 30 feet deep. "The ground in the center was invisable to the eye owing to the many dead & dying Blacks piled upon one another," Verdery wrote. Once the Rebels stopped the Federals, they crushed the heads of Union wounded with rifle butts. "Well dear Sister," Verdery concluded, "I have witnessed a truly *Bloody Sight a perfect massacre* nearly a Black Flag fight." The Crater battle was not one of the bloodiest engagements of the war, but it was one of the most vicious. The brutality of the fighting had its roots in the long-standing animosity between Southern whites and blacks—the one group fighting for a slaveholding republic, the other for Union and freedom for those still held in bondage.[1]

In a war that erupted over the future of slavery in North America, the Confederate army served as the shield and sword of the peculiar institution. Slavery ended only after four years of bloody conflict in which more than 260,000 white Southern troops died.[2] The war did not end because of Confederates guilt,[3] and it did not end because Southern whites believed human bondage an inefficient and outmoded economic system. Nor did it end because of the passage of the Thirteenth Amendment. Slavery ended because the North defeated a Confederacy that would not abandon human bondage without war.

To understand slavery during the Civil War, historians must explore its role in the lives of Confederate soldiers. This work examines slavery's role in the creation of both Confederate identity and Confederate war strategy. In the first instance, slavery and men's desire to protect a "white man's government" played a central role in the formation of the Confederacy. Southern troops had a complex relationship with slavery, both ideologically and in their day-to-day interactions. On the one hand, slavery was an abstraction, a subject of argument, and one that many Southerners loudly defended against abolitionists. On the other hand, whether or not one was a member of the master class, slavery created intimate, though not necessarily benign, relationships between whites and blacks. In the second instance, that of Confederate war strategy, I show that the Rebel army's reliance upon, and protection of, slavery had a profound effect on military strategy. From the invasion of the border states in 1862 to acquire more slave territory, to the 1862 "Twenty Slave Law," to slave impressment, to the refusal of Confederates to recognize black troops as prisoners of war, the army worked to assure the protection of slavery.

This book adds to the corpus of studies that combine military and social history as a means of understanding Rebel troops. The first scholarly monograph on the Confederate soldier was written by Tennessee-born Bell Wiley. In *The Life of Johnny Reb,* published in 1943, Wiley examined the lives of the Confederacy's "common" troops while placing them in a modern war context. Grunts in World War II could have found much in common with Wiley's soldiers—the long campaigns far from home, bad food, longing for loved ones, and the joys of recreation. *The Life of Johnny Reb,* however, does not focus on Confederates' political convictions, let alone their views on slavery.

Wiley's view of Southern history was not a whitewashed one. His first monograph had been *Southern Negroes, 1861–1865.* But these first two books were as segregated in subject matter as the Jim Crow South in which he lived. Wiley himself was a liberal Democrat who eventually denounced racial injustice, but Wiley's Confederates do not seem to have fought for a nation dedicated to perpetuating slavery. "Yanks and Rebs were far more alike than not," Wiley claimed in a 1971 foreword to *The Life of Johnny Reb.*[4] In contrast to what Wiley wrote, the fundamental difference between "Yanks" and "Rebs" was that Yanks lived in a free North, while Rebs lived in a slaveholding South.

In a field loaded with "top-down" narratives of military campaigns and biographies of politicians and generals, Wiley's work inspired future social historians. But it was not until a generation after his studies of the Civil War appeared that scholars began stressing the importance of politics and ideology in the worldviews of American soldiers. Such works were the product of what has been termed the New Social History of the 1960s and 1970s. Taking their cue from other military historians, scholars of the Civil War unleashed what Joseph Glatthaar has dubbed the New Civil War History.[5] These studies, often at the communal or state level, examined not just "common soldiers," but relationships between soldiers and the societies that produced and supported them. By looking at battles as well as the home front, scholars offered new insights into the Confederate experience.

The New Civil War History made soldiers' motivations often as important as their actions. Yet, even in this period of "New" historical scholarship, Confederate soldiers' views of slavery went mostly unexamined. In *Attack and Die,* an influential and controversial work written in 1982, Grady McWhiney and Perry Jamieson argued that Confederates lost the war because of an ingrained Celtic tradition that was wedded to costly offensive tactics. Such a thesis, regardless of its validity as an explanation for Southern defeat, leaves little room for the importance of slavery in the Confederate war effort. The Celts, after all, never owned four million slaves.

The scholarship on Civil War soldiers that emerged in the 1980s often employed a comparative approach. Gerald Linderman's *Embattled Courage* examined soldiers North and South, concluding that men fought out of a sense of communal pride and pressure. Troops feared that showing cowardice might ruin them in the eyes of their comrades, who usually were from the same state or town, or in the eyes of those at home, who would hear about their conduct on the battlefield. Linderman's work, however, although it provides much insight into soldiers' psyches, does not examine the role of slavery within that mindset.

Soldiers Blue and Gray, written by James Robertson in 1988, is yet another comparative study. In summarizing Southern white men's attitudes as they went to war, Robertson wrote: "Contrary to popular Northern belief, the average Southerner was not fighting for slavery. Owning slaves, and profiting from their labor, were attributes only of the upper classes who constituted a very small percentage of the South's population. Most . . . took musket in hand to defend their homeland."[6] Robertson is correct that most soldiers were not slaveholders, but he neglects to say that hundreds of thousands of masters and men from slave-owning families marched with the Confederate armies.

Another Civil War monograph written in 1988, Reid Mitchell's *Civil War Soldiers,* does addresses slavery in depth, noting that "racism and the fear of insurrection motivated some volunteers" and that "examples of racism and Confederate loyalty are straightforward and easy to understand." Yet Mitchell also warns that racism operated on Confederates in "complicated ways." Despite that warning, *Civil War Soldiers* is more concerned with how Northerners perceived slavery during the war than with how Southerners did.[7]

Despite the rise of the New Military History, studies of great commanders have remained a staple of Civil War scholarship. These works have allowed historians to make generalizations concerning the political relationship between generals and their men. In his 1995 study of Robert E. Lee, Charles Roland cited "letters Confederate soldiers wrote from the battlefield" when he asserted that "Lee was accurate in saying that Southerners had not fought for the purpose of preserving slavery." Roland conceded that a soldier's defense of states' rights, liberty, or family often signified "a defense of slavery too," but he was wrong to say that soldiers did not write about slavery often, or defend it strongly, in their letters home.[8] Roland's comments about Lee's troops highlight the need for more in-depth scholarship concerning how men viewed their place in the war and the world of slavery.

By the 1990s, historians were looking more intently at the political convictions of the "common" Confederate soldier. James McPherson's *What They Fought For* and *For Cause and Comrades* emphasized slavery's vital role in motivating men to go to war. As McPherson depicts them, soldiers were similar in many ways, since they were all Americans, but it was slavery that drove the wedge between North and South. McPherson rejects the notion, put forward by Bell Wiley, that soldiers were not ideologically minded. They were "intensely aware of the issues at stake and passionately concerned about them," argues McPherson. "Men often discussed slavery when articulating why they fought."[9] According to McPherson, Confederates remained mostly proslavery throughout the war, whereas Union troops mostly began the war anti-abolitionist or indifferent to slavery's evils but came to see slavery's destruction as necessary to achieve Union victory.

Scholars do not agree on how slavery affected men's combat motivations. J. Tracy Power has argued that in the last year of the war, Confederate troops "seldom gave much thought to ... the institution of slavery."¹⁰ In *All That Makes a Man,* Stephen Berry makes a similar argument when he says that protecting human bondage did not play a large role in men's view of the Confederate mission—that "slavery could not give him a reason to march." Rather, it was love and personal ambition that motivated Southern elites to defend their honor on the battlefield.¹¹ It is true that men were far more likely to write about bad food, disease, lousy weather, homesickness, and longing for a sweetheart than they were slavery. But to remove slavery from the Confederate mindset depoliticizes the most political of events: warfare. As Clausewitz noted in the early nineteenth century, war is politics by other means. The conflict that erupted over a debate over slavery demands that historians examine how the South continued that debate in wartime.

In contrast to Power and Berry, Chandra Manning's *What This Cruel War Was Over* makes explicit the importance of slavery in the Northern and Southern mindset. For Confederates, "slavery was worth fighting for because it served many fundamentally important purposes that white men considered vital to themselves and their families." Other historians, however, have been more equivocal about using slavery to construct Confederate identity. Jason Phillips notes that the Confederacy's "ethos stemmed from more than slavery." His study, *Diehard Rebels,* emphasizes religion far more than slavery as a central aspect of the Confederate experience. "Many slave owners," he notes, "believed in southern invincibility, but diehards cannot be summarized as planters angered by emancipation. . . . Slave ownership did not predispose a trooper to have an optimistic view of the battles he fought or heard about through the grapevine."¹²

Other scholars have shown that fighting to uphold the Southern racial order went beyond personal slaveholding. "At the core," Glatthaar notes in his study of the Army of Northern Virginia, "virtually all . . . citizen-soldiers shared the same fundamental beliefs in the rightness of secession and slavery." Aaron Sheehan-Dean, in another study of wartime Virginia, has reached a similar conclusion, asserting, "It should come as no surprise that slavery played an important role in motivating men to enlist and serve in Confederate armies." Very often, historians have used the words of Confederates who rushed to recruiting stations in the spring and summer of 1861 as representative of the views of those who enlisted later. But as Kenneth Noe has demonstrated, slavery was "just as important to later enlisters as to the earliest firebrands."¹³

Historians have recently examined slavery's importance in shaping

Confederate ideology, but the subject deserves book-length treatment. The present work builds upon the New Social and New Civil War History by examining how slavery affected privates and officers alike. To create their slaveholding republic, Confederates had to overcome great challenges. Rebels expected that they would triumph, and for a while they believed winning one decisive battle would assure their independence. When that did not happen, and as the war took more lives, destroyed more property, and disrupted more families, they continued to defend human bondage, ideologically and by force of arms. Events show that slavery became more important than ever for men adjusting to the profound changes the war wrought on their society.

This book adds not just to the scholarship of the Civil War soldier, but also to the surprisingly limited number of works that examine slavery within the Confederacy.[14] My examination of thousands of letters by hundreds of soldiers illustrates that even men who were not explicitly proslavery in 1861 feared what abolitionism meant for Southern "rights" and "institutions." When Confederates realized that the war would not end in ninety days, they did not cease talking about slavery. Most did not write extensive proslavery polemics, as John C. Calhoun, Thomas R. Dew, and George Fitzhugh had before them. One can see Confederate soldiers' proslavery convictions in their words, but even more telling were their actions. By "actions," I do not refer simply to combat, though in waging war, Confederates hoped to protect slavery. Rather, these pages explore the many ways Rebels suppported slavery at the individual and group level.

The protection of the institution of slavery also profoundly affected Confederate military policy. In a South that prized individual liberty and states' rights ideology, it was the Confederacy that passed the first conscription law in American history. It was followed six months later by another, which included the infamous "Twenty Slave Law" permitting one white man on every plantation to avoid military service. Most Civil War soldiers were volunteers, but in 1862, the Confederacy realized it needed men to protect its communities from insurrection and invasion. Yet the Confederacy was not content to remain on the defensive when it came to establishing a slaveholding republic. In 1861 and 1862, Southerners hoped to conquer three border states—Missouri, Maryland, and Kentucky—that had enormous resources in men, matériel, and slave wealth. For Confederates to defeat the forces of abolition, it needed to consolidate power, conserve resources, and enlist as many men as possible.

Lincoln's Emancipation Proclamation, issued soon after Lee's retreat from Antietam, further united Confederate soldiers against the Northern war effort. For the rest of the conflict, Southern white men faced the possibility of battling "Negro" troops, and they reserved their greatest wrath for black units at places like Plymouth, Fort Pillow, and the Crater. Rebel armies also served as de facto slave patrols that shot, captured, and punished thousands of runaway slaves and some free blacks. Even very late into the war, Confederate troops continued to believe in ultimate victory—the triumph of their nation and of proslavery ideology.

In undertaking as large a topic as understanding the thoughts and motivations of large armies of men, Civil War scholars endeavor to solve the problem by relying upon what they call a "representative sample" of the sources.[15] James McPherson, for example, used the letters and diaries of 429 Confederates in the research for his book *For Cause and Comrades*. According to McPherson, only 20 percent of the men in his sample "avowed explicit proslavery purposes," but none of them dissented from such views.[16] My study, while addressing proslavery thought, does not quantify racial thinking. Contrary to McPherson's findings, my own research shows that many Confederates expressed views dissenting from strong proslavery convictions. Those who supported black enlistment into the Confederate army, for example, had views at odds with the proslavery status quo, and there were probably thousands of men in Lee's army alone who thought that way. Most Confederates adhered to proslavery principles when the war began, and many, if not most, were still wedded to such ideas when Lee surrendered. Nevertheless, the war led many to change their views on slavery, even if it did not destroy their belief in the inherent inferiority of black people and the notion that African Americans were best kept enslaved.

This book sheds light not only on the Confederate experience, it furthers the study of racial attitudes in the South. By present-day standards, Confederates were virulently racist. Yet, exploring their racism independent of the institution of slavery does little to further our understanding of the Confederate soldier or the nineteenth-century South. Most nineteenth-century white people, North or South, were racist.[17] As cruel and dehumanizing as slavery was, Southern whites could boast of an intimacy with black people that was rare or nonexistent in the North. The relationships that created this intimacy—whether in the case of whites and blacks working alongside each other in the fields or of a planter hiring an African American wet nurse for his children—existed on white people's terms. But proslavery arguments about Northerners' racism and their brutal treatment of free blacks led some Southern whites to think that they had created the best of white-black societies. It is no wonder that they were perplexed and outraged by Northern criticism of their "institutions." For Confederates, it was the North's free soil, free labor, free men ideology that was strange, not slavery—a practice that had existed since time immemorial.

This study is anecdotal in nature. The use of anecdotes to make definitive claims about slavery has its perils, but anecdotes also illustrate, better than most other evidence, the complex, often contradictory nature of the Confederate soldier. Anecdotal evidence, furthermore, shows that similar patterns of thought existed throughout the Southern army. Virginia's Robert E. Lee and Tennessee's Nathan Bedford Forrest were men of very different background and temperament. Even so, they fought for the same cause. Lee was far more diplomatic than the volatile Forrest, and he waged a very different kind of war, but both were unsympathetic toward abolitionists and black Union soldiers. Both men were exemplars of offensive warfare, a strategy that affected not only their battlefield tactics but their attitudes toward slavery. They were shrewd at using impressed black military laborers, and wherever their armies marched, their troops became a threat to the lives and freedom of black people. In 1864, Forrest's soldiers massacred black troops at the infamous battle at Fort Pillow. But it was Lee's forces that unleashed an even greater fury against African Americans at the Crater. As leaders, Lee and Forrest well represented the men who served under them.

One, therefore, can see similar currents of thought in the prosecution of the war in both the Eastern and Western Theatres. In 1863, Confederates in the West were the first to confront black troops in significant numbers, but their reaction to them was similar to that of the men who later battled black troops in the East. East or West, Confederates vowed to show blacks troops no quarter. Nor were the voices urging the enlistment of slaves into the Rebel army isolated to one portion of the Confederacy. In December 1863, Patrick Cleburne of the Army of Tennessee was the first Confederate general to make an extensive case for the enlistment of black troops, a plan never supported by his superiors. But later in the war, in the Army of Northern Virginia, the spirit of Cleburne's proposal lived on. Men engaged in an intense debate about whether or not they should enlist slaves, and with the support of Robert E. Lee, the Confederate Congress adopted the measure.

This study includes not only the words of troops who fought in different theaters of the war, it also endeavors to provide the words of a large cross-section of those troops, from privates to officers, whenever possible. Civil War scholars invariably need to address the biases in surviv-

INTRODUCTION

ing manuscripts, which mostly are from the ranks of the better-educated, more-literate, and economically prosperous officers. Officers were more likely than their subordinates to own slaves. Yet, many slave-owners had little or nothing to say about slavery, while many non-slaveholders did. Nor did a man's rank determine his views toward the institution. Some scholars, such as Chandra Manning and J. Tracy Power, have emphasized the "common" soldier's role in the war. In my own study, such an approach proved impossible, especially with respect to my discussion of the army's policies regarding impressed slaves and its decisions concerning black Union soldiers. Officers, not privates, were the ones who formulated the strategies for winning the war. In this book, therefore, I endeavor to employ a democratic approach to the sources, even if those sources, cumulatively, did not provide a perfect cross-section of Southern white male society.

In contrast to other works on the Confederate soldier, this book uses both wartime and postwar sources in an effort to contrast what men thought during the conflict and what they thought afterward. One must approach all sources with caution, especially those written decades after an event, but comparing wartime and postwar writings reveals that men's perception of slavery changed over time. After the war, former Confederates were far more likely to romanticize the conflict and the institution of slavery, and they mostly rejected the notion that Confederates fought to preserve human bondage.

Whether Confederates wrote during or after the war, it was important to separate the men's rhetoric from the wartime reality. Their views of slavery were important, but that is not to say the perception *was* the reality. Black Southerners' overwhelming preference for the Union over the Confederacy disproved Southern whites' belief in slaves' undying loyalty toward their masters. As delusional as Southern whites might have been concerning the true nature of the master-slave relationship, they acted on the assumptions of proslavery ideology. Proslavery theorists argued that masters had done blacks a favor by enslaving them, as they were deemed inferior in intellect and the "children" of "uncivilized" Africans. Entrenched notions about African Americans led Confederates to express surprise, horror, and betrayal when servants fled. They were even more shocked when many of these same slaves took up arms against them.

Given their fears that defeat would mean the collapse of the racial order, Confederate troops continued to believe slavery was worth defending, and more so, that they *could* defend it. True, tens of thousands of slaves fled their masters, but Confederates could boast of countless slaves engaged in building earthworks, hauling and unloading wagons, serving in hospitals, and cooking and washing in camps. Despite the changes wrought by the war, men did not abandon their proslavery views. They believed that African Americans—whether factory workers in Richmond, field hands in North Carolina, or teamsters in Tennessee—were best kept in bondage. By looking at the Confederate army's attitudes and policies toward enslaved people, we can see how the end of slavery unfolded in the United States. The Union eventually won the war and abolished human bondage, but Confederates did not relinquish slavery quietly.

· 1 ·

"The Question of Slavery"
CONFEDERATE SOLDIERS AND THE
SOUTHERN CAUSE, 1861–1862

By April 1862, most of the men who served in the Confederate army had already enlisted. Others joined later, and still more found themselves drafted, but examining men's words in the first year of the war allows us to understand why they fought for the South. When it came to the "question of slavery," Rebel soldiers expressed proslavery views that included fears of abolitionism and slave revolt, and worries that the North sought to eradicate white Southerners' political power. Men often spoke vaguely of defending their "rights," but they understood that the right to own slaves was one of the most important. White Southerners had argued with Northerners for decades about slavery's future in the United States. Secession and war were the Confederacy's answer to the "question of slavery."

South Carolinians were the first Southerners to find themselves part of a new slaveholding republic. On 20 December 1860, South Carolina's secession convention—in a climax to the state's history as the most radical Southern state—voted unanimously to leave the Union.[1] In what was now the Republic of South Carolina, Confederate soldiers knew how important slavery was. William Grimball, who came from a slaveholding family and served in the First South Carolina Artillery, spoke plainly about why his people chose secession. He said property holders were "united with *few* exceptions in the belief that now a stand must be made for African slavery or it is forever lost." Grimball was equally clear about the stresses that secession placed on his state. He warned his sister that when she returned home, she would find "your father with a loaded pistol, your brothers with loaded pistols." People were armed to "protect themselves and their families from dishonor and death," as well as against the United States sending "incendiaries to stir up the slaves to poison & murder us."[2]

South Carolinians knew that they could not defeat the United States alone. Once South Carolina had become a "sovereign state," wrote John L. Agurs—who served in the Sixth South Carolina Infantry—"evry other slaveholding state should do as S.C. has done." South Carolinians, he believed, had seceded rather than submit to a "Black Republican" president.[3] South Carolina would soon gain allies, but the other cotton states did not secede all at once. And despite Agurs's wish, not every slave state joined the Confederacy. Nevertheless, by the time Lincoln gave his inauguration address, seven states had seceded. In February 1861, in Montgomery, Alabama, the Confederate States drew up a constitution, which gave slavery permanent sanction within its borders and guaranteed slavery's legality in any future state or territory. Although the Confederate Constitution banned the foreign slave trade, the South's blueprint for government laid out a strong, proslavery state apparatus.[4]

Confederates were constructing a new nation that reflected their proslavery principles. For Louisianan William Henry King, secession was a rejection of Northerners' view of the Constitution and what he felt was misguided antislavery feeling. King would have been content with the Constitution and the Union his ancestors had lived under, but, he noted, "our Northern brethren ... were not content with *them,* claiming, when the subject of African servitude as it existed in the Southern States, was under consideration, there was a 'higher law than the Constitution—the law of conscience.'"[5]

Not all Confederates, however, even those from the Deep South, accepted secession unthinkingly or unconditionally. In March 1861, South Carolinian Samuel Elias Mays asked: "What are we fighting for? Why should I take up arms against the Union?" His family's ties to the Union were strong. His father had served in the Indian wars of the 1830s and his grandfather in the Revolution and War of 1812. He came from a slave-owning family, but he was not enthusiastic about disunion. Nevertheless, along with hundreds of thousands of Southerners, he joined the Confederate army.[6] Even if Mays was hesitant about secession, he had direct ties to slavery, ties which undoubtedly affected his decision to join the army.

In 1860 in the South, 384,000 people, roughly 5 percent of the population, owned at least one slave. In the seven original Confederate States, 36.7 percent of households owned slaves, as did 25 percent of households in the states that joined in the spring and summer of 1861.[7] When compared to non-slaveholders who joined the Confederate army, men of the master class were overrepresented. In his research on the Army of Northern Virginia, Joseph Glatthaar has shown that one in ten enlisted men owned slaves (double the percentage of slave owners in the population as a whole), and half of officers did so. A historian of John Bell Hood's Texas Brigade asserted that two-thirds of the officers in that unit were slaveholders. Men's connection to slavery was not limited to personal slave ownership, however. Glatthaar has put the percentage of men who lived in slaveholding families at 36 percent, and if one also considers men's economic ties to slavery, whether through the hiring of slaves or selling goods to planters and other slaveholders, the percentage of men directly engaged in the slave economy rises much higher.[8]

Whether or not men owned African Americans, Confederate soldiers believed that slavery was an economically beneficial, divinely ordained institution that maintained a racially structured social order in the South. The North, with its antislavery Republican Party, threatened their interests. Ferdinand Boesel, who served in the Fourth Texas Cavalry, said the North was fighting not to save the Union, but to free the slaves, "so the blacks can subdue 6 million whites." As did many Confederates, he feared subjugation, and he had little sympathy for the plight of African Americans, claiming they had little to complain about. They had "an easy life compared to a day laborer in Germany," he wrote. Were it not for slaves, "the South would be a desert ... [and] no white man could live there."[9] For him, a South without slavery was a land not worth living in.

Confederate forces fired on Fort Sumter on 12 April 1861, and Virginia seceded five days later. The states of Arkansas, North Carolina, and Tennessee followed soon after (on 6 May, 20 May, and 8 June, respectively). Radical, plantation-heavy South Carolina had been the first state to secede, but tardiness in leaving the Union did not mean that states in the Upper South were not committed to secession and the defense of slavery. In April 1861, Arkansas soldier William Crow said, "The south has not got yet what she seceeded for." In considering what had led to secession, he said, "the first pretent was the loss of slave property."[10] Fears of Republicans limiting or abolishing slavery put men like Crow on the defensive. In April 1861, the South had not yet lost any slaves to Northern decree or seizure, but in Virginia, Pvt. William H. Baxter, who would serve in the Twelfth Virginia, was certain about the wisdom of secession. "The South is right," he wrote, and he believed disunion was the "only alternative."[11]

Secessionists needed the Upper South. Virginia was the largest slave state, both in white and black population, and according to Confederate service records, Virginia sent the most men of any Southern state to the Rebel army.[12] Richmond, which became the Confederate capital, was a major industrial and commercial center. In the antebellum period, it produced a considerable amount of flour, and in wartime, its Tredegar Iron Works made more than half the cannons that would help tear apart the "Yankee invaders." Virginia also had symbolic importance, given its intellectual and military tradition going back to Jefferson and Washington. Virginia, furthermore, was the engine of the domestic slave trade. On average, Virginia plantations were smaller than those of Mississippi or South Carolina, but there were more slaveholders per capita in the "Old Dominion" than in the cotton, rice, and sugar regions of the Deep South. Virginia had nearly half a million slaves in 1860, and every year its people shipped thousands of slaves from pens in Alexandria and Richmond to Deep South plantations.[13]

With strong ties to slavery, Virginians shared the convictions of the Lower South. After the war, Gen. Henry A. Wise—governor of Virginia during John Brown's assault on Harpers Ferry and a major player in Virginia's decision to secede—wrote that with the rise of Northern radicalism, "the fate of the slavery of the colored race was sealed, and it could not secure any guarantees for the future; and if the Constitution could be set aside and violated in respect to the right of slave property, it could be as to any right or possession whatever."[14] Wise accurately summarized the views of Virginia men in 1861. On the day the war began, Georgia officer Henry Constantine Wayne, in words that did not fall on deaf ears, wrote to Jeb Stuart about the need for Virginia and the other slave states to join with the Deep South. The Confederate Constitution, he stated, was the same as the Constitution of 1787, with "some improvements." The new government would exclude the abolitionists, thus removing "all political controversies that tend to sectionalism." In his eyes, Southerners were defending their rights and property, whereas the North had forgotten about questions of "race, intelligence, cultivation, and Government."[15] Virginians could not ignore such calls. In February 1861, John Apperson, who would serve as a surgeon in the Stonewall Brigade, heard a speaker denouncing "Northern aggression" and the violation of Southern principles. He also derided the practice of escaped slaves being "harboured by northern fools." Of the address, Apperson concluded, "I am for him and with him in sentiment."[16]

Another Virginian was more playful when considering secession. Henry K. Ramsey, who would join an artillery unit, cast Virginia in the role of Hamlet. "To submit or not to submit, that is the question," he wrote, wondering "Whether 'tis nobler in the south to suffer/The abuse and slander of a fanatic North/Or to take up arms against a sea of wrongs."

Seceding, Ramsey continued, would end the "calumnies and innumerable abuses/That our institution is the object of." The "fanatic North" meant the forces of abolition, and the "institution" he spoke of was, of course, slavery. Virginia, he concluded, must avoid the "rule of Black Republicans" and becoming a "slave to such a government."[17]

Ramsey had fun with Virginia's dilemma, but his play on Hamlet's soliloquy accurately reflected widespread feeling among Southerners, who believed they must stop the abolitionists before they wrecked slavery and Southern society. In March 1861, John Preston Sheffey, who served as an officer in the Eighth Virginia Cavalry, wrote of the possibility of other states joining the Confederacy. Virginia had not yet seceded, but Sheffey thought reunion impossible. "The mutual hatred of the North & South now is too deep, too irradicable," he asserted. Reunion would prove "too degrading, too disgraceful, to be endured by the proud slaveocracy of the gallant South."[18]

Among non-slaveholders—and in contrast to the cliché of the Civil War being a conflict of brother against brother or father against son—political allegiances were heavily based on close family ties. Charles Trueheart, still studying at the University of Virginia in March 1861, wrote that a comrade's parents were large planters and "very warm Secessionists" who could not bear to live in Virginia if it did not secede. Were Virginia to remain in the Union, they would instead flee to the Deep South, believing it more devoted to slavery and secession.[19] Despite the fears expressed by the parents of Trueheart's friend, when the conflict ended, Virginians could not say that they had not strongly supported slavery and secession.

Carter McKim Louthan, a Virginian who served in the Stonewall Brigade, wrote amid the secession crisis about the rapid turn of events in his native state. Shortly after Lincoln's election, Carter, whose father was a large slaveholder, said he had no sympathy for extremists. But by late January 1861, he expressed concern over Republican antislavery leaders, especially William Seward. Once South Carolina fired on Fort Sumter, Louthan said, "I now want Virginia to secede immediately and to put her unflinching veto upon the policy of coercion." Louthan thought Virginia must defeat tyranny, and he believed men would fight for their altars, firesides, and homes. Virginians could not bear seeing "their sisters of the South invaded by abolition hordes without lending a helping hand."[20]

That "helping hand" proved enormous. The industrial might and large population of Virginia was crucial in enabling the Confederacy to make war. Virginia also produced some of the most gifted generals of the Southern army, including Robert E. Lee, Stonewall Jackson, and Jeb Stuart. But

Virginia's Southern neighbor, North Carolina, also contributed much to the war effort. North Carolina sent 137,000 men to the Southern armies, and later in the war, the port of Wilmington, North Carolina, became the last lifeline of Lee's army.[21] As did soldiers from other states, North Carolinians spoke of fighting for "rights" and "institutions." Common were the words of Pvt. John Pegram of the Twenty-Second North Carolina, who said he would like to stay home but thought it better to fight for his rights, property, children, and friends. Fighting for "rights," "property," and "liberty" usually served as euphemisms for defending slavery. In April 1861, before North Carolina had seceded from the Union, John R. Lowrey, who served in the North Carolina Camp Guards, was ready to fight the "abominable rebels & abolitions, who are trying to deprive us of our liberties."[22]

White Southerners hotly debated secession, not just in the Upper South states of Virginia and North Carolina, but also in the border states of Missouri, Kentucky, and Maryland, where approximately 500,000 slaves lived in 1860. The border states ultimately did not join the Confederacy, but they sent thousands of troops to Rebel camps. In 1861, M. Jeff Thompson, a Virginia-born partisan who earned the nickname "Swamp Fox of the Confederacy," discussed slavery, the "one great question now before the American people." Thompson was rare among Confederate soldiers in making specific reference to how proslavery theory affected his own ideas. In his memoirs, he noted that his thoughts after Lincoln's election were influenced by Edmund Ruffin's 1859 writings on race. Indeed, in the year leading up to John Brown's raid, Ruffin had written several articles in the proslavery magazine *De Bow's Review* warning that emancipation would destroy the white and black races.[23]

Shortly after Lincoln's election, Thompson addressed his fellow Missourians. He ably summarized the tenets of the proslavery argument and the Confederate mission. He agreed with William Seward, who believed in an "irrepressible conflict," but Thompson's politics were very different from Seward's. He warned listeners that Northerners were preaching abolition from "a thousand pulpits" and legislature halls. Thompson did not want Southerners to remain passive in the face of Northerners who had "kindled the torch of a servile insurrection." Rather, he urged Southerners to stand up immediately and demand their rights. He did not want to debate the morality of slavery, but his address put slavery in a positive light. Thompson declared that Southern whites had a duty to keep mentally inferior black people in bondage. What choice did whites have but to "provide for [slaves'] comfort and happiness," he asked. As slaves, black people contributed to the "power, glory, comfort and wealth of not only our nation, but of the world." Concerning Northern antislavery efforts, he would not yield to "blind and wicked fanaticism."[24]

Thompson's words added to widespread fears of slave revolts breaking out in the South after Lincoln's election. In the midst of the secession crisis, slaves did not flee or rebel violently against their masters in great numbers. Only after the Federals began penetrating the South did slaves resist their masters' authority in unprecedented numbers. Before then, however, in 1860, from Texas to Georgia, nervous whites feared that slaves were plotting against them.[25] As usual, white Southerners hoped violence would prove the best means of asserting racial control. In March 1861, Frank Voss, a Marylander who would soon join the Confederate infantry, wrote in Virginia of a rumored slave insurrection. Armed with a six-shooter, he said he was ready to "kill every *Nigger* I meet."[26]

In the summer of 1861, in Adams County, Mississippi, near Natchez, whites uncovered a plot that might have been on the scale of the Turner Revolt or the Denmark Vesey Conspiracy. Whether the planned uprising was a widespread threat, whites crushed it, though they left little record of what occurred.[27] Months after the plot's discovery, masters were still punishing slaves. "I sincerely hope that the insurrection has been effectively put down," wrote William H. Ker to his sister in the fall of 1861. Ker, serving in a Mississippi cavalry unit, said the failed rebellion should serve as a lesson to people in Natchez, whose servants, he believed, had too much freedom. In Ker's opinion, his family's slaves were much better behaved, though he doubted whether they were entirely faithful. "Thank God that none of *ours* have been implicated in this sad affair," he said. Writing from camp in Virginia, Ker was happy to hear that whites had swiftly punished the guilty, or as he put it, that "the last of the wretches have been hung."[28]

Whether in the Upcountry or Lowcountry, Upper South or Lower, Confederates feared not just a black uprising, but a slave insurrection led by white men. John Brown's failed plot in 1859 had led to heightened anxieties of another black-white rebellion. Whites usually considered their own slaves loyal and their white neighbors firmly anti-abolitionist, but they believed antislavery forces had a shadowy character.[29] Northerners, they worried, would incite blacks, turning the home front into a bloody carnival. In June 1861, John David Workman, who was at seminary but would soon join the Ninth Louisiana, anticipated revolt in a "great many places" in Louisiana. Workman wrote of an aborted insurrection in St. Martin's Parish in which authorities had arrested forty slaves. That two white men had led the uprising troubled him even more. Confederates hanged one of the men, but the other escaped. In August 1861, another soldier wrote of unrest in Jefferson County, Alabama, in which "400 negroes was to rise in rebellion against the white people & kill them all." The slaves apparently had the help of sympathetic whites. Nothing came of the plot, but he worried that because he lived in mountainous country, slaves were more difficult to monitor.[30] That same month, North Carolina soldier Charles Liebermann described a suspicious Southerner who tried to talk blacks into rebelling. "Death will be his doom," he warned, if the man were guilty of such actions.[31]

One intense fear among Confederate soldiers was the possible violation of Southern white women. In May 1861, one soldier wrote from Ringgold, Georgia, where he had heard about the hanging of white and black conspirators. The guilty men had "even selected whom they would make their wives among the young ladies."[32] In September 1861, John J. Good, a Texan, wrote of a camp slave who was executed for assaulting a white woman. A jury of local citizens, which he dubiously described as "impartial," had tried the slave and the convicted man had confessed under the gallows.[33] One can doubt whether "justice" was indeed handed out or whether the confession was coerced. What is more important is that once the war began, Confederates were more concerned than ever about the loss of racial control threatening the safety of their white families and communities.

Confederate troops' fear of slave unrest was one aspect of Southern white racial attitudes that shaped their political, religious, and social outlook. In looking at soldiers' letters and diaries, one does not find proslavery thinking on a par with the writings of John C. Calhoun or James Henry Hammond. Nor does one find ideas similar to those of George Fitzhugh, who, as C. Vann Woodward has pointed out, lambasted any society that supported free labor, suggesting that even white people were suited for slavery.[34] Soldiers rarely engaged in such detailed arguments about slavery, but their thoughts on the institution reveal that these men, even if they were not slaveholders themselves, believed that owning blacks was the birthright of all white men.

In attempting to categorize Southerners' complicated, often paradoxical views of slavery and race, historians have categorized their attitudes toward human bondage as either a "necessary evil" or a "positive good." In the former, which is epitomized by Thomas Jefferson, slavery was cast as a burden. Jefferson compared slavery to holding a wolf by the ears: you did not like it, but you dared not let it go. He believed that, over time, slavery would die off, and that white Southerners should control the pace of emancipation. Some former Confederates, from Pvt. William Fletcher to Gen. Robert E. Lee, believed slavery would have died out had the North left it alone.[35] Although some men considered slavery a "necessary evil," many of those who welcomed its demise usually did so after the Confederacy's defeat, not while it still had substantial military power. In the same way as Thomas Jefferson, ex-soldiers qualified their laments about slavery to the point of meaninglessness. Jefferson did not believe that black people were the intellectual equals of whites, and he freed only a few of his 200 slaves upon his death. Jefferson claimed to dislike slavery, but he made no effort to eradicate it in the South. Confederate soldiers would also have preferred to delay emancipation indefinitely. Richard Maury, the son of Gen. Dabney Maury, a Virginian who served in the Western Theater, wrote about his father, saying in regards to slavery that Virginians were in "no manner responsible." Even so, Maury considered the institution "the happiest and best for the negro," though not necessarily for the master. Summarizing his father's views toward extinguishing slavery, he asserted, "I think [he] favoured gradual, very gradual emancipation." Gradual, indeed. For generations, Southerners had said they wanted to control when and how they would destroy slavery, and they did not want its abolition as long as they lived.[36]

One of the most influential aspects of the proslavery argument was its religious foundation. Far more Confederate soldiers heard ministers preach proslavery ideas from their pulpits than ever read the writings of Calhoun, Hammond, Dew, or Fitzhugh. Other men, in the Protestant tradition, read and interpreted the Bible for themselves. Alfred Ringgold Gibbons, from Georgia, remembered reading his Bible while a prisoner of war, "not so much that I might become more righteous but . . . in order that I might be well versed on the question of slavery."[37] In using the Bible to justify their proslavery position, Southern whites often cited the Israelite's practice of enslaving their enemies. They also claimed that black people had the mark of "Ham" (even though the Bible makes no explicit reference to Ham being black), as an explanation for why African Americans were only fit for slavery. If they used the New Testament for their justifications, they quoted Paul's words, "Servants obey in all things your masters," and argued that because Jesus never denounced slavery, he had given tacit approval of it.[38]

Southern preachers staunchly defended slavery and the Confederate cause. In 1861, James Sinclair, a North Carolina clergyman who volunteered for the army, urged Confederates to show the "fanatics" of the

North that "we have not followed cunningly devised fables, [and] that [we] have taught our people certain principles and doctrines in relation to the institution of Slavery." After years of preaching the righteousness of human bondage, he said, "we are now prepared with our lives and fortunes to endorse the same."[39] The North and South both claimed to have God's blessing, but Confederates, acting on the idea that the Bible supported human bondage, believed they were "in the right." Misguided Northern Congressmen, said a Confederate chaplain, were in favor of an "anti-slavery Constitution, an anti-slavery Bible, and an anti-slavery God!!" To remedy such a situation, he believed, Southerners must rely on "the God of Battles."[40]

In wartime, Southern camps were the scene of various revivals, especially as Confederate fortunes worsened after the defeats of summer and fall 1863. Confederates, however, did not want to see slave religion altered in a way that challenged white authority. In addition to thinking they were saving the souls of their slaves, white Southerners believed religion to be an invaluable form of social control. Blacks could worship, as long as it was under the supervision of the master class, and Confederates hoped biblical teachings would instill docility rather than rebelliousness. In May 1862, John Wightman, the pastor of Trinity Church in Charleston, wrote to John C. Pemberton, asking that the army not interfere with the practice of religion among blacks. Wightman expressed the prevailing proslavery view of most Southern clergy. "I am convinced that religion creates the strongest tie between servant and master," he said, "and that the ministry thereby constitute the strongest police of municipal and of domestic order." As long as Southerners maintained a proslavery faith, he could "expect to check insubordination" among blacks. Otherwise, events might stir slaves with "false hopes of liberation . . . to congregate in idleness, or to seek employment in villainy."[41] For Confederates, Christianity was a path to spiritual freedom, but it should not prove so liberating as to make servants leave their masters. After all, they claimed to have had slaves' best interests at heart, and they wanted the military to make sure their version of religion endured.

Most Confederate troops did not express biblical justifications for slavery, but they heard others preach them. In 1862, Bishop Stephen Elliott, a South Carolina–born Georgian who became the only Confederate bishop of the Protestant Episcopal Church, preached on the "dominant race" and the "subject race." Elliott reminded his countrymen that, for generations, Christians of the "dominant race" had led Africans to "culture," "elevation," and "salvation."[42] Indeed, Confederates believed whites had been given a special mission in bringing black people across the Atlantic to America, where most Africans had become Christians. For Elliott and others, the Christian South must use its churches and religious teachings to maintain slavery.

Some Confederates, regardless of their proslavery views, were willing to let God decide whether or not human bondage should survive. In 1861, Lt. William Cowper Nelson, of Mississippi, wrote about hearing a sermon that closed with these words from Psalms 34:15–16: "The eyes of the Lord are over the righteous, and his ears are open to their prayers." Nelson did not repeat verse 16 in his letter, which speaks of God turning his face against evildoers, but he said it applied to abolitionists. Nelson had no problems with slavery—during the war, he kept a servant with him in camp—but he speculated on God's role in the conflict, and he was clear about the link between slavery and the meaning of the war: "I have thought that this war was ordered by Providence, as a means of settling definitely and conclusively the question of slavery." If slavery did have divine sanction, he believed, the Confederacy would achieve its independence and have slavery as "its great distinctive feature."[43] Were slavery not good, Nelson thought, God would abolish it in the course of the war. He did not say the South should abolish slavery, but was instead willing to let God decide the issue.

Rather than grapple with the divinely ordained aspects of slavery, Confederates were more likely to write of their immediate fears of abolitionism spreading in the South. From the 1830s onward, Northern abolitionists had become more vocal, and in the generation before the Civil War, the South had engaged in an aggressive campaign to purge itself of any antislavery believers. In response to the bloody 1831 Nat Turner Revolt in Virginia and the increasing visibility of reformers such as William Lloyd Garrison, antislavery societies disappeared or were driven out of existence in the South. Southern legislators tightened slave laws at the local level, and Congress instituted a "gag rule" on slavery debate. Southern states also outlawed the distribution of abolitionist literature. Confederates soldiers were familiar with Garrison's anti-slavery newspaper, the *Liberator*, first published in 1831, and whether or not they themselves were slaveholders, they feared the abolitionists.

Perhaps the most influential abolitionist of the 1850s was Harriet Beecher Stowe, whose novel *Uncle Tom's Cabin,* published in 1852, contributed greatly to the turbulence of that decade. Her book brought the horrors of slavery to millions of Northerners, while at the same time alienating white Southerners, who branded it as merely antislavery propaganda—fiction in more ways than one. Long after the novel's publication, Confederate veterans claimed that it was *Uncle Tom's Cabin* that had caused the war, and they accused Stowe of misrepresenting the South and slavery. Georgia cavalryman A. R. Gibbons recalled that it was during his time as a prisoner of war that he realized how ignorant Northern troops were about slavery. They asked him, much to his dismay, whether black people were "driven up at night and corralled in pens like mules," and he concluded that they could only have come to their "knowledge" of slavery from Stowe's book.[44] The Louisiana memoirist Douglas John Cater agreed about the influence of *Uncle Tom's Cabin,* noting that Stowe's book had "deluged our country in blood."[45] Another postwar writer, James Huffman, who served in the Tenth Virginia Infantry, remembered that fellow troops distributed Northern Sunday School papers among the camp. In them, he saw depictions of masters whipping their slaves, the kinds of "black falsehoods" Stowe had made popular. Her book, Huffman concluded, was pure propaganda.[46]

Other than Harriet Beecher Stowe, the abolitionist Confederates most denounced was John Brown, whose raid on Harpers Ferry had served as a violent conclusion to the troubled 1850s. Brown's mission, to unleash a Southernwide slave revolt, failed, and Virginia authorities hanged him for treason. Some Northerners lauded Brown as a martyr, but Southerners recoiled in horror. The war that erupted roughly a year and a half later, said the surgeon Thomas F. Wood, was "the natural sequence of John Brown's raid."[47] Few Americans ever considered themselves abolitionists, and even fewer of them were as fanatical as Brown, but Confederate troops believed that the clamor created by the antislavery issue gave the South no choice but to secede. Brown's raid seemed evidence of the North's plans to abolish slavery everywhere.

Confederate soldiers were determined not to let that happen. Writing from Harpers Ferry in May 1861, Edward Dorr Tracy, a Georgian who enlisted in an Alabama regiment and who would rise to the rank of general, said of Northern troops, "If any more of the John Brown family should conceive the idea of paying us a visit we will endeavor to give them a warmer reception than the John 1st was treated to."[48] In 1861, for Confederate soldiers, recent events, from Brown's raid to Lincoln's election, only validated their fears of abolitionism. From their point of view, no one could dissuade them from believing that all Yankees were, or would soon become, the enemies of slavery. Confederate soldiers thought they had no choice but to fight.

As Confederate soldiers seized arms in 1861, the very word "abolitionist" became a weapon, similar to when soldiers would shout the names of battles at attacking troops. Calling Northern troops "abolitionists" probably fired up the Southern troops as much as it likely angered the Yankees. Most Northerners were not antislavery when the war began, and would have hated being grouped with the likes of Stowe or Garrison. In 1862, Gen. P. G. T. Beauregard, a southern Louisiana planter, urged that all Confederate documents should refer to the Northern forces as "abolitionists," which he did in his own reports.[49] Rebel soldiers were so virulently anti-abolitionist that they even accused some parts of the Confederacy where support for secession was not that strong, such as eastern Tennessee, of being "abolitionist."[50]

Prominent commanders in the Confederate army were not above manipulating men's fears of abolition and the atrocities that might be committed by slaves. The story of James Longstreet, a Confederate commander born in South Carolina and raised in Alabama, is instructive. During Reconstruction, Longstreet joined the Republican Party. Because of his alliance with the "Party of Lincoln," and the fact that he had criticized Lee's decisions at Gettysburg, he became a pariah in the South. In 1894, he recalled, albeit inaccurately, that when the conflict broke out, most U.S. army officers were pro-Southern. He claimed that they "generally believed that the people of the South had just cause for complaint against the encroachment in respect to their slave property, guaranteed by the supreme law of the land."[51] While many U.S. officers may have sympathized with the South, such sympathy did not necessarily translate into Confederate loyalty. Longstreet was one of a small minority of United States officers who resigned to join the Rebel military.[52]

Longstreet nevertheless was among those Southerners who felt the need to defend slavery and racial control on the battlefield. Shortly before the Seven Days Battles, he warned his troops about abolitionism. The North, he charged, wanted to "make the negro your equal by declaring his freedom," and he claimed Northerners "care not for the blood of babes nor carnage of innocent women which servile insurrection thus stirred up may bring upon their heads." The Yankees were "encouraging the lust of his hirelings to the dishonor and violation of those Southern women." In this way, Longstreet sought to plant in the minds of the Confederate soldiers images of slaves let loose on innocent and dutiful Southern white women, and he hoped his men would prevent such atrocities. "If ever men were called upon to defend the beloved daughters of their country," he said, "*that* now is our duty."[53]

By 1861, Confederate soldiers saw that their greatest abolitionist enemy was not Harriet Beecher Stowe or John Brown, but Abraham Lincoln himself. As they saw it, Lincoln's election represented a Northern mandate to crush slavery.[54] Confederate soldiers wrote of slaves who, despite certain misconceptions concerning the Union president, understood Lincoln's antislavery attitudes and the possibility of emancipation. Roderick McMillan, who worked as a plantation overseer before serving in the Thirty-Eighth North Carolina Infantry, warned his sister in May 1861 of slaves who believed Lincoln would free them. He wrote that one small boy had even asked him if Lincoln was black.[55] The boy's mistake might have been innocent, but it shows how much Confederates worried that enslaved people were in league with Lincoln. Lincoln and the abolitionists quickly became "outlaws" in the eyes of the Confederates. A few weeks before the First Battle of Bull Run, one man called upon Confederate soldiers to fight abolitionism, saying Lincoln was a traitor to the South. "Arnold or Judas, why they were white men compared to this scoundrel," he asserted. He offered a $20,000 bounty for Lincoln's head, or the heads of Lincoln's "pet Kangaroos" and "Abolition Devils."[56]

Lincoln, though he remained consistently antislavery to that time, had never advocated abolition: the immediate release of the slaves with no compensation to slave owners. Even well into the war, Lincoln urged caution, promoting the colonization of blacks as perhaps the best way to settle the race issue within the United States. Upon his election in 1861, Lincoln had no intention of freeing the slaves. Nevertheless, Confederate troops depicted him as the embodiment of antislavery fanaticism. For them, Lincoln was more dangerous than any other antislavery advocate, because he controlled the army and it was the U.S. military that would subjugate the South. Only after the war did the Alabama sociologist and soldier Daniel R. Hundley apologize for his vitriol against Abraham Lincoln, whose assassination made some former Confederates reflect on their earlier hatred for the U.S. president.[57] Most Rebels, however, were unapologetic about their dislike of Lincoln. In wartime, they believed the Union president and his armies deserved no mercy.

White Southerners' fears of a Lincoln presidency were not just based on their imaginings that black people and white abolitionists would henceforth roam the Southern countryside to commit violent acts. They held economic concerns as well. Republicans wanted to exclude slavery from the new territories, which caused Southerners to fear that they would not then be able to share in the fruits of the western lands.[58] Once Republicans had barred slavery from the territories, Southerners feared, the eradication of slavery everywhere would soon follow, leaving the South bankrupt and in ruin. "Is it nothing to yell about that we are prevented from carrying our property into the common territory of the United States[?]," asked South Carolinian William H. Grimball of his sister shortly after Lincoln's election. Confederate troops knew that the Yankees' looms were supplied by the South's cotton, and that Northern merchants and industrialists had made their fortunes from Southern slavery. In December 1861, one soldier placed the origins of the war in Yankee greed: the North hoped to undermine Southerners' profit margins.[59]

Confederates' fears were not illogical. Lincoln and other Republicans had indeed made clear their belief that slavery was both economically unsound and morally repugnant. However, just because Republicans hoped to block the expansion of slavery did not mean they necessarily wanted to destroy it within the South. In his March 1861 inaugural address, Lincoln reassured Southerners that he had no intention of eliminating slavery where it already existed. Lincoln had supported the Corwin Amendment—put forth by Ohio Republican Congressman Thomas Corwin—that would have given slavery permanent sanction in the South. Had it passed, it would have added a proslavery thirteenth amendment to the Constitution. Both the House and Senate passed Corwin's bill, but it was never ratified by the states. Despite Lincoln's desire for compromise, he was adamant about prohibiting slavery in the territories. Confederates mistakenly believed his election gave him a free hand in dealing with the South. Confederate soldiers, as with many Southern politicians, took Lincoln's stance on slavery to its logical, albeit extremist, end—preventing slavery from entering the territories would eventually lead to its abolition.[60]

For Confederates, abolitionism was merely one of the North's reform-minded "isms" which they believed would destroy Southern white political power. E. J. Ellis, a captain in the Sixteenth Louisiana, believed Confederates fought to defeat the "authors of Mormonism, free lovism, spiritualism, and all the isms of sin and iniquity that have desecrated our country for the past 30 years."[61] Other than abolitionism, perhaps the most frightening "ism" was "free lovism," which by definition made interracial sex socially acceptable. White Southerners worried that loosening the chains of slavery would result in a greater instance of black-on-white sex. Thomas Jefferson, although we now know that he fathered illegitimate slave children with Sally Hemings, once called such "amalgamation" degrading, unpatriotic, and a betrayal of the human character.[62] For worried masters, slavery might be seen as a somewhat "civilizing" force among black laborers, but the same masters feared that emancipation would unleash debasing and destructive forces. As did Jefferson, Confederate troops detested the idea of amalgamation, and they were not above taunting their Yankee opponents with remarks about interracial union. During the Vicksburg campaign, one Confederate soldier noted that the men with him would ask the Federals "geeringly if they had all gotten negro wives yet & how they liked them."[63] Any Southerner could bait a Northerner by suggesting a reductio ad absurdum: free the slave and he will bed your wife, daughter, or sister.

White Southerners did not necessarily find race-mixing unacceptable, so long as it occurred between white men and black women. Masters and other lustful white men raped slaves with impunity, even if their wives or other family members disapproved. Since slave status was inherited from one's mother, the illegitimate children of white men and slave women were doomed to a life of servitude. White males could perhaps never fully suppress their desire to "seduce" black women. "Is Caroline's child half white or not?," Gen. Henry Wise casually asked about a servant in 1862.[64] Race-mixing in itself did not always shock white Southerners. They would not ostracize a black woman for having a racially mixed child, since having mulatto children served to perpetuate the institution. But they would shun a white woman who had borne the child of a black man. Black-white sex existed, but only on Southern white men's terms.[65]

Fears of amalgamation resulted not merely from Victorian attitudes toward sex, but from Confederate soldiers' belief in the inherent superiority of a strong and homogeneous white population. For them, slaves were a part of their culture, but they were inferior human beings, if they were considered human at all. They saw the North as being filled with foreigners and "half-breeds," creatures worse than slaves. Black people were—as the proslavery argument went—well fed, well clothed, and provided for in their old age. Yankee industrialists, in contrast, disposed of their workers, especially immigrants, once they were too old or too unfit for work. As he marched through Maryland during the Antietam campaign, one soldier took note of the "poor devils" he saw along the way. They were "infernal foreigners, fit only for *slaves* and lives of vice and crime. Irish and *Dutch* by the thousand."[66] The more they saw of the Federals, the more Confederate soldiers saw them as uncouth, uncultured, and followers of misguided abolitionists.

The North had experienced a much greater influx of foreigners in the years before the war, but the white South contained many people of Irish, Scottish, English, German, and French lineage. Confederates liked to ridicule Northerners with Irish or German accents, but one of their best generals, Patrick Cleburne, was also an Irish immigrant. Southern Louisiana was just one part of a Confederacy that exhibited a great ethnic diversity. The Confederacy's secretary of state, Judah Benjamin, who came from New Orleans, was Jewish, and the popular P. G. T. Beauregard was a Creole. James McPherson has asserted that immigrants were actually overrepresented in the Confederate army and underrepresented in the Union army.[67] Nevertheless, Confederates' awareness of the large numbers of immigrants in the North—and the strange-sounding men from Ireland and Germany that they encountered during the war—led them to believe otherwise.[68]

Despite Southern ethnic diversity, Confederate soldiers created an identity based on what they believed were the fundamental differences between themselves and Northerners. The North, they imagined, was a land of abused factory workers, effete clerks, greedy shop owners, unintelligible foreigners, and lowly free black people. Southerners never thought that such a mix of Irish and "Dutch" immigrants, and, later, "Negro" soldiers, could ever defeat the Confederate army. The South's strength and character, Confederates were convinced, lay in its English and Scottish stock. In contrast, Southern men supposedly had military pedigrees that went back centuries—to the descendants of those who had "wrested the Magna Carta from King John."[69] One Confederate soldier—with the good Celtic name of Carlton McCarthy—wrote that the Federals used hirelings to win their battles. After the war, McCarthy subscribed to the Lost Cause view that said the South had been beaten only by the sheer weight of Northern numbers. Men of "white, black, olive, and brown" skin, McCarthy asserted, had "gathered from every quarter of the earth by steamer loads" to overwhelm the South.[70] Confederates knew that the North had an advantage in numbers, but they believed Union soldiers lacked the aggressive cavalier and Celtic spirit. They had faith in their population of fighting men, whose ancestors had fought on English and Scottish battlefields generations before.[71]

Some men's belief in the connection to some mystic Celtic warrior heritage meant far less to them than notions of their own racial superiority. Soldiering was not just about being a man, it was about being a *white* man. Confederate troops believed that in the battle against racial equality and unruly African Americans, their most sacred charge was to defend their honor and their manhood, and the honor of Southern women. Confederate soldiers were convinced that they were better than any "Negro." Alex Spence came from an Arkansas family that owned several slaves. In the army, he felt that it was not enough that others treated him like a man. He expected his treatment to reflect a level of courtesy shown toward white men. As he sailed to war in May 1861, he complained that his officers ought to treat their soldiers "like *free and white men*."[72] In January 1862, when a Florida soldier said some white men should have had black skin, he meant it as an insult.[73] In his eyes, real men did their duty; they did not abandon their post or succumb to dishonorable impulses. Soldiers believed that blacks were good workers, and a black man might even be considered a beloved "family member." But generations of servitude had deprived the slave of his honor and his manliness. Black servants thus represented what white men must not become. That "Negroes" were slaves suggested they had acted in ways that made them less than men. For Confederate troops, a true man would never have fallen into a state of servitude, the most dishonorable of conditions. Rebel soldiers sought to prevent the Yankees from doing to them what Southerners had done to black people for generations.

Through combat, Southern white men would prove their abilities and their worthiness to remain free. "Are we a generation of driveling, sniveling, degraded slaves?" asked Sterling Price of a group of Missourians in November 1861. Price—the governor of Missouri in the 1850s and perhaps most famous for his invasion of that state in late 1864—thought that men must defend their rights, given from God, and volunteer for what was a noble and necessary cause. Only then could Confederates avoid bondage. Price said in 1861 that he would opt for death (though he died in 1867) rather than allow white Southerners to endure enslavement.[74] For much of the war, many Confederates believed that surrender or defeat were not options. Liberty for the slave meant slavery for Southern whites.

The white Southern desire for liberty, Confederate soldiers believed, was as pure as the intentions of the North were evil. "Black Republicans" and their "Negro" allies wanted to violate the Southern republic, turning it into a land of enslaved men, fallen women, and mongrel offspring. Confederate troops believed they must protect themselves against a government that would be more despotic than the cruelest plantation owner.[75] One Virginian in the Stonewall Brigade vowed to fight as long as "the abominable flag of despotism hovers over a fort on Southern soil." He feared becoming a slave to the North, which would prove to be "the most degraded slavery."[76] White Southerners were convinced that slavery had made them freer than Northerners. Thus, subjugation at the hands of the Union would prove a far worse form of slavery than that practiced by the Southern master class. Confederates saw freedom as a zero-sum game: the only way for the "Negro" to win his liberty was at the expense of the white man's freedom. Gen. Lafayette McLaws, a Georgian who fought in the Army of Northern Virginia, believed that if the North were to win, Southerners would become a "poor despised race," their condition worse than that of the "meanest negro."[77]

Confederates feared that the more they resisted, the stronger would be the chains of subjugation and tyranny imposed by the North. Independence, therefore, became more urgent as the possibility of enslavement became more real. Lincoln's election proved cause enough for secession, and once the war began, Confederates believed that their army would be the only thing between independence and defeat, liberty and slavery. Soldiers would take up where the antebellum politicians had left off. In 1861, Confederates were finished with the political work of defending slavery; Southern troops would now carry out politics by other means.

Confederates did not see the contradiction, any more than Southerners had in 1776, in fearing their own enslavement while maintaining and prolonging the slavery of others. "I am in the battlefield to fight for my liberty," the slaveholding Louisiana soldier Isaac Hall wrote to his wife. "I am fighting for you all and for our Negroes and country."[78] Confederate troops believed that resisting tyranny, even while protecting slavery, would uphold the Revolutionary tradition. Lincoln's election, feared one South Carolinian, signified the end of liberty. In contrast, it was the Confederacy that truly honored the nation's founding fathers.[79] Slavery did not detract from soldiers' political mission; rather, it provided continuity between the struggle of 1776 and that of 1861. In November 1862, a soldier recalled Washington's relationship with a trusted servant who had followed his master not only into war, but also into retirement.[80] Anything approaching the quiet existence of the pre-war days would not materialize in the South for some time, but up until the end, Confederates still imagined returning to their former bucolic life, just as the heroes of the Revolution had done, only this time beneath the banner of an independent republic consisting entirely of slave states.

Soldiers often sounded as defiant a tone as Patrick Henry, who once exhorted "Give me liberty or give me death," and by death he meant suicide.[81] When they finally saw that the war would end in defeat, most Confederates did not kill themselves, although some did.[82] Earlier in the war, however, they saw little room for compromise. "*We can* and *we must* succeed," said one Alabaman who served on General Longstreet's staff, in February 1862. Referring to the Second Continental Congress's "Declaration of the Causes and Necessity of Taking Up Arms," written by Thomas Jefferson and John Dickinson in 1775, he noted: "'Better to die free men, than to live slaves.'"[83] Such sentiments were not uniquely Southern, but Confederates believed the idea had more immediacy for them. In September 1861, in a single letter to his wife, Georgia soldier Will McKee mentioned "liberty" four times. McKee's notion of liberty was not in the abstract: it had a racial element. He said he loved his home but if he had to be "the equal with a niger I had rather never come home, better me fall in the struggle for it."[84] Southern independence, Confederates believed, would allow them to avoid the specter of racial equality while at the same time assuring their freedom from Yankee rule.

Confederate men may have tried to live up to Patrick Henry's rhetoric, but they were far more dubious of the Revolutionary notion of equality among men. The conservative politician John Randolph of Roanoke had once said: "I love liberty. I hate equality." Confederate soldiers believed they treated "Negroes" better than Northerners did, but they too rejected egalitarian thinking. In 1861, Gen. Howell Cobb—as strong a supporter of slavery as anyone—created a list of the North's transgressions, including the United States' supposed attempt to create equality between the races.[85] In the view of Confederate troops, were equality to occur, Northerners would achieve it only through duress.

Throughout 1861 and into 1862, the Confederate soldier fought for many things—honor, adventure, camaraderie, and states' rights. Some had personal reasons for fighting, but their *political* reasons were firmly wedded to a proslavery ideology. Southern troops believed that Lincoln's election jeopardized slavery, and during the war they fought to maintain racial control through the perpetuation of human bondage. They did not want abolition, and certainly not any leveling between blacks and whites. The proslavery argument had made a deep impression on the minds of Rebel soldiers. In 1861 and 1862, articulating the Confederate cause in the language of liberty and slavery, and playing on the South's racial fears, motivated the men to fight. In 1861, the rush of Southerners to recruiting stations underscored their overwhelming early support for the Confederacy and the institution of slavery.

· 2 ·

PLANTERS AND YEOMEN, OFFICERS AND PRIVATES
RACE, CLASS, AND CONFEDERATE SOLDIERS

Proslavery thinking did not always assure harmony among white Southerners. As the Civil War ground on and took increasingly more lives, the struggle to create a white man's government led many Confederates to question whether protecting slavery was helping or hurting their cause, and whether planters had an unfair advantage in affecting government policy. Confederate troops sometimes complained they felt like "slaves" to the government, and that it was a "rich man's war, poor man's fight." But throughout the war, there remained solidarity between planters and yeomen.[1]

Confederate soldiers had many reasons for objecting to their politicians' conduct of the war effort; and thousands, whether because of class resentment, the need to care for families back home, or a simple belief in the inevitability of defeat, deserted their posts in wartime and never returned. Nevertheless, for most of the war, before defeatism and battlefield losses wrecked the South's ability to wage war, Confederate troops fought hard against Federal forces. Despite the internal problems that slavery and conscription caused, Rebels believed being subjugated by a "Yankee-Negro" alliance would prove far worse than the injustices and mismanagement within the Confederacy itself. Some troops harbored resentments toward the master class, but they understood the important role planters had in the army and the government. Yeomen and planters worked together in their efforts to maintain slavery and win the war.

Eric Foner has written, "The Confederate government molded its policies to protect the interests of the planter class."[2] If he is correct, why would soldiers, most of whom did not own slaves, support a war in which planters had the most to gain? The previous chapter has addressed that question in its analysis of Confederate ideology. The answer also lays in the economic, political, and social nature of the Old South—a paradoxical world in which universal manhood suffrage and egalitarian Jacksonian notions existed alongside the horrible, thoroughly undemocratic institution of slavery. Southerners lived in an antebellum world in which planters had a disproportionate share of the wealth, which translated into disproportionately greater political influence. Yet Southern yeomen supported the planters politically because of a shared belief in the need for racial control. The antebellum bonds between yeomen and planters, slaveholders and non-slaveholders, continued during the Confederacy. Privates relied on their officers in the same way that yeomen depended on antebellum planters.

As contradictory as it seems for Confederates to have believed in democracy and slaveholding simultaneously, white Southerners did not see the two institutions as incompatible. Most Confederate soldiers had come of age in the wake of the Jacksonian Era, a period in which the South's political structure became more democratic for adult white males, even as slavery became more entrenched. To a present-day observer, the Old South looks oppressive—suffrage and other rights were based on traditional notions of the "proper" (read, subservient) place of women, blacks, and Native Americans. But to a foreign observer of the mid-nineteenth century, the South could seem a very democratic place. In contrast to England and other European countries, the Southern states had no aristocracy. And unlike England before its Great Reform Act of 1832, the South did not suffer from an unjust, rotten borough system. In the late 1820s, most adult white Southern males could vote, and they helped elect, and then reelect, the leader of the "common man," Andrew Jackson. Jackson, a planter, general, duelist, and president, was anything but a "common man." But his presidency and the entire Jacksonian Era—and, more specifically, Indian Removal, the acquisition and settling of western territories, and advances in markets, transportation, and technology—gave white Southerners new opportunities. Along with them came the expansion of slavery, which made white men feel more secure in their economic and political liberties. With the firing on Fort Sumter in 1861, the South was trying to protect the gains it had made in the previous generation. As one historian has said, the Civil War was the playing out of a "Jacksonian drama."[3]

The planters, who owned most of the South's slaves, competed with the far more numerous yeoman farmers, who owned a much smaller proportion of the slave population, for greater wealth and political power. But despite the economic disparities that existed in the South by 1860, planters and yeomen found unity through slavery, which assured, at least in theory, that white men would never work at the bottom rungs of society as long as black men occupied that social position. Black workers, as South Carolina's Senator James Henry Hammond argued in the 1850s, made up a "mudsill" class that performed the most thankless duties and undertook the hardest, least rewarding tasks. Men like Hammond believed that it was slavery that kept whites on an equal footing.

Was Hammond correct in asserting that white Southerners benefited from the slave economy more than their Northern counterparts did from free labor? Southern farms, many of which were dedicated to plantation agriculture, were larger than those in the North. With the help of millions of slaves, crops of rice, cotton, and sugar made Southern agriculture more lucrative than it was above the Mason-Dixon Line. But as Gavin Wright has noted, "It is surely an exaggeration to describe the rural North as a homogenous, egalitarian society of freeholding farmers, but that region was much closer to such an ideal than was the South." Wright, however, dismisses the idea of "planter domination of the small farmers in the sense of the exercise of power or control." He notes that "Southern wealth holdings were not substantially more concentrated than those of the Northern economy as a whole." Southern farms were unquestionably larger and more valuable than Northern ones, though they were not necessarily more efficient. Still, antebellum Southern wealth was considerable. On the eve of the Civil War, the South—if one counts slaves as wealth, and not as people with whom to divide wealth—was one of the four wealthiest "nations" in the world. White Southerners surely were never equal. But there was enough wealth in the South to ensure political solidarity among white men.[4]

White Southerners' collective desire to own slaves meant that planters and yeomen had much in common—economically, politically, and culturally. The historian George Fredrickson, citing the Swedish sociologist Pierre L. van den Bergh, has described the Southern political order as a one of *Herrenvolk* democracy, a system that assured white equality would survive as long as its foundation rested on black servitude.[5] Yet, despite what its most vocal advocates claimed, slavery did not make whites equal or provide them with the same economic opportunities.[6] In the antebellum period, although Southern politics gave way to more democratic ways of thinking, planters still held considerable and disproportionate economic and political sway. Nor was the influence of the largest slaveholders confined to the plantation regions.[7] There were fewer than fifty thousand Southern planters (defined as those who owned twenty or more slaves), but yeomen were still willing to follow their political lead.[8] As Stephanie McCurry has shown, in three South Carolina counties—Barnwell (in the Middle Country), Darlington (in the Middle Country), and Beaufort (in the Tidewater)—antebellum politicians were overwhelmingly of the planter class. McCurry determined that 72 percent of the representatives and 92 percent of the senators from those counties were planters.

South Carolina was not atypical. As Mark Wetherington has shown in his study of wiregrass Georgia, planters there wielded great power. In the 1850s, in Black Belt Pulaski County, all but one of the state's representatives were planters, and in White Belt Irwin County, 85 percent of the men who served as senators and representatives in the state legislature from 1830 to 1860 were planters. Clearly, non-slaveholders and slave-owning yeomen looked to the planters to provide leadership. Such political participation was reflected in the Confederate legislature as well. Planters made up 40 percent of the first Confederate Congress, and nearly a quarter of them owned more than fifty slaves.[9]

Even in the wealthiest slaveholding regions—as was the case in the South Carolina Lowcountry, where slaveholders controlled the vast majority of the wealth—yeomen and planters were able to forge what Stephanie McCurry has called a "workable alliance."[10] Yeomen and planters were not only engaged in the same markets, they had a shared belief in the absolute need for racial control. South Carolina was home to the bloodiest colonial slave revolt, the Stono Rebellion. And the 1822 Denmark Vesey Conspiracy terrified whites there, setting the tone for antebellum racial politics. As the Civil War approached, poor and wealthier whites believed they must tighten the chains of slavery on Southern blacks ever tighter.

South Carolina became synonymous with radical politics and the proslavery argument as put forth by Calhoun, Hammond, and others, but white Southerners in other states, in plantation and non-plantation districts alike, also understood the need for racial control. As Mark Wetherington has shown, the yeomen of Georgia's Wiregrass Region supported the Confederacy because they agreed with the planters on the goodness of slavery and the need for a docile black population. "Race consciousness," Wetherington has written, "had more influence in shaping plain folk ideology and motivation to support secession and war than class consciousness."[11] Self-interest, therefore, helps explain why non-slaveholding privates followed planter and slave-owning officers into battle. For much of the war, soldiers elected their own lower-echelon officers, and they were usually slaveholders. Southern whites saw the planters as natural political and military leaders.[12] Southerners hoped to share in the prosperity that independence would bring, and in order to win their freedom from Northern rule, they needed the planter class. John Henry Cowin, an Alabama soldier serving in the Army of Northern Virginia cheered that "planters about Greensboro [Alabama] say we shall never be in want of money, but . . . we have only to let it be known. Hurrah!"[13]

One astute contemporary observer of Southern society was Daniel R. Hundley of Alabama. His 1860 work, *Social Relations in Our Southern States,* has become a classic study of antebellum Southern society. Unlike his contemporaries, like Abraham Lincoln, Hundley believed that true democracy could coexist alongside slavery. Hundley made it clear that the South, in contrast to what Northerners thought, was not made up merely of slaves, poor whites, and planters, and he emphasized the important role the yeomen played in their society. Planters were powerful, but they depended on the yeomen, who made up the majority of the voters and slaveholders in the South. Hundley did not see the Southern system, whether in its yeomen-planter alliance or in the workings of slavery, as perfect. But he did not think any society or institution was perfect. The South had its share of planter "aristocrats," he noted, but it also gave yeomen, through land and slave ownership and the right to vote, a great degree of independence.[14]

Hundley's writings shed much light on how Southern society could create a cohesive and formidable army. "They only require the right sort of leaders," Hundley said, "officers under whom they are willing to fight, and in whose mettle and abilities they have perfect confidence." Hundley had in mind Zachary Taylor, but he could have been describing Robert E. Lee. "Southern born himself," he said of Taylor, "and Southern bred, plain and unostentatious in his manners, and at all times cool and determined in the hour of danger; his soldiers loved the *man,* while they respected and trusted the *general.* Noble old Soldier!"[15] Hundley's defense of the South did not consist of idle words. In 1861, he served on a slave patrol in Louisiana, and he later joined the Confederate army, where he rose to the rank of colonel. Captured in 1864, he endured a Yankee prison for the last year of the war.

Men like Hundley argued that even though slaveholding was not equally distributed among white Southerners, all men could take advantage of the economic opportunities slavery created. Writers, from Hundley to James De Bow, claimed that social relations in the South benefited from slavery. In *De Bow's Review,* which had the widest circulation of any Southern magazine at the time, a reader could find an ongoing defense of slavery. "I think it but easy to show," said De Bow in 1860, "that the interest of the poorest non-slaveholder among us, is to make common cause with, and die in the last trenches in defence of, the slave property of his more favored neighbor."[16] For many soldiers in the Confederate army, De Bow's words about dying "in the last trenches" were prophetic. Confederates did not necessarily like the idea of fighting for another man's slaves, but they understood that slaveholding was a path to prosperity in the South. The institution was worth keeping despite the inequalities it created.

Robert E. Lee, the Confederacy's greatest general, was sometimes referred to as another George Washington—an "aristocrat" of the Virginia "gentry." Since the South never had a lineage-based class system, "aristocracy" and "gentry" are inaccurate ways to describe the actual makeup of its society. But such terms suggested the power that men such as Lee—who, like Washington, was a soldier and planter—possessed in the Old South.[17] Planters and yeomen found much common ground on race, but Confederates understood the tensions that existed between republican ideals and the "aristocracy" that the plantation economy created. In 1863, one officer wrote his wife not only about his difficulty obtaining a "body servant", but also his problems in trying to lead his men without acting too much the aristocrat. "I am needing a boy very badly yet," South Carolinian David Jackson Logan complained. "I am entirely too dependent or my notions are rather too *aristocratic*. I can command the respect when I have to depend upon my men to cook my meals for me, and find no other officers do it scarcely in the regiment."[18] Logan might have worried about his aristocratic tendencies, but others did not. As Thomas Green wrote from Petersburg, Virginia, in 1865, "It pays sometimes for a soldier to have a genteel appearance."[19] Shrewd officers tried to find a balance between sharing in the experiences of the common soldier and maintaining the dignity and authority befitting a superior, who was very often a member of the planter class. Robert E. Lee, who preferred living in a tent rather than in a house while in camp, performed this balancing act well. Confederate leaders had to be careful about upsetting the democratic sensibilities of the yeomen.

Soldiers, however, did not always have faith in the workings of Southern society. In November 1861, in Texas, Rudolf Coreth found himself feeling out of place among officers and enlisted men who were "almost all planters" and who "only went to war to lead quite a comfortable life."[20] Lt. Charles Liebermann, serving in the Thirteenth North Carolina Infantry, epitomized the alliance, albeit sometimes a troubled one, Confederate soldiers had with the planters. In December 1861, he questioned the patriotism of the large slaveholders in his unit, and their decision to burn valuable cotton stockpiles to keep them out of Northern hands. The planters probably were wise to destroy crops that the Federals might have seized, but Liebermann did not believe burning cotton compared to putting one's life in danger. Nevertheless, he acknowledged the vital role "King Cotton" played in the conflict. One day he said slaveholders did not do enough for their country, and on another day he wrote, "We have got the very staples which command the markets of all the civilized world."[21] For Liebermann, Europe could not function without cotton, and in 1861 he was among those who believed the Old World would side with the South. The Confederacy's future rested on the shoulders of the planter class.

Planters had influence disproportionate to their numbers, but soldiers believed the most palpable inequalities in the South existed between free men and slaves, not among whites. Slavery had created considerable leveling in the South, and thus within the Confederate army. "The very flower of the South are engaged in this war," wrote Louisiana soldier D. P. Gibson in 1861. "Companies are not formed of the lower calsses [sic] . . . as in other wars."[22] For soldiers, race, rather than class, provided the most powerful force for creating their identities as soldiers.[23] For some soldiers, the conditions of army life caused them to wonder if their cause was worthwhile, but more common than the cries of "rich man's war, poor man's fight" were soldiers' complaints that the military made them feel less than white.

Troops often used black people as the most ready point of comparison for the trials of soldiering, and their use of "Negro" metaphors reflect both individual complaints and unit morale. In Confederate eyes, the question became how long could one remain a "slave" and still fight for the "rights" and "liberties" of free white men?[24] Likening oneself to a "Negro" was not always negative. In January 1862, Felix Guilford, writing from winter quarters at Camp Pickens, Virginia, described Manassas as the muddiest place he had ever seen, but he went on to say that his men had worked to build comfortable shelters of oak logs and boards daubed with clay. Guilford continued, "Our camp would make the nicest free negro vilage you ever saw." As the war progressed, soldiers continued to see their experiences in racial terms. In the fall of 1863, for example, Pvt. J. P. Cannon wrote that, while on the march, he and his comrades sang like "niggers at a corn-shucking."[25]

One is more likely to read of soldiers complaining than singing, and they frequently compared their unpleasant experiences to slavery and black people. Confederates used "Negro" metaphors to describe everything from a man's grimy appearance ("black as a negro"), to his lack of money ("I am like the Negro who when he first saw a piano-forte said he intended to have one if it cost five dollars"), to theft in camp (to steal "a quarter off a dead nigger's eyes"), to physical maladies (lips "as thick as a Negroes"), to the "blackness" of corpses on the battlefield. Such metaphors were also frequently used to describe army discipline and the need to respect authority.[26] The longer some Confederates stayed in the army, the easier seemed the lives of black workers back home. As the South Carolina cavalryman James Michael Barr griped in December 1863, "If we could only get two lbs. of bacon we could do pretty well. My Negroes need not complain."[27] Men found that army life—from performing menial labor, to eating poor food, to enduring harsh discipline—made them feel too much like slaves. "I want to see you all," wrote a North Carolinian to his wife, adding, "I am bound tighter than any Negro."[28] Complained another, "A Solgers life is ahard life, it is true a life of Slavery." A prolonged illness led one suffering Alabaman to compare himself to a black person: he yearned to be free, his poor health having become a kind of enslavement, which made him feel "no more than a negroe."[29]

Complaints did not necessarily come only from men who were of the middling or lower classes; nor did a soldier's criticism of officers mean that he was uncritical of his comrades. Frank L. Richardson, from a Louisiana planter family, found the transition to army life difficult. In September 1861, he complained that it was "a great deal worse than that of a common field negro." Commissioned officers, he said, acted "just like the owners of slaves on plantations they have nothing to do but strut about dress fine and enjoy themselves." But he also complained that most of the common soldiers "have to be treated as negros or they will not obey," and he had little sympathy for a certain "very low set of men" made up of "low Irish and the scum of creation."[30] Richardson eventually got used to army life, but he never lost his contempt for his lower-class countrymen. In October 1862, recovering in a hospital in Knoxville, Tennessee, he complained of comrades whose English was "almost as bad as the cornfield negroes." They apparently had "as much knowledge as these same honest natives of Africa of writing or reading."[31] Describing class differences through the use of racial metaphors was not unusual for a Confederate soldier, especially one from the planter class. Still, Richardson's complaints do not suggest a lack of faith in the Confederate cause. He knew who his real enemy was, as evidenced by his letter in the summer of 1864, in which he wrote about his encounters with black Union troops and the damage they had done in Pattersonville, Louisiana, southeast of New Orleans.³² The forces of abolition were far more threatening to Richardson than class differences.

Confederates compared themselves and others to black people throughout the war. These analogies between Rebels and African Americans are instructive, but they do not hold up completely. Confederates believed that combat provided them with opportunities that could never be available to blacks workers: they had paths to promotion that were impossible for the slave population; they could take pride in their battlefield victories and the accomplishments of their comrades, whereas no "unit pride" existed among black workers; a slave was bound for life, a soldier only for the duration of the war; and their officers had more respect for their white subordinates than masters did for their slaves. Soldiers, after all, could not be sold or prevented from marrying. Whites had far less reason than slaves to fear a loss of their manhood.

The men's use of black and "Negro" metaphors nevertheless provide insight into the racial mindset of Confederate soldiers and their support for the war effort. It was understood that a contented soldier enabled the machinery of war to function, just as white Southerners believed a "happy" slave made the farm or plantation operate efficiently. A master could perhaps not win his servant's love, but he could hope for respect, or at least to keep his blacks in fear. An officer, similarly, wanted soldiers to obey and admire him, just as a master wanted black workers to appreciate him as more than a provider and disciplinarian. A sadistic master was as hated as a sadistic officer, and he would arouse the ire of those he offended and of others around him, becoming a menace to the institution, whether it was the army or slavery.

In 1861 and early 1862—and, to a lesser extent, later in the war—soldiers complained of harsh discipline and having to take orders, which tested the resolve of an army made up of individualistic farmers and small merchants. For many soldiers, obedience was for slaves, not white men. In May 1861, John B. Pendleton of the Twenty-Third Virginia complained to his wife that his plight was a hundred times worse than that of "any negro in our community," and that his condition would improve only if it were fifty times as bad. He took comfort, nevertheless, in fighting for country, liberty, and family.³³ To say that soldiering was worse than slavery by a factor of ten said less about the misery of human bondage, or the army, than it did about Confederates' sensitivity to obeying authority. Many soldiers' complaints were mere grumbling—harsh words uttered by those far from their homes and loved ones. They complained because they felt they could do little else to alleviate the stress of low pay, bad food, capricious officers, and thoughts of impending death in battle. For men to compare themselves with slaves was an act of hyperbole, similar to the popular hyperbole that one Southerner could whip ten Yankees. In June 1861, Pvt. S. B. Gulledge, serving in the Thirteenth Mississippi Infantry, wrote that he and his men were "being treated worse than negroes," but, like John B. Pendleton, he endured his hardships. In time, Gulledge wrote, he hoped he could "get a Yankee skalp."[34] The Alabama soldier Miller W. Francis perhaps best summarized Confederates' mixed feelings about the army in 1861, when he wrote: "A privates life is a hard one. They are worse than Negroes." But as long as he had good officers, life proved tolerable. Luckily, he did have "kind and indulgent" officers.[35]

A soldier might compare himself to a black worker on the Red or Chattahoochee Rivers, but provided there was no combat or marching, the average day in the army did not approach the misery that slaves suffered cutting Louisiana sugarcane or toiling in Georgia's rice paddies.[36] Soldiers nevertheless understood that they would have to work harder than ever to win the war. Gen. Clement A. Evans wrote to his wife in 1861, saying, "Do not stint yourself on anything you want. I am willing to work like a Negro to make you happy."[37] Confederates often considered slaves "rascals," prone to loafing or shirking their duties. But the fact that white troops equated hard labor with "Negro work" suggests that, contrary to proslavery ideology, which spoke of carefree, loyal, and contented "darkies," they were willing to acknowledge that slavery was a tedious, exhausting, and demoralizing condition. In May 1862, in discussing his recent labors, Edwin H. Fay, a Louisiana cavalryman, likened himself to a slave *and* a mule.[38] Living as they did in a nation of small farmers and common laborers, Confederates were not strangers to physical activity, but slaves and blackness were crucial in describing the trials of soldiering.

As did slaves, Confederate soldiers saw that they often had to defer to arbitrary authority. At times, it seemed best if a soldier could hide himself away. "One fellow even wished that he was a dog," William Kinzer of the Fourth Virginia Infantry wrote in 1861, "so that he could get to sleep in the chimney corner at home." As for himself, he said, "I have often wished I was a negro for a while."[39] For some Confederates, the only thing worse than being a slave was their own condition as a white soldier, as they found themselves suffering as never before, falling ill or risking death for the cause. Comparing their situation to that of slaves was not always justified, but it was understandable for men used to living in a slave society. Only slaves, they believed, could have understood such misery.

Men discovered the Confederate army was not always a kind master. It reduced them to waiting for the quartermaster to issue their clothes, just as slaves waited for their masters to clothe and feed them.[40] The physical appearance of Confederate troops—many of whom marched barefoot during Lee's 1862 invasion of Maryland—was often substandard, and the army did not always make up for such deficiencies. In August 1861, Alabama soldier John Henry Cowin obtained some shoes only to find they were of "low-quartered bad leather," which was "made for negro women for Sunday shoes." Two weeks later, he noted how camp life reminded him of similar times on the plantation. All the men had "clean clothes on, faces washed and hair combed just like the negroes. If we were only as well off as they I would be satisfied, for they have warm and dry houses to stay in, plenty to eat and good warm clothes." Still, he did not find his condition unbearable. He said he had enough to eat and wear, but "[did] not [have] the houses."[41] Confederate troops looked to those at home for additional food, money, and better clothing. In their view, a nation that could not care for its soldiers was a weak one, just as a negligent or penurious master was. For critics of the government, unfortunately, what was available at home was often little better than what the authorities could provide. In August 1861, the Louisianan Charles Batchelor wrote to his mother to ask for white lindsey, a cheap fabric known as "Negro cloth." The war had created shortages that made men settle for inferior material, even what was known to be worn by slaves.[42]

Even Confederate rations, which usually consisted of corn and pork, seemed as monotonous as a slave's diet. Rebel troops could have claimed that their food was even worse than that of black people—slaves, at least, never had to eat the dreaded hardtack. In 1862, the Virginia soldier William T. Casey complained of the government furnishing him with only a little flour and fatty meat "that is so very strong that it will knock a man down as far as fifty yards if he does not hold to a post like grim death to a dead negro."[43] Soldiers frequently wrote about the lack of food in camp, and its poor quality once it was available. One Confederate recalled that while he was a prisoner, the Yankees issued fatty bacon, which the men called "Cincinnati chicken," and black molasses, known as "nigger foot." In April 1862, another soldier, not a prisoner, grumbled that his pickled beef was so bad, "even our negroes will not eat."[44] Despite their treatment being "worse than negroes" and having had nothing to eat for two days, the Georgia captain Ujanirtus Allen spoke of his comrades' "contempt" for whiners in the ranks. "It is an old adage that some men would grumble to be hung," he wrote. "The greatest disafectants have always been men of no social standing, and whose fare here was better than they provided for themselves at home."[45]

In 1861 and early 1862, many Confederates anticipated a quick end to the conflict. With one decisive battle, they would destroy the Yankee army. Much to their disappointment, they found they would have to drill for hours, march for miles, and eat lousy food before they could even engage the Federal forces. "Common men" were becoming professional soldiers, though they often did not like the transformation.[46] For them, camp conditions smacked too much of black servitude. Confederates imagined the chivalric charge, not the prolonged campaigns and ongoing sacrifices inherent in modern war. The men grew frustrated with having to humble themselves before other white men in a slavelike manner. Some officers, furthermore, apparently were not worthy of such deference. In 1861, John Henry Cowin complained of superiors who "have not the common sense of a regular corn field negro."[47]

When a soldier did not obey his officers, the repercussions could prove extreme. Long after the war, Pvt. Sam Watkins, who served in the First Tennessee Infantry of the Army of Tennessee, recounted the whipping of a comrade. The scene could have doubled as a depiction of slave punishment. When a man was whipped and branded for going absent without leave, Watkins said, the regiment would be called out to watch the man kneel down and have his head shaved. Then, he wrote, "a strapping fellow with a big rawhide would make the blood flow and spurt at every lick, the wretch begging and howling like a hound, and then he was branded with a red hot iron with the letter D on both hips." For Watkins, the parallels were obvious. "No pack of hounds under the master's lash, or body of penitentiary convicts," he concluded, "were ever under greater surveillance. We were tenfold worse than slaves." Watkins clearly was shocked at such a display, but he never deserted. In fact, he served in all the Army of Tennessee's major battles.[48]

The naked show of military force made Sam Watkins recoil in horror, but Confederates understood the necessity of maintaining discipline. "I find from observation that white men require watching as much so as negroes," said John Henry Cowin. "I think there are many who ought have masters to watch over them at all times."[49] In early 1862, the Florida infantryman Robert Watson wrote of the election of officers in camp.

A candidate made the mistake of saying that "white men... must be treated like niggers." Such an assertion was a lapse in judgment for an aspiring officer, who should never have compared his comrades to "niggers." Even so, since no one ran against him, he won election to the rank of lieutenant.[50]

Rebel troops knew that officers should not act in the same manner as a slaveholder toward his chattels, but they also understood that they must sacrifice many freedoms for the sake of the cause. In the first months of the war, some men found the discipline of army life actually created unity among whites. Confederates formed good relationships amid the hardships of soldiering. In August 1861, the Louisianan John Foster referred to his fellow "Niggers" in camp. His officers were "masters" and "overseers." His "overseer," he was happy to report, did not drink, and he described his "drivers"—sergeants, most likely—as "good bad & indifferent."[51] Confederate soldiers wanted leaders who were just. They elected their company-level officers, and they did not want their superiors to abuse their authority or think of themselves as better than privates. Rebel troops did not reject authority on principle; they rejected the use of excessive authority. Even if officers were stern, as long as they were capable, troops found they could serve under them without sacrificing their faith in independence, honor, and manliness.

In April 1862 with the passage of the Conscription Act, the nature of the war and the makeup of the Confederate army changed. By that time, some original one-year enlistments were expiring. The Confederacy would face a crisis should thousands of its troops choose not to reenlist. The South thus passed a conscription bill to keep men in the army, where they were desperately needed as the spring campaigns began. Early 1862 was a bad time for the Confederacy. In the West, the Rebels lost critical strongholds along the Mississippi at Forts Henry and Donelson and Island No. 10, and they had also lost the large city and port of New Orleans. At the bloodbath at Shiloh in early April, over just two days, the Confederacy lost not only its hold on Tennessee, it also took 10,000 casualties and lost one of its highest-ranking generals, Albert Sidney Johnston. The South clearly needed to take stronger measures to keep its muster rolls full, and volunteering would not be enough.

The Conscription Act called for all men between the ages of 18 and 35 and not engaged in "essential" jobs to serve in the military for three years or until the war ended. Those who could hire a substitute to fight in their place did not have to enlist. Those who had already enlisted under the old one-year system must remain. As a concession, the Confederacy promised sixty-day furloughs for its troops, reenlistment bonuses, and it now allowed soldiers to elect officers at the company level.[52]

The bill was immediately controversial, which should come as no surprise, as it represented the first draft in American history. Many soldiers were unhappy with the idea of conscription. They found, as with slaves fated to a life of servitude, that the draft gave them no choice about remaining in the army. For some independent-minded, liberty-loving Confederate troops, it smacked of tyranny. Charles Liebermann wrote of conscription that it "deserves the hearty condemnation of every freeman, as it is nothing but an act of military despotism in violation of every republican principle."[53] Some soldiers were suspicious of the government's motives in passing the bill. They also questioned the loyalty of the upper classes, who could hire substitutes. Prominent politicians also voiced their opposition. In May 1862, Joseph E. Brown, the governor of Georgia, complained to Gen. Howell Cobb (a man Jefferson Davis hoped would garner citizens' approval for conscription), saying that the draft violated state sovereignty. Brown said that he might approve of conscription in an emergency, but that he felt none had arisen. And furthermore, wrote Brown, the Confederacy's problem was not just in obtaining men, it was in arming them.[54] In June, one Georgia soldier applauded Brown, saying it would be "a great deal better if we had Old Joe at the head of our government."[55]

Confederate soldiers had gone off to war proud of their Jacksonian political culture, which assured white liberty by ensuring that blacks would remain enslaved. Conscription left many troops resentful of what they saw as a planter-dominated Confederacy, and theirs were not just idle complaints. For the rest of the war, in some communities, but especially in the hill country and mountainous regions where fewer slaves lived, men violently opposed Confederate authority. Many others deserted, which worked to undermine Confederate unity. With the April 1862 draft, the Confederacy seemingly allowed class divisions to weaken the war effort.[56]

When the Confederate Congress first passed the Conscription Act, however, many Confederate soldiers supported the measure. In April 1862, G. H. Tichenor, who served in a Tennessee regiment, wrote that the draft was "talked of now more than anything else." But he concluded, "Some are in favor & some are a pose [sic] to it."[57] His words do not suggest that there were loud cries against conscription. Other men were clearer in their support, though they wanted the Confederacy to assure them that all classes of men would fight for their country. Before the draft was passed, the North Carolinian slaveholder James L. Reid had written, "The poor ought to go and the rich too." When the bill finally passed, some actually met it enthusiastically. "I think that is the best law ever passed by the Confederate Congress," said an Arkansas soldier in May 1862. He believed too many men were "laying around home and enjoying all the Comforts . . . while we are undergoing all the hardships of Camp life." Louisiana Capt. E. J. Ellis, writing from Mississippi in July 1862, stressed, *"We need every man for the approaching struggle* which in a few months will decide our fate" (Ellis's emphasis).[58] For many Confederate soldiers, the government should do whatever necessary to ward off Federal forces, and they in turn would courageously accept the challenge of Confederate service. Conservatives might have believed that in a war supposedly fought for states' rights, the central government should lack the power to keep men in the army against their will, but Rebel troops believed that winning the war superseded all other concerns. One North Carolinian rejected the idea, which the Conscription Act allowed, of hiring a man to fight in his place. If a man hired a substitute, he might arouse the ire of his community. This soldier feared that others would think such a man was "too cowardly, afraid of the Yankees," and unwilling to accept "death before dishonor."[59]

The pressure for men not to leave the army before the war had been won stemmed from white Southerners' notions of honor and manliness.[60] But Southern loyalty also had a racial element. Those who avoided conscription would look like lowly "Negroes," men who had no sense of pride or duty. Anyone who took the first opportunity to leave the military was considered not much of a soldier, and not much of a man either. Pvt. Peter Dekle noted that some troops had obtained exemptions, but he did not envy them. "I will be asshaim to go and then cared of like a negro just to get out of service," he said. He vowed to "stay till I cant stand it and then get a discharge honerably." Dekle found that military service tested his resolve, for how could one act like a soldier when the army treated him as a slave? Although tired of the service, for "we are thought no more of here than dogs especially privates they are not treated half as well as a negro," he was still willing to remain until he could leave by honorable means.[61]

William H. Tripp, who commanded the Fortieth North Carolina Infantry, ably summarized Confederates' mixed response to the draft, which engendered feelings of anger, reluctance, resignation, patriotism, and duty. In May 1862, Tripp wrote to his wife about a possible furlough. He did not want to "sneek home like a runaway for fear not so much of the Yankees as our own people." He said he had opposed "damnable" secession, but added, "I also acknowledge the right of any people to rebel when they are oppressed," and for that reason, he expected to fight "until we have . . . our independence." Tripp then turned to the matter of his slaves at home. Were they to behave well, he said, when he returned home, each "shall have a nice present."[62]

Men like Tripp not only discussed politics in their letters home, but also their concern, however paternal, for the management of their slaves. With so many men in the army, Confederate soldiers had to be sure that their slaves would remain under control behind the lines. Before the war, Southern whites had feared that they were vulnerable to slave rebellion, and this anxiety persisted throughout the war. From North Carolina, in February 1862, Gen. Richard Gatlin hoped to station two companies locally to give white people protection against their slaves. But for many citizens, the promise of protection was not good enough—they wanted guarantees.[63] In October 1862, Governor John G. Shorter of Alabama wrote to Jefferson Davis reminding him that there were few white men left to guard the plantations. In some areas of Alabama, only one white man remained for every thousand slaves. He wrote of "a spirit of insubordination" that had descended upon the countryside, and he worried about the fall of Mobile and subsequent Federal control of the rivers. Concerning the effect on the slave population were the state to be overrun, Shorter concluded, "The probable result I need not depict."[64]

Other Confederates preferred to downplay any possibility of slave revolt, thinking that such worries were merely a manifestation of an overactive white imagination.[65] Yet even before the war, in many areas of the South—such as in the rice regions of Georgia and South Carolina and in the Mississippi Delta—there were ten or even twenty slaves for every white person. For many Confederates, the potential threat to white people was obvious. "My two brothers . . . are in the encampment here, and my negroes at home require some attention," one North Carolinian wrote in May 1861.[66] With most white Confederate men of military age in the service, slaves enjoyed less supervision on plantations and farms, and many whites feared that their black workers would abuse these new freedoms. Soldiers needed their wives to keep order at home in their absence. Confederate troops wanted to have confidence in their spouses, but on the whole, they understood that more men were needed to protect their loved ones and other civilians. In June 1861, Roderick McMillan, who worked as an overseer before he joined the Thirty-Eighth North Carolina, told his brother John that "some one will have to stay at home for I fear the

Devil will get in the negroes . . . for they are beginning to runaway pretty fast."[67]

Early in the war, rumors and fears of slave insurrection had led state and local governments to more closely monitor the black population. Some counties beefed up slave patrols, while state governors handed out weapons to any man who wanted to make sure that the blacks remained docile. As Armstead Robinson has argued in his study of the Mississippi Valley, after the start of the conflict, some Southern governors actually denied arms and men to the Confederacy, even if they could have been used to better meet the Federal threat. The fear of black unrest, Robinson asserted, fatally undermined Confederate mobilization in the first crucial months of the war.[68]

The governors' reluctance to hand over men and matériel to the Confederacy, however, was not based solely on fears of slave unrest or on a selfish dedication to the ideology of states' rights. The governors also had understandable concerns about a military invasion from the Federals. Governor Pettus of Mississippi, for example, certainly frustrated Jefferson Davis's efforts at consolidating military resources, but the Confederacy faced a strategic problem. From the war's outset, there were thousands of miles of territory to defend, a long border with the Union, and it was also critical to hold onto the Mississippi River, which could become an invasion route for U.S. vessels (which is exactly what happened later in the war). On the one hand, Robinson suggests that if the Confederacy had chosen to consolidate its forces early in the war, it may have been able to mount a stronger offensive against Washington, although the outcome of such an offense is unknowable. On the other hand, if the Confederacy had not chosen to contest every inch of territory, this might have allowed for more rapid penetration into its heartland, which would have resulted in a much easier victory for Federal forces.

Regardless of what strategy the Rebel military took, it could not take for granted the docility of enslaved people. In October 1862, the Confederacy passed a second draft bill (known as the "Twenty Slave Law") that allowed one white male to stay behind on plantations with twenty or more slaves. The Confederacy already allowed various exemptions for mail carriers and postmasters, teachers and professors, miners, salt-makers, druggists, manufacturers, railroad workers, newspaper editors (one editor per paper), telegraph operators, and cobblers. Men could also avoid service by hiring a substitute, another advantage for those with money.

As Mark Weitz has shown, the advent of the "Twenty Slave Law" alienated many non-slaveholders.[69] Some troops believed their government had disregarded the planter-yeomen alliance, depriving poor whites of their liberty at the expense of pleasing the larger slaveholders. Some men had little interest in further preventing disorder among blacks, which may have resulted from their belief that blacks were inherently docile or because they dismissed planters' concerns. In October 1862, one Georgia soldier voiced his disapproval in the pages of the *Atlanta Southern Confederacy,* which supported the planter exemption. "What say you to the poor white man who has *ten children* all dependant upon him?" the writer asked. "Shall he be exempt? No, you answer, 'go fight for the negroes of your neighbor, because it elevates you in society.'"[70] Such words did not suggest a lack of support for the war effort, but rather that the Confederacy must acknowledge the sacrifices of non-slaveholders and protect Southern communities through fairer means. Confederate troops were clearly interested in defending slavery, but they wanted their government to use manpower sensibly to assure that goal.

Nevertheless, many Confederate troops were irate about the "Twenty Slave Law." In October 1862, Heber Bennett, serving in a Louisiana artillery unit, said the planter exemption was "about to caus a rebelion in camps."[71] His men apparently were livid over the government passing laws that favored the upper classes. Still, no such rebellion occurred. The rhetoric, however, was heated among the Rebels. In February 1863, the Louisiana private John A. Harris wondered why the rich were considered better overseers than the poor. After all, had antebellum politicians not said that slavery made white men equal? It seemed to him that planter-friendly politics ruled the Confederacy. Perhaps the Confederate government should not have thought of one man's "property" as being more valuable as another's.[72]

One war song decried the class element at work in the war:

> At every large plantation,
> Or negro holder's yard,
> Just to save their property,
> The Generals place a guard,
> The sentry is instructed,
> To let no *Private* pass,
> The rich man's house and table,
> Are *fixed* to *suit* the *brass.*

> Chorus:
> I hate to quit this story,
> So beautiful and true,
> But the poor man and the widow,
> Must have a line or two,
> For these no guards are stationed,
> Their fences often burnt,
> Their property molested,
> As long ago you've learned.[73]

The Confederate draft was unprecedented in America, and it was the poorer Southerner who was first to see the preferential treatment extended to the wealthy, which led to a bitter response. Some believed that the planters who chose not to serve were unpatriotic, even cowardly.[74] In August 1863, Gen. Daniel Ruggles, then commanding eastern Louisiana, complained of not enough men coming into the army. Discontent among smaller property owners, he believed, had led to the decline in patriotism, and the large landholders had not set a good example. He believed the planters should have to make greater sacrifices; otherwise, they would alienate the non-slaveholders.[75] In December 1863, the embittered North Carolina officer Caleb Hobson wrote of his hatred toward the planters, men whom he believed felt no compunction to fight. They were nothing more than "Tories," and he would like to have seen them hanged.[76]

The "Twenty Slave Law" aroused opposition among some Confederates, but in actuality, it did not allow many men to win exemptions. Regarding overseers, the law affected only states that lacked statutes requiring their presence on plantations, and the number of men who took advantage of the "Twenty Slave" clause proved small. Roughly 38,000 overseers lived in the South in 1860. Only 200 in Virginia, 120 in North Carolina, and 201 in Georgia won wartime exemptions. The Confederacy did excuse 300 South Carolina overseers—a high number considering the state's population was well below Virginia's, but South Carolina had a much higher concentration of plantations.[77] Although some overseers gained exemption, their numbers were a mere fraction of the overseers who remained in the army.

Long after the war, Sam Watkins wrote passionately about the discontent with the exemption. "It gave us the blues," he wrote of the "Twenty Slave Law." For the rest of the war, he claimed, the Confederate soldier was no more than "a machine, a conscript." With the planter exemption, he said, the troops' "last hope had set. They hated war. To their minds the South was a great tyrant, and the Confederacy a fraud. They were deserting by [the] thousands."[78] There was some truth in what Watkins said. Aaron Sheehan-Dean has shown that 1862, the year of the first two draft bills, was the worst year for desertion from within Virginia units.[79] Sam Watkins was correct to say that men were deserting in large numbers at that time. During Lee's invasion of Maryland, in September, many Confederates abandoned their units along the march. By the time Lee fought at Antietam, he had only 40,000 troops, far less than the 85,000 he had commanded at the Seven Days Battles.

Lee's straggling problem was temporary, and it had less to do with class conflict than with the bloodiness and exhausting pace of the summer 1862 campaigns. In some parts of the Confederacy, men might have left the ranks because of what they felt were unjust concessions to the planters, but they voted with their feet only briefly. Following weeks of rest and resupply after the Antietam campaign, by the December 1862 battle of Fredericksburg, Lee's troop count had rebounded to 74,000 men, almost twice as many as had fought at Antietam. Sam Watkins account, in hindsight, of how detrimental the "Twenty Slave Law" had been cannot be considered the last work on the measure's effect. In the fall of 1862, at least one soldier was no longer upset over the measure. It was "extremely liberal," he said, and "does tardy justice to planters." He was not irked at planters gaining exemptions, though the fact that newspaper editors could obtain them did anger him.[80]

In 1863 and 1864, because of manpower shortages, the Confederacy granted fewer and fewer exemptions. Over time, the Confederacy became a more centralized government, giving military officials not only conscription power but also the authority to impress food, horses, and slaves. In October 1863, after the Confederacy had suffered serious reverses at Gettysburg and the loss of Vicksburg, the South Carolinian William H. Grimball wrote, "I confess myself in favor of a Revolutionary military dictatorship with Davis as Dictator." For him, the Confederate Congress had too much power and the Confederacy must "disregard the old ideas fit for order & quiet and accept the conditions imposed by a terrible and a mortal struggle."[81] The South Carolina soldier David J. Logan was also eager to see the Confederate government exert more authority. "Let no man of Conscript age be relieved from his duty to his country and himself by the votes of our people at home," he wrote in November 1863.[82]

The planter exemption undoubtedly created class tensions within the Confederacy, and by late 1862 the war was testing whether the South had the non-slaveholders' interests in mind when it had passed the legislation. For the most part, however, conscription and the planter exemption did not fatally undermine soldier morale. Tens of thousands of Confederates deserted during the war, but they did not do so chiefly because of anger over planter privileges. As historians have shown, troops in South Carolina regiments were most likely to desert because of Confederate reverses, not the government's supposed planter favoritism.[83] Deserters may have harbored class resentments that factored into their decision to leave the army, but they were willing to support the Confederacy as long as it could win victories. Even in areas where desertion proved considerable, as in Floyd County, Virginia, slavery did not play a major role in Confederate disloyalty. Men instead were driven to leave the army because of family hardships and suffering that they felt they could not alleviate in any other manner.[84]

Overall, troops agreed about the need to save slavery and maintain the racial status quo, even if it sometimes gave an advantage to the planter class. Those men likely to desert did not do so just because of the "Twenty Slave Law." Confederate defeats, not legislation that exempted some men from service, is what led to desertions. Areas like eastern Tennessee, western Virginia, and the hill country of the Deep South, were exceptional because of their anti-Confederate attitudes, not because they harbored anti-slavery views.

Southern soldiers did not necessarily have to be strong proslavery men to fight and die for the Confederate cause. But the more proslavery a Confederate was, the more likely he would remain loyal to his country. The papers of diehard Confederates in published and archival manuscript sources far outweigh those of men who were unpatriotic or rejected Confederate authority, especially deserters. It is difficult make generalizations about why men left the ranks, but the writings of one deserter are instructive. "I will be glad to see an end to slavery," said Philip Van Buskirk, who had once served in the Thirteenth Virginia Infantry. He believed black people were best suited to bondage, but he did not think Southern whites were fit masters. The whole slave community, he asserted, was one of debauchery that degraded white and black, young and old.[85] Van Buskirk obviously had little to gain from a Confederate victory, and his attitudes were unlikely to change along with the rise and fall of Rebel fortunes.

In the North, many Union soldiers, originally unsympathetic toward the abolitionists, became more antislavery over the course of the war, though their change of heart did nothing to mitigate their racist attitudes. Their feeling was that if emancipation would hasten the demise of the Confederacy, then they were for it. The Confederacy had a greater problem. Antislavery Confederates, like Van Buskirk, made up a very small number of enlistees, and they would not become more proslavery as the war ground on. Given this dynamic, the Rebel government's policies concerning the draft and conscription could not hope to embolden those men, even though they shared the Confederacy's vision for a proslavery republic.

Soldiers' loyalties transcended the problems that slavery caused for the Confederacy. The army may have made troops feel like second-class citizens, but in the South, as it had in the antebellum era, race trumped class. It seems logical that soldiers, the vast majority of whom did not own slaves, would question the fairness of having to fight for a government that gave privileges to the planters. Few men, however, wanted a Confederacy without slavery, which allowed all classes to share in the prosperity it created. When he wrote his memoirs after the war, Col. Irvine C. Walker, a South Carolinian who served in the Western Theater, talked about how his family was of the merchant class, not the planter class. Even so, he stressed that fact that merchants and planters could run in the same social circles. The refinement, prosperity, education, and culture he enjoyed allowed him to cross the "dividing line into the so called higher class."[86]

In contrast to those like Sam Watkins, who believed the conflict became a "rich man's war, poor man's fight," some Confederates were not convinced that the wealthier classes had not done their fair share. In his memoirs, one veteran wrote, "Instead of being, as Andy Johnson said, 'the rich man's war and the poor man's fight,' the better class of the South suffered and endured out of all proportion."[87] The planter exemption angered some soldiers, but most thought more in terms of black and white than of rich and poor. One can make too much of soldiers' discontent with planters and slaveholders. Most nineteenth-century Americans were not from the wealthy classes, and Confederate soldiers were no exception. Their struggle was about protecting slavery—the so-called "rich man's war"—and they knew that going in. Had the Confederacy won more victories, the planter exemption would have aroused even less grumbling than it did.

Troops occasionally spoke ill of wealthy planters, but if they did not own their own slaves, they would have wanted to, and if they already did own slaves, they would have wanted to own more. Confederates avoided class conflict. Poorer whites emulated and admired the planters. The New

Testament told the Southerner to love his neighbor, but it was the Protestant work ethic that taught him to outdo his neighbor. If they could rise to the master class, white Southerners knew, their lives would be made easier. Slaveholding meant wealth. In September 1863, during a particularly hard march from Atlanta, the Georgia sharpshooter William R. Montgomery claimed he would have given "a small negro" to get some rest.[88] For soldiers, "Negroes" were as good as money and slaveholders seemingly had both in abundance. In actuality, even the largest planters had difficulty remaining solvent, but for all the paternalistic posturing by proslavery advocates who thought slavery more an inherited obligation than a financial investment, Southerners knew that slave-owning led to prosperity. Soldiers supported the Confederacy because of the security that slavery provided them. "No doubt we shall be poor and Stricken people," said the slaveholding soldier James Stubbs in June 1862, but he was not discouraged. "I have only Now My Boy Sam My Two Horses and My Government pay." A man could be optimistic as long as he had a slave, a horse, and money to see him through.[89]

The Confederacy was not deaf to the complaints of its citizens, but the government's repeal of substitute and exemption clauses in the draft—in late 1863 and early 1864, respectively—had more to do with the need for men than with the complaints of the non-slaveholders. As one historian has recently argued, Confederates did not necessarily see the hiring of a substitute as unpatriotic.[90] Yet, late in 1863 the government struck down the substitute clause. This pleased one soldier, who wrote that "the wealthy man who owned money and negroes enough to keep his precious carcas out of the reach of the Yankee" was now "reduced to the level of the poor man." The abolition of the substitute clause, he believed, would raise spirits within the army. All Confederate soldiers would now be on a more equal footing.[91]

In 1863 and 1864, the war increasingly became a "rich man's fight." In 1863, tax-in-kind and impressment laws significantly impacted the planters. In February 1864, the Confederacy passed the last of its three Conscription Acts. The South by then needed as many soldiers as it could get. All white men between the age of seventeen and fifty were now eligible for the draft. The new bill did not allow exemptions for planters, though overseers could be exempt under certain conditions. The Confederate Congress also made 20,000 slaves subject to conscription for use in non-combat roles.[92]

Manpower and discipline problems continued into 1864 and 1865. Nevertheless, for the rest of the war, Lee would have between 60,000 and

65,000 men at the start of each spring's campaign season.[93] When Johnston confronted Sherman in Atlanta in May 1864, he had more troops than Confederates had mustered at Shiloh, Vicksburg, Murfreesboro, or Chattanooga. Rebel muster rolls rose and fell at various points in the war. It is simply not true that they began an irreversible decline with the passage of the first conscription bill.

Early in the war, soldiers compared their plight to that of slaves, but such comparisons only reveal that they thought more in racial than in class terms. The war put pressure on the political and social bonds among whites, and it tested the limits of men's willingness to sacrifice their liberty for a slaveholding republic. Conscription led some Southerners to complain of a "rich man's war, poor man's fight," but it did not cause army discipline to collapse. Soldiers wanted to become planters, if not serve under them. The greatest of Confederate officers, from Lee and Jackson to Forrest to Beauregard, were slaveholders, and they answered to a commander in chief who was a Mississippi planter. In the Confederacy, there were unpatriotic planters and patriotic ones, non-slaveholder deserters and slave-less yeomen who fought until the war's bloody end. Slavery served as a mark of prosperity and prestige, the most common path in the South to economic and political advancement. In the process, it often instilled martial values in those who owned, bought, and sold black people. Confederate troops found unity in the institution of slavery.

· 3 ·

THE GREATEST OF MASTERS
THE CONFEDERATE ARMY AND THE IMPRESSMENT OF BLACK LABOR

The Confederate draft forced Southern troops to remain in the army against their will. Slaves were by definition compelled to serve, but in 1863, they too became conscripts of a sort. In March 1863, the Confederacy passed an impressment law giving commanders power to use slaves for military work. Impressment proved a controversial aspect of the Confederacy's massive effort to use black workers to aid the war effort. From the war's beginning, the army found itself in a power struggle with masters who did not want their property taken and commanders who needed slaves for military work. Impressment created tensions between two powerful segments of the Confederacy—planters and officers—who depended on slave labor. Far from revealing that Southerners were fatalistic about emancipation, impressment showed the military's commitment to, and continued reliance upon, human bondage.

The Confederacy's use of impressed slaves resulted from an increasingly serious military situation requiring the army to have reliable black labor. It was also a result of the government's increasing centralization. "States' rights ideology," one historian has recently written, "eventually lost to a more expansive vision of the Confederate central state."[1] The Confederacy passed a white conscription law after the South had suffered defeats in early 1862. The army found black laborers invaluable, and by March 1863, the Confederate government had the power to impress them into service. The Rebel military became the greatest of masters, but many civilians did not like the army's strong-arm tactics, which infringed upon their property rights. As a result, the Confederate army had to work hard to supply its camps with black workers, while at the same time not asking slaveholders to sacrifice too much.

After the war, some former Rebels complained about the Confederate government's impressment policy and the disadvantage the South bore in trying to control its slave population. In his memoirs, Richard Taylor said, "It was a curious feature of the war that the Southern people would cheerfully send their sons to battle, but kept their slaves out of danger."[2] Another Confederate noted that slavery "gave the Federal Government a great advantage in the prosecution of the war and imposed additional cares and responsibilities upon those charged with ... military operations in the South."[3] Such sentiments, written after the war, tended to revise the important role slaves played in the Confederate army. During the war, white Southerners believed strongly in slavery's advantages. Blacks made up the majority of agricultural and industrial workers in the South, enabling 80 percent of Southern white adult males to serve in the army. Slavery was a "tower of strength to the South," wrote the *Montgomery Advertiser* in 1861, "really one of the most effective weapons employed against the union by the South." With slaves freeing white men to fight, Confederate armies were two-thirds the size of Union ones.[4] The advantages of slave labor were offset to some degree by the flight of thousands of slaves to the Union armies. Confederates, however, adapted to the realities of wartime. Confederate industry, for one, used slaves in innovative ways.[5] As Edward Ayers has asserted, by 1863, when the Confederate Congress made impressment official practice, slavery "remained a crucial weapon of the Confederacy." Ayers notes that slavery's role "not only remained undiminished but actually grew as white Southerners saw their men killed, maimed, and lost in [battle]."[6]

Early in the war, Confederates realized that they must mobilize all their resources. As Capt. E. John Ellis wrote in March 1862, "Every man, woman or child, negro or dog in the South that wants to submit ought to be hung up to the nearest limb as soon as possible."[7] Southerners saw that they had to mobilize their slaves effectively to military advantage or Northerners would use them against them. The Confederate army employed blacks by the tens of thousands, to build and repair fortifications and railroads, and as haulers, teamsters, and ditch diggers. Slaves also served alongside medical workers. "I have all hands at work cleaning and whitewashing at the Hospital," said a surgeon a few weeks before the battle of Chancellorsville. "Today the Medical Director sent me 12 negroes extra."[8] Slave labor made the Confederacy function, as it had the antebellum South.

Some historians, however, have argued that the Confederacy's impressment policy failed because of the refusal of planters and state officials to provide blacks to the military. Confederates' opposition to letting go of their slaves, they contend, created serious divisions within the

South.[9] The editors of *Freedom: A Documentary History of Emancipation* concluded that impressment "divided [Confederates], exacerbating conflicts that pitted state officials against national officials, national officials against army officers, army officers against slaveholders, and slaveholders against nonslaveholders."[10] Impressment certainly caused divisions within the Confederacy, and as a logistical measure it was far from perfect. The Confederate army, nevertheless, received thousands of slaves from Southern masters who although often unhappy about the taking of their slaves, were not necessarily resistant to it.[11] The relationship between the army and slaveholders was often tense, but planters and smaller slaveholders gave much support to the military. Their grumblings about impressment were similar to privates' gripes about conscription: they did not always like the undemocratic nature of the army, but they feared that defeat and abolition would be far worse. Through impressment and obtaining of slaves by other means, the Confederacy was able to delay the advance of Federal armies.

A vital form of military labor involved the building of fortifications and entrenchments. The advantages of using earth and timber to stop bullets seems obvious, but early in the conflict, Southerners saw taking cover as unmanly. Robert E. Lee won the sobriquet "King of Spades" for digging in during the Seven Days Campaign.[12] Men's attitudes toward defensive tactics would change, and when they did, Rebel troops preferred that slaves do the digging. The vast majority of Confederates were farmers accustomed to hard labor, but troops felt that their duty was to fight rather than dig trenches or perform slavelike tasks.[13] Writing near Jackson, Mississippi, shortly after Vicksburg fell, one soldier was plain about how he and his comrades occupied themselves while the slaves worked: "We layed around & took it easy."[14] Commanders tried to get their soldiers to work as hard as the slaves, but officers found that their men disliked anything approaching "Negro work." Whites would apparently do hard labor only if coerced. The Louisiana infantryman Robert H. Miller wrote that he had overseen black workers, "but never yet did I see anything work like white men when the fear of the guard house is before their eyes."[15]

Generations of involuntary servitude, Rebel troops believed, made blacks ideal for doing the labor required to fortify towns and strengthen defenses. And as their officers reasoned, why suffer soldiers' complaints when black laborers could take their place putting up sandbags and constructing earthworks? Blacks, they believed, were more manageable and efficient, more used to difficult conditions and white supervision. Also, they were not only better workers, Confederates claimed, they were more expendable. Masters, who expected compensation for slaves who died from overwork, were unhappy when they lost valuable property. But most Confederates did not own slaves. For them, a dead black worker was better than a dead white one. One South Carolinian was blunt: "If the negro men had been enlisted to do all this hard manual labor, there would have been more white soldiers living at the close of the war, and fewer negro men to vote the radical ticket."[16]

Slaves were used to build fortifications at such vital strongholds as Richmond, Fort Henry and Fort Donelson, Island No. 10, Vicksburg, Port Hudson, Wilmington, and Mobile. The government did not authorize the impressment of slaves until the middle of the war, but even before then, officers had forced thousands of black workers into service. Often, the work they performed was on a much larger scale than the work at any antebellum plantation. Few masters owned more than fifty or a hundred slaves, but in September 1862, P. G. T. Beauregard, then commanding coastal defenses in South Carolina and Georgia, wrote of fourteen hundred slaves working on the defenses at Savannah. Other areas could also boast of massive work projects. That May, an officer wrote to Joseph E. Johnston, saying that he had seventy-five hundred slaves at work at Mobile—so many slaves that he could not feed them all. Richmond, furthermore, was the scene of constant fortification projects. In late May 1862, one soldier wrote of three thousand slaves at work throwing up breastworks, and in the spring of 1863, W. C. Corsan, an English traveler, estimated that between four and six thousand slaves were at work on the railways running into the Rebel capital.[17]

Early in the war, appealing to patriotism and volunteerism had been enough to get Confederates to turn over their slaves. In January 1861, Hugh Mercer, commanding the Georgia militia, noted that "patriotic planters" in Savannah had provided Confederates with a large force of slaves.[18] As other Southern states prepared for war, they too used black laborers. In April 1861, the North Carolina overseer and soldier Roderick McMillan wrote of the excitement that ensued when black workers were sent to Forts Johnston and Caswell—part of the Wilmington defenses. Fifty African Americans had already gone and more were to follow. McMillan said he never expected to see "negroes Volunteering their services in defence of the country." His employer, a physician, had called for volunteers, and two of his "best hands" had stepped forward. The scene, McMillan concluded, was enough "to make the stoutest heart shrink."[19]

Once it became clear that the Rebel victories in the summer of 1861 would not end the war, the Confederacy took more serious measures to use slaves to protect its citizens. In January 1862, the South Carolina soldier William Grimball wrote that the generals agreed that planters should remove their slaves from threatened areas to designated safety zones.[20] Planters expected protection, but military officials also wanted slaveholders' cooperation in helping fight the war. Officers learned that slaveholders were not always quick to fill their quotas for black workers. In December 1861, in Tennessee, Jeremy Francis Gilmer, an engineering officer, complained to his superiors that he had not obtained enough laborers around Nashville.[21] Local citizens had contracted many black workers until the end of the year, which impeded progress in building defenses.

Just as masters could not necessarily obtain the laborers they needed, Confederates also discovered that slaves were not always available. In late December 1861, Isham Harris, who would serve in the army after his term ended, complained that his agents had not obtained enough black laborers. Harris wrote Western Department commander Albert Sidney Johnston to say that he had obtained two hundred slaves but that he wanted three times that many.[22]

In Virginia, commanders also were experiencing shortages. In May 1861, John B. Magruder, then a colonel, had his forces building fortifications to stop the Federal approach to Richmond, but he had to send slaves back to their masters, as promised.[23] Magruder was not alone in suffering labor shortages. In Virginia, in response to hesitant slaveholders, George B. Cosby, an engineer serving in Williamsburg, reassured planters that the military would treat their slaves well, provide them with rations, and pay their masters fifty cents a day. Despite his efforts, problems continued. And without black workers, Cosby was unable to place his heavy guns in position. He complained about having to dismiss some slaves whose term of service had expired, and decided to exert more pressure on the planters. In addition to using slaves, Cosby also wanted to force free blacks into service to deepen ditches, thicken parapets, and put up traverses. With only a few hundred additional men, he hoped he could complete the work at Williamsburg in a few days.[24]

In August 1861, a soldier encamped near Richmond noticed that the only laborers he saw throwing up breastworks were black.[25] The use of so many black laborers denuded the plantations, making harvesting and planting more difficult for masters. In late January 1862, John Magruder—by then promoted to major general for his performance at Big Bethel the previous June, and now defending Yorktown—said he had impressed nearby slaves repeatedly, which he thought too much of a strain on local slaveholders. Were he to impress slaves again, he worried about complaints flooding the War Department. Magruder—aware of the resistance of some planters, who were cognizant of the delays in collecting black workers, and realizing Congress's inability to pay for lost slaves—advised against ordering slave impressments in the local counties. Furthermore, Magruder did not want the authorities to appear heavy-handed, thus offending those citizens who held only tepid Confederate loyalties. Despite unhappiness among some planters, Magruder believed that Virginians approved of the impressment policy.[26]

Why? Patriotism was a factor. Some masters thought giving up slaves, even involuntarily, helped their country. The answer also lay in slaveholders' financial worries. When commanders hired out slaves, masters incurred any attendant losses. But if the slaves were impressed, the army had to compensate slaveholders. Thus, some planters saw the financial wisdom in the army taking much-needed African Americans. Given the support among officers and planters for impressment, in February 1862, the army gave Magruder—still at Yorktown—authority to seize slaves for work on fortifications on the peninsula between the James and York Rivers. The army also subjected free workers to impressment.[27]

Some Confederates, uncomfortable with measures that threatened their property, complained. John Tyler Jr., the son of the ex-president and a congressman himself, and Col. Hill Carter of the Fifty-Second Virginia Militia, wanted greater assurances "against possible contingencies of loss," since some impressed slaves never returned home.[28] The problem was not unique to Virginia. In November 1862, James C. Marcom, serving in North Carolina, found nothing much new to write about except "the death of a little negro—one of the conscripts Negroes."[29]

Despite imperfections with the impressment system, Confederates saw it as not just attractive, but necessary. With Yankee armies on the offensive, the Rebels needed all the workers they could get. By April, Ulysses S. Grant was rolling through Tennessee and George McClellan was moving his massive army across eastern Virginia. Both John Magruder and D. H. Hill—serving with Magruder's troops—wrote to their superiors for more black workers. Hill complained of his men's exhaustion. They had worked too hard to supply the army with guns, forage, and commissary stores. Hill had drawn slaves from the outworks in order to relieve his troops, but he needed more. Many had reported sick and were of no use to him.[30]

Some Confederates were unhappy with impressment measures. In

March 1862, writing from South Carolina, a pessimistic John C. Pemberton, then commander of South Carolina, Georgia, and Florida, spoke of the uncertain cooperation between civilians and the military. Pemberton knew he could not exclusively rely on slaveholders to furnish chattels voluntarily. Too many masters, he said, had acted according to their "individual interest."[31] In April 1862, Pemberton saw the Confederates lose Fort Pulaski, which guarded the sea approaches to Savannah. The Georgia soldier Augustus Adamson complained that his commanders had bungled the fight for Pulaski. He thought they could have better used their men and their slave laborers. Adamson chided the commander at Pulaski, Alexander R. Lawton—a South Carolinian who had studied at Harvard Law School before the war—as an "Abolitionist." Lawton, he asserted, "could have had five hundred Negroes fortifying the Fort," but had chosen otherwise, with poor results.[32]

In May 1862, Pemberton—stationed in his headquarters in Charleston and not wanting to repeat the loss of Pulaski—directed planters to furnish slaves "free of charge" for coastal defenses. A few weeks later, he worried that the work on Fort Jackson would stop without additional slave laborers. Masters were understandably hesitant to give up their slaves, thinking their chattels might fall into Federal hands or die from Confederate mistreatment. In July, Pemberton nevertheless believed he should put 1,600 slaves to work at Charleston and elsewhere for at least two months.[33]

The South Carolina diarist Mary Chesnut wrote of the tensions between military officials and civilians along the coastal regions: "Every man is in Virginia and the eastern part of South Carolina in revolt because old men and boys are ordered out as a reserve corps—and worst of all, sacred property, that is, negroes, seized and sent to work on fortifications along the coastline."[34] Problems existed, but neither Virginia nor South Carolina was "in revolt." Despite the difficulties they had in dealing with masters, commanders continued taking slaveholders' black labor. After the fall of Forts Henry and Donelson, Gen. William Withers, writing from Richmond, said the only way to resist further advances out west was "by the surplus slave labor of the South." If the government used slaves, he continued, "immense results could be surely and speedily accomplished." In the Mississippi Valley, he believed slavery was losing its "patriarchal character."[35] The army must exploit its slave population for the peculiar institution and the Confederacy to survive.

Not all Confederate officers supported impressment. Gen. Howell Cobb of Georgia, one of the foremost proponents of the racial status quo, did not object outright to the use of black laborers (he thought slaves best served as gatherers of corn and fodder), but he did not want the Confederacy to make impressment official policy.[36] In August 1862, Cobb, an experienced politician sensitive to the complaints of his constituents, complained to the secretary of war about soldiers seizing slaves in Georgia. Citizens were "willing to make any and all sacrifices, but they like to see reason and common sense in the officials of Government," he noted.[37] Cobb's Confederate credentials are beyond question—he was the president of the Confederate Constitutional Convention—but he was at times critical of his government upsetting the usual workings of slavery. Cobb's conservatism would remain consistent. He was not only reluctant to see the army impress slaves, later in the war he would oppose the enlistment of black troops. Cobb worried that greater slave impressments would upset long-held Southern white property rights.

Cobb opposed impressment on principle, but most commanders did not. For them, military urgency trumped individual property rights. In late April 1862, stationed in Corinth, Mississippi, General Beauregard gave David Bullock Harris, then commander at Vicksburg, power to seize slaves to help with fortifications.[38] And far out west in Arkansas, Col. William H. Parsons of the Twelfth Texas Cavalry issued his Special Orders No. 65, allowing officers to obtain "by impressment if necessary a sufficient no. of negroes" to fix a bridge at Bayou De View between Little Rock and Memphis.[39]

In contrast to Howell Cobb, Confederate civilians had concerns, not about the principle of impressment, but its practice. Catherine Edmondston, a diarist and the wife of a prominent North Carolina planter, complained of slaves being impressed in Petersburg, Virginia. Writing from Raleigh, she said there were "negroes enough on James River whom their owners would be glad to employ & keep from the domination of the Yankees." Edmondston feared Confederates might take slaves near her home, where they were needed to gather crops, but she saw the sensibility of putting slaves under the care of the army rather than let the Yankees seize them.[40] Commanders, Edmondston believed, needed to pursue impressment sensibly.

In February 1863, writing from Richmond, where there were roughly ten thousand slaves at work, the North Carolina engineer Jeremy Francis Gilmer wanted to stop the "onerous requisitions for labor." He knew slaves were needed to make Lee's army and the city of Richmond secure, but he did not want to interfere with the harvest. In the future, he wrote, he wanted "such calls as light as possible."[41] Gilmer clearly sought to avoid problems with planters and farmers. The Confederate army, however, did not always arouse slaveholder opposition. In August 1862, Hugh Mercer wrote from Savannah about masters who "cheerfully" provided workers to the military, even if there were also "selfish individuals" who had "made all sorts of frivolous objections." Some masters had refused outright to furnish any workers. Even so, slave owners were not seriously undermining the military's efforts.[42] In November 1862, General Beauregard wrote South Carolina governor Francis Pickens to say that planters had "done nobly" in providing the army with slaves. Beauregard noted, however, that "they must not stop three-quarters of the way." In his view, were the army to succeed, Confederates must wholly support the war effort, and apparently white soldiers were not working hard enough. Slave laborers, Beauregard said, "would leave the troops to attend to their legitimate duties of drill and guard." His men, he lamented, "object most strenuously to work with spades and shovels; they will do it in very pressing emergencies, but on ordinary occasions do more grumbling than work."[43]

Confederate officers needed the help of black laborers. In February 1863, a month before Congress passed the impressment law, Thomas Jordan, serving on Beauregard's staff, praised the slaveholders who "have ever been found alive to the impulses of duty." Such words softened the blow when he asked in the same sentence for three thousand additional slaves.[44] In North Carolina, in March 1863, Leonidas L. Polk (not to be confused with his more famous uncle, Bishop Polk) noted that the "people very generously responded to the call." Some slaveholders gave their workers to the army understanding that the slaves were to be returned in four weeks. Polk, however, was disappointed that many of the larger slave owners had sent no workers.[45]

Masters made concerted efforts to help the army, but commanders wanted and needed more men, black and white. In late November 1862, Gen. Gustavus W. Smith—commanding between the Rappahannock and Cape Fear Rivers—complained to Robert E. Lee that he had obtained only 3,330 of the 4,500 black workers that had been promised him for work at Wilmington. Though he was writing from Richmond, not Wilmington, Smith wanted more troops as well as 5,000 additional black workers. Despite his complaints, Smith had received about 75 percent of the workers he had asked for, which was close to the percentage of white men who enlisted in the Confederacy during the war.[46]

The Confederate military could not have achieved such results without coercion. In April 1862, it instituted a draft. In October, it issued another. The army tried to persuade slaveholders to provide chattels voluntarily and temporarily, and some argued that slaves were safer in camp than elsewhere. The Confederacy's appeals were not free of threats. "If owners shall fail or refuse to comply with this request," warned Gideon Pillow in reference to Alabama planters in March 1863, "they need not complain . . . if they should be robbed of their negro property."[47] Some politicians did not appreciate commanders acting as if they were the ultimate authority. In South Carolina, Governor Francis Pickens wrote to General Beauregard in November 1862 concerning black workers who were not "assigned to the control or command of practical men." As did other politicians, Pickens complained that the military had unequally drained slaves from districts, and that they had been kept them longer than expected, which led to "derangement" in gathering crops.[48] Beauregard lamented having to mediate between state authorities and the Confederate government, a problem that would test the diplomatic skills of officers for the rest of the war.[49]

On 26 March 1863, because of white soldiers' refusal to do menial labor, the inconsistent efforts on the part of masters and governors to furnish slaves, and the general labor shortages and stresses of war, the Confederate Congress passed a slave impressment law. The Confederacy knew that most Southern states had no statutes concerning impressment. Congress hoped the bill would enable the war effort to run more efficiently. By March 1863, the Confederate government rightly understood that it had to keep its priorities in order: use its enlisted men to hold key positions rather than waste them in building fortifications or trenches, work that blacks could do, or acquiesce to the masters or state officials who did not want to give up black workers to the Rebel army.

The impressment of slaves raised the question of whether Confederates could legally seize free blacks, who numbered about 260,000 in the South in 1860. Free blacks had always lived in something of a limbo in the South. They were not slaves, but they did not have the legal rights or economic opportunities whites possessed. Southern whites never seemed to know what to do with them. The same proved true in wartime. Free blacks, because of their skin color, never became Confederate troops, with the brief exception in 1861 of the Louisiana Native Guards (who never served in combat for the Confederacy, which failed to provide the regiment with muskets or uniforms).[50]

Virginia had the largest free black population in the Confederacy, numbering roughly 58,000 people. Its legislature dealt with the issue of free black labor versus slave labor by passing three laws. The first subjected free black men to the Confederate draft (though they would serve in noncombat roles only); the second placed limits on the number of slaves authorities could impress; and the third law exempted enslaved agricultural laborers. By March 1863, commanders in Virginia had the power to force both free and enslaved workers into service.[51] The day before the Confederate Congress passed its slave impressment law, Robert E. Lee had written the secretary of war, James Seddon, to argue that both free and enslaved workers were needed on fortifications and railroads, which would allow him to deploy more soldiers.[52] Neither Lee nor other Confederate commanders, however, used many free blacks on military work projects.

One of the problems was logistical. Of the 28,000 free black males in Virginia, only 5,000 were of military age. By the time the Confederacy passed its impressment law, half of these men were already engaged in military-related tasks, from mining to hospital work. That left a relatively small number of free black workers that authorities could draw upon. Another problem was legal. The Confederate impressment act applied only to "property," and since free blacks were not property, Southern armies could not impress them into service.[53]

Free blacks were far fewer in number than enslaved African Americans, but some Confederates believed they were an underutilized labor source. In November 1863, with whites conscripted and slaves impressed into service, Francis Parker, a provost marshal in Georgetown, South Carolina, wondered why the "free man of color ... enjoys the increased profits of his business and makes money, whilst the white man does the hard work of the day." He decried such "inequality and injustice," asking that free blacks do "menial and much of the mechanical service" for the army. They should serve as cooks, cobblers, teamsters, and nurses, all for a "moderate rate of wages," the kinds of work white men did not like to do.[54]

The use of free blacks proved to be a lost opportunity for the Confederacy. Rebel leaders all too often liked to think of the Confederacy in terms of free white Southerners and enslaved African Americans. Free blacks enjoyed greater freedom than slaves, but they were not as free as whites. Confederate authorities would not let them fight in their armies, nor would they force them to work against their will. Very often, Confederates bent the proslavery ideology to meet the needs of the war effort. But when it came to the tens of thousands of free black males of military age, Rebel leaders were content to let them remain in limbo.

Strategically, the passage of the impressment law helped commanders gather much-needed workers. It also aroused more complaints than ever from masters. "I regret very much the impressment of your property," wrote Claudius L. Goodwin, a South Carolinian serving on Wade Hampton's staff, to an anxious Virginia master. An impressment officer "should satisfy himself that there is a 'sufficiency for family and plantation use.'" Even so, Goodwin conceded that the officer "may have transcended his orders." He enclosed a "certificate of protection" in order to ward off future problems.[55]

Complaints were not confined to civilians. From Jackson, Mississippi, in April 1863, one colonel wrote to John C. Pemberton—then commanding Mississippi, Tennessee, and eastern Louisiana—to note that crops were "so backward" that he thought officials should send slaves home to help with planting. He worried that cotton production would cease indefinitely, adding that he should not have to say that citizens needed corn.[56] With the tax-in-kind taking effect in 1863, masters felt pressed enough without having to hand over slaves to the military. The army could not rely on the volunteering of slaves alone, but masters believed they had more of a right to keep their slaves than the military had to take them.

In addition to the demands of the harvest, masters had concerns for the health and safety of their slaves. Many planters complied with impressment, but the Confederacy's promises of good treatment of slaves, or of compensatory payment, were not always kept. In May 1862, the Virginia slaveholder L. H. Minor complained of Confederate troops using his runaways on work projects. Federal forces were not the only soldiers who employed escaped slaves.[57]

Whether because of disease, flight, or capture by soldiers, many slaves never returned home, and it might take years before a master received compensation. The Virginia slaveholder James H. Evans waited until 1865 to see a $1,000 payment for the October 1862 loss of "Elijah," a slave who had worked on fortifications.[58] Confederates expected some slaves would undergo great danger in the service of the rebellion. In June 1862, the South Carolina soldier John J. Jefcoat heard of the shelling of black workers in Charleston by the Yankees.[59]

Impressed black workers, even more than normal field hands, endured harsh working conditions.[60] Some officers tried to feed black workers adequately and care for their well-being. In September 1861, the Virginia staff officer Charles H. Dimmock complained to North Carolina governor Henry T. Clark of "needy & ragged Negroes, that demands prompt action." He said his laborers were free blacks, not slaves, and that they had received neither salary nor clothing for months. They were a "miserable squalid set," he wrote. "The alacrity with which these poor creatures work, & the sadness of their appearance, has weighed upon me like a night-mare."[61] No white man would have wanted to die in the place of a "Negro," but that did not mean he always lacked sympathy for them. In Texas, in November 1863, for example, one officer complained his slaves needed better clothing.[62]

Confederate officers had good reason to care for their workers, but most slaves did not receive the care masters and conscientious commanders would have liked. One officer suggests why. In June 1863, David Harris, the chief engineer at Charleston, defended his department against accusations of slave mistreatment.[63] He admitted that blacks were working overtime, but this was because agents were unable to gather enough of them. And slaves were not productive, he noted, after thirty days of labor. Strenuous work, limited diet, and homesickness had weakened them, and until the army furnished commanders with sufficient numbers, blacks would suffer. Harris wanted servants to be kept longer, up to sixty days, and he considered whether masters should have the option of substituting one worker for another.[64] Early in the war, grumbling privates had complained that the army was turning them into slaves. Now, ironically, black laborers were becoming more like white soldiers. The army impressed some in a manner similar to conscription, substituted others, and kept them as long as the military required. Slaves were never impressed for the duration of the war, as were whites, but they too served for long periods in the army.

Concerning impressment, commanders preferred to deal with Confederate rather than state officials. In July 1863, Hugh Mercer, serving in Savannah, said his agents had gone as far as Mississippi to gather slaves. He appealed to Georgia governor Joseph E. Brown for more black workers. Not expecting success, he went over the head of the governor to obtain the needed labor. He wrote the secretary of war, James Seddon, saying that were he able to impress slaves, he could buy Savannah "at a cheap rate even if it cost them the labor of a thousand slaves yearly as long as the war may last."[65]

When it came to providing the military with slaves, North Carolina's governor Zebulon Vance—who, like Brown, had a reputation as an uncooperative Confederate—was caught between citizens who thought he impressed too many slaves and officers who thought he provided too few. In January 1863, the planter and politician William A. Smith complained to Vance about "the Governor with his bob tail malish demanding half of our able bodied slaves, which the Confeds have had for seven weeks."[66] A few weeks later, Secretary Seddon asked Vance for more black laborers for work on a railroad between Virginia and North Carolina. "Full hires shall be paid," he promised, "and every care possible shall be taken to provide for the comfort and safety of the slaves." Vance was slow in complying, saying he did not want to impress any slaves. He suggested that the government call upon free blacks. He told Seddon he would help collect workers, but his tone was uncooperative.[67]

In April 1863, Vance wrote to Seddon complaining of the "impossibility to prevent a famine" should Confederates take too many slaves. Vance was protecting the interests of North Carolina, but he created other problems. In May, he asked Gen. William Whiting, who was constructing works at Wilmington, to return impressed slaves to their owners. Vance and Whiting bickered with one another for months. Vance worried Whiting had used too many slaves, while Whiting feared a labor shortage would threaten Wilmington, a vital port. In June 1863, Whiting unburdened himself to D. H. Hill. "What little aid I can give I will," he said, though he lamented, "I expect to need it sorely myself." Vance, he wrote, was "calling in all the negro labor, which much embarrasses me." Whiting was worried about an attack by land or sea, and said he did not have enough forces to hold off either.[68] Wilmington, however, would hold out until February 1865.

As Federal threats mounted, slaveholders tried to move their slaves out of danger. Some took them from one town or neighborhood to another; others drove them across state lines. Writing from Petersburg, Virginia, in 1862, one soldier explained that "people are coming to town bringing negroes and other moveables at a rate you can form no idea of."[69] The reason, he said, was because the Yankees had been "plundering" nearby Garysville. Much further south, in Mississippi, another Confederate wrote his father, "I am at a loss what to do," noting it would cost four or five hundred dollars to bring his slaves to Virginia. He was anxious about them catching measles or whooping cough "at the very worst season of the year." He even thought of moving his slaves to Texas, but knew he could not attend to such a task himself.[70]

In North Carolina, Confederates noted the movement of slaves away from the coastal regions—which were most vulnerable to Federal invasion, and where there was a higher concentration of slaves—to the mountains, where slavery was thriving. An elderly civilian slaveholder and North Carolinian noted, "The yankies has been near tarborough and the People move their cotton and negroes from the lower Counties up the country." As John Inscoe and Gordon McKinney have concluded, slavery in Appalachia "proved so resilient" that few Upcountry people believed it would die until the final weeks of the war.[71]

Some planters and governors opposed impressment, but the Confederate military remained committed to it, for officers believed blacks were better workers than white men. In April 1863, the chief engineer at Galveston noted how the slaves were sweating in the sawmills, cutting and carrying sod, and hauling timber and iron. "The work of soldiers," he said, "amounts to very little, as the officers seem to have no control whatever over their men." In his eyes, "The number of soldiers at work is about 100 men, whose work amount to 10 negroes' work."[72] That an officer believed black labor was superior to white labor by a factor of ten was a damning indictment of Rebel soldiers, who apparently had internalized the racial hierarchy concerning work. Stationed at Secessionville in November 1863, a South Carolinian wrote that blacks working on fortifications "have done more in the last 3 months than all that ever has been done before."[73] Wherever they could find it, officers preferred using nonwhite labor. In May 1863, writing from Fort Brown, Texas, a quartermaster wanted to use not only black laborers for hauling cotton, he wanted Mexican teamsters, too.[74]

Not only were black men better workers than whites, Southerners saw that African Americans in Confederate camps were less likely to be taken or lured away by Federal forces than they were elsewhere. In July 1863, the Alabama slaveholder W. C. Bibb offered a quarter of his black workers to the army, thinking his slaves would be safer under the watch of soldiers than they were with him. Northerners, in his eyes, easily manipulated black people. Were slaves to come in contact with the enemy, the Federals might enlist them.[75]

In August 1863, during the Charleston campaign, one soldier wrote of the "picturesque sight at [Fort] Gregg: the grim bastions looming up, the lurid glare of camp fires lighting up the swarthy faces of our Southern soldiers, and an endless string of stalwart negroes busily carrying bags of sand."[76] Confederates, however, did not always get needed slave labor easily. In July 1863, James C. Marcom, serving in North Carolina, wrote of the poor turnout of black workers near Raleigh (which had 1,621 slaves and 466 free blacks in 1860), where "2 white men and 13 negroes were all that came."[77] Given such manpower shortages, and with the South's military fortunes worsening with defeats at Gettysburg and Vicksburg, some wanted the government to go further. In August 1863, the South Carolina planter A. P. Hayne submitted a plan to Jefferson Davis to place a hundred black workers, equal to a company, into each regiment.[78] That same month, Jonathan Watson, a citizen of Meridian, Mississippi, urged that slaves replace white workers at hospitals and at railroads. They could also serve as wagon drivers, pioneers, sappers, and miners, he wrote. The Federals, he noted, were already using slaves against the Confederacy—at Memphis and Corinth, there were thousands taking drill. He wrote of the possibility of the slaves "being made pretty good soldiers," and he thought it better to use blacks than allow the North to use them. "Under judicious treatment," Watson believed, "the army is really the safest place for the negroes."[79] The Texan William H. Neblett would have agreed. After predicting that agents would take some of his slaves, he said, "It would be best to let Sam and Joe go." Because they were likely to flee to the Yankees, he believed they would "probably be safer with the [Confederate] army than at home."[80]

In November 1863, the South Carolina slaveholder and staff officer Samuel W. Melton emphasized the crucial role slavery still played in the war effort. In his eyes, slavery made "our 8,000,000 . . . equal to the 20,000,000 of the North." One might question whether slavery gave the South parity with the Northern war machine, but Melton believed the Confederacy needed to expand its black labor force. For him, the problem lay in adapting "our peculiar system of labor . . . to relieve the fighting population from the obligations of production and manufacture." Just as slaves had for generations saved many white Southerners from digging ditches, cleaning stables, making supper, splitting hands on cotton stalks, and getting tuberculosis in factories, they could now allow whites to do what Confederates saw as the noble work of war: the fighting.[81] Realists such as Melton believed that the government must take on greater powers. From his hospital bed in 1864, one Texan argued that the army should use all nearby blacks to repair the Confederacy's supply roads. But, he lamented, "the powers that be will wait a week or ten days & then do what they could as well do today."[82] Even Confederates who did not oppose the use of slaves in the army might worry about whether the Rebel government could or would use them effectively.

In June 1863, the Confederate government put John Magruder, commanding the District of Texas, in charge of an impressment bureau, designed to make sure that masters furnished more slaves to the army.[83] Slaveholders might not like it, but the Confederate army believed it to be a necessary measure. For commanders, the alternatives—defeat and subjugation—were far worse. As the war became even more destructive, and thus threatened more and more households, some planters and smaller slaveholders hesitated to relinquish black workers. "Slavery is a most delicate question," the Virginia staff officer Samuel S. Anderson, serving in Texas, wrote to Magruder, noting that in some parts of Texas, "the production is so varied that free labor is very profitable." He believed it better that Magruder appeal to planter patriotism rather than resort to impressment. State elections were coming up in August and the army's seizing of slaves would prove a controversial issue. Better to leave a touchy issue aside, Anderson reasoned, when trying to win over voters; otherwise, staunch Confederates might face defeat from the opponents of Jefferson Davis and his policies.[84]

In response to the impending loss of Vicksburg and Port Hudson, Magruder wanted to protect Texas against invasion. He appealed to planters for slaves to help with fortifications, assuring them that the army would not move them west of the San Antonio River.[85] Magruder wanted to fortify Niblett's Bluff, a port city on the Louisiana side of the Sabine River, which served as a roadway for Confederates traveling from Louisiana to Houston and other points in southeast Texas. Niblett's Bluff technically was in Louisiana, but Magruder had authority there as well as in Texas.

Long after the war, the former staff officer A. G. Dickinson said of Magruder, "Texas owes him a debt of gratitude," for he "saved the State from invasion, and therefore gave to it that prosperity which it now enjoys." Near Niblett's Bluff, Magruder wanted authorities to stop and put to work all black men in the area. He and his men had little luck in getting slaveholders to provide servants voluntarily. Magruder, who had experienced similar problems earlier in the war in Virginia, now had more to consider than planters' hurt feelings. He feared Federal troops in northern Texas and western Louisiana would draw his own men from the coast, the defense of which was essential to keep slaves, cotton, railroads, and sugar in Confederate hands. He wanted to concentrate his forces, and he needed slaves to do it. Thankfully for Magruder, the Confederates thwarted a Union attack at Sabine Pass, where General Banks had hoped to gain a foothold in order to attack Niblett's Bluff and later Beaumont and Houston.[86]

Confederate success in Texas underscored the benefits of a reliable supply of black labor. Yet, despite problems in Texas and elsewhere, masters were still supportive of the Confederacy. Said a War Department employee, Robert Kean, about Alabama: "Heretofore a negro could not be got for work connected with the army for any price. Now men are offering them and are proposing to use them as soldiers." Kean was happy to see masters give slaves to the army, but he was dubious of black men becoming troops. He thought it "bad policy," and he was hopeful the army could use blacks as teamsters, builders of fortifications, cooks, and at all other "menial offices of the army."[87] For white Confederates, African Americans were best kept at work and out of uniform.

In September 1863, Kirby Smith, commanding the trans-Mississippi region, received good news. He said Texas planters, understanding such calls would fall on masters equally, were cooperating with impressment officials. "The public-spirited man," Smith said, "objects that his unpatriotic neighbor should receive the protection of the Government without adding his quota to its support." Masters wanted men of equal means to furnish slaves at the same rate, and they hoped Confederate officials would practice impressment fairly. With the Federal threat ever increasing, Smith believed the idea that "slave property is uncertain has been gradually gaining ground in the public mind." In his view, it was better that the army impress thousands of slaves in Texas rather than let them fall into enemy hands.[88]

John Magruder did not support Kirby Smith's plan, which he thought put an unfair burden on Texas planters. Rather, he believed Texans and Louisianans should both furnish more slaves. Magruder noted that he had not lost many slaves in his Texas District, nor had he impressed many. To change the Confederacy's policy to one based on impressment would result, he wrote in October 1863, in masters finding no "home for their slaves," which would cause "great confusion." Magruder believed the impressment bureau was working well for the first time, and he did not want Kirby Smith or "interested parties (planters from Louisiana or elsewhere)" to interfere. Magruder worried that if impressment was the sole policy for acquiring black laborers, it would anger masters, who might flee beyond the reach of Confederate authorities.[89]

Magruder's efforts to control impressment in Texas were part of the Confederacy's larger attempt to create a workable bureaucracy. In October 1863, Samuel Cooper, the highest-ranking general in the Confederacy and Jefferson Davis's military advisor, issued a special order based on the Confederate Congress's impressment law. Cooper said commanders could take slaves from plantations dedicated to the production of grain only "in cases of urgent necessity." The order, however, put heavy demands on masters to furnish slaves when needed. Those who were slow in doing so, without reason, could have their slaves detained an extra month. Masters could send overseers to the army, but officers had the power to dismiss them for misconduct. In return, those who provided slaves on demand would receive $20 a month for each worker. Were a slave to die, "a board of experts" would decide his value, but a master could not hold the military responsible for slaves killed "by the act of God, or by disease existing when the slave is received by Confederate authorities." Such measures underscored the fact that by 1863, the army had a contract with the states for black labor, the largest such contract in the history of American slavery. The Confederacy now had a board to determine a slave's worth and was not responsible for a slave struck by lightning, washed away in a flood, or otherwise taken by Providence. If it were not obvious by then, slave owners now knew who came first: the owner, the state government, or the Confederate army.[90] Confederates dealt the best they could with the new measures. Long before General Cooper issued new measures, the South Carolina soldier William Grimball wrote to his father about drawing up an affidavit concerning the loss of a slave named Henry. He wanted his father to use care, but he lamented "the tedious process of legislative compensation."[91]

Confederate commanders not only ordered the impressment of slaves, they also demanded masters move chattels out of harm's way. In December 1863, the Texas soldier Rudolf Coreth wrote of General Magruder forcing planters and their slaves to move seventy-five miles inland. Coreth worried about the loss of crops due to neglect, and of worried slaves consuming more than they were producing and eating provisions intended for the army.[92]

The Confederacy's loss of Vicksburg, Port Hudson, and Chattanooga worsened an already difficult military situation. As the defeats mounted, the army demanded greater impressment power. In Mobile, in December 1863, local masters were angry that the army kept slaves at work for too long. However, Von Sheliha, an engineer, blamed the planters. Masters had hesitated to send slaves, he said, and then complained when they were not quickly returned. He also dismissed accusations that Rebel soldiers mistreated blacks. For Sheliha, the problem again lay with masters, whose overseers were "not always men who deserve the confidence of their employers." The number of sick men under his command was not excessive, but he felt the Confederacy should placate worried masters by increasing slaves' pay to $30 a month (with the planters providing rations). Sheliha's plans, however, went further. He wanted the Confederacy to create a permanent force of black workers. "The advantages of such an organization," he concluded in December 1863, "are too obvious for me to venture."[93] Sheliha would never see such a body created, but the Confederacy did take steps to create a permanent black labor force. In February 1864, the Congress passed a third draft bill, which allowed for the conscription of 20,000 slaves, effectively a corps, for use as teamsters and cooks. The Confederacy, however, never created an official corps of black workers.

By February 1864, Richard Taylor, then commanding western Louisiana, grew fatalistic about slavery in his district. Taylor, a wealthy Louisiana sugar planter before the war, had no doubts about the goodness of slavery. But he understood firsthand how the war had weakened it. In 1863, the Yankees had plundered Taylor's plantation, "Fashion," making off with livestock and horses, hogsheads of sugar, and scores of slaves. Taylor knew the limits of slave loyalty, and when it came to impressing black workers, he also saw difficulties. On the one hand, to rely upon masters to volunteer their servants was to risk a labor shortage, and with it a weaker military that might lose more Confederate territory. On the other hand, if the army resorted to impressment, Taylor believed there would be a "general stampede" of masters to Texas, where they could find more lenient polices under Magruder's leadership. Taylor, ultimately, thought impressment unwise. On this point, he differed with his superior, Kirby Smith. But then again, the men rarely agreed on anything.[94]

Taylor was nervous about his superior's impressment policies, but disagreement over how to best deal with slaves did not suggest chaos within the command structure or inherent weaknesses in the Confederate army. As 1864 began, Southern forces were still formidable. That year perhaps proved to be the most decisive in the history of North American slavery, for it was in 1864 that the Confederate army would break under the pressure of Union offensives. Confederates, who faced ever greater shortages of troops and supplies, relied increasingly on impressment, and they had considerable success in getting needed slaves. Black workers did not fend off Grant's huge armies directly, but they continued to help Confederates build forts and make entrenchments.

In February 1864, Virginia governor William "Extra Billy" Smith, formerly a Rebel general, used appeals and threats to assure citizens sent slaves to authorities. The "first duty of the citizen is to unite in the public defence," he said to the people of Lunenburg County, reminding them that unlike other parts of his state, Lunenburg had not suffered from Yankees burning homes, food shortages, or slaves being taken. Now he hoped they would "cheerfully" respond to calls for black workers, but if they did not, he threatened that officials might "impress the necessary labour to insure the obligation."[95]

Well into 1864, many Rebel soldiers remained optimistic about the survival of the Confederacy and the institution of slavery. For them, impressment was just another means of preserving slavery in the long run. The Louisiana colonel James C. Beard, who took part in the Red River campaign, was hopeful about his men's chances against the Yankees. Even so, he advised his father-in-law to "send off" all of his male slaves, believing that the "safest thing" would be if they served as cooks and teamsters. Another Louisianan, the sugar planter Alfred Weeks, who did not serve in Confederate forces until very late in the war, moved his slaves to Texas. In May 1864, he still had confidence in the Rebel military. "I do not think . . . that we will lose our negroes," he wrote. "The Confederate States must succeed and if we can keep [slaves] from the enemy we will save them. I feel hopeful & confident and know that we never can be subjugated."[96] Masters might have moved slaves out of the Union's way, but it was not necessarily because they were contemptuous of authority or pessimistic about Southern independence.

Commanders continued shuffling thousands of needed black workers into the army. In January 1864, Gen. Leonidas Polk, commanding in Mississippi after his fallout with Braxton Bragg after the battle of Chickamauga, said he had sent five thousand slaves to Mobile. That summer, the North would capture Mobile Bay, though the city itself would remain in Confederate hands until after Lee's surrender.[97] Confederates in Mobile obtained thousands of slaves to bolster the city's defenses, but in Polk's theater of operations, all was not well. By 1864, Mississippi was "in a most deplorable condition."[98] Yet, that summer, the ever resourceful Nathan Bedford Forrest continued to gather slaves. In August, he planned on getting five hundred for the works around Grenada and Graysport.[99] But as the year went on, officers had greater difficulty obtaining slave labor, and, for that matter, manpower in general.

Officers continued to make appeals to civilians, and they made it clear how impressed labor would help the war effort. "With the work of two hundred negroes I can in fifteen days strengthen the position as to hold it against any raiding party," said Col. Benjamin Farinholt to the citizens of Charlotte and Halifax, Virginia. In a 4 July appeal, he said he needed slaves "at once," for their work would "be the means of saving you[r] farms and homes from desolation and the foul presence of the enemy's vandals." He said farmers had no reason to refuse him—as they were between planting and harvesting season—and he wanted blacks to help citizens avoid the fate of others in Virginia.[100]

As Farinholt made calls on Virginians, William T. Sherman's army moved into the heart of Georgia, where slaves had become part of the Confederate campaign to defend Atlanta. One soldier recalled how Gen. Joseph E. Johnston called for 12,000 blacks to act as teamsters and cooks.

The need for such a large number underscored the dire state of the Confederate military and the limits of what the government could do. The impressment of 12,000 slaves was a fantastic number, constituting a small army of laborers. The Confederacy never furnished so many slaves at one time for any general, even Robert E. Lee, and such numbers were difficult to meet in 1864. Johnston never got his 12,000 slaves, but black laborers were an important part of the campaign. "We expect to make a stand of three or four days at this place," wrote the Georgian Eugene Verdery on Independence Day 1864, "so as to enable the negro forces engaged in building our last line to do it effectively."[101]

Once Sherman occupied Atlanta, he marched to the coast rather than finish off the limping Army of Tennessee. Coastal cities in Georgia and the Carolinas became vulnerable. The previous year, while commanding at Charleston, General Beauregard had complained that his "constant appeals" were not enough to obtain the 2,500 slaves per month he requested. Instead, he had only received an average of 330.[102] In 1864, Beauregard was busy in Virginia holding off Butler's and, later, Grant's forces. Sam Jones, who had served in various theaters, succeeded him as commander of South Carolina, Georgia, and Florida. Headquartered in Charleston in June 1864, Jones asked planters to send slaves to the military, provided it did not interfere with rice harvesting. Jones would not impress black workers, but rather hire them out, and he promised that the military would treat them well. His ranks were depleted of labor. Where 2,000 slaves were needed, his agents obtained only nine; where 200 were required, he had only a dozen. "I cannot order the impressment of negroes in those States which have taken action on this subject," General Jones complained.[103] As did many commanders, he had enough confidence in the survival and necessity of slavery to keep demanding black workers from local masters. But he did not always get the numbers of slaves he wanted.

In September 1864, Robert E. Lee, whose army lay pinned down at Petersburg, knew he must enlist black workers to an extent greater than Congress had authorized. In his eyes, the February draft bill, which had allowed for the use of 20,000 slaves in the army, had not proven effective. "It seems to me," he wrote Jefferson Davis, "that we must choose between employing negroes ourselves or having them employed against us." The general's thinking foreshadowed that of early 1865, when he favored enlisting blacks into the army. Every slave that fled to Union lines took away a laborer from the Confederacy and added one to the Federals. In September 1864, Lee reported that he needed 5,000 black laborers for his army—and that meant 5,000 white troops could remain at the front. As Lee saw it, the February Conscription Act gave impressment power not to Secretary Seddon, but to commanding officers, and he wanted to use slaves not just for military work, but anywhere where they might free up white soldiers. Lee asked the Confederacy to create a corps of black workers to cut wood and perform roadwork, and he wanted them to be exclusively slaves: no free blacks or contract laborers. Late in the war, Lee saw that his army had to rely more than ever on slave labor.[104]

In late September 1864, Seddon said he would impress 20,000 slaves, as authorized by Congress, to help General Lee. "Many advantages," Seddon believed "would result from this system in enabling us to preserve better order and exercise more care and supervision over the negroes so employed." The machinery of war, however, was not working. In October, Lee told Seddon that the slaves he needed had not arrived. Were they not to come, he warned, "it will be very difficult for us to maintain ourselves." Despite Lee's desperate situation at Petersburg, Seddon complained of problems raising more white troops and an entire corps of impressed workers.[105] In December, Lee further complained that only 2,000 of the 5,000 slaves he requested were in camp. It was a formidable number of workers, but Lee was not satisfied for he had not received enough men to replace his white teamsters. Instead, he had only enough to supply A. P. Hill's Third Corps and part of a division. Lee was not alone in understanding what a lack of black laborers meant for Confederates. In late December 1864, James Longstreet worried that the army would have to abandon a line of defenses unless it put black workers on it.[106]

Lee, Longstreet, and others never received the slaves they requested. They made considerable efforts to get them, but by the fall of 1864, even the seemingly supernatural Nathan Bedford Forrest could no longer work miracles. Forrest reported his failure to provide all the slaves that Richard Taylor, then commanding eastern Louisiana, Mississippi, and Alabama, needed in his theater of combat. Forrest had captured roughly 1,000 slaves, and he sent about 800 to Taylor.[107] By then, however, the war was going badly for the Confederacy. Impressed slaves mattered little when Sherman's forces were marching unopposed through Georgia.

Union victories meant not just the flight of slaves to Federal lines, but the flight of masters. In November 1864, writing from Lewisville, Arkansas, in the southwestern portion of that state, John Magruder estimated that slaveholders had taken 150,000 chattels from Missouri and Arkansas to Texas during the war. Given the vast number of slaves in his region, he wanted to impress more black workers, even though he worried it might alienate the planters. If slave owners fled to Texas, he reasoned, they were still within Confederate borders, and thus still under his control. Magruder had not lost faith in slave labor. "My judgment tells me the negroes are absolutely necessary," he wrote in November 1864.[108]

In February 1865, Mississippi authorities ordered officers not to disturb slaves working on railroads used for military transportation.[109] The Confederacy was in its death throes, but commanders were still making policy concerning the use of slaves in the army. In March, Nathan Bedford Forrest ordered that all wagon drivers in his forces were to be black. In addition, every ten men were to be allowed one black cook, and no officer could claim a slave that was not in his immediate service.[110] Such orders had little importance given that the war would soon end, but they underscore the Confederate army's continued reliance upon human bondage.

Until the end of the war, Confederates used as many slaves as possible for their defenses. In 1865, the campaign for Spanish Fort, which guarded Mobile, had little bearing on events elsewhere, but Federal forces spent much blood to take it. On 5 April, a worried Confederate officer complained that he needed "more heavy guns, more mortars, more axes, more negroes."[111] Spanish Fort surrendered three days later, a day before Lee capitulated at Appomattox.

The Confederacy's decision to impress slaves was a natural and logical, albeit controversial, one. Thousands of slaves, doing the hard labor they had performed for generations, kept Confederate armies in the field. Rebels often considered blacks lazy, but the army knew that they had performed the most menial and difficult work in the South. In resorting to impressment, the Confederacy faced one of the many dilemmas it confronted during the war: how to use the South's vast resources without violating individual property rights. It also questioned how Southerners could best govern slavery while defending Confederate strongholds.

Southerners faced not just ideological challenges, but logistical difficulties. Whether or not they worked slaves in the army, or kept them at home, they were merely transferring the labor force, not employing unused resources. Every slave used in the army allowed one soldier to serve at the front, but it also meant the absence of one more slave on the farm or plantation. Slaves were rarely idle. Their usefulness to the South depended on where and when they worked, not on whether or not they worked. When they were under white supervision, and even when they were not, blacks provided the main source of labor for the Confederacy. Rebel leaders understood that slaves were not a perfect means of labor, but they were an essential one. Without slaves, white men could not have fought in the numbers they did for the South.

Confederates applied antebellum laws and custom as much as possible to the contingencies of war, but the conflict led to the passage of new laws governing the peculiar institution. The authorities hoped that the people would understand that impressment was only a wartime measure. Confederate soldiers interfered with the usual workings of slavery, but they did not want to change the institution fundamentally. The issue of impressment did not lead Confederates to question the validity and practicality of human bondage, only how best to keep it alive without starving the war effort.

· 4 ·

"SEND ME THE NEGRO BOY"
CONFEDERATE SOLDIERS AND THE
NEED FOR SLAVES IN CAMP

The conscription of able-bodied white troops and the impressment of slaves into the Rebel armies were two instances of the Confederacy exerting unprecedented power in the South. Throughout the war, Confederates hoped to strike a balance between the forces of states' rights and centralization, volunteerism and coercion, the free market and government intrusion into the economy. Many slaves who served in the Confederate army were impressed from Southern masters, but when Irby Goodwin Scott entered the army in 1861, he brought two slaves with him. They were among only six slaves who shared the camp with his entire unit, but on the whole, in Rebel armies, black workers literally represented a division of labor. When Lee's forces invaded Pennsylvania, the Army of Northern Virginia had roughly 6,000 African Americans with them. None of them were soldiers.[1] The Confederate military proved to be a place where blacks could alleviate Rebel soldiers from a multitude of tasks and where Southern whites could exert greater control over slaves.

Confederate troops found a safe haven for slaves by having them share their tents, messes, and firesides, and as Joseph Glatthaar has noted in his study of the Army of Northern Virginia, the peculiar institution "represented a world of contradictions to Rebels."[2] Indeed, Confederates' relationship with slaves and camp and with those back home revealed the tensions that existed in being treated both as human and as property, as valuable and as expendable, as a beloved friend and as merely a servant. And as was the case with impressment and conscription, the war challenged the normal workings of slavery and Confederates' faith in the institution. In Rebel camps, slaves weathered the uncertainties of the market and the difficulties of combat while also being under their master's control. Camp slaves were dear to soldiers, but even beloved body servants—immortalized in wartime letters and postwar literature—were valuable only if they were useful, obedient, and cost effective.

The more conventional the Confederate unit, the more slaves played a part in its operations. In the Army of Northern Virginia and the Army of Tennessee, for example, one would expect to find more slaves per white man than would be found in a guerilla unit located in the trans-Mississippi, or in a unit of home guards hunting down deserters in North Carolina. In comparison to most Confederate forces, Lee's army was of much greater size and stability, and geographically, for most of the war, it remained within the one-hundred-mile corridor between Richmond and Washington. Months would pass during which Lee's men were not engaged in significant fighting. In such "quiet" periods, soldiers could run their camps like small Southern communities, in which slaves would be expected to perform domestic functions. But camp slaves were a part of every theater of Confederate operations. Body servants were in the army at the demand of their masters, not the government, so their presence depended on the willingness of slaveholders to put their chattels in harm's way. The less domesticated the camp environment, the less sense it made for a master to have what was, in essence, a domestic worker with him.

In many ways, Confederate soldiers found that the army proved a good home for African Americans, who could help with washing, cooking, cleaning, and the upkeep of animals. Men frequently wrote to family members about their need for a servant, although they also wanted to be sure that their servant would be manageable. The Mississippian Ruffin Thomson wrote at length about the faithfulness of his servant, "Press." Despite the risks, he believed Press was safe with him in camp. In June 1862, Thomson worried about the possible loss of Vicksburg, but were that to happen, he said, Press "will be better with me than at home."[3] Soldiers thought of slaves much as they did any other military resource. Using the logic of defending interior lines, Confederate troops knew that a loss of territory was not necessarily detrimental to their cause—the less land the Confederacy had, the less it had to defend. Similarly, the fewer numbers of slaves the Confederacy had to worry about, the more they could control those nearby. Soldiers could do very little about blacks hundreds of miles away, but they could keep watch over those serving alongside them. In April 1863, Pvt. Eugene Verdery of the Sixty-Third Georgia complained that he had "suffer[ed] a great deal of inconvenience in not having a servant," especially during his recent illness. Verdery hoped to convince his father that a body servant would be safe in the army. "They have never captured a negro from Savannah," he wrote of the Federals who had occupied territory in the southeastern Confederacy but had not yet taken Savannah. Even as fortunes turned against the Confederacy in 1863, men still had faith in the army's ability to keep its slaves under control. "*Be certain* and send me the negro boy," the Arkansan Alex Spence wrote in March 1864 from Georgia. "A negro I think is safer in the Army than anywhere else now."[4]

In the early days of the war, slavery as an institution remained relatively untouched, and Southern whites thought of the conflict as a great adventure. In the mind of many Confederates, the spirit of the antebellum world lived on. In 1861, some Confederates continued to depict the South as a land of plenty where blacks remained dutiful slaves. A mother writing from Charlottesville, Virginia, wrote that the "servants *all* look well and cheered so do both Master and mistress—splendid crops—said to be the best in the neighborhood."[5] Confederate soldiers' control over their slaves, however, proved to be far more tenuous than most Rebels admitted. The war created problems for masters at every level. Soldiers attempted to adapt to the changes the conflict wrought on their society without losing faith in slavery. Just as black workers were essential to the antebellum South, their cooperation and productivity were vital in wartime. Thousands of slaves performed many roles in the army. Some undertook the dangerous, grueling, and essential work of building fortifications. Others had "lighter" duties as body servants and cooks.

Body servants were a luxury that most Confederates could not afford, but they were not a rarity. Regardless of where they were stationed, Southern troops enjoyed having body servants with them, and others enjoyed having blacks in camp, even if they did not own any slaves themselves. A body servant answered to his master, not the Confederate government, and it was the individual soldier, not the quartermaster department, who cared for him. For Confederate troops, a servant who could make a good cup of coffee or biscuit, or appear with a dry blanket after a soldier had slept too long in the rain, was well worth the trouble. A slave's companionship and labor alleviated the miseries and tedium of camp life.[6] "In a fort," wrote William H. Grimball, serving along the South Carolina coast, "a servant is very important as he performs the varius duties of chambermaid, butler, and bootblack."[7] Some Confederate troops enjoyed the "good life," as servants completed the more unpleasant tasks required to keep the army functioning. As one soldier put it, slaves performed "incalculable services."[8]

Such "services" were often not essential. After all, soldiers could have made their own meals and saddled their own horses. But most Confederates preferred African Americans as cooks, foragers, musicians, teamsters, and animal drivers.[9] Richard Taylor believed his slave—who could light a fire in an instant, make good coffee, and was an excellent cook—was invaluable.[10] Body servants gave Confederates a sense of continuity between the period before the war and the present, and what was more, they provided a taste of the soldier's cherished domestic life.

Confederate troops entered the army untrained and undisciplined; only with hard work and dedication did they become good soldiers. Some slaves also needed time to adjust to their responsibilities in the army. In November 1863 Mississippi Pvt. Harry Lewis referred to his servant as "cornfieldish," by which he meant lacking the graces that one might expect from a domestic worker. Nevertheless, Lewis also thought his servant was "industrious" and believed he "likes his work." Stationed in Rapidan, Virginia, in the fall of 1863, the men in Lewis's mess apparently consisted of only five soldiers, but there were also four slaves.[11] The Confederate army usually did not have such a high ratio of slaves to troops, but when soldiers were not campaigning, servants were more easily kept at hand. Contrary to the myth of the Lost Cause which glorified the barefoot and perpetually undersupplied Confederate troops, the Rebels enjoyed many of the pleasures of living in what was, by nineteenth-century standards, a wealthy society. The Confederacy was less urban and less industrialized than the North, but when the war began—and even later—secessionists were able to maintain the high standard of living that slaveholding made possible.

In the Confederacy, despite the intrusion of the central government into the economy, slavery remained subject to market forces. The Rebel camps were no different. Not all camp servants worked for free; nor were all of them slaves. Many blacks in camp were free workers who expected payment from the individual soldiers they served.[12] It was also common for slaves to receive money. The amount of payment differed greatly depending on the state of the war effort, location, and work performed. In August 1862, one Mississippi soldier wrote of a servant who received $4 for a week of washing and cooking. Payment for servant labor sometimes exceeded a private's monthly pay of $11 (increased to $13 in 1864). Privates could not afford to hire a servant on an army salary alone. Instead, most servants were either owned by one of the commissioned officers—who made far more money—or belonged to a soldier's white family, who sent him along when the son entered the army. Since servants were not hired by the army for domestic duties, individual troops, or a group of soldiers, had to pay for them. And as the war went on, nearly everything in the Confederacy became more expensive, including hired hands. In October 1864, Pvt. William A. Penn of the Twenty-Fourth Virginia Infantry and from a prominent tobacco growing family, was prepared to pay his slave $50, or even $100 to do the washing tasks for him and his mess. That may sound like a lot of money, but one should bear in mind that Penn was also planning to spend $50 on a blanket.[13]

The practice of paying slaves was not new. The antebellum hiring system had been an important part of the slave economy, in which many black people could sometimes keep a portion of their earnings.[14] Slaves also had other ways of making money. On plantations, some masters gave slaves cash bonuses and gifts, and many servants grew produce and raised livestock for sale. In Confederate camps, slaves made money for performing a variety of tasks, from mailing letters, selling apples, and providing wakeup calls, to running barbershops.[15] According to one veteran, servants in camp supposedly had little reason to steal, because they had enough money of their own. His own slave, Jim, supposedly had as much as $1,000 of his own money. Such an amount was uncommon, but it is clear that servants sometimes possessed large amounts of money.[16]

It is clear that some slaves were shrewd in their financial dealings with soldiers. Confederates often complained about sutlers gouging them, but whites were not the only people known for charging high prices to troops. Writing from Petersburg, Virginia, in June 1862, one Confederate complained that "the negroes sell us pies two and three about as big as a pound of soap after a weeks washing for a quarter and onions five cents a piece."[17] Some Confederates might have mistaken a servant's taking advantage of his master for plain stupidity. In December 1862, the North Carolina officer Thomas Toon wrote of giving his slave, Wesly, five dollars to get something to eat. After a long wait, Wesly returned armed with a turkey and a "little chicken (too little to wean)." Toon, clearly disappointed, thought the price he had paid was far too much. He wondered whether Wesly could "break Jeff Davis in a short time." It is likely that Wesly paid less for the food than he claimed and then pocketed some of the change. Toon, however, assumed it was Wesley's bad judgment that had cost him too much money.[18]

Even if slaves might occasionally take advantage of their master's trust, they were highly prized workers. For Southern whites, men were supposed to fight, not clean dishes or make meals. Confederates especially valued servants who could make good food. One said he was "lost without a cook," while another said, redundantly, that he almost "perished to death" in his servant's absence.[19] Some camp slaves might have "spoiled the broth" as a way of resisting their white masters; others might simply have been bad cooks.[20] For the most part, Confederate troops thought slaves cooked and performed their duties well, which left soldiers more time to concentrate on fighting or recreation.

With the aid of slaves, some men lived perhaps too well. The Louisianan James Stubbs had no shame about the pleasures of the army. In October 1862, he kept three horses, "at the expense of the government," and possessed "as many servants as I choose or can afford to have." He spoke of "two who are attentive to all my wants." One, named Dandy, came in the morning, made a fire, prepared the water for washing, cleaned Stubbs's boots, brushed his clothes, and "seems to take pleasure in doing all for me." The other, Sam, fed and attended to Stubbs's horses while Dandy made breakfast, which consisted of biscuits and butter, coffee and York River Spots, "well pickled & cured." Stubbs asked, "What better can a soldier desire?"[21] It was rare, but some men could reproduce in camp the life of a privileged master. They perhaps even had an easier life than they had enjoyed in the antebellum period.

Most men, however, found that the war made their lives much harder, and slaves sometimes created divisions among the troops. Men formed tight bonds in camp, but comradeship did not always ensure that troops would share their servants with others. Masters, after all, paid good money for their workers, so why should they share a cook or body servant with others? One soldier wrote of his captain's unpopular decision to have the soldiers' personal cooks prepare meals for the entire company. Some opposed the idea and threatened to send their slaves home.[22]

There were servants who belonged to overindulgent or selfish masters, but in the Confederate army, black workers had a communal function. They were usually attached to a company or regiment as much as they were to their owners, and servants were helpful, not just in cooking food, but in finding it.[23] In contrast to the Lost Cause myth of ragged, scarecrow Rebels bravely fighting on despite inadequate provisions and incompetent quartermasters, white Southern troops often ate well, and slaves' resourcefulness helped supplement their rations. In May 1862, the Louisiana cavalryman Edwin H. Fay said he had not seen meat for three days, except when camp servants had killed some hogs. But three years later, Fay was stationed in an area where ducks were so abundant that slaves brought them in by the "horseback loads." Throughout the war, Confederate troops wrote of slaves foraging for cornbread, chickens, apples, peaches, and watermelons in the countryside in order to feed themselves and hungry soldiers.[24]

Such bounty was usually had at the expense of nearby communities. As two historians have written, the Confederate army "depended almost entirely on military seizure from its citizens to support itself."[25] Charles Powell devoted a good portion of his memoir to his servant, Wright, "a young mulatto." Powell had brought Wright to Georgia during the Atlanta campaign. While there, using a photograph of his master as identification, Wright had searched the countryside for food, often returning "laden with delicacies such [as] milk, butter, light bread buttered, sausage, backbones, and even dried fruit and honey and preserves." For his services, Wright "was a favorite with all the Battalion." Powell seemed convinced that Wright always asked permission for what food he obtained. And maybe he did. But other Confederate masters encouraged theft, looked the other way when it happened, or asked no questions after it took place.[26]

Soldiers often faced the ethical dilemma of stealing. In 1862, Tally Simpson wrote of a servant who came across an unfenced cornfield. That the place was unprotected made the moral question of whether to taking some corn more ambivalent. After his slave had returned with arms full of food, however, Simpson relented.[27] The need to survive made whites act in ways that undermined the ideal of the "Southern gentleman," and Confederate troops did not necessarily enjoy immunity when they stole from a black person either. In 1862, one soldier wrote of a comrade having been punished for taking a slave's watch.[28] After the war, the Louisiana infantryman Maj. Silas T. Grisamore remembered a soldier swiping a melon from a slave, who caught him before he could jump onto a train. The soldier was lucky not to have been crushed underneath the locomotive, though the melon was not so fortunate.[29] In Confederate eyes, blacks were not to take advantage of the freedoms the war gave them, but neither should whites act in a way that might threaten the master-slave relationship.

George Washington once dryly noted that his slaves drank more of his wine than he did. Slaves, indeed, were often accused of thievery that ranged from the theft of petty items to the taking of more expensive property, such as horses. Many masters did not fret over minor theft, considering it an unfortunate part of slaveholding. Slaves knew stealing was risky, but they likely felt they were taking what was owed them; regardless, stealing could not compare with a master's theft of a black person's body, time, and labor. The chaos of war undoubtedly made some slaves bolder in their efforts to undermine their master's authority. The Virginia sergeant Robert W. Parker wrote of slaves stealing men's horses near his camp. He also wrote of slave children taking sweetcakes from his haversack. Parker did not seem angered by such actions, but other Confederates were less forgiving. In 1863, Arthur Fremantle, a British observer of the war, witnessed two Confederate troops pound a slave with ramrods after the slave had tried to abscond with his master's horses.[30]

Few Confederate memoirs detail the day-to-day miseries of camp life. The army usually failed to live up to the "moonlight and magnolias" myth of the Old South. Wartime letters and diaries, in contrast, do depict the unpleasant side of soldiering. As with armies throughout history, the Confederate army was always running short of something. The troops tried to keep their servants relatively well clothed and fed, which was not always easy, yet masters did not want to think that slaves ate better than they did. "I must admonish you not to be extravagent in weighing out meat to the negros," said Georgian James L. Reid to his wife. He wanted her to distribute five pounds of meat to each for two weeks. Soldiers were on half rations, he noted, "and [we] must not feed the negros so high as heretofore."[31]

On 4 March 1864, the Confederate army issued General Orders No. 28, which concerned the issuing of rations. Among other things, the order said that commissioned officers would receive one ration per day, the same as enlisted men. The order said nothing about body servants. Commanders in Lee's Second Corps, including Richard Ewell, Jubal Early, Stephen Ramseur, and John B. Gordon, protested. A decrease in rations would effectively take food out of a body servant's mouth, and possibly their own. Their 19 March letter declared that it was "absolutely necessary that officers should keep servants," noting that regulations prevented enlisted men from serving in "menial capacities." Confederates who had dug ditches, cooked meals, washed dishes, and cleaned camps for almost three years might have disagreed with that statement. But it showed how Confederates, especially officers, preferred that servants do such tasks. Some officers believed that having to pay for slaves' provisions from outside sources placed a financial burden on them. Apparently, even when officers had money, they could not always find food and clothing among the locals. "The country in which we operate," the officers noted, "is almost entirely denuded of supplies, the citizens having barely enough for their own support and no surplus for sale."[32]

Among the generals who signed the 19 March letter was the North

Carolinian Stephen Dodson Ramseur. In 1853, Ramseur had decried the wickedness of slave trading, but with the rise of the Republican Party, he now denounced abolitionism, calling slavery "the *greatest blessing* both for master & slave, that could have been bestowed upon us." Ramseur's father was a planter, and Ramseur himself traded slaves during the war. In January 1864, he wrote his brother, saying that those at home should limit slaves' rations to a quarter-pound of meat or less per day if they had vegetables. "Our whole people should do this," he said, "& send the surplus to the army." To do so would allow whites to eat better, and it would in theory allow officers to purchase rations for slaves serving with them. William A. Graham Jr., another North Carolinian, also disliked General Orders No. 28. He noted that officers were too important to care for their own horses or share their food. "It is not right to starve [an officer]," he complained, "by making him divide his ration with his negro."[33]

The debate about Confederates feeding blacks in camp only underscored the importance of slaves' work for the war effort. Southern troops, however, did not always think of "Negroes" as menial workers or merely another mouth to feed. Soldiers often praised body servants and spoke of their bravery under fire. During the Atlanta campaign, Alabaman Wallace Comer said his servant, Burrell, "is one negroe I have seen that is not much afraid of the bullets." He added that Burrell "staid with me all day yesterday when I was on Picket."[34] White or black, noncombatants had a much lower chance of dying during the Civil War than soldiers, but Burrell's proximity to the fighting was dangerous enough.

After the war, veterans ignored or forgot the bravery that black men had shown in the army. Instead, they told funny stories about their servants as a means of injecting comedy into what would otherwise have been a dry memoir or reminiscence. Confederates depicted black people as victims of fate or as comical bystanders. The stories about them often involved their exposure to danger, and in such accounts, the slaves handled themselves much differently than Wallace Comer's slave Burrell had. Some servants were said to have been apprehended as they were astride runaway horses, while others—with eyes bulging, mouths agape, and mouthing dialect-heavy appeals to "de Lawd"—were depicted as running away from the whistling of artillery fire or the snap of bullets. In these stories, Confederate veterans repeatedly indulged in the "Sambo" stereotype, portraying blacks as blunderers and buffoons. Such exaggerations of slave behavior served an important purpose in the white world. They made white soldiers look braver and more in control, thus reinforcing Confederates' belief that fighting was the domain of white men.[35]

Soldiers could be callous masters at times, but they also wrote of slaves in ways that suggest they did not merely think of them as children or property. "How sad and gloomy I feel, after hearing the sad news of the death of poor Rachel," wrote William B. G. Andrews to his family in the late summer of 1864. Rachel's death left him heartbroken, "for if ever there was a servant in the world that I wa[s] devoted to it was her."[36] Another soldier wrote of how a dead servant's body had been cared for in camp. "I had him washed by Charles and another servant," wrote the South Carolina soldier Lewis Grimball, "and dressed him in a full suit of Black with shirt Collar Stock &c and laid him out." When it came to the loss of a valued servant, however, the affected soldier was also well aware of the economic advantages he had enjoyed as a result of owning another human being. Lewis Grimball's brother, William, wrote of the death of another slave, Alfred. "I was sorry to hear of Old Alfred's death," he wrote to his father in April 1863, but added, coldly, that Alfred was "pecuniarily no loss to you."[37]

Confederates clearly could be upset by the death of a valued slave, but their feelings were often more about how a servant's passing would affect the white household's workload than any deep regret over the loss of a human being. A slave's death was more an inconvenience than an occasion for expressing prolonged grief. The Virginia infantryman Col. James Francis Preston wrote about the death of his servant, which left him in need of a "steady, *sober* man & good servant who knows something about gardening if possible." He also wanted to make sure any new servant could be "managed by a lady." He was prepared to hire a slave, if need be, at any "reasonable" or "unreasonable" price.[38]

The practice of hiring a slave was far more common than an outright sale. In 1860, a prime black worker could cost a potential buyer well over a thousand dollars. Hiring was far cheaper for men who needed a black laborer only temporarily, and most slaves hired as unskilled workers were contracted for only a year or less. In late 1861, one Confederate wrote of paying $160 for the hire of three slaves for the next year, but he had to sell some cotton before he could hire any workers.[39] In the vulnerable wartime slave market, hiring proved a good alternative to buying and selling. Caleb McCurdy, traveling with Lee's army in March 1863, was sanguine about slavery's future. Regarding his slaves, he said, "If we gain our independence they will be very good property for they will bring a big price." After the Confederate setbacks of that year, he was less optimistic, but he was still concerned about making as much money as possible. In December 1863, he complained of the depreciated Confederate currency.

The riskiness of doing business made him conclude that "the idea of hiring them out is a bad one but preferable to any other way of disposing of them."[40]

Even after the Confederate reverses of 1863, Rebel soldiers continued to buy and sell, hire and hire out their slaves. In January 1864, the South Carolina soldier John Jefcoat learned that he could hire two slaves for $150 each, and later that summer, another soldier wrote to his wife about a slave named Albert, saying, "Keep him and if not send him back or else hire him out for he is not worth any thing to me were [sic] he is."[41] From the Petersburg trenches, Lewis Warlick wanted his father to sell his property, except for his slaves. "I dont think the negros ought to be sold as they can be hired out," he wrote.[42]

Despite their concerns about the economics of slavery, masters in the army were not immune to paternalistic feelings. Yet Confederates claimed that the white-black relationship rested not merely on obligations toward their workers, but on genuine love and affection. They often closed letters with friendly "howdies" to slaves; others went even further. "My best love to all the servants," said one letter writer from Camp Caroline in Virginia, in 1861. "Tell them I will finish the war as soon as I can and wish to see them all."[43] The intimacy between some white and black people followed them from cradle to grave. In 1862, shortly before the battle of Fredericksburg, Ruffin Thomson, a planter's son serving in a Mississippi regiment, wrote of his servant Preston's final moments, resting "with his head in my lap." Thomson wrote of making a bed of straw for Preston and then walking away to make breakfast. When he returned, Preston was dead. The night before, Preston had talked of dying and "seemed reconciled." Thomson was hurt by his servant's death, thinking him a "good boy." He felt as if he had "lost a companion." He then wrapped Preston inside a blanket and buried him in a musket box. Preston, he concluded, received a "soldiers burial."[44]

More often, Confederates wrote of slaves caring for masters who had become casualties of war. A slave might roam the battlefield to look for a missing soldier, or to procure a coffin after his master's death. One soldier remembered he was "much touched" at the attention two slaves showed Maj. John Pelham, the young, promising artillery officer killed at Kelly's Ford, Virginia, in March 1863. For Confederates, nothing better signified the benign relationship between the races than a slave shedding tears at a white man's passing.[45] Shortly after the battle of Fredericksburg, William S. Carter heard the gruesome details concerning his brother, Capt. James H. Carter, who died from an artillery head wound. Carter was reassured that his brother's death had been instantaneous. "Too much praise can not be awarded to the perseverance and constancy of his servant boy Jim," he learned, who had brought the body back to Richmond.[46]

In life and death, masters expected servants to remain loyal. In 1863, Charles C. Jones, a colonel from Georgia, noted that his father had dressed on the morning of his death with his trusted servant at hand. A large gathering of whites and blacks attended the funeral. In Old South terms, it was a fitting memorial, one similar to that of South Carolina Senator James Henry Hammond, a vocal advocate of "King Cotton," who died in 1864 with his hymn-singing slaves at his bedside. Confederate soldiers were not of the same generation as Hammond, but they too expected their servants to mourn their death.[47] When Gen. Howell Cobb died in 1870, it was said that his former servants attended, "and there were but few more sincere and afflicted mourners at his grave than those negroes."[48]

Were black people genuine in their grief? In some cases, slaves probably did have genuine feelings for their Confederate masters. Slaves, however, would rather have been free than live a life where they were defined, and very often treated, as property. The historian Peter Kolchin has concluded, "Although some slaves were truly attached to their owners and grieved at their deaths, much of the proverbial distress at their masters' passing reflected anxiety over their *own* fate rather than sadness over that of their owners."[49] Such anxiety did not disappear in wartime, when a master's death could have immediate and dire consequences for his servants. A slaveholder's passing might lead to the breaking up of his slaves' families if debts remained unpaid, or workers might be parceled out to other white family members.

African Americans, regardless of what Confederate soldiers wrote, cheered for Union victory. The fact that hundreds of thousands of slaves fled their owners in wartime casts serious doubt on the depth of their emotional ties to their Southern white families. Yet slaves apparently were good at convincing whites that the opposite was true—a deception that fueled Confederates' belief that slavery was worth keeping. After all, white Southerners believed that if black people seemed content with enslavement and spoke well of their masters, what reason could there be to end human bondage?

Nevertheless, Confederates made great efforts to keep blacks under their control, although, when a slave disobeyed, some masters refrained from physical punishment, thinking that harsh discipline could go too far. Fred Fleet wrote of a fellow Virginian, Gen. Henry Wise, who forced a "disloyal" servant to assist him in his garden as punishment.[50] James

Yates of the Sixteenth Mississippi Infantry spoke of his reluctance to use the lash, believing reasoning with slaves had its advantages. "I would whip them when they needed it," he said, though he admitted, "I do not know if talking would not do as much good." Some men were even compassionate toward slaves who were already in trouble. In April 1864, the Virginia artillerist James Ward Stuart witnessed the capture and imprisonment of a slave for trying to escape from his master in eastern Tennessee. Stuart bought the freezing slave a blanket, even though it cost him fifteen dollars, more than a private's monthly salary.[51]

Physical punishment, nevertheless, had a prominent place in slave society, and the Confederate army was no different. John R. Lowrey, who served in the North Carolina Camp Guards, wrote in July 1862 to his mother about her need to discipline the slaves at home. "You must whip some of the laziness out of old Levi," he told her, "and make him work." Camp slaves were also a problem. John Lane Stuart of the Forty-Ninth North Carolina wrote of some black women bringing his regiment pork, which reputedly contained dog meat. Lane said the women were given thirty-nine lashes each. "I dont think they will Bring any more Dog stew to the 49th soon again," he concluded. Southern troops were more than willing to punish slaves on the spot, or advise those on the home front to do the same.[52]

One soldier, writing from White Bluff, Georgia, told his mother that he wanted a man back home to "go to my house and give jack a good whipping." He added, "I dont want my negroes to be impudent to any one but especially to my brothers or father or any of my immediat family and I want him to make him know his place."[53] Anger could grip even the kindest of masters. Gen. William Pender, a religious man who criticized slavery, agreed with most of the claims of *Uncle Tom's Cabin*. But in September 1862, even he wrote about whipping one of his servants.[54]

Soldiers punished slaves not only to maintain discipline in camp, but to assure obedience to white women back home. Charged with running the farm or plantation while their husbands were away, wives were not always successful in getting servants to obey, and Confederate soldiers tried to remedy such situations. William T. Nelson, who served in the Fifty-Seventh North Carolina, owned several slaves. His wife, Anne, oversaw them while her husband was at war. Anne had frequent trouble with one slave named George. By November 1862, Nelson had had enough. "Dear you said in your last [letter] that georg agrevated you do not sufer it just get some one to tie him and whip him good." Nelson assured her, "I will give him as much more when I get home."[55]

CONFEDERATE SOLDIERS AND THE NEED FOR SLAVES IN CAMP

Confederate soldiers thought of themselves as fair men, but whether or not they administered physical punishment themselves, they were not strangers to it. In December 1863, Pvt. Grant Taylor, serving in the Fortieth Alabama, wrote of a beating that resulted in the death of a servant. What was the slave's offense? He had stolen liquor, gotten drunk, and "cursed and sauced" his master. A few months later, Taylor wrote of his regiment hanging two black men. He was not sure of their crime, but said it was "enough to cause them to be hung."[56] Taylor's terse words reinforced a fact of the Old South: Southern law rarely punished white men for disciplining slaves in a manner other masters might have thought excessive.

In the antebellum period, as a gesture of their generosity, masters might give slaves gifts, a day off, or a pass to visit another plantation or farm. But for white Southerners, one man's kindness was another man's weakness. Some Confederate soldiers regretted their own generosity. In October 1861, William R. Carter, serving at Yorktown, wrote to his father about the problems he had with his slave, Alleck, who had left him without permission. Carter partially blamed the "low" soldiers in camp who "have carried off a great many negroes." But he also chastised himself for thinking Alleck was loyal because of his good conduct when Carter had been sick. He was convinced that "kindness will not do always." He was prepared to "deal harshly with him" and regretted he had ever brought Alleck from Mississippi to be with him. Carter wanted his father to choose the manner of punishment, suggesting Alleck be placed in "the pits." Regardless, he did not want Alleck to roam about "public places or works," nor did he want his father to hire him out.[57]

Soldiers occasionally rewarded their slaves, but they were convinced punishment was even more necessary to maintain racial control. For some whites, discipline was done in the manner of "fathers" correcting their "children." Nineteenth-century parents and other adults did not hesitate to physically punish children. In the world of slavery, given its basis in racial violence and the chattel principle, Southern whites beat enslaved people worse than they would have their own children. Masters would not kill a slave except under extreme circumstances, but they might threaten them for any misbehavior.

Some threats to punish slaves were perhaps more literal than others.[58] Black people probably knew when their masters were truly threatening them and when they were merely blowing off steam. Some warnings, however, were stark. A white man need not tell anyone the consequences of a black man raping a white woman, but masters set other guidelines for slaves' sex lives. The Louisianan Edwin H. Fay wanted one of his female servants to bring another valuable worker into the world. If she did not, he threatened to whip her "most to death or sell her to the meanest man I can find on [the] Red River." He had bought her for breeding purposes, yet she had not produced children. He had little patience with a slave who was not "virtuous" but would not get pregnant.[59]

Despite the cruelty slavery bred, in the form of maiming, murder, and rape, for black families, the selling of loved ones proved the most horrible aspect of bondage. The lash scarred some slaves physically, but the mental and emotional toll of a sale "down the river" proved far worse. Some Confederates were reluctant to separate black couples, but if necessary, the need for money overrode concern for maintaining slave families. A conscientious master wanted whites and blacks to see him as kind and generous. Still, there were perhaps two million slaves sold in interstate transactions in the antebellum period, a number roughly equal to half of all slaves living in the South in 1860. Such sales destroyed marriages (even if they were not legally recognized) and tore children from parents and other family members. In the Upper South, as Peter Kolchin has noted, "about one first marriage in three was broken by forced separation and close to half of all children were separated from at least one parent." The Deep South did not see as many families broken up by sale, but that was because it imported more slaves than it exported.[60]

Masters might not have to relinquish their slaves, but if pressed, or if they believed prices had peaked, they would sell them. In April 1863, one soldier preferred not to unload some of his slaves, but believed he had already suffered enough because of "tenderness."[61] That same month, the Virginian William Beverley Pettit, who was having problems with slave theft, was hesitant to sell any of his workers, but not because of moral considerations. His pocketbook was his chief concern. "To be sure they are selling very high now," he wrote to his wife, "but so is everything else and they are priced really comparatively low." He urged her to wait and keep their slaves at work growing the corn, oats, peas, and potatoes that kept Pettit financially sound.[62]

Protests against sales usually went unheeded. In December 1863, James Barrow wrote testily to his father about not keeping a slave couple together. "I thought that you would leave the purchase of the negro woman to my discretion," he complained. "She is sold . . . so it is too late." Riley, the groom-to-be in this interrupted slave marriage, was a servant who enjoyed a good reputation in his Florida community. Despite his closeness to whites, market forces, not paternalism, had dictated his future.[63]

CONFEDERATE SOLDIERS AND THE NEED FOR SLAVES IN CAMP

Confederates soldiers accepted the sale of slaves as a regular practice. The South Carolinian Arthur Grimball wrote in March 1863, "Pa has sold the Negroes very well and I am very glad he did so," adding, "They were undoubtably a great deal of annoyance to him and when sick or dead a great loss." His brother, Berkley, also heard of the sale. Berkley was not concerned about the slaves' welfare so much as the amount his father received for them. "I wish you had sold them at auction," he wrote. "I think you would have got more for the negroes."[64] In wartime throughout the Confederacy, the wheeling and dealing of the slave economy continued. Concerning the selling of slaves in April 1863, the Georgian R. H. Brooks was blunt. "Let the hyest bidder take them," he concluded, "but I do not care I am willing any way."[65]

After the war, Confederates played down the necessity and desirability of selling slaves. A master's loyalty to his chattels, white Southerners claimed, outweighed market forces.[66] The reality was that the Southern economy depended on the frequent buying and selling of human beings. Slave owners were not absentee masters, but anxious capitalists focused on the workings of the market. The vast majority of white Southerners did not have enough slaves to avoid hard work or the close supervision of chattels, and even if they did, they did not possess enough to free themselves from economic concerns. Pvt. Marcus Toney remembered his unusual status in 1860: he owned homes in Tennessee and Virginia, both of which had black workers.[67] A more typical master was a small farmer who owned one makeshift dwelling, five or fewer workers, and who worried about his family getting enough food. Nor was slaveholding a fixed condition. Men frequently entered and exited the master class. A slave had a better chance of being hired by a master than being sold by him.[68]

No matter how many slaves they owned, masters aspired to greater things. Two years before he bled to death at the Battle of Shiloh, Albert Sidney Johnston had articulated the Southern man's version of the pursuit of happiness. "I was a planter in a small way with ideas of expansion," he wrote. Had his plans been realized, they would have provided "the means of 'an accumulation of wealth beyond the dreams of avarice.'"[69] The cotton boom of the 1850s had led many Southerners to believe economic good times would continue into the 1860s. On the eve of secession, cotton growers approached the coming years with optimism, not fear.[70] In wartime, slave-trading and speculation did not halt. In fact, such activities became even more frantic. "I am told that cotton has taken a great rise all over the country," wrote the South Carolina cavalryman Simon P. Wingard to his wife in July 1862. "If you can get fifteen cents for our few pounds," he advised her, "sell it—for cotton will fall soon. This war is not near closed and as soon as people find it so, cotton will come down."[71] The unstable Rebel economy ruined some Confederates. Others found the war kept the market vibrant and attractive, albeit risky. The Civil War destabilized the Southern economy, but it also presented opportunities for shrewd masters and would-be slaveholders.

Despite fluctuating prices and shortages, for most of the war the slave market showed resilience.[72] In 1860, the average slave had brought $1,500 in Virginia and a "prime field hand" in New Orleans had brought $1,800. In July 1862, one South Carolina soldier wrote to his wife about how slaves, Confederate bonds, and cotton "have all jumped up tremendously in Charleston." More than a year later, he saw prices for slaves in Richmond as high as $4,000 or $5,000.[73] In 1863, Arthur Fremantle wrote of Texans constantly speaking of slave prices. They said an able-bodied male went for $2,500 and a seamstress for $3,500. Most Southerners could not afford such costly workers, but many Confederate soldiers nevertheless found the money to purchase slaves in wartime.[74]

By the end of 1861, the Texas artillerist John J. Good was skeptical about the Confederacy's ability to keep the economy stable, reasoning that no government "has ever yet paid at par its revolutionary liabilities." He wanted his father-in-law to sell land for slaves, and he noted that some people were putting slave prices low but land prices high.[75] In April 1862, another Confederate wrote of a comrade who asked his factor for money. The Federals apparently had left him with only two slaves that he could mortgage.[76] Keeping one's eye on slavery served as a gauge for Confederates' fortunes and their financial standing. As the Union armies penetrated the South, Confederate troops worried about the war upsetting the usual pattern of buying and selling slaves.[77] By late 1862, slave markets in some states had suffered disruption, but elsewhere they had not. That October, Charles C. Jones had enough confidence in the economy to buy a plantation in middle Georgia, a 1,400-acre spread at ten dollars per acre. He saw the need for four additional slave dwellings, but was pleased with the overseer's house, gin house, corncribs, and the existing servant houses.[78]

In 1863, even after the issuing of the Emancipation Proclamation, many Confederates continued to thrive as slaveholders. William H. Grimball heard rumors of a man who had recently bought a house outside Columbia, South Carolina. The man apparently was spending $140,000 to decorate the grounds and had given his daughter a birthday present of $30,000 in cash, most of which she planned to give to her local church.

"How excessevely grand all this sounds," Grimball wrote, expressing his belief that the "novi homines" were becoming the new aristocracy of South Carolina. Grimball himself was from a family that owned thirteen slaves, but he, along with most Confederates, could only dream of such wealth. Yet the "aristocracy," especially in a state like South Carolina, gave Confederates a lifestyle to which they could aspire.[79]

In November 1862, the Louisianan James Stubbs said he did not want to separate some of his slaves. He had an emotional attachment to them, but what was most important was the safety of his investment. As with any manager, he was careful about maintaining good morale. He feared that a male slave, John, had heard rumors about his master's debts, which might make him fear that he could be sold. John might decide to flee with his "Molly" before that happened. Worried, Stubbs vowed to keep the couple together. He resolved to buy John, whom he thought a good and faithful servant—one better than Molly—even at "an extravagant price." "I never deceive my negroes," Stubbs wrote, "as I have never done children either my . . . own or others."[80]

Men like Stubbs were determined to remain masters of the black race. They did not believe that the war had negatively affected the institution of slavery. In hindsight, it is easy to see that by November 1862 Union victories had effectively freed thousands of slaves, and that the Lincoln administration was moving, albeit cautiously, toward freeing all people in bondage. But even as the conflict threatened their livelihood, many masters still enjoyed good times, and slavery remained central to their lives. "It is a great relief to me to hear," said Archibald Bolling, a Virginia artillerist, in January 1863, "that my negroes . . . are a pecuniary advantage & a comfort too." The more the Confederacy kept to its normal practice of buying and selling, lending and borrowing, the better. And Bolling wrote home happily of having recently paid a debt.[81]

During the war, Confederates, as Southerners had for generations, sought new frontiers for slavery. In December 1862, the Arkansan E. P. Petty described his home state as "awful," "forlorn," and "God forsaken." Everyone, it seemed, was leaving for Texas and taking their slaves with them.[82] By the 1850s, less than two decades after statehood, Texas had become a state where those who produced cattle, cotton, and sugar cane prospered. Slavery went hand-in-hand with Texas's growth. Black workers had become a valuable commodity. In January 1859, writing from Austin, William D. Howard, who would die at the Second Battle of Bull Run, complained that it was "almost impossible to hire negroes here at any price."[83] In wartime, investment in Texas also thrived. In March 1862, writing from Corinth, Mississippi, Frank Richardson, the son of a Louisiana planter, asked whether his father had shipped any sugar to Texas, where planters had made "quite [large] speculations at it." Texas became a haven for masters. In September 1863, William Nugent wrote that his wife might want to go to Texas. He wanted her to do anything rather than live, as she presently did, near a camp of "demoralized" black Federal troops.[84]

Texas survived the war relatively unscathed. When Robert E. Lee surrendered, Texas had more hard money than the rest of the Confederacy combined.[85] In September 1863, John B. Magruder, commander of the District of Texas, wrote that the Federals were planning an invasion of the state. In response, he believed planters should move their chattels inland. The Federals did invade the state in its spring 1864 Red River campaign.[86]

The Union's 1864 campaign failed, however, and Texas fought on for several months after the Army of Northern Virginia had capitulated at Appomattox. "Juneteenth," a memorable day in black history, honors 19 June 1865, the day the authorities announced emancipation in Texas. Texas's isolation meant that Confederate slavery survived there longer than anywhere else.

Confederates in other states were too far from Texas to seek refuge there, but they too moved slaves to safer communities. In 1863, a soldier in the Sixteenth Mississippi Infantry wrote to his mother about moving their slaves in the wake of Nathaniel Banks's raid in southern Mississippi. He urged her to take their servants into Alabama.[87] Elsewhere, masters, even if only psychologically, delayed black freedom as long as they could. In early 1863, the Mississippi cavalryman Edwin H. Fay was not concerned with emancipation, but rather how slavery would fare once hostilities ceased. In January, Fay was optimistic that slaves were going to be worth "2 & 3000 a piece when this war is over."[88] When he wrote those words, Lee's surrender was a long way off. That February, Theophilus Perry of the Twenty-Eighth Texas Cavalry heard there was an effective freeze on the market. A high demand for black workers still existed, but buyers were exercising caution. In many areas, the Union army had seized slaves, or black people had escaped to Union lines, both of which disrupted the slave market.[89] Even so, Confederates were eager to hire or buy slaves for work in camp and at home. "Pay almost any price rather than not get [a slave]," wrote the Virginia general Elisha Paxton in April 1863.[90] A few months earlier, the Arkansan Lt. William W. Garner urged his wife to purchase a servant. "A negro is as certain as Confederate money," he wrote, and he wanted to keep buying them. He would have done so himself, but could not obtain a leave of absence to do it.[91]

In July 1863, the Confederates suffered serious reverses at Vicksburg and Gettysburg, but Alabama infantryman James Simpson in the Army of Northern Virginia was not too concerned about the possibility of a financial collapse. He spoke to his wife about buying a slave and new house. "I am glad to hear that you have succeeded in getting a negro," said Simpson. His wife had "made a very good bargain, Considering the present prices." Simpson was not sure he wanted to keep the slave woman for very long, thinking it better to "settle for her hire" at the end of the month. Regardless, he hoped his wife knew how to control her new property. "Let her know you are Mistress," he warned her, "for if you let her get the advantage at first it will be hard to cure her." Confederate troops wanted to remain the undisputed masters of the battlefield and of the black race.[92]

Many whites believed they could avoid the perils of speculating in the market. The South Carolinian Alexander Fewell considered selling some of his slaves in February 1863. His potential buyer offered $3,800, but he wanted $4,000. He was tempted to accept the offering price, but begged off, thinking prices would go higher. He was not alone. Some men had everything invested in slavery and the fruits of it. "I intend to keep my last dollar invested in tobacco, cotton, & Negroes," said the Alabaman James Francis in March 1863.[93] For such men, the Confederacy's collapse would result in something far more devastating than the defeat of states' rights ideology.

Some men's faith in the market was an extension of their patriotism; others were opportunists taking advantage of masters' fears over uncertain economic forces. Writing from Louisiana in June 1863, Theophilus Perry was angered that citizens were "getting rich & buying negroes" while men in the army were barefoot, poorly shod, and wearing clothes they had not changed in weeks. "I have an insufferable hatred for many men at home," he said. "They are such base demagogue & hypocrits."[94] But whatever their political leanings—and despite protestations from men like Perry—these men were acting as masters always had. As the North Carolinian Pvt. John W. Reese boasted to his wife in February 1863, "It is A Grate time for Speculatan."[95]

In wartime, markets fluctuated and Northerners threatened to undo the whole slaveholding enterprise in a single blow. For masters, the contingencies of war added to the problems they faced in an agrarian economy. Given that they might die in the army, slaveholding soldiers wanted to get their finances in order, making as much money for themselves or their families before they were killed or succumbed to disease. Even better-off slaveholders understood the gravity of their financial situation. In March 1863, Theophilus Perry told his wife that he did not want government money for his slaves. "Negro" property was more reliable legal tender. "For Gods sake," he told her, "buy our freedom from our creditors." He was happy to get whatever he could on the market, but Perry would not live to see the end of the war. He was killed in the 1864 Red River campaign. In November 1863, he had written his will, in which he left the care of his slaves to his wife.[96] It was a timely decision, and it showed that unless the Yankees took their slaves, Confederate soldiers, even in death, wanted to keep blacks tied to the soil.

After the serious Confederate losses of 1863, troops still sold slaves at a profit. Even in Virginia, one of the most ravaged of states, men from the Sixteenth Mississippi Infantry noted that masters continued to get high prices for chattels.[97] And given the persistent high demand, some men seemed only concerned with making money. In June 1864, writing from Arkansas, Gen. Joseph O. Shelby, himself a Kentucky slaveholder, wrote of citizens in Virginia taking a loyalty oath to the United States and then hiring out their slaves. In his theater of combat, cotton speculation went hand-in-hand with "marked fraud." Were such activities to continue, he said, "it will be better to abandon this country altogether."[98] For General Shelby, though a war was raging, it was still incumbent upon men to act ethically. They should not make a profit at the expense of the Confederate cause.

Later in the war, some soldiers grew dubious of their nation's ability to survive and wanted to unload their slaves, who were diminishing in value. Others chose to buy slaves regardless of the economic difficulties. "I have talked with Clawson about his negro," wrote the South Carolina soldier David Logan in August 1863. Clawson was ready to take either $3,000 in Confederate bonds or Logan's note for $1,500. Concerning his financial situation, Logan complained, "I am a fat man no more it seems." What is interesting is not that he faced financial hardship, but that in the face of what he called "the vale of darkness," Logan chose to buy rather than sell slaves. A few weeks later, he complained that "the trifling scoundrels at home who are depreciating our currency, are doing more against our cause than all of Lincoln's fleets and armies.[99] Logan complained not of the desirability of slavery, but of the fact that his countrymen were not doing their utmost to support the cause, and by extension, his economic ventures.

CONFEDERATE SOLDIERS AND THE NEED FOR SLAVES IN CAMP

In 1864, slaveholders were helped somewhat by the Confederacy's attempts at economic reform. That February, the Confederate Congress passed the Currency Reform Act, which sought to increase the value of its money by decreasing the number of notes in circulation. The Confederacy was successful in eliminating much of its paper currency, and therefore in curbing inflation. It was not until the military reverses of late 1864 that the Confederate treasury reverted to printing vast amounts of paper money. But the 1864 measure helped stabilize the cost of various goods, among them the cost of slaves.[100]

In 1864, for those with investments in black workers, prices did fall in some areas, but the cost of purchasing slaves, along with most other items, remained prohibitive. In February 1864, an Arkansas lieutenant, Robert C. Gilliam, wrote of a slave auction where a "white woman" (a light-skinned woman of mixed race), an infant, her mother, and her husband brought $13,000 to the bidding. Most Confederates did not have that much to spend. The persistent demand for slaves, combined with economic measures in Richmond, kept prices high. Many areas of the Confederacy suffered great losses long before Lee's surrender, but slaveholders did not always expect disaster. Lieutenant Gilliam hoped that the country would soon find itself in a state of "peace and safety," even if he did not know when that would happen. In the meantime, he asked, "what had better be done?" What he did was attend to everyday activities concerning the farm and the slaves that worked there under his mother's management.[101]

The slave market grew increasingly risky, but continued to find buyers and sellers. Some tried to locate areas of the South where threats to slavery as an institution were few or nonexistent. In early 1864, writing from a Maryland prison, James Anderson said, "I am grateful that there is yet territory accessible to us where the 'peculiar institution' still exists, and I hope you may *all* be able to move to it in case this state be forever lost to the Confederacy."[102]

Joseph Glatthaar has written that in 1864 the problem of slaves escaping "led to a significant decline in body servants, as well as a shift from the use of slaves to the employment of free blacks." Glatthaar has also noted that in Virginia by 1864, slavery was "no longer viable."[103] However, many soldiers, inside and outside Virginia, still had confidence in slavery's viability. One way Confederates believed they could protect slaves was to keep them in the army. The Georgia private James Paul Verdery wrote from the Petersburg trenches in October 1864, saying that he needed a slave to help with his washing and cooking. Eighteen months earlier, while serving in Georgia, he had observed that the Federals had not captured any slaves from Savannah. Now, in Virginia, he expressed a similar faith in the dependability of slavery. He said he had neither the time nor the money—getting his shirts cleaned was costing him a dollar per garment, he complained—and he assured his family that a servant would be safe with him. "There is no possible chance of his getting to the Yankees," Verdery wrote optimistically. Time and again during the war, slaves had found their way to the Federal lines. Verdery, nevertheless, planned on keeping his servant three miles behind the front, with the officer's servants. "Out of the many negros in this army I havn't known one to even try to make his escape to the enemy since I have been here," he noted. The servants in his regiment, he claimed, were "well contented."[104]

Elsewhere, however, slaves were not so "well contented," as they fled masters or aided Yankee forces. Yet, the Confederate soldiers languishing at Petersburg tried to remain masters of their slaves. That August, Thomas Strayhorn of the Twenty-Seventh North Carolina was upset to hear about a servant named Ellen "cutting up with the Parks family." He would have preferred to go home to whip her himself, but he decided he would instead sell her. He warned that he might "trade [her] for real estate," and he made it clear that "I don't want money now unless it is gold or silver."[105]

By November 1864, the Confederacy had suffered crushing defeats at Mobile Bay, Atlanta, and in the Shenandoah Valley, while Lee remained trapped at Petersburg. Most important of all, President Lincoln—whose political future had seemed dim as recently as August—was poised to win reelection. In October, Gen. Clement A. Evans, serving in Lee's army, wanted to sell his slaves and was happy to exchange them for real estate.[106] He believed that land would prove to be a much safer bet than other "property." When it came to choosing between losing a slave's supposed love for his master or the cash value of a servant, Confederates chose the latter and unloaded their slaves on any willing buyer. White loyalty to black workers was usually only skin deep. As ultimate defeat seemed more possible, slaveholders began to calculate how emancipation might affect their finances. "We have not grown rich before the war began," said the Georgian Samuel Wiley to his wife in November 1864, "and are rapidly going down hill now." He placed the blame for his economic woes on "the presence and expense of an idle, lazy, sickly, deceitful, discontented family of negroes." His assessment of his slaves' behavior contrasted with that of other white Southerners who, in the Lost Cause literature of the postwar era, preferred to remember their contented, happy, and helpful

CONFEDERATE SOLDIERS AND THE NEED FOR SLAVES IN CAMP

servants. To Wiley, his slaves instead acted like a sponge, soaking up his profits. A few had served him well, but that was not enough to brighten his spirits.[107] Adding to Wiley's troubles were Confederate taxation and the high prices that were crippling the economy. War was hell in more ways than one. Even those who did not have their homes burned by the Yankees were facing ruin.

Nevertheless, Confederate soldiers found that if slaves were no longer their most valuable commodity, they were still worth more than Confederate money. In November 1864, Pvt. Spencer Barnes wrote to his sister from New Market, Virginia, about his mother possibly selling some of his slaves. He concluded, "The money you would get for them would not do you any good."[108] As defeat loomed and many areas of the South had become dangerous for whites living among blacks, Confederates squeezed every dollar they could from the peculiar institution, whether by selling their slaves or hiring them out. The Louisiana infantryman Maj. Hugh W. Montgomery hoped in January 1865, "We may be able to get some work out of the negroes & make some money."[109] In March 1865, Edwin Fay wrote that he had tried to buy a slave girl but the sellers had insisted on specie, "and at very high prices at that."[110] The Confederate fortunes worsened and masters scrambled to move, sell, or hire out their chattels. Yet even into the last days of the war, some were not convinced that slavery was doomed. In April 1865, a hopeful U. G. Owen, serving in the Army of Tennessee, wrote of General Johnston's good prospects against the Federals even if Richmond fell. Were Lee's army to move to North Carolina, he would try to move his father's slaves further south, but he did not imagine he could get to it.[111]

Thousands of slaves served in the Confederate camps. They were not soldiers, but they were essential to the running of the Rebel army. The relationship that existed between whites and blacks in the military was an extension of Old South society. The war often tested the strength of the bonds that tied slaves to their masters, and at times broke them down. Nevertheless, for most of the war, Confederate troops had faith in their ability to control the race and in the economic viability of slavery. As long as there were formidable Confederate armies, white Southerners believed slavery could survive.

· 5 ·

"WE CRUSHED THEIR FREEDOM"
EMANCIPATION AND THE PROBLEM OF SLAVE LOYALTY

In July 1863, the Federal army raided Adams Run, South Carolina, near Charleston. With the arrival of troops came the freeing of slaves. "My Plantation will very soon become a wilderness," complained Henry H. Manigault, a civilian who owned dozens of black workers. All but two had left him. Before they fled, they broke open a trunk, stole clothes, and robbed a neighboring colonel's plantation "of everything." They even ripped apart feather beds to make rough sacks to carry away their booty. The Confederate soldier Lewis Grimball wrote of the destruction and its aftermath. Concerning his uncle Henry, he said, he looked "ten years older since the loss of his negroes." Despite his losses, Grimball's uncle was fatalistic about the flight of his slaves, saying he had "lost them just a little sooner than every body else." Lewis Grimball concluded, "This seems rather poor consolation."[1]

Thousands of Southern masters would find themselves in the same situation as Grimball's uncle. For them, the breakdown of slavery was not a matter of *if* it would happen, but *when*. By 1863, the United States had made emancipation an official war aim, worsening an already difficult situation for Confederates, who were trying to win their independence and maintain racial control. Lincoln's Emancipation Proclamation, even though it gave hope to millions of slaves, spurred Confederates to make more-concerted efforts against Union forces, and it led them to a closer embrace of slavery.[2] Through the use of force and the help of "loyal" black people, Confederate troops were confident they could assure the survival of human bondage. Rebel troops believed they could prevent the freeing of the slaves, not only because of the inner divisions within the Union concerning abolition, but because they had faith in the South's long-standing resourcefulness in controlling the black population.

Historians have often shown how slaves resisted their masters and opposed white Southerners' authority. Without ignoring the importance of resistance and agency among slaves, one should remember that black people faced practical and psychological boundaries that prevented them from throwing off their chains. Through laws constricting black mobility, statutes preventing slave literacy, and the use of mounted patrols and individual acts of punishment, white Southerners had worked hard, though not always successfully, to keep black people enslaved. In the antebellum period, the difficulties inherent in slaves gaining their freedom were evident in the lack of successful slave revolts and the relatively small number of runaways that ever made it to Northern soil.[3] Moreover, slaves did not challenge their masters' power out of fear of destroying families or upsetting kin ties. During the Civil War, hundreds of thousands of slaves fled to the Yankees, but many more remained where they lived and worked. Enslaved people understood that the Federals could not liberate them all instantly, or necessarily help them once they were free. Wherever the Federal army held ground, slaves gained their liberty, but elsewhere, black people had to find other ways to challenge their Confederate masters, if they challenged them at all, and could only hope for an eventual Union triumph.

What is important in discussing Confederate soldiers and emancipation is not the fact that many slaves resisted their masters or that their actions weakened the Rebel cause; rather, it is the effect of black resistance on Southern troops' morale and the conduct of the war effort. Many slaves absconded in wartime, but Confederate soldiers continued to believe that black people were more loyal to the Confederacy than to the Union. Most of the rebelliousness whites encountered in African Americans' behavior was not deemed to be serious, or was only serious because the Federals had lured slaves away with false promises. Given the formidable strength of the Confederate military well into 1864, Rebel troops were confident that they could contain disloyalty among the slave population. Black people were not always reliable, but Confederate soldiers believed that they could control them and maintain slavery indefinitely.

After the war, veterans forgot or downplayed the difficulty the Confederacy had experienced in trying to control its black population. In veterans' eyes, the slaves had been loyal "darkies" who never seriously challenged their masters' authority and who remained true to their white "families." In 1912, the magazine *Confederate Veteran* asserted that in wartime the devotion of black people had had "no equal in all history" and that whites should dedicate statues to these slaves, who had proven to be valuable Confederates.[4] As the former soldier James Dinkins pointed out, in the case of Fort Mill, South Carolinians had erected a monument to blacks who had served in the war. "It is a beautiful shaft," Dinkins noted, "and stands near the Confederate Monument."[5] Such memorials revealed much, not only the abundance of paternalistic memories of the war, but also the politics of the Jim Crow South: conforming to the demands of a segregated society, these historical markers were separated from one another along racial lines.

Whether in memoirs or in monuments, former Rebels acknowledged the important role of black people in the Civil War, as long as it was on Southern whites' terms. The "faithful" slave became an integral part of Lost Cause mythology and postwar memory. Long after the conflict, some veterans liked to have their pictures taken alongside their former servants.[6] Other black men, who were considered the equals of white Confederates, even attended reunion meetings.[7] "They shared with us our hardships, and at times even our dangers," remembered George Baylor concerning his black comrades. They "entered into our sports and jests, and never were more joyous than when taking part with us in our horse races."[8] In reality, slaves had flocked to Union forces whenever possible, but former Confederates preferred remembering the loyal "old time darkies," just as they preferred to remember the battles of Chickamauga and Chancellorsville rather than those at Franklin and Five Forks.[9]

In soldiers' postwar writings, slaves' loyalty occasionally took extreme forms. One involved black men who followed Confederate troops into captivity.[10] One veteran recalled an imprisoned black man who was, as he put it, a "hardened dyed-in-the-wool rebel."[11] No Confederate soldier wished to suffer in a United States prison, and any slave who entered prison with him proved that, more than just a dedicated slave, he was a loyal Confederate. Some enslaved people, separated from Confederates by the chaos of war, apparently made extraordinary efforts to return to their masters. One soldier remembered a slave named "Box" who swam a river in order to return to the Southern lines. For Confederates, his was only one example of the many ways slaves showed their support for the cause. Other slaves cheered as "their" troops marched toward the front; hid food, jewelry, silver, horses, and money from marauding Yankees; and tended wounded soldiers or carried others to safety. They also gave Southern troops valuable information about the enemy. Black people were the eyes and ears of the countryside, and they might serve as "Paul Reveres" sounding the alarm, as did one girl who yelled the "Yankees is cummin'" at the approach of Northern troops.[12]

In their remembrances, Confederate troops convinced themselves that during the war, peace had reigned on the home front, which proved that good relations existed between black and white people. After all, they reasoned, no Nat Turners had emerged during the course of the conflict. "The conduct of the slaves ... was extraordinary," said Alabama Col. William C. Oates in his memoirs. "Not a single case of murder, rape, or outrage occurred during the entire war." Oates's words were in keeping with the spirit of the Lost Cause mythology. In wartime, Confederates had been quick to suspect slaves of plotting against them or of raping and murdering whites. Whether black men were guilty of such crimes is another matter. But for Oates and many others remembering the war, slaves became, by their very nature and experience, averse to revolting against their masters.[13]

The reality was very different. Throughout their history, slaves, in large and small ways, resisted masters. On farms and plantations, slaves broke equipment, feigned illness, slowed or stopped work, and stole from whites. Occasionally, they plotted revolts. Running away, however, was the most prevalent form of serious rebellion. The historians John Hope Franklin and Loren Schweninger have estimated that by 1860, masters could expect 50,000 slaves to flee annually—the majority young male field workers (although most never made it very far).[14] During the war, hundreds of thousands of black people escaped to Union lines, some because they wanted to reunite with loved ones, others because they wanted to live under Federal protection, and still others simply to free themselves from a master's control.

Exact figures concerning the number of wartime runaways are unknown. Abraham Lincoln and his secretary of war, William Seward, concluded that the Union armies had seized about 200,000 slaves. Historians have offered higher estimates, however, that range from 500,000 to 1,000,000.[15] To put such numbers in perspective, one should note that in 1861 the Confederacy contained approximately 3.5 million slaves. If a million slaves did indeed flee during the war, they represented a large percentage, albeit still a minority of the total number of slaves in 1860. Whatever their actual number, the slaves who escaped seriously undermined the Confederacy's capacity to make war.[16]

Enslaved people wanted a Union victory, but they were careful to disguise their hopes from their masters. They adopted a watch-and-wait posture regarding emancipation. Just as a "loyal" slave did not necessarily love the Confederacy, a "disloyal" servant might not love the United States. After all, when the war broke out, a half-million slaves still lived in Missouri, Kentucky, and Maryland, all of which would remain in the

Union. Even in the states that had abolished slavery, African Americans could encounter racism and anti-black laws that sought to keep them "in their place." Many slaves were willing to risk their lives and families for the safety of the Union army, but others were slower in challenging their masters.[17] Because of black peoples' divided allegiances to home, family, and the Union cause, Rebel soldiers witnessed enough "loyal" behavior to think that slaves would remain true to their owners and supportive of the South. They were not always right in their assumption, but they were correct to assert that many, if not most, enslaved people remained governable in wartime.

Since the war did not affect slavery much in 1861, Confederate soldiers were not at all pessimistic about its future. They were more likely to write of good health, abundant crops, and well-behaved servants than they were of slave revolts. In their eyes, black and white Southerners alike seemed jubilant about the new Confederate nation. In June 1861, one soldier wrote of his long journey from Texas to Virginia. On passing the Tennessee-Virginia border, he described seeing beaming crowds of men, women, and children. Black field workers waved to the men and seemed "as enthusiastic as the whites." In the early months of the war, some Mississippi soldiers trusted a slave enough to give him a double-barreled shotgun, with which he said he was ready to kill a few Yankees.[18]

Confederate soldiers believed that the slaves supported their cause, but they worried that Union soldiers would destroy this supposed harmony between whites and blacks. Long before Lincoln issued the Emancipation Proclamation, Northerners had taken a hard line toward Southern civilians. Often, they would not make the distinction between loyal slaves, who preferred to stay with their masters, and disloyal ones, who were happy to find sanctuary within Union lines.[19] No slave owner seemed safe from the Union army. "They are doing a regular Negro stealing business on the coast," said Gen. Clement A. Evans, writing from Savannah in November 1861. A local planter had tried to get his 300 slaves to follow him into the interior, Evans noted, but they would not go. "Some troops were sent from here to force them off but I have not heard the result," he said.[20]

From the outset of the war, despite the Federal army's practice of seizing slaves, emancipation was not inevitable. Some antislavery Northerners were cautious about feeing any slaves, while other Union supporters chose not to free the blacks under their control, either because of racism, expediency, or respect for the law. While serving in Missouri, in November 1861, Gen. Henry Halleck issued General Order No. 3, which actually barred fugitive slaves from his lines.[21] Halleck was not alone in hoping to avoid the slavery issue. Democrats such as George B. McClellan and Don Carlos Buell ordered the return of "disloyal" runaways to their owners.

Despite their frequent denunciation of the enemy as abolitionist, Confederate troops could not help but notice the lack of an antislavery spirit among Northern troops. "The Yankees are selling the negroes back to their masters on the eastern shore of Virginia," said William Tripp, writing from Fort Fisher, North Carolina, in May 1862, "and you know how they will fare after having run off and sold back to their original owners."[22] Even prominent Republicans would not tolerate commanders who went faster than the president on the subject of taking slaves. Lincoln would not be rushed into sanctioning emancipation, and he reprimanded officers who freed slaves on their own authority.

As the war ground on, the United States made greater efforts to strike at slavery, and black Southerners' willingness to support the Union grew more obvious. Most of the enslaved people the Federals took in the early months of the war had lived in the coastal regions, which were the most susceptible to Northern invasion. The Union's capture of the Sea Islands off the coasts of South Carolina and Georgia, in November 1861, allowed the North to invade the Deep South. With Federal victory came the liberation of slaves. One soldier said Beaufort, South Carolina, was "completely gutted by the Negroes, the houses pillaged, ornaments destroyed, the women wearing their mistress' best apparel, the men rioting over their masters' wine." He was not sure whether such transgressions were the work of "town Negroes" or "thieves from the country."[23] Regardless, Southern whites were seeing the effects of war on the institution of slavery.

The Sea Islands, however, represented only a small portion of the Confederacy. The Union had much more territory to conquer before it could defeat secession and eradicate slavery. Early in 1862, Confederate soldiers still fervently believed in their cause, in their army's ability to defend slavery, and in the "loyalty" of African Americans, but as the year progressed, the Union army brought increased destruction on the South. One Virginian found that his servant, Dick, had gone missing, but wrote, "I do not think he would stay with the Yankees unless forced to do so."[24] As long as the Confederacy could fight, its men did not think that slavery was doomed. If the South were to fail, wrote Samuel Burney, serving in Virginia, "negroes will be no property at all." But, he confidently added, "this will never be." He had faith in the South's ultimate triumph, thinking the Yankees could never "subjugate such white people."[25]

The Union's taking of New Orleans, Forts Henry and Donelson, and Island No. 10 in early 1862 dealt strong blows to the secessionist cause in the West. After its defeat at Shiloh, the Confederate Army of Mississippi retreated farther south to Corinth. Soon after, the Union army took Memphis, and it was prepared to wreak further havoc on the Mississippi River Valley, which for a generation had been "slavery's center of gravity."[26] But it was a different story in the East. In early 1862, the Union armies were able to conquer some parts of the Confederate coastline, but it proved more difficult for Northerners to free slaves and destroy plantations in the interior. And Confederates believed that even in Union-controlled areas, Federal measures would not necessarily be effective. In February 1862, the South Carolina soldier Milton Leverett made a dire prediction about slaves under Northern masters when he expressed his belief that the freedmen at Beaufort were going to have a "tough time of it." The Yankees, he believed, would make no cotton.[27] Black freedom, Confederates thought, would mean little if the Federals could not improve the lot of the average slave or use abandoned land as capably as Confederates had. Furthermore, the North's efforts would prove fruitless were the South to emerge victorious.

In 1862, when it became obvious that the Confederacy would not surrender without a long, bitter fight, the North's war against Southern civilians became harsher, and complaints about Federal depredations, including the taking of slaves and the seizing of other property, grew more common. The chivalric adventure of 1861 had become a modern conflict that affected all aspects of Confederate society. The events of 1862 showed Southerners that the Yankees were adopting an increasingly "hard war" policy toward noncombatants, which, when combined with everyday hardships, created disruption on Southern farms and plantations and wherever Confederate soldiers were stationed. Slaves, like other types of property, became part of the spoils of war for the invading Northerners. Writing from Louisiana in April 1862, John Hall of the Twenty-Seventh Louisiana Infantry expressed faith in his slaves' dedication to him. Concerning his servants, he said, "Tell them all I confide my trust in them, that one day they may see their Masters face, and bless the hour of his arrival."[28]

By the spring and summer of 1862, it became clear that the Federals would now seize slaves, just as they had earlier taken pigs, chickens, and household valuables. Confederates made a distinction between slaves who had fled on their own and those who had been reluctant to flee. And indeed, Federals at times seemed to have taken black workers who may not have wanted to leave their masters' care.[29] Northern politicians, furthermore, began to worry that some officers were acting too zealously. In

May, Gen. David Hunter, an abolitionist commanding the Department of the South (which encompassed South Carolina, Georgia, and Florida), acted to liberate slaves in his theater of operations, but President Lincoln overruled him, claiming he had acted without orders. Lincoln was not yet ready to endorse the blanket freeing of slaves. Indeed, at that point, the Union had not yet been able to agree on its policy toward slave emancipation. Edward W. Drummond, a Northern-born Confederate, looked on gleefully as Lincoln overturned Hunter's order. "It is the best thing that could have happened for the South," he wrote. Drummond thought Hunter's actions would strengthen Confederate resistance, making a "division at the North and in a measure demoralize the Federal Army."[30]

Despite Hunter's failed attempt, Northerners were increasingly moving toward an emancipation policy. In June 1862, the well-informed Texan James C. Bates saw that the United States Congress, with the passage of the Second Confiscation Act, had moved another step toward abolition.[31] The bill expanded the powers of the first Confiscation Act by allowing Union troops to seize property from any Confederate, and it enabled black males to enlist in the Union army. The Federal government was not slow in implementing the law. Well before the Emancipation Proclamation, Confederate troops had begun to see blacks in Federal uniform.[32]

By July 1862, Lincoln had made his decision on emancipation, even though he did not make it public immediately.[33] Many Northerners already had been working to crush the antebellum status quo, and Confederate soldiers noted the change in attitudes. In August, the Confederate chaplain Joseph Durkin wrote of how Federal soldiers had broken a farmer's fence and than had not let the farmer's servants fix it until he had paid them a regular wage for doing so.[34] Rebels who now believed that slavery might be vulnerable now spoke about receiving money for their chattels. "The Yankees should pay for every negro they have stolen during the War," wrote one sergeant.[35] His idea of receiving compensation for his freed slaves was not unrealistic. When the U.S. Congress had voted to free slaves living in Washington, D.C., in April 1862, masters there has been compensated for their chattels. But in the summer of 1862, the Lincoln decided that rebellious masters would receive nothing for their emancipated slaves if they did not renew their allegiance to the United States by the end of that year. Lincoln would wait until after the Battle of Antietam, however, before he made his decision public.

By the summer of 1862, Confederates believed that the army needed to take more aggressive measures to keep slaves under control. That July, Gen. Gideon J. Pillow—relegated to an obscure command after his shameful conduct at Fort Donelson—wrote to Jefferson Davis. The Federals, he said, were not only plundering houses, stealing corn, meat, and stock, but they were sweeping slaves out of Arkansas. "They shoot the negroes attempting to escape," he wrote of Union troops, "and handcuff and chain those refusing to go." Pillow was an example of a Confederate soldier who believed that the slaves did not welcome the Federal army. And it was true that Northern soldiers certainly were capable at times of being as cruel toward African Americans as Confederates were. But Southern troops mistakenly believed that slaves were far more reluctant than they actually were to cross into Yankee lines. Still, the tenuousness of slave "loyalty" reinforced Confederates' belief in the need to act more aggressively toward the Union. Convinced that many slaves did not wish to follow the Union soldiers to freedom, and not wanting to remain passive in the face of the Federal army's aggressive tactics, Pillow, for one, believed that the Confederacy should retaliate.[36] And for him, the best means of protecting slavery lay in taking the offensive.

At various points in 1861 and 1862, the Confederate army invaded the states of Missouri, Maryland, and Kentucky, where approximately 500,000 enslaved people lived. Since Confederates believed that it was the issue of slavery that united Southerners against the North, they thought that all it would take was a push from their gallant army to move the border states into the secessionist camp. However, taking them proved not to be so easy. Confederates were successful at the August 1861 battle of Wilson's Creek in Missouri, a victory that led the Rebel Congress to admit that state into the Confederacy a few months later. The Southern military, however, never established a permanent hold on Missouri, which made it impossible for the secessionists to maintain a viable government there. After the March 1862 battle of Pea Ridge, Arkansas, fought near the Missouri border, the defeated Confederates abandoned, at least temporarily, any plans for another invasion of Missouri.

In September 1862, after Confederate victories at the Seven Days Battles and Second Manassas, and amid the controversy in the North surrounding black liberation, the Army of Northern Virginia invaded Maryland. "Maryland belongs to the Confederacy," one hopeful soldier had said in late April 1861, and such a spirit still existed among many Southerners well into 1862.[37] Confederates knew that the firing on Fort Sumter had led four states—Virginia, Arkansas, North Carolina, and Tennessee— to secede. Perhaps another impressive show of strength might bring in more. However, as the Confederate army marched through Union territory, Lee's men encountered unfriendly civilians. Most Marylanders, they discovered, were not secessionists. One soldier met a man who said he would never raise his hand against the Confederates and planned to go south, purchase slaves, and settle.[38] But the man represented a minority opinion. More Marylanders were hostile about the Confederacy's decision to invade their state. One soldier described Middletown as "the bitterest abolition hole in the state," noting that he might as well have been marching through Massachusetts or Vermont.[39] Marylanders on the whole were not abolitionists, and many had Confederate sympathies, but they did not want to secede.

Lee's drive into Maryland went down to defeat. After his army's bloody repulse at Antietam, his forces retreated into Virginia. Confederates, however, saw it more as a temporary setback than evidence that their nation's "high tide" had crested. Rebel troops remained hopeful. "The invasion of Maryland has saved our property for the present," said one officer.[40] Lee's invasion, indeed, had taken some pressure off Virginia, which had suffered much loss of crops, livestock, and slaves. But if Lee's march north had saved Confederate property "for the present," five days after the Union victory at Antietam, Abraham Lincoln's issuance of the Emancipation Proclamation put things in doubt again. The president's executive order would allow the Federal army to strike at Confederates' most valuable property—their slaves—with impunity.

The North's decision to emancipate the slaves infuriated many Confederates. "Curse the Lincoln proclamation!" exclaimed the prominent slaveholder Gen. Henry Wise. According to William Watson, a Scottish-born soldier who served in a Louisiana regiment in the Western Theater, the proclamation aroused "excitement and indignation."[41] Lincoln's measure was a direct attack on the Southern social order. For Confederates, the loss of other kinds of property was bad enough—but one could replace silverware or livestock or grow more feed to replenish the family stocks. But slaves were not like dinner knives, animals, or corn; they could rise up and rebel against their Southern white masters. Even long after the war's end, there were veterans who were still incensed by what they saw as the Union's attempt to incite servile insurrection.[42]

In the wake of the Emancipation Proclamation, black people did not go through the countryside slitting white people's throats or shooting them in their beds, as many Confederates worried. Even Northerners did not want any insurrections to occur. Confederate troops' fears, nevertheless, were intense, and in the context of the time, understandable. Never before had the U.S. government given black people such license. Most Confederate soldiers had not been alive at the time of the Nat Turner

Revolt or the revolution in Haiti (St. Domingue), but the stories of slave uprisings had taken on the character of ghost stories, scaring white Southerners who feared any hint of insurrection.[43] Gen. Moxley Sorrel, a Georgian who served on Gen. James Longstreet's staff, was not old enough to remember the revolt in Haiti, but his grandfather—a French soldier who served on the island at the time—was.[44] Sorrel was like many Confederate soldiers who had inherited their parents' and grandparents' fears of black violence, and to them, in the fall of 1862 Lincoln seemed to have opened the door to racial Armageddon.

Despite their defeat at Antietam and the Emancipation Proclamation, Confederate soldiers did not expect the war to end any time soon. There would be much hard fighting before either side surrendered.[45] In the fall of 1862, Braxton Bragg's Army of Mississippi tried to seize Kentucky, which, with 200,000 slaves, had the largest slave population of any non-Confederate state. From the war's beginning, Confederates had kept a close eye on events in Kentucky. In the fall of 1861, Daniel C. Govan—a North Carolina-born general and planter who was living in Arkansas when the war broke out—wrote that the situation in Kentucky was "lamentable and heartrending," and that the "abolition incendiary" was driving citizens from their homes. That same month, a North Carolina officer heard complaints from a man in western Tennessee about Kentuckians carrying slaves into his state. He cursed such masters because "they dont go back to fight for their homes." Such insults were designed to make Kentuckians look like cowards. More importantly, Confederates believed that Kentuckians' failure to "fight for their homes" gave the South justification for invading the state.[46]

In 1862, Simon Bolivar Buckner, who was born in Kentucky and joined the Confederate army after the Union's occupation of his home state in 1861, took part in the Army of Mississippi's invasion. That September, his appeals to his fellow Kentuckians used the central ideas of Confederate ideology. In his view, the Federal army had subjected Kentuckians to unlawful searches, had overrun their houses, and had made their women perform "menial services." In Buckner's eyes, the North sought to free the slaves at the expense of enslaving white people.[47] Buckner and other soldiers expected that Kentuckians would welcome the Confederate invaders.

At the 8 October battle of Perryville, the Army of Mississippi, under Gen. Braxton Bragg and Gen. Leonidas Polk, was defeated by the forces of Gen. Don Carlos Buell and Gen. Alexander McCook. The Confederate army then began a slow retreat from Union soil. Kentucky slaves remained Union slaves.

The Kentucky general Humphrey Marshall, who had fought along the Kentucky border before commanding troops in Bragg's invasion force, was disappointed. Writing from the safety of Abingdon, Virginia, a few counties distant from the Kentucky line, his letter to Secretary of War George Randolph illuminates what Confederates had hoped to accomplish on Union soil. He still thought that Kentuckians would in the future defect to the Southern cause, and he hoped they would bring slaves and other property with them. However, the Confederate army would have to establish a foothold in Kentucky before the Rebels could take advantage of the state's slave-generated wealth. For Marshall and others, clearly, turning back the forces of emancipation and amalgamation depended on the strength of Confederate arms—in Kentucky and elsewhere.[48]

Confederate soldiers, despite their recent defeats in the late summer and fall of 1862, believed Lincoln and the Republicans had miscalculated in making the war about re-union *and* emancipation. They were convinced that Union supporters would prove to be as anti-abolitionist as Confederate troops and oppose black freedom en masse. Even after his expulsion from Maryland, Robert E. Lee thought that the Democrats might make gains in the United States Congress, which would strengthen the Northern antiwar movement.[49] The Democrats did well in that fall's elections, but nothing approaching a coup occurred in Washington.

Confederates knew there was considerable opposition to the Emancipation Proclamation in the North. When Lincoln was first elected, it was easy for Southerners to think that the Republican president had received a mandate to crush slavery. By January 1863, however, Southerners had a more nuanced view of their enemy. They still had much ill feeling toward Northerners and their efforts to liberate the slaves, but many Confederates had seen, either first hand or in the press, that the Union was far from unified on racial matters. Rebels and Yankees often fraternized, and Northern troops usually spoke freely about what they thought of blacks. A Confederate soldier could also easily obtain copies of Northern newspapers, where, for example, he could read the racist editorials of the *New York World,* or the vitriolic opinions readers wrote concerning Lincoln's slavery policy. Indeed, many of those who fought in Lincoln's army did not approve of their president's efforts to free the slaves and recruit them into the Union army. They wanted the conflict to remain a white man's fight. That did not mean they liked slavery; it simply meant that many Union troops wanted the United States, win or lose, to remain a white man's country.

Despite such anti-Lincoln feeling in the North, however, it was clear to Confederates that the Republicans were bent on emancipation.[50] Before the Emancipation Proclamation, Confederates had expected that any efforts at emancipation would divide the North while at the same uniting the South. In the fall of 1862 and in early 1863, Confederate troops heard reports of Union soldiers who openly denounced emancipation, even deserting their units or changing their allegiance to the South. "There is general dissatisfaction in the North and more especially in the West, against Lincoln's Emancipation proclimation," said the Louisianan D. P. Gibson. In January 1863, a North Carolinian stationed in Wilmington heard a rumor that people in Kentucky and Illinois were calling upon Union troops to "resist Lincoln" because of the Emancipation Proclamation.[51]

But Lincoln's policies never lost him the loyalty of his party or his army. Many Northern troops were opposed to emancipation at first, but they eventually realized that freeing the slaves would weaken the Confederate war effort and help shorten the war. Even a general as prejudiced against blacks as William T. Sherman never waivered in his belief that secession was treason and that extreme measures, including the abolition of slavery, were needed to crush the Confederacy. In the fall of 1864, despite the horrible costs the Union had paid in bloodshed, Union soldiers in the Army of the Potomac overwhelmingly supported Lincoln for reelection.[52]

But the election of 1864 was far off when Lincoln issued the Emancipation Proclamation. And the measure led not to a loosening of Confederates' allegiance to both slavery and a white man's government, but to a firmer commitment to both. In December 1862, Capt. E. John Ellis believed that Confederates were fighting for all white Americans. Were the South to lose, "Lincoln & the negroes alone would be free." By trying to free the slaves, he believed, the North was only enslaving itself. "Will her people," asked Ellis a few months later, "stand while the bolts are fastened and the chains riveted which must bind them to slavery?"[53] Lincoln, he asserted, was a tyrant, a czar, a sultan, an emperor. By increasing his power, the Union president thought he could crush the South. Yet Ellis was convinced that Lincoln would have to do more than simply declare that the slaves were now free.

The Rebels were aware of how slavery affected foreign policy. John Foster wrote to his brother in August 1862, saying that England was against the Confederacy and wanted to kill slavery. France, he thought, did not want to interfere in the war, nor would Russia, which was busy with its own recent emancipation, the freeing of the serfs in 1861, and did not care much about the American conflict. Yet by February 1863, Foster had changed his mind. He then thought that slavery would not hurt the Confederacy abroad. "Europe does not entertain any friendly views toward our institution of slavery," he wrote to his father, "but [will support us] in spite of their hatred to the Negro question."[54] His hopes were not baseless. The English were skeptical of the North's motives behind emancipation and of its ability to win the war, and they were repulsed by Northern racism.[55] In early 1863, it seemed that Confederates had good reason to think that emancipation at the North's hands was not inevitable. Yet, despite the existence of pro-Confederate opinion in English cities like Liverpool (which depended much on the cotton trade), and in the pages of the *London Times*, the Confederacy never received diplomatic recognition from England.

The Confederacy's failed Union invasions in late-1862 gave the North an opportunity to take advantage of its improved military and diplomatic situation. The passage of the Emancipation Proclamation made the Mississippi private Ruffin Thomson feel increasingly isolated from world opinion. It was "folly to look for any aid other than our good right arms," he wrote to his planter father about foreign nations. The peculiar institution, he said, "makes them all enemies, actively or passively." The Confederacy's greatest asset, he asserted, was King Cotton, but he was angry that Britain seemed to have no problem with using the South's cotton, even as it denounced the institution of slavery. Once the Confederacy had proven victorious, his countrymen might "repay the cotton-loving, slave-hating Britan for his hostile sentiments towards us now."[56]

Emancipation officially took effect on 1 January 1863, and in the year that followed thousands of slaves fled or otherwise fell into Union hands. Historians have often described 1863 as a turning point in the war. The issuing of the Emancipation Proclamation, they have argued, combined with Northern victories at Vicksburg and Gettysburg, spelled doom for the Southern cause. Confederate soldiers, however, did not necessarily see it that way. In early 1863, their military situation seemed stable if not bright. Lee's forces had soundly defeated Burnside's men at Fredericksburg, and in Tennessee, Braxton Bragg's army had fought Rosecrans's men to a draw at Murfreesboro. Furthermore, Grant's campaign against the vital stronghold at Vicksburg had come to nothing.

In hindsight, one can easily see how the issuance of the Emancipation

Proclamation spelled the downfall of slavery, destroyed any chance for diplomatic recognition for the Confederacy, and led to the withering of Southern military power. In November 1862, a slaveholding Texas soldier warned his wife that when emancipation took effect in January, "you dont know what disturbance may occur."[57] Yet, despite widespread fears of insurrection, slaves did not rise up once emancipation became official. "January has passed quietly in spite of Lincolns diabolical Proclamation," wrote Edwin Taliaferro, an officer on Gen. Lafayette McLaws's staff. "I can not help feeling some anxiety," he admitted, but he did not believe "that it will have any bad effect on those of our servants who have so far remained faithful."[58] The secretary of the Confederacy's War Department, John B. Jones, also wrote of the slaves' loyalty: they had been working on fortifications around Richmond, he said, singing happily. He believed that they had "no faith in the efficacy of Lincoln's Emancipation."[59] One might easily have interpreted their happiness as signaling their *faith* in emancipation, but men like Jones saw black people's behavior in a pro-Confederate light.

Even so, Southern whites had not entirely abandoned their fears of slave revolt. Worries about black-on-white violence persisted in varying degrees for the rest of the war. In asserting that African Americans were loyal, some Confederates might have been simply suppressing anxieties about their slaves. They dismissed the efficacy of the Emancipation Proclamation and clung to misguided notions of enslaved people's inherent docility. Others, however, were aware that maintaining race control lay not solely in preventing slave revolts. A more pressing crisis was the flight of slaves by the hundreds and thousands. When it came to emancipation, Confederates were not dealing with another St. Domingue revolt, but with something closer to the pages of Exodus.

In response, Confederates gave more credence to stories about black people who were divided over whether to flee their masters. "I see from the papers that a good many negroes have gone to the Yankees," wrote the Louisiana captain E. John Ellis. Three had left his regiment, but his own servant, Stewart, had not, and Ellis believed that nothing could lure his slave away. One of his comrades asked Stewart about whether or not he would leave. Stewart, not surprisingly, and wisely, said he had no intention of fleeing. Had he claimed otherwise, he would have incurred much closer supervision of his actions or perhaps even suffered a whipping. His master, however, believed he understood why Stewart remained loyal. Stewart said he had seen "many free niggers" in Louisville and Cincinnati and none of them had as good clothes or as much money as he did.

Also, Ellis had taken care of Stewart the previous Christmas when he had been sick. "Im not fool enough to want to leave my master dats certin," Stewart said, and presumably he was not foolish enough to say so even had he wanted to.[60] Confederates expected that most slaves would remain loyal to their owners. The flight of another man's slave proved troubling, but the flight of one's own slave was a crisis. Luckily for men like Ellis, it always seemed it was another man's slaves who were escaping or rebelling.

Confederates believed black people fled only because the Federals gave them false assurances of good treatment. Lincoln and his cohorts, they were convinced, had worked a spell over the slaves that was causing them to drift away, entranced, from their caring white masters. The Virginia cavalryman Wayland Dunaway recalled that an older black man was disappointed to hear of a slave girl who did not welcome the "year of jubilee." He told her, "You's a fool, gal, not to go where there's a plenty to eat and nothing to do."[61] Confederate troops, however, understood such reluctance. Northerners might promise much to slaves, but they would fail to provide for them. Blacks who fled might find themselves in a much worse situation than before. John Milton Hubbard, a veteran of the war, recalled an instance when Confederate soldiers had captured a packed corral of slaves. "They were a dirty and ragged lot," he said, "who were content to grasp at the mere shadow of freedom."[62]

In late 1864, after being captured at Franklin, one Confederate was marched past freed people outside Nashville. He shrugged off the insults he suffered from these men, women, and children, but he was shocked at their living conditions. The freed peoples' huts were "less commodious than the cabins of the most rigid and cruel slave-driver in the South. They were dirty and disorderly in their dress in fact furnished no evidence that in their freedom, they had been elevated one degree above their natural status."[63] It's not hard to understand why Confederates emphasized the negative aspects of the transition from slavery to freedom. But even if their depictions of the freed people's material conditions were accurate, they missed the larger point: slaves were willing to endure such hardship so long as they were free.

Confederates were not mistaken in that many Northerners were guilty of abusing or neglecting black people. As many as a quarter of the freedmen in some Federal camps died from disease and a lack of medical care. Circumstances became so bad that the authorities even returned some of these slaves to the care of the local planters.[64] The former slaves, furthermore, were victims of rape and other brutal acts. Confederate soldiers concluded that slaves who left their masters were gambling with their very lives, or at least their well-being. In the eyes of white Southerners, masters had at least cared for their servants; the Yankees, in contrast, were indifferent to their plight. One soldier recalled a female slave who became a prostitute after winning her freedom; her clients supposedly were mostly Northern men.[65]

Some slaves may have regretted their decision to flee their masters. Confederate soldiers, however, were not willing to take any chances when it came to letting slaves obtain a taste of freedom. In the spring and summer of 1863, the Confederate army realized that it had to act more aggressively to keep their slaves in line. Throughout the South, Rebel troops dealt harshly with any black people who expressed their desire for freedom. "If you catch the scoundrels who run away," advised a Louisianan, John Foster, in April 1863, "swing them up to the first tree as they will give too much trouble among the rest."[66]

In April 1863, Ira J. Smith, involved in the campaign to retake the Mississippi River town of Helena, Arkansas—which had fallen to Union forces in the summer of 1862—wrote of twenty Rebel scouts disguising themselves as Yankees in order to obtain information from sixty slaves, who were "brought in." What the scouts discovered shocked Private Smith: slaves wanted to rob from, murder, or imprison their owners. In response, the Confederates "sent home some of the young negroes" and hoped to ship the other rebellious slaves to Little Rock—roughly 120 miles to the west and still under Rebel control. If what Smith had learned was indicative of slaves' attitudes elsewhere, he believed that they may as well "let them go free." Even so, the Rebel attack on Helena went forward as planned. The Union forces, outnumbered two to one, still defeated the Confederates at Helena in July, and Little Rock would fall two months later. But these defeats would not end the fighting in Arkansas, nor would they stop Confederate attempts to maintain racial control in that state or elsewhere.[67]

Confederates understood that force, not persuasion or abstract proslavery arguments, was the most powerful means of turning back emancipation. In 1863, in order to retrieve slaves and destroy Unionists' property, the Rebel army planned raids on plantations along the Mississippi. In August 1863, Gen. William Hicks Jackson, a Tennessee cavalry commander serving in Mississippi, was ordered to use a "strong body of cavalry" in the Natchez region, where they were to burn cotton and "awe unruly negroes." By intimidating black people and through the use of force, Confederates hoped to placate whites and subdue rebellious slaves.[68]

Far from Mississippi, Confederates were acting more aggressively to seize African Americans—slave and free. During the Gettysburg campaign, which brought Lee's men onto the free soil of southern Pennsylvania, the Army of Northern Virginia unleashed its wrath upon Northern civilians, black as well as white. The soldiers had few qualms about slavery, and Lee's men, as Stonewall Jackson's had earlier in the war, rounded up as many black people as possible.[69] One historian has noted that for the Confederates it was "a regular slave hunt." Captured blacks became part of the spoils of war. The North Carolinian James Albright was not serving in the Army of Northern Virginia, but he was happy to hear of Lee's raid into the North. "If we could only devastate Ohio and Pennsylvania," he mused, "it might bring the abolitionists to their senses." Fighting devils with fire, as he put it, was "the only way to win the war."[70] Among those captured by Lee's men were newly escaped Virginia slaves who had fled to Pennsylvania, as well as free blacks.[71] The Gettysburg campaign showed that Confederates, especially when in Union territory, were willing to use the Southern military as a weapon for race control.

In addition to giving Confederates a chance to enslave black people, Lee's second invasion of Union territory also became a test case for servants' support for the Southern cause. How would blacks traveling with the Army of Northern Virginia act when on free soil? In theory, African Americans would have easy opportunities to flee, but Confederate soldiers noted that they did not do so. As they saw it, some blacks were loyal to the army in ways that went beyond quietly performing their duties. At Mercersburg, Pennsylvania, the surgeon Thomas Fanning Wood wrote home about a slave who avoided the calls of some "abolition women" to seek refuge with the locals. It is unlikely, however, that a slave would have attempted an escape with so many Confederate soldiers nearby. It would have been an invitation to recapture and punishment—at worst, a suicide mission. The slave's "choice" to remain with the Confederate army might not have been much of a choice at all. Wood nevertheless believed that even in the absence of thousands of armed white Southerners, blacks would not have fled, nor would Yankees have welcomed them. Wood noted that when another slave asked for bread from a local woman, he heard that she "didn't cook for nasty niggers."[72]

Confederates were probably more accurate in noting Pennsylvanians' dislike of black people—the North was no stranger to virulent racism—than they were in their assumption that slaves had no desire for freedom. Even so, they penned numerous stories of slave loyalty during the Gettysburg campaign. They saw that black people shunned the Pennsylvanians, even if they were promised liberation, and they were convinced the North had no charms for servants accustomed to Southern ways. One slave told his master that he did not like Pennsylvania because he saw "no black folks," and other slaves seemed to enjoy plundering Union territory as much as Confederate troops did.[73]

Despite displays of black "loyalty" in Pennsylvania, during the war Confederate soldiers were witness to the greatest defection of slaves in American history, and every year brought thousands more slaves to Union lines. In September 1863, one officer wrote of the difficulty in seizing black people who had disappeared into the wilderness around the Combahee River in South Carolina. He had set dogs on the trail of missing slaves, with no luck.[74] Troops, furthermore, were not always enthusiastic about disciplining servants or capturing runaways. Appointed the task of hunting down blacks who had absconded with some animals, Robert Hamilton Williams, an English-born partisan ranger who fought in the Far Western Theater, remembered, "I knew the thing was a humbug, but orders had to be obeyed."[75] Another soldier recalled that he felt "much ashamed" at having to apprehend such "poor creatures" as he was told to capture. He did his duty, nevertheless, and returned the slaves to camp.[76]

In 1863, efforts at controlling slaves were hampered by Confederate military failures. The Rebel army lost control of the Mississippi River after its July defeats at Vicksburg and Port Hudson. One soldier captured at Vicksburg was quickly introduced to the Northern way of war. He wrote of actions "quite grating to my feelings towit negroes on guard... saluting [whites] all on an equality."[77] The loss of these strongholds on the Mississippi set the tone for operations in the Western Theater: military defeats meant the loss of thousands more slaves. Yankees sometimes seized hundreds of them at a time from plantations and towns, and as much as Confederates hated to admit it, most blacks were happy to leave.

Yet even after their defeats of the summer of 1863, and much evidence that Northerners and slaves embraced emancipation, Confederate soldiers would not accept the end of human bondage. In August, the Mississippian William Nugent, serving in the West, expected the Union to return slaves to their plantations. That Confederates believed such things was why the Union government had issued the Emancipation Proclamation in the first place: it wanted to make masters pay for having waged war against the United States. Nugent, nevertheless, believed that the United States would accomplish more by turning back the clock to 1860 "than by five years hard fighting."[78] Confederate soldiers' antebellum way of thinking died hard. As the war continued, becoming bloodier and more destructive, maintaining slavery still proved to be a central concern for Confederate troops.

In June 1863, William H. Grimball, serving in South Carolina, downplayed the massive loss of slaves in his theater of war, saying "the loss to the Individual is much greater than to the country. People value pecuniarily so high sentiments & ornaments." He believed his own family's plantation, "Grove," was in little danger (though the family had already shut down operations there).[79] Emancipation might lead to the disappearance of slaves, but it did not necessarily undermine men's faith in the war effort. Confederate troops still had much trust in the cause and in the power of the military to achieve a slaveholding republic. In late 1863, E. John Ellis, who was from a slaveholding family, said one's duty in the army must include keeping "the negroes in proper subjugation."[80] Even men who did not own chattels knew the South's fortunes rested on slavery. "I own no slaves," William Nugent wrote to his wife in September 1863. She obviously knew he did not, but he wanted his wife to understand that he could speak without "any motive of self interest." Although he was not a slaveholder, he refused to let the peculiar institution go. A South without slavery served no purpose. "We can only live & exist by this species of labor," he said, "and hence I am willing to continue the fight to the last."[81]

In addition to the flight or capture of slaves, Confederates faced other types of resistance by black people. Lt. William Grimball, serving in the First South Carolina Artillery, wrote from the defenses of Charleston in November 1863 concerning a servant who stole $30 from him. He said "the scoundrel" had passed himself off as a free black man, but that he actually belonged to a master "from whom he purloined $2300." William sent the servant to the guard house, but problems for the Grimballs persisted. William's brother, Arthur, serving in another South Carolina artillery unit, guarding Charleston, had a slave steal a comb from him and then flee. The servant then apparently set fire to a home and robbed others of clothing, money, geese, and a saddle. "Little did I think I had a miniature [Jeb] Stuart or [John Hunt] Morgan waiting one me," Arthur quipped. If that were not enough, William and Arthur's father received a letter in May 1864 telling him that the losses on the Grimball plantation, which slaves had damaged, came to at least $20,000.[82]

With the coming of the 1864 campaign season, some Confederates hoped to overcome the major defeats of 1863. The Alabama soldier

Thomas W. Francis began 1864 with the loss of his slaves. Writing from Mississippi, he was fatalistic about his situation, saying, "It is the beginning of what we may expect from our Negroes." He then predicted, "At least one half of the [male slaves] in the country will leave and try to get with the Yankees, and I expect that a large portion of them will succeed." As did many Confederates, he thought slaves who had fled were "deluded" and would regret their decision. He believed the slaves on his plantation were untrustworthy, but apparently did not think it was the case for all of his servants, as he repeatedly made requests throughout that year for his family to send him a servant.[83]

In 1864, Confederate troops believed that the Union's most concerted effort to subdue the South would occur before Northerners went to the polls in the fall.[84] Lincoln wanted to win the war as quickly as possible, and his new commander of the Union armies, Ulysses S. Grant, had a plan for total victory involving simultaneous offensives in every major theater. Increased pressure on the Confederate army meant increased stress on the master class. The Alabama infantryman Reuben Vaughan Kidd remembered one raid undertaken in his home state that year. "It was impossible to keep from the negroes their owners' dismay and dread," he wrote.[85] Such a fact did not mean that the Confederacy would lose, but the edifice of slavery was cracking. In 1864, slavery was becoming more precarious. Incidents unusual if not unheard of before the war had become common. After nearly three years of bloody warfare, some Confederates saw that slavery was proving untenable, and many became fatalistic about its future.[86]

Soldiers, however, adapted to the new conditions. Slavery had always faced challenges. For generations, Southerners had altered the institution in order to meet new conditions, not to mention new threats. During the Revolution, Southern whites had endured the English army's capturing of slaves. Fifty years later, they had seen the rise of vocal abolitionists. Now, amid civil war, slavery was undergoing greater stresses than ever, but soldiers continued to believe that their victory would entail a permanent defeat of abolitionism. As the spring campaigns approached, the South Carolinian Samuel Mays found that spirits were still high in the Army of Northern Virginia. "How long are they going to stand it?" he wondered about the men in the ranks. "They have but little direct interest in this contest as few are slave holders, and they are fighting for the pure love of country."[87] Even if most Confederates did not own slaves, they feared the results of a Northern victory. In March, Reuben Allen Pierson, an infantryman serving in Virginia in the Ninth Louisiana, said he would accept "everlasting war in preference to a union with a people who condescend to equalize themselves with the poor, ignorant & only half civilized negro."[88] Every Confederate victory brought Southern whites closer to the slaveholding republic they wanted, and with the reelection of Lincoln at stake, the battles of 1864 would likely decide the conflict. "As for my part I expect to fight till the bitter end," said a North Carolina soldier, writing from Greenville. "I never knew before what we was fighting for," he continued, "but now I know we are fighting against equalizing our selves with the darkies."[89]

Were Confederate troops to hold back the Yankees, they would crush what they saw as the perverse plans of Lincoln and the abolitionists to free the slaves and promote race-mixing. Still, soldiers had to struggle harder than ever to prevent what they saw as the evils of emancipation. They knew they must not only defeat Grant's armies, but they also must re-enslave black people, one slave or one group of slaves at a time. In March 1864, Jerome Yates wrote of the flight of servants across a river to Federal lines. They were prepared to escape, he wrote, but "we crushed their freedom in the bud by marching them across the river."[90] The troops believed that as long as they were vigilant, they could defeat the "abolitionist" Yankees and prevent the flight of slaves to Union forces. "I should not be surprised if the next Presidential Campaign will settle the thing," said Cpl. Fred A. Brode, serving in the Washington Artillery, in July 1864. "I do not believe that the people in the North will stand it [anymore]," he asserted. "They are getting tired of the war I think."[91]

Given the resilience of the Rebel army, Confederate troops could not accept defeat or emancipation as foregone conclusions. Well into 1864, Rebel soldiers still found slave disloyalty inexplicable. While on the march toward Washington during Jubal Early's raid on the capital, Capt. Robert E. Park, a Georgian serving in an Alabama regiment, wrote about his cook, Charles, leaving him. "I sent him off to cook a chicken and some biscuits, and he failed to put in an appearance any more," he noted in his diary. Park believed Charles had been "enticed away or forcibly detained by some negro worshipper, as he had always been prompt and faithful, and seemed much attached to me." He found his servant's disappearance odd, but rather than see it as a result of the unpleasantness of slavery, he believed Charles's disloyalty was the result of Yankee duplicity.[92]

Unlike Capt. Park, other Confederate troops quickly learned the new realities of the master-slave relationship. "A negro can't be trusted a tall

[sic]," said a soldier near Petersburg in June 1864.[93] The loss of slaves had proven a great hardship for many. "It seems hard to realize," said Fred Fleet, writing to his father from the Petersburg trenches in September, "that all of the servants are away and you are so dependent on others for labor in order to have food." He had written letters in 1862 about his uncle's slaves running away. Being from a Virginia family with large holdings of slaves, he always had reason for nervousness.[94] Now, his fears were coming true.

At places such as Kennesaw Mountain, Georgia, and the Crater, outside Petersburg, Confederates had shown how viciously they could still defend Southern soil from Yankee advances. But in the late summer of 1864, they suffered disheartening defeats at Atlanta and Mobile Bay. Nevertheless, the Rebels took comfort in knowing that Hood's and Lee's large armies were still intact. And slaves still made up a significant portion of those forces. In September 1864, Robert Park wrote of the meals that servants brought to him and his comrades. He claimed that none of the "seductive promises" of the Yankees could induce the slaves to leave their "life-long friends and homes."[95] As late as October 1864, one Confederate wrote, "For the negroes—it seems to me a bad move to take them from Virginia, they are safest here—specially as they would be unwilling to go."[96] The history of the war in the East up to that point suggests otherwise. Northern Virginia had suffered the most devastation of any Confederate-held area. Such words, nevertheless, showed that soldiers still believed that the army could protect slavery. There were black people who had actually returned to Confederate lines, and the Rebels saw this as an endorsement of slave society. Even in the fall of 1864, Confederate troops were not convinced of the inevitability of emancipation.

While Grant kept Lee occupied in Virginia, William Tecumseh Sherman marched through Georgia, causing devastation that spurred or worsened slave rebelliousness. The Yankee forces seized many black people, and other slaves abandoned or neglected their duties. Confederate troops felt their loss. "Negroes all been run off from hospital," said James Bates, while recovering from wounds received in the Atlanta campaign. In July 1864, he lamented that there was "no cook & nothing to eat."[97] Not all slaves were so bold as to abandon their masters. General Sherman did not want them following his army, which helps explain why many servants chose not to seek out the Federals. Some Confederate soldiers remembered blacks who hid family valuables or were loyal in other ways.[98] One Rebel recalled how his father panicked at Sherman's approach, taking all the trunks he could find before he fled, leaving several black workers in charge of the abandoned plantation. Some of his slaves did seek the Union army's protection, but they eventually returned to the plantation after the war.[99]

Even after serious reverses in Georgia, Confederates continued to resist rather than submit to Northern armies. John Bell Hood had abandoned Atlanta on 1 September 1864 (the Yankees entered the city the next day), but Sherman's order to evict citizens from the city was for him unbearable. In letters to Sherman, Hood bitterly objected to the Union commander's behavior. He promised that the South would fight on. "Better die a thousand deaths than submit to live under you or your Government and your negro allies," he wrote. General Hood was not the man to defeat Sherman. Nevertheless, the Federal army's actions made some Confederates even more resolved to win.[100]

In October, one Tennessee soldier, writing from Virginia, explained why he fought on. He feared that defeat would mean "disgrace, dishonor & slavery forever."[101] Amid the destruction of 1864, Confederate troops directed their hatred toward the "abolitionist" Abraham Lincoln, who was up for reelection. By the fall, it seemed that the last chance for the South lay in the North electing the Democrat, George B. McClellan, as president. Confederates hoped, as they had in the fall of 1862, that Northern Democrats, who were running on a peace and anti-emancipation platform, would end the war. As Daniel Hundley wrote in his diary, the Republican government, as Confederates had warned since 1861, was subverting the liberty of its very defenders. A McClellan victory, he believed, might restore the status quo antebellum: a united nation with slavery intact. Yet even those who supported McClellan's bid for the presidency found reason for hope in a Lincoln triumph. A Republican victory, the Texan James Bates believed, might embolden Confederates. Without being ironic, he supported Lincoln, thinking his policy of confiscation and emancipation would unite white Southerners and assure their independence.[102]

Lincoln's reelection meant the continuation of the war, which, by November 1864, was going very badly for the Confederacy. Lee remained stymied at Petersburg, Sherman was wreaking havoc as he marched to the Atlantic, and Phil Sheridan's army had cleared the Shenandoah Valley of Confederate forces. After Lincoln's victory, Rebel soldiers' letters took on a more desperate and depressed tone. In Virginia, a Confederate wrote of how those at home "may be stripped of everything—negroes stolen away—stocks and provisions all taken—all your clothing destroyed—

your house burned."¹⁰³ By late 1864, emancipation had not necessarily stripped soldiers of their slaves, but it had destroyed the kind of mastery white Southerners once enjoyed.

Some men denied they were fighting for slavery. George Stedman, suffering in a Yankee prison, said that Confederates wished there was "not a negro in the south. The negro is the soldier's enemy. He cannot visit his home within the federal lines because of the spies in his household.... Negro slavery is the least element in the strife."¹⁰⁴ Yet Confederate soldiers were still not willing to let slavery go. The most willing of white Southerners might have advocated gradual or partial emancipation, but most did not go even that far. In the trenches at Petersburg, in December 1864, Fred Fleet expressed his belief that the Confederates were fighting foremost for independence and "our very lives." He also took the "positive good" view of human bondage. He did not consider it a "moral or political evil." On the contrary, he believed it a "divine institution" which had brought black people out of savagery. Fleet even thought the South should reopen the African slave trade. Since its constitution had banned it in 1861, the Confederacy could not enact such a measure, but Fleet's words show his continued belief in the inherent righteousness of slavery. The Union had seized countless slaves, and many more black people had fled to Northern lines, but Fleet still thought human bondage could and should survive.¹⁰⁵

Even after the passage of the Thirteenth Amendment on 31 January 1865, Abraham Lincoln was willing to consider either compensated or gradual emancipation if they would end the war.¹⁰⁶ Had they laid down their arms earlier than they did, Southerners might have been able to keep slavery in some form, but they were determined to keep the institution on their own terms as long as they felt they could achieve victory. In February 1865, after the conference at Hampton Roads—in which Union and Confederate diplomats failed to achieve a negotiated cease-fire—the artillerist William Poague was upset that Lincoln had "exploded the peace bubble." The news, he noted, invigorated Confederates to the point of indignation. They could again rally around their hatred of Lincoln and were ready to accept "protracted, never ending war, with all its evils and distress," rather than become "slaves to Yankeedom."¹⁰⁷

The advent of emancipation, whether by Lincoln's order or as a natural outcome of the war, led many slaves to flee their masters. Confederates found that blacks were often dubious allies of the Southern war effort, and despite the disruption that emancipation caused, even late into the war, troops believed that most slaves remained loyal and believed that the Confederate army could maintain control over the institution. "Slavery is gone up," said Willie Milling, writing from Shreveport, Louisiana, in May 1865.[108] His assessment, even after the Confederacy itself had succumbed, reflects just how slow white Southerners were to accept slavery's demise. For most of the war, despite the evidence of slave flight, and despite the Emancipation Proclamation, Rebel troops continued to believe that they could hold back the tide of abolition.

· 6 ·

ON BATTLEFIELDS AND IN PRISONS
CONFEDERATE SOLDIERS CONFRONT BLACK UNION TROOPS

With the Emancipation Proclamation came the North's use of black Union troops to help crush the Confederacy. By the spring of 1863, the United States had organized some black regiments, and it had thousands of volunteers ready to fill others. Over the course of the war, 180,000 African Americans, most of them former slaves, served in the Union army. In 1863, Confederates found, much to their dismay, that colored troops were now invading the South. Rebels who had joined the ranks with dreams of Walter Scott–like glory, found their chivalry tested when they confronted black men in battle. Confederates treated black regiments with little of the respect they often showed Northern whites, and over the course of the war, they promised "no quarter" when they fought them.[1] Most Confederates never confronted black soldiers in battle. But with their manhood and combat reputations, not to mention slavery and the Southern social order at stake, Confederates found that racially charged combat proved to be the bitterest fighting in a very bitter war. It was the kind of combat they must win were the Confederates to succeed as defenders of a slaveholding nation.

From the war's beginning, Southerners vowed to treat Northerners without restraint, and such grim assurances were not always racial in tone. Confederates often spoke of flying the black flag or showing no quarter toward any Northerner. In their eyes, Yankees were abolitionists and they must pay dearly for waging war against the South. In March 1863, Henry Semple, an Alabaman in the Army of Tennessee, wrote from Tullahoma, Tennessee, about the recent depredations by the Yankees. He complained of Northern troops having taken the "unwilling as well as the willing" slaves from a house in northwestern Alabama. In response, he said, his men had refused to take prisoners and those who were captured would be shot if they were not "keeping up." Flying the black flag would become common.²

The fighting between Confederates and black Federals was not the beginning of racial violence in the South. Slavery had always depended on coerced labor, armed patrols, and corporal punishment. Whatever their disposition, masters had always had control over their servants' bodies, rewarding or punishing them according to their whims. But Confederate soldiers were different. A master might only have to discipline a slave for a minor act of rebelliousness, but Southern troops were fighting for their lives. Slave owners sometimes killed or maimed a slave for some infraction, but in wartime, Confederate troops believed they had much more to lose if they did not stop black soldiers from invading their communities. Thus, the killing often spun out of control and devolved into massacres. Merely defeating "Negroes" was often not enough to satisfy Confederate soldiers.

For some Confederates, such interracial combat took on the characteristics of a race war. The South Carolina cavalryman U. R. Brooks remembered the savagery of engagements between white and black soldiers. "Comrades, did you ever fight negroes in the war?" he asked. "Well," he continued, "if so, did you notice that your guns would shoot faster and straighter than ever before? Did you ever see a comrade after he had surrendered to a negro soldier, and if so, where? And did you ever take a negro soldier prisoner, and if so, what did you do with him? I never saw one captured nor one after he was captured. General Sherman says 'war's hell,' and we found race prejudice to be strong there."³

For some, by 1863 the war had become more destructive, even biblical, in nature. That March, concerning recent raids by black and white Union troops, the Florida soldier Winston Stephens called upon God, who, "being our helper," would clear out the invaders.⁴ Confederate soldiers believed that they must inflict Jehovah-like wrath on the "Yankee-Negro" alliance. Most felt up to the task. Daniel R. Hundley, the author of the influential *Social Relations in Our Southern States*, drew on another antebellum book, *Armageddon, or the United States in Prophecy*, written by S. D. Baldwin in the 1850s, to bolster his belief that the fighting between black and white troops was echoed in the words of the prophet Ezekiel. Hundley saw the North in the role of Gog, an invading power that worshipped a false god, whereas the South was the true Israel. As depicted in Ezekiel 38:5, alongside the armies of Gog were "'Ethiopia and Libya . . .; all of them with shield and helmet.'"⁵ As Hundley interpreted the Old

Testament, the presence of black Union soldiers on the battlefield embodied the spirit of the ancient armies of Ethiopia and Libya. For him, the war had the characteristics of a racial Armageddon.

To some extent, Confederate soldiers' behavior was predictable. In their eyes, black soldiers were rebels and the opposite of the docile plantation "Sambo." Historians have ably described the many engagements in which African Americans were slaughtered at Confederate hands.[6] However, it is also important to examine the extent to which the North's use of black soldiers affected Confederate military policy and white Southern racial thinking. The Confederates initially thought they could defeat the black soldiers with little effort, and they never acknowledged the decisive role African Americans played in the conflict. Even so, they could not ignore the fact that black Union troops changed the character of the war. On battlefields and in prisons, African Americans effectively challenged white Southerners' ideas of racial mastery.

By 1862, the Southern military had grown concerned about the Union's move toward a harder war, a full-scale assault against civilian property, slave or otherwise.[7] In May 1861, Benjamin Butler, later known as "the Beast" among disgusted Confederates, declared that seized slaves were "contraband of war."[8] Butler did not free any slaves outright, but he would not return them to their masters either; and his actions were part of a growing trend toward the United States using former slaves in its army. Two months later, the United States Congress passed the Confiscation Act, which allowed Northern troops to capture slaves that had been used for military purposes against the Union. Early in 1862, Congress abolished slavery in the territories and in the nation's capital, and in July came the Second Confiscation Act, which allowed Union soldiers to seize property used in aid of the Confederacy. The act also deemed slaves who came into Northern lines as "captives of war" who "shall be forever free," which then, as free men, allowed them to join the United States army.[9]

Gen. John Pope, once he took command of the Army of Virginia in the summer of 1862, declared that he would not hesitate to confiscate Rebel property, and that he would also take harsher measures to combat guerrilla warriors. Pope's orders concerning guerrillas, and the people who harbored them, ultimately were not enforced, but his attitude toward Confederate property was widely shared by Northerners. Pope never enjoyed the success of a Grant or Sherman, but his policies showed that Union commanders were employing stronger tactics to defeat the Confederacy. One North Carolina soldier from a planter family feared that Pope's measures would give the Yankees license to "seduce and arm our

Slaves," and he added, "It will be time for Southrons to steel the heart to misery and rush with keen edged weapons to the conflict."[10] A Northern officer did not have to attack slavery directly for Confederates to reach the logical conclusion that further efforts to destroy the Rebel war effort would entail an attack on human bondage. And they were prepared to retaliate against those who would interfere with slavery.

For Confederates, commanders who liberated and armed slaves were criminals inciting insurrection. In late July 1862, Governor John Letcher of Virginia wrote George Randolph, the Confederate secretary of war, concerning such men. The Confederacy, he believed, must punish black soldiers, their officers, and any Federal who attacked slavery. Randolph knew the Yankees were not merely striking at masters in Virginia, but at the Southern nation as a whole.[11] Letcher's concerns were not ignored. By the summer of 1862, the Confederacy had issued stern warnings to those Northerners instituting a "get tough" policy in the South. In August, the Confederacy angrily responded to David Hunter's decision to emancipate and arm slaves in the southeastern Confederacy. General Orders No. 60, which stated that Confederates would retaliate against Federal "crimes and outrages" was issued. The Confederates saw Hunter as not just an enemy, but an outlaw, and Jefferson Davis himself would determine the time and the place of his execution.[12]

By summer 1862, despite Confederates' attempts to keep the war a white man's fight, black troops were playing an increasingly important role in the struggle. Some African Americans had already fought in battles. In August, a Texas soldier wrote of a "good many Negroes" engaged in a skirmish in Arkansas.[13] In response to the increasing presence of blacks in the Union army, the Davis government refused to recognize them as combatants, but it did not know how to treat them beyond that. Confederates, unsure of their government's policy toward "colored troops," looked to their commanders and political leaders for guidance.

On 22 September 1862, Lincoln issued his Preliminary Emancipation Proclamation, which made black freedom an official Union war aim. The proclamation did not guarantee the end of slavery in the United States—Lee's surrender would do that—but it changed the character of the war. In response, the Confederacy developed its own policy for dealing with black troops. The result was that Confederates, who saw African Americans foremost as slaves, would treat them with severity. In November, the Alabama colonel Jonathan R. F. Tattnall, commanding the Twenty-Ninth Alabama Infantry, wrote to Gen. John H. Forney, commander of southern Alabama and western Florida, to say that he had ordered the shooting of blacks found in arms with "abolition troops," or who served as guides. Confederates had few qualms about murdering black men, but they were far more hesitant about killing whites in cold blood. Writing from Mobile, General Forney urged Tattnall to hang rather than shoot black troops or guides, a punishment he apparently deemed more appropriate for traitors and spies. He did not authorize the murder of white troops.[14]

Confederate commanders subsequently wondered what they should do with captured black soldiers, or perhaps whether they should take them prisoner at all. On 14 November, Hugh Mercer, in charge at Savannah, wrote his superiors, saying that he had captured "six [slaves] in Federal uniform with arms (muskets) in their hands." Rather than sell one of the men, named Manuel, back into slavery, Mercer suggested that "these negroes be made an example of." General Beauregard, commanding the Carolina and Georgia coasts, wrote Secretary Seddon about the matter. Seddon believed that Mercer should execute Manuel, but before he issued a death sentence, he wanted to discuss it with Jefferson Davis.[15] After consulting with the president, Seddon reminded Beauregard that slaves in "flagrant rebellion" were subject to harsh penalties in all the Confederate states. Seddon foreshadowed the Davis administration's December 1862 proclamation, which asserted that Confederates would not recognize blacks as prisoners of war. The only fitting punishment, Seddon concluded, was summary execution. Seddon, however, included a caveat. He wanted officers to weigh such executions carefully, in order to avoid "possible abuse of this grave power." Seddon worried that soldiers might kill black troops because of "immediate excitement" or "over-zeal"; General Mercer, therefore, should use his power discriminately and judiciously.[16]

In December, Jefferson Davis issued an official statement about his nation's conduct toward captured black troops. One could call it an "Anti-Emancipation Proclamation." Davis's proclamation, which was issued with Ben Butler and his black soldiers in mind, declared that the Confederate army would return to slavery any black man found in Federal uniform. It would also turn over to state authorities any slaves found aiding Northern units; and it would do the same with white officers of "colored" regiments. The threat of handing over Federals to the states was vague but threatening. It essentially meant that Confederates would, at the very least, remand black men to slavery, and at worst, execute them and their white commanders for inciting servile insurrection.[17]

Davis's decision partly was a concession to states' rights. Rather than have Confederate officials execute black troops, the president left any decision on punishment to the states. At another level, delegation to the states freed the Confederate government of the attendant legal work. The Confederacy did not have in 1862, nor would it ever have, a national court system, even though the Confederate Constitution called for one.[18] Thus, no Supreme Court was in place to review the laws that mandated the return of former slaves in Federal uniform to their masters, or the execution of white officers. Davis instead let the states decide how to deal with these prisoners. The Confederates may have questioned why it was necessary to adjust their laws in order to deal with captured blacks. Indeed, for them, taking a soft line toward black soldiers would undermine the legal and ideological foundations of human bondage and a white man's government.

To Northern minds, the execution of white or black Union soldiers violated the unwritten code of battle (the Union would not issue its Lieber Code, outlining the army's code of conduct, until April 1863), regardless of what Jefferson Davis said. Confederates, in contrast, said Northerners should not have been surprised that Rebels did not consider blacks the equal of whites merely because they were now in uniform. Confederates believed that the North had exceeded the bounds of reasonable conduct by using black people to destroy slavery, and the result, as Davis wrote in his December proclamation, was a "servile war ... far exceeding in horrors the most merciless atrocities of the savages." Confederates felt that they could not tolerate black "savages" terrorizing the countryside.[19]

Some Confederates wisely saw that Jefferson Davis's hard line toward black troops would cause problems. Robert Kean, who served in Longstreet's corps before he became a War Department employee, feared that the state courts did not have the authority to punish prisoners of war. And he thought Davis's measures would result in "renewing the ferocity of the war and exasperating those who were being driven over to sympathy with us against the Abolitionists."[20]

Other Confederates were ready for the coming escalation of violence. After hearing Davis's December 1862 proclamation, the South Carolina artillerist Clayton Huger believed that the Federals would "probably retaliate by hanging ... our officers." Yet, if Davis's actions should incur Yankee retribution, his president's conduct would make Huger support the Confederacy even more. His nation could withstand any punishment Northerners might unleash in response, he thought, since he believed that Southerners captured more prisoners and outfought the Yankees in any case. In his mind, the North's experiment in using black soldiers would fail.[21] Confederates would later discover that it was the Union that best withstood attrition, but before that cruel truth emerged, they believed they could beat back any Northern troops, black or otherwise.

Davis's proclamation might have angered the Northerners, but it did not intimidate them. In April 1863, Gen. David Hunter wrote to Jefferson Davis complaining that the Confederates had killed blacks and sold others into slavery, acts that went "against the laws of war and humanity." As retaliation, he promised to execute the highest-ranking Confederate officer in his possession. Hunter would not allow the enemy to murder his men or sell them "into a slavery worse than death."[22] For him, responsibility for the execution of prisoners of war would fall on the Confederates, not the Federals.[23] Hunter's views were supported by officials in Washington. In July 1863, Abraham Lincoln promised to execute one Confederate soldier for every Federal in a black regiment killed after being captured. He would also place a Confederate soldier at hard labor for every white or black Union soldier who was made to labor for the South.[24] The Confederacy might distinguish between black and white prisoners, but the Federals would not.

The Confederacy, which quickly learned of Lincoln's order, did not pursue the official no-quarter policy any further. In addition to having aroused Federal retaliation, the rebellion's stance toward black soldiers and their officers posed other problems. For one, it probably confused more commanders than it helped. Southerners preferred to think of all black people as slaves, but as the Confederate treasury secretary Christopher Memminger noted in July 1863, what would the army do with captured free blacks? At that point in time, nearly half of the Union's "colored" soldiers had never been slaves. Were Confederates to treat them as slaves, inciting insurrection? And how would the Confederacy control its army's actions toward black units?[25] The Davis administration could not adequately answer such questions. Also, it gave at best mixed messages to its troops regarding the treatment of black soldiers. In August 1863, James Seddon, at Davis's urging, wrote that black troops should not have prisoner-of-war status, but rather than execute them, he recommended putting them at hard labor. Beyond that, the government left decision making to its commanders. "Each case must depend upon its circumstances," Seddon wrote, "and as the two govts will have different classes to deal with it is not seen how a definite answer can be given."[26]

The Confederate government did not pursue an official "take-no-prisoners" policy toward black troops, but if any soldier had forgotten how important victory was, President Davis reminded him. In an August 1863 address to the troops, he expounded on the terror and destruction the

Yankees had brought to the South. He warned of Federals who would "incite servile insurrection and light the fires of incendiarism whenever they can reach your homes." The Northern troops had worked to "debauch the inferior race, hitherto docile and contented, by promising indulgence of the vilest passions as the price of treachery." Davis's words were intended to conjure images of black soldiers murdering and raping white women. One Rebel soldier was "greatly enthused" by the address. "If there is a man now in the Confederacy who is unwilling or fails to do his duty," he said, "he should be branded as a *traitor* or *coward*."[27]

More important than the speeches of Confederate politicians concerning black men's potential for violence were the effects of decades of proslavery ideology on Southern whites' desire for racial control. President Davis proved unwilling to sanction the murder of Federal prisoners of war, but the Confederate armies operated on a de facto "no-quarter" policy. On the battlefield, officers and common soldiers found they could act with impunity. Confederate law did not dissuade them, and Federal law could not touch them.

Some commanders were unwilling to raise the black flag and descend into racial killing. In late August 1863, Joseph E. Johnston, commanding the Department of the West, wrote Stephen D. Lee—in charge of Mississippi cavalry—concerning a supposed massacre of twenty-two black Federals and a white officer. The men, Johnston wrote, were "put to death in cold blood and without form of law." If the report was true, Johnston wanted to bring the men to trial.[28] His memorandum suggests that he did not necessarily protest the killing of the Federal troops, but rather that the Confederates had punished them without due process of law. Other Confederates also prevented attempts to execute black soldiers. They believed they should return blacks to slavery, where they could renew the ties that had bound them to the white South. Black soldiers, so the thinking went, would realize the error of their ways if they were welcomed back into the Confederate fold. During the Confederacy's summer 1863 campaign along the Mississippi, James Seddon informed Edmund Kirby Smith—whose isolated Trans-Mississippi Theater would become known as "Kirby Smithdom"—that many Northern troops along the river were black. Seddon gave "suggestions," rather than orders, about how to deal with them. Confederates should act with leniency toward blacks, but as for whites, they "had better be dealt with red-handed on the field or immediately thereafter." Black troops, he believed, were mere dupes, "deluded victims of the hypocrisy and malignity of the enemy." Therefore, they "should not be driven to desperation, but received readily to mercy, and encouraged to submit and return to their masters."[29] Once they were under the care of their former slaveholders, he believed, blacks would find contentment.

Such a policy gave the Confederacy's war against black soldiers a patina of paternalism. As James Seddon believed, the former slaves could not have fled willingly—rather, they were tools of the Yankees. For Confederates, since their society was superior to the free North, blacks must have joined the Yankees only under duress. Thus, just as masters should avoid punishing their slave "children" unnecessarily, Confederate troops should spare black troops the worst kinds of punishment. For Seddon, a servant who fled deserved swift justice, but a dead one was useless. "Negroes" might stray, but Confederates should not execute them.

Confederates serving in the West were the first to fight African Americans in significant engagements. In the summer of 1863, black troops fought along the Mississippi River at such places as Port Hudson and Milliken's Bend in Louisiana. Black soldiers' efforts did not come without great cost. As one Southerner wrote home in June 1863, "Let the negroes know how the Yankees put the negro soldiers in the front at Port Hudson when nearly a whole Reg. was killed."[30] Confederates wanted those still enslaved to know that the North only used them for cannon fodder. Such stories, whether true or not, served as a cautionary tale: slaves at home should not join the Union army. An Arkansas soldier heard that Northerners did not bury the blacks they killed in battle, and other Southern troops reported that blacks did not always enter the service willingly. In March 1863, one cavalryman serving in Florida said that local Federals were gathering up blacks and hanging those who would not fight.[31]

Black units were fighting hard in important battles, but the vast majority of Confederates had not encountered any black troops. And they were not convinced, anymore than most Northerners were, that blacks could make good troops. For Rebel troops, blacks seemed better marauders than soldiers. Confederates could imagine ex-slaves destroying property and assaulting civilians—as they had in slave insurrections, however rare—but not marching well or dressing ranks amid withering fire. Robert E. Lee's men, for example, prided themselves on supposedly not plundering the countryside during the Gettysburg campaign. Gen. Clement A. Evans noted, in contrast, the behavior of black troops under Col. James Montgomery, who put Darien, Georgia, to the torch around the same time. Rather than resort to such barbarity, Evans said his own men helped save a Pennsylvania home from burning down.[32] His implication was that Confederates were gentlemen. To expect black troops to act like them was absurd.

Despite the challenges they faced from racist Northern comrades and proslavery Rebels vowing to give them "no quarter," black men did use their guns successfully against Confederates. White Southerners were as determined to keep their way of life, and the racial foundation of their society, intact, as blacks were determined to destroy it. Black troops showed courage on the battlefield, but for Confederates, African Americans were cowards—field hands, not soldiers. "Darkies," one Confederate wrote after the war, "understood the use of the hoe better than the fire-lock."[33] Early in 1863, when Gen. Gabriel James Rains—a veteran of the Seven Days Battles and the Confederacy's torpedo expert—heard about the North's use of black soldiers, he told John B. Jones, a War Department employee, that blacks could not fight and would always run away.[34]

By 1864, many black troops were not only fighting, but serving behind the lines as prison guards. Racial tensions in prisoner-of-war camps compounded already bitter animosity between Union and Confederate soldiers. Early in the year, before he began his campaign against Robert E. Lee, Ulysses S. Grant ended the prisoner exchange. In his memoirs, Jubal Early objected to Grant's policy, which he saw as punitive.[35] Early's assumption was correct, though the killing and wounding of Confederates was already punishing the Southern military—and besides, punishing them was the whole point. Grant understood that the South could not stand a war of attrition: a Confederate prisoner was almost as good as a dead one. By that point, the Union had mostly stopped the exchange because of Confederates' refusal to recognize blacks as combatants. As early as August 1863, one Southerner saw it coming. "God help the unfortunate ones," he said of those who would have to live under the new prison system.[36]

In Union prison camps, Confederates had the chance to reflect on the meaning of the war and the role race played in the conflict. In the fall of 1863, the partisan commander M. Jeff Thompson, who had been captured and temporarily sent to Johnson's Island in Ohio, wrote to a Northern colonel that he had "no right to discuss politics." Yet, the next day, he wrote to George D. Prentice, editor of the *Louisville Journal*, about politics, namely, the two possible outcomes of the war. One was the recognition of Confederate independence. The other was far more ominous: "*Extermination of the White Race at the South,* as preached by the abolitionists."[37]

Such fears reinforced the hatred felt by many Confederates toward their black prison guards. Capt. John O'Brien remembered how much he and his men disliked the "everlasting nigger" who "busted up the whole thing"—meaning the prisoner exchange. Angry comrades, he wrote, cursed the "whole nigger race from Ham down." O'Brien lashed out at white Yankees, too. In the reductio ad absurdum many Southerners drew upon, he thought that because Northerners extended greater rights to African Americans, that meant that they wanted to marry black women. O'Brien reserved the utmost contempt, however, for black troops. In roughly a paragraph, he used the word "nigger" six times when accounting for their role in the prison camps.[38] His racial diatribe was about as vitriolic as any when discussing blacks in the Civil War.

In prisons, Confederate soldiers saw black prison guards as crueler than white ones and believed them worse than any slaveholder. From Jacksonville, Florida, to Fort Pulaski, Georgia, to Fort Delaware, Delaware, to Point Lookout, Maryland, Confederates agreed that their black prison guards were terrible.[39] Masters, Southerners knew, had financial incentives to keep their chattels alive, but in wartime life was cheap. For the least infraction, black prison guards might shoot or starve their prisoners. Confederates believed they were as powerless as one could be, and the fact that their guards were black proved to be a further humiliation. Feelings of powerlessness would fuel postwar rage against African Americans. It was perhaps not surprising that in Alamance County, North Carolina, the Klan consisted of men from companies who had been guarded by black soldiers at Point Lookout.[40] The highest compliment troops could give their captors was faint praise. One Confederate said that blacks would shoot a man at the slightest provocation, but that they treated the inmates better than their white officers.[41]

In late January 1865, one Confederate was willing to have authorities exchange him for black troops.[42] But before the war seemed lost, most Southerners refused to acknowledge blacks as equals in any way. In February 1864, in a defiant, though futile resistance, the Alabama officer John Washington Inzer said he would always hate the United States flag and vowed never to marry any woman who honored it. Inzer was adamant about not recognizing blacks as soldiers, yet he could write, "Man, however vile, whatever his perils, whatever his destination, was born Free and loves Liberty."[43] Such a claim, as ironic as it may seem, was in keeping with the long-held Southern belief that freedom did not extend to black people. For Confederates, the existence of African American troops violated their fundamental ideas of racial superiority.

Confederates tried hard to portray black guards as primitive brutes, which included detailed descriptions of them as having especially black skin. The Alabama infantryman Robert Park, imprisoned at Fort Pulaski, depicted one of Benjamin Butler's contrabands as "coal-black" and "brutal-looking." Anthony Michael Keiley, who served in the Army of Northern Virginia before being captured, remembered walking past an "odorous Congo, with a claymore two-thirds his length," who had a "Nubian nose." Keiley said, "Like every other negro soldier I met ... he was as black as Mason's 'Challenge,' and as surly looking a dog as ever brake bread."[44] In fact, African American troops were not as uniformly dark as Confederates depicted them. In the black Fifty-Fifth Massachusetts Infantry Regiment, for example, 430 of the 980 enlisted men were of mixed-race ancestry.[45] Confederates, however, did not describe "colored" troops that way. They wrote instead of "Negroes" who seemed right off the boat from Africa, a falsehood that rejected both the complexity of race in America—namely the reality of interracial sex in the South—and the multigenerational American ancestry of Southern slaves. Confederates suggested that black troops were all the same and that their dark skin reflected a blacker, more primitive, indeed, *more African* character. Only white Southerners, they implied, were true Americans. For Confederates, black troops appeared as dark as they expected a man from Africa to look, and in their view, dark skin color reflected a depraved moral character. Black soldiers apparently had no white blood in their veins, and thus—as white Southerners were convinced—little of what made men civilized. Most black Union soldiers had indeed been slaves at one time, but Confederates acted as if they were a type of "Negro" they had never seen before.

Confederates described black Union soldiers not only as primitive looking, but primitive of mind. Confederates believed that just below the surface of black soldiers' martial, authoritarian demeanor was the ignorance and subservient instincts of the plantation "darkie." "The negro *never* loses the instinctive respect which he feels for the Southern man," said E. John Ellis in his reminiscences. In his eyes, a black soldier would never prove to be a white man's superior, no matter how much temporary power he wielded. Confederates believed that whether or not they lost the war, the inverted racial roles of Yankee prison camps would not last.[46]

Point Lookout (officially called Camp Hoffman), located in Maryland and the largest Union prison camp, was notorious for racial tensions. In reading wartime letters, one finds little evidence of this, mostly because during the war, prisoner-of-war letters were censored by Northern officials. To reconstruct conditions there, one is forced, then, to rely on postwar reminiscences and recollections—some of which aimed to counter the misconception that only Northerners suffered in Civil War prisons. Despite their attempts, Confederates who suffered at Point Lookout could not make it seem worse than the most infamous prison: Andersonville. Of the 41,000 men imprisoned at Andersonville (officially called Camp Sumter), approximately 13,000 died; whereas at Point Lookout, 4,000 of the 52,000 men there perished. Nor were physical conditions between the two camps comparable. At Andersonville, men suffered from overcrowding, disease, poor sanitation, and shortages of provisions. In contrast, Confederates at Point Lookout benefited from a more temperate climate and a better Union supply system. Despite their shortcomings, at Federal prisons, the authorities could care for prisoners of war much better than Rebel officials could.[47]

M. Jeff Thompson described the hospital at Point Lookout as the "most comfortable and convenient . . . I had seen during the war."[48] Life at Point Lookout, materially at least, was not bad as at other prisons, but Confederates were successful in painting a thoroughly dismal portrait of it. Mostly, they emphasized the cruelty of their black guards. In May 1864, one North Carolinian noted that his black guards were "mean as hell."[49] According to one Confederate, the men policing the grounds were so brutal that authorities had to remove them. Black troops forced skeletal men, at the point of the bayonet, to march at the double-quick, which sometimes took place in the middle of the night. They also compelled prisoners to carry black guards on their backs, or to pray for Abraham Lincoln. With Victorian restraint, the Virginia infantryman Charles T. Loehr alluded to jokes blacks told at Point Lookout that "decency would not permit me to mention."[50]

Among the most notorious crimes at Point Lookout was the unprovoked shooting of prisoners, which led Confederates to conclude that Northerners should not have trusted African Americans with guns. Blacks apparently shot each other accidentally, and one even shot himself. A. M. Keiley wrote of the cold-blooded murder of a "poor, feeble old man named Potts . . . one of the most harmless creatures in the pen."[51] Another wrote of a "sort of rivalry among [the black troops] to distinguish themselves by shooting some of us." In April 1864, a black sentinel killed a Virginia soldier, and later that month, guards shot another inmate.[52] According to a former Point Lookout inmate, Rev. John Malachi, the black guards would shout, "Rats to you holes, or I will shoot you," before they fired. At one point, Malachi had to jump into a barrel of water to avoid getting hurt.[53]

CONFEDERATE SOLDIERS CONFRONT BLACK UNION TROOPS

In one of the war's many ironies, imprisoned Confederates rebelled in small ways, much as slaves had done for generations, and were still doing, on the plantation. The North Carolina infantryman Bartlett Malone wrote of fellow Confederates at Point Lookout who stole a guard's knapsack which had his sweetheart's picture in it.[54] The testing of Federal troops' patience could prove more serious. One Confederate told a white soldier that "the negro was superior to the Yankee, and that all [Northerners] ever knew [they] learned from them." Such words played on Northern prejudice. Yankees did not like to hear that they were the inferior of a black man, and they might overreact to such barbs. The quarrel between the guard and his Confederate prisoner apparently resulted in the killing of the latter.[55]

Just as the Union could not stop the execution of black soldiers from occurring at Rebels' hands, the Confederacy could do little about the excesses at Federal prisons. In June 1864, Robert E. Lee considered sending a force to liberate the prisoners at Point Lookout. Lee knew most of the garrison was composed of black soldiers, and he believed that the Federals' commander was a poor one. A "stubborn resistance . . . may not reasonably be expected," Lee concluded. Confederates, however, never mounted an effort to take the fort.[56] The North's mistreatment of prisoners at Point Lookout continued, though not on the same scale as existed at Andersonville or other, more notorious prison camps.

The end of the prisoner exchange in the spring of 1864 made the Civil War increasingly bitter, and the North's use of black troops on the battlefield and in prison camps united Confederates against their enemy. But before April 1864, the Confederate army's refusal to take prisoners had not been widely denounced in the North. This would change with the Rebel attack on Fort Pillow, where there occurred the most infamous—but not necessarily the worst—massacre of African Americans during the war. At the 12 April battle, Nathan Bedford Forrest's men overran the Federal position at Pillow, roughly a day's ride north from Memphis along the Mississippi. There, they killed dozens of men, some white, most of them black, as they tried to surrender or escape. The engagement achieved instant notoriety, and the North's Joint Committee on the Conduct of the War investigated.[57] As one black survivor recalled, a Confederate private had said that "all the colored boys that could escape had best to do so by all means, for General Forrest was going to burn or whip them to death after they got farther south." According to one Rebel, the Confederates had been insulted by black troops before the battle, and when combined with white Southerners' natural desire to maintain racial control, they made sure that the "colored" soldiers paid for their insolence.[58]

The testimony about Fort Pillow proved to be controversial, for disagreement arose even among Federal troops about what happened. But it is clear that the Union troops were killed as they surrendered or shortly after. Through the years, analysis of Confederate conduct at Pillow has often focused on Forrest's role.[59] After the battle, he said, infamously, "It is hoped that these facts will demonstrate to the Northern people that negro soldiers cannot cope with Southerners." Whether or not Forrest directed the massacre, most Confederates were willing to murder blacks without orders. The sight of "Negro" troops, said one, "stirred the bosoms of our soldiers with courageous madness."[60]

The Confederates justified the massacre in several ways. One was tactical. As one veteran claimed, using rather circular logic, the reason the Federals fled from Fort Pillow was because they expected no quarter, and since they did so, Confederates had no choice but to take no prisoners. Union troops apparently would have done better to stay their ground, but they knew what kind of treatment they could expect from their enemy. For the Confederates, to kill a man in flight was not cold-blooded. In their eyes, they were forced to slay Northerners who would not surrender. Another even more important reason for the massacre lay in Confederate soldiers' racial thinking. After the war, James Dinkins, who had served in the Tennessee cavalry during the war, discussed white Southerners' attitudes toward blacks: slaves were property, he noted, and thus soldiers treated African Americans like "a refractory horse or child."[61] Confederate troops reasoned that no one could blame them for their conduct at Fort Pillow.

In 1864, battlefield atrocities combined with stories of crimes committed against Southern civilians intensified interracial combat. Before April ended, other brutal fighting took place between black Federals and Confederates in Arkansas at Poison Spring and Jenkins' Ferry. At both battles, Southern troops were in control of the field afterward. As with Forrest's triumph at Fort Pillow, however, these Confederate successes did not have much effect on the war's outcome. They were at best a morale booster for Confederates, but they also underscored the viciousness of white-black combat. The Arkansas soldier Robert M. Rodgers remembered pouring a heavy fire into black troops at Jenkins' Ferry, the last battle in the Union's botched Red River campaign. He said that the Confederates mowed blacks down "by the score." After his men retook a battery that the black Federals had seized earlier in the battle, he wrote of "what might be termed 'negro killin.'" Rodgers might have exaggerated the extent of the carnage at Jenkins' Ferry (he estimated Federal casualties at 1,000, which is likely too high), but he did not exaggerate the rage that accompanied Rebel attacks on black troops.[62]

Massacres were not confined to the Western Theater. Confederates everywhere expected both sides to raise the black flag. The Louisiana infantryman Henry Handerson marched toward Fredericksburg in early 1864, where he saw some of General Burnside's black troops. His comrades said it was "extremely likely that they would massacre us on sight." Handerson did not believe it; he thought the troops no more insulting or intimidating than white ones. Confederate and Union soldiers instead merely viewed one another with "mutual curiosity and dislike."[63] Handerson's encounter with the African Americans was bloodless, but Confederates had reason to fear retribution for their actions at Fort Pillow and elsewhere.[64] Over the spring and summer, Civil War combat reached a new height of bloodiness and ferocity.

In April 1864, at the battle of Plymouth, North Carolina, black soldiers again fared far worse than the Confederates did. "There were a good many prisoners taken at Plymouth about 3000 in all, amongst them a good many negroes," wrote Clayton Coleman, a North Carolina soldier. He added that "our men did not take any negroes with arms, but killed them all." He also looked to see if any of his father's slaves were among those captured, but "didn't recognize a single one."[65] Confederates in North Carolina were as vicious as those in Tennessee and Arkansas had been in their conduct toward African Americans.[66]

For Confederates, Northern troops were offensive and villainous by nature, but the threat of black Federals violating Southern white women cut at a deeper level.[67] Whether or not white Southerners feared assaults on their women because of what Wilbur Cash has called a "rape complex," Confederates wrote of black-on-white sex crimes.[68] Writing from Petersburg, Virginia, in early July, the South Carolina soldier John Jefcoat wrote of Confederates turning back "the Raiders" who had taken white prisoners and slaves, stolen horses, and made off with carriages. He also noted that they committed "the worst of cruelty uppon the woman an childrin and would alow the Negroes with themselfs to Ravish the Most Respectable ladies of verginia. I think such theaves and Robers should be killed and not taken prisners."[69] Such stories worsened already intense Confederate fears of a loss of racial control in the South.

By the summer of 1864, troops were exhausted from the vicious battles and other hardships that had become customary in Civil War campaigns.

Rumors of enemy atrocities only fed their anger toward the Federals. Some evidence of blacks committing crimes against white women was credible; other stories were more dubious. The veracity of such news did not matter. One soldier heard from an ambulance driver, who heard it from a "trustworthy lady," that a "big black negro" went to one of "the most respected young ladies in the city" and offered her money for sex. His reaction was typical: every nerve in his body was prepared for vengeance. He wanted to raise the black flag and "let slip the dogs of war."[70]

Combat between black and white Civil War soldiers reached a climax at the 30 July 1864 Battle of the Crater. After months of heavy fighting, Lee's and Grant's armies were locked in a stalemate at Petersburg, Virginia, an important rail junction roughly a day's march south of Richmond. To break the deadlock, Grant's men spent weeks mining under the Confederate works. They stuffed tons of gunpowder in the tunnels, and on 30 July lit the fuses. The tremendous blast shocked the Confederate army and created a temporary hole in the Southern lines. The Union, however, frittered away its initial advantage. It took an hour for the Federals to launch their attack, and once they advanced, many troops went into the Crater rather than around it. The Confederates rallied and reformed their lines, pouring a deadly fire into the Union troops huddled at the bottom of the huge pit the mine had created. The Confederates won the battle and inflicted 3,800 casualties on the black and white Union forces.[71] With the North's failure, the siege at Petersburg continued.

The struggle in the Crater had much historical significance. The North missed a great opportunity to break the Confederate line, which resulted in the prolongation of the siege. It also proved to be the bloodiest battle in which black soldiers in the Army of the Potomac took part. It was not the first battle in Virginia in which blacks had fought. At the battle of Wilson's Wharf (or Fort Pocahontas) on 24 May, approximately 1,800 black troops had fought off a larger force under the cavalryman Fitzhugh Lee. Before the Crater fight, however, Grant had worried about public opinion. Were blacks to fail, he reasoned, racist Northerners—among them his friend William T. Sherman—might think them incapable of winning victories, or that Grant was merely using them as cannon fodder. Regardless, many Federals did not want to see black troops alive or dead on the battlefield. After the Battle of the Crater, one Confederate noted the "loathing with which the Yankees took up and bore to the ditches [and] prepared the offensive remains of their African soldiers."[72]

Black soldiers at the Crater went into battle vowing to avenge their comrades. They cried "Remember Fort Pillow!" as they emerged from their trenches to attack.⁷³ But at the Crater, black soldiers—as they had at Fort Pillow, Jenkins' Ferry, and Plymouth—suffered a sound defeat. "No man asked, no man gave quarter," remembered the Virginian W. Gordon McCabe. "The slorter of Negroes was awful," said Cpl. Andrew S. Barksdale, a Virginia artillerist.⁷⁴ Most Confederates had never seen "colored" soldiers before. The sight of black troops aroused in them feelings of shock, outrage, and desperation.

At the Crater, the Rebels agreed that the battle was among the most vicious and bloody they had seen, which was telling, considering the carnage of the previous months in Virginia at the Wilderness, Spotsylvania, and Cold Harbor. "The negroes were piled up in our ditches six deep," said one North Carolinian. "The blood ran in streams from their worthless carcasses."⁷⁵ The fighting was savage, not only because of the racial element involved, but because Confederates wanted to prevent a breakthrough in the Petersburg defenses. Had they failed, Petersburg and Richmond might have fallen much sooner than they did.

Confederates were enraged when they saw black units taking part in the attack. James Thomas Perry of the Seventeenth Virginia Infantry noted that Burnside's corps was made up of "negroes and mongrels." For Southern troops, the black Federal units represented abolitionism at its most threatening.⁷⁶ The Alabama infantryman and planter Alfred Lewis Scott remembered he was more upset at whites having armed the black soldiers who charged him than the black troops themselves. Most Confederates, however, were not.⁷⁷ Their astonishment quickly turned into rage against the "colored" regiments. Col. William Stewart remembered the excitement he felt as the Yankees advanced. "I never felt more like fighting in my life," he wrote. "Our comrades had been slaughtered in a most inhuman and brutal manner, and slaves were trampling over their mangled and bleeding corpses."⁷⁸ That Stewart called his attackers "slaves" was inaccurate—all slaves were freed upon enlistment in a "colored" regiment—but fitting, since Confederates considered black troops slaves in rebellion against their masters. It did not matter that the Confederate government did not take this line officially. Seeing their white comrades falling before black troops, Confederates were eager for vengeance. In their eyes, they were witnessing a disturbing and violent betrayal of the Southern racial order.

The Battle of the Crater resulted in the greatest massacre of black troops during the Civil War.⁷⁹ Accounts are grisly. Hand-to-hand encounters were rare in the Civil War, but not at the Crater. Black troops were so packed together at the bottom of the pit that Rebels could easily club or bayonet many of them.[80] The closeness and brutality of combat proved similar to other engagements between white and black troops. But at the Crater blacks were shown even less mercy. As was the case with the veterans of Fort Pillow and elsewhere, the Confederates were unapologetic. A Georgia soldier serving in Mahone's division wrote of the "indiscriminate butchery" that occurred. In actuality, the butchery was quite discriminate, as "hardly a negro remained to tell the story." He knew what happened was awful, but he said it was "perfectly right." Confederates should not have captured a single black soldier, he concluded.[81]

The Rebel troops—stirred by the "excitement of battle," as one eyewitness said—engaged the enemy with unusual ferocity.[82] Confederate officers either could not or would not stop the butchery. Andrew Barksdale wrote after the Battle of the Crater that William Mahone, whose division halted the Union attack, had said, "Men for God's sake observe humanity, and don't be so destructive to life."[83] But according to F. R. Callaway's memoirs, Mahone, who became a hero for saving the Confederate position at Petersburg, gave his men contradictory orders. Callaway recalled Mahone riding along the lines asking his soldiers to cease firing, only to utter in a low voice, "Boys, kill everyone of those niggers."[84] Whether or not General Mahone whispered such a command to his troops, before he led his vicious counterattack, he let his men know they were fighting black troops who were giving no quarter.[85]

One historian of the Crater has recently written, "Although General Mahone had ordered the men to show no quarter to their enemies, he tried to check the killing of prisoners being marched to the rear."[86] But as was the case with Nathan Bedford Forrest, Mahone did not have to give orders for his men to show "no quarter." The Confederates were willing to do it on their own, and their officers were at best indifferent to the butchery. On the whole, soldiers did not wish to take captives. "It gows mighty against our boys to take Negro prisoners," said Corporal Barksdale. "They would never do it," he said, "if General Lee had not ordered it to be done."[87] It was Mahone, however, not Lee, who was closest to the fighting, and neither Mahone nor Lee ever censured Rebel troops for their conduct at the Crater.

Confederates' postwar recollections of the Crater fighting did not ignore the horrors there, but years after the event, former Rebels were more likely to disassociate themselves from the massacre, saying they were not among the butchers. In one of his accounts, Mahone not only did not discuss the massacre, he failed to even mention that blacks were there.[88] Other Confederates were clearer in saying that they were not guilty of atrocities. "Oh boys, let the poor devils alone," Alfred Lewis Scott remembered saying to his comrades.[89] In contrast to the barbarity he saw around him, the South Carolina artillerist John Cheves Haskell portrayed himself as humane. According to his memoirs, his role at the battle was one of a moderator, a voice of reason against the unjustified bloodshed. He saved one black prisoner from being taken behind the lines and shot, and he reunited another with his old master.[90] Col. William Stewart apparently was decent enough to give a drink to a black soldier who had been torn apart by artillery. With his legs blown off, the wounded soldier had made a crude tent of three muskets and a cloth to shield himself from the sun. However, heat, shock, and his wounds took their toll. The taste of Stewart's water, as well intentioned as it was, finished him.[91]

Whether or not they were guilty of massacring black soldiers, Confederates did not see their behavior at the Crater—as violent and desperate as it might have been—as dishonorable. They could not say as much for the white Federals, who went to extreme lengths to avoid the fate of their fellow black troops. John Haskell remembered catching an officer who had removed his insignia and had tried to pass himself off as a private so that he would not be killed for leading the black soldiers into battle.[92] Another Confederate remembered how the Federals had killed their own black troops. After the war, he spoke with a man who confessed to such murders. While hiding in a bombproof shelter, he and a handful of other whites had supposedly murdered fourteen African Americans.[93] The account seems shocking, even dubious, considering that it is a Confederate who is recounting a Northern veterans' memory of an event from long ago. Even so, more than one Confederate remembered that Federal officers had killed black troops. John Haskell wrote of a Union man who had "dashed out the brains of a colored soldier." Afterward, he saw a disgusted Confederate put the man to death. At the Crater, white Southerners justified the killing of black soldiers after they had captured them. Such actions were done in the heat of battle, when their passions were high. Haskell, however, found it despicable that a Federal soldier, and an officer at that, could kill one of his own men in order to save himself.[94]

One can only estimate how many black troops were massacred at the Crater. The historian Bryce Suderow has put the number at more than 200, with the actual figure perhaps closer to 400. Whatever the number, the butchery was extensive. "The negroes were wiped clean out," said one Confederate, and his Southern comrades filled a long ditch with black and white bodies piled three deep. It was a grim, ignominious fate for the Federal forces.[95]

The oft-quoted Col. William Pegram wrote that the slaughter was "perfectly right as a matter of policy." Atrocities at the Crater, however, were not part of any military policy. Confederates' actions were more intuitive than anything else. As one soldier wrote from Virginia in June 1863, "If [blacks] fight with spirit, and ever meet our Reg't, the carnage will be frightful. I believe our men would fight a Brigade of them without flinching." Confederates at the Crater seem to have fulfilled this dark prophecy.[96]

The Rebels were determined that black troops should fare worse than white Union soldiers, and men in the Army of Northern Virginia were no less determined, and no less violent, than their western counterparts. Robert E. Lee was a very different man from Nathan Bedford Forrest, but the men in his ranks were equal to those under Forrest's command in their hatred of black soldiers. Lee was in many respects a kind, Christian man, but his job was to kill, wound, or capture as many Federals as possible. The West was a frontier compared to the eastern states, but that did not make the war in Virginia more humane. On the whole, battles there were larger, and casualties higher. Unfortunately for African Americans, the massacres were worse. Confederates did not have to pursue an official no-quarter policy in order to ensure that black soldiers suffered harsh treatment.

The reaction of the Confederate troops after the Battle of the Crater proved to be similar to that of Forrest after the slaughter at Fort Pillow: they were convinced that "Negro" soldiers could not cope with white Southerners. One soldier wrote home to say the black units "fought desperately but our brave boys was never born to be whipped by negroes."[97] Col. Daniel R. Hundley of the Thirty-First Alabama did not take part in the Crater butchery, but he had feelings of both pity and contempt, writing of the "recent cowardice of the poor blacks."[98] The Mississippi private Daniel Holt attributed the Federal soldiers' poor showing to black men's servile nature. They had been slaves since they had inhabited Africa, he said, and in something of a non sequitur, he claimed that no men in "religious or economic slavery" could develop the "highest qualities."[99] He mentioned Christ's liberating power as a remedy, but he perhaps forgot that most black Southerners were Christians. No matter. In his view, they would always be slaves, the descendants of pagan savages from Africa.

Had black troops been good fighters, Confederates reasoned, they would have avoided disaster at the Crater. Some reported finding blacks drunk. "Colored" troops apparently were so inept and cowardly that they could not face the Confederate guns sober. It was customary for some soldiers to have a drink before battle to steady their nerves, and black men were not the only ones to be accused of drunkenness during the war. But for Confederate troops it seemed fitting to find African Americans inebriated.[100] Nor was the Crater the only occasion where Confederates wrote of black troops hitting the bottle. In December 1864, Edmund F. Stone, stuck in the Petersburg trenches, wrote that he witnessed black troops drinking, even at their peril. The Confederates fired on "unsuspecting blacks" who apparently were more interested in their whiskey than in monitoring the enemy's movements.[101]

Other Confederates were more generous when considering why the Union attack failed at the Crater. They saw poor leadership and bad timing, not cowardice, as the cause. Black soldiers had not been the first choice to lead the charge, one Confederate asserted, but last-minute replacements, and they might even have succeeded had the North not waited so long after the mine explosion.[102] Some Southerners could appreciate how the blacks conducted themselves in the field. A month after the battle, Charles W. Trueheart wrote, "The negroes who were wounded and lay there for 36 hours before they were attended to, bore their sufferings much better than the [white] Yankees."[103] Perhaps blacks were not as cowardly as Confederates troops believed. They were capable of bearing suffering well and dying a "good death."[104]

Despite acts of bravery on the part of black Federals, Confederates mostly believed that when under adversity, "colored" soldiers would revert to their slavish ways, begging for capture rather than dying with honor.[105] John Haskell said he did not take part in the massacre, but he almost killed a black soldier who came at him with a bayonet. In the language of a "rice field Gullah," he wrote, years later, his attacker threw up his hands and surrendered, asking to be spared. Haskell said he had no intention of killing him. His captive supposedly said he would gladly return to the fields where he would prove to be a "faithful worker." Haskell instead sent him to the rear to help in the hospitals. For Confederate troops, once a slave, always a slave.[106] Haskell was not the only soldier who wrote of men playing "Sambo" in order to avoid death. According to Pvt. Charles Trueheart, black troops fell on their knees, prayed for mercy, and asked for water in "a most abjectly submissive tone."[107] Rebel troops believed that black soldiers who took a "Sambo" posture were the antithesis of Confederates' avowal, in the spirit of Patrick Henry, to seize their liberty or die trying.

Black troops understandably played "Sambo" in order to avoid retribution, but their behavior after the battle did not reflect upon their viciousness during it. One North Carolina soldier said that the "Negros fought Well." Private Trueheart, who said that the troops had reverted to "Sambos," believed they had also fought "with an obstinacy that was really surprising; and held their ground till our fellows came to close quarters and knocked them in the head with muskets, or bayoneted them." Another soldier tried to explain why the black troops screamed "no quarter" one minute and played "Sambo" the next. "I'll wager that if the enemy had got the upper hand of us," he said, "they would have sung an entirely different song."[108]

Whether or not they thought black men fought well, Confederate soldiers did not treat them as they did white Federals. They believed that black men were slaves, and that those who took up arms against the South deserved no mercy. In late 1864, Confederate forces were still fighting to maintain the racial status quo. They believed they could deal to all blacks and their white officers the sort of violence they had inflicted at the Crater. For them, the war was not yet lost and neither was slavery. They still had hopes of assuring that the "bottom rail" remained on the bottom. At the Crater, Confederates took pride that they had defeated the duplicitous, "mongrel" Yankee forces. The Federals could explode a mine in order to win Petersburg, but Confederates would not allow their passage into the city so easily, and in their view—as with field hands pleading with "massah" to avoid a whipping—blacks begged for mercy when Confederates had the upper hand.

After the Battle of the Crater, one Confederate noted that there was "scarcely a day but some of them come over & ask to be sent back to their masters." The Confederates believed African Americans wanted nothing more to do with what they considered a "white folks fight."[109] In fact, the Crater did not undermine black troops' commitment to the Union. It did, however, contribute to the gloom among white Northerners. By August 1864, the North's prospects for victory looked bleak. Grant had not taken Richmond, nor had Sherman taken Atlanta. That month, President Lincoln confided to his administration that he did not think he would win reelection.

Outside Petersburg, Lee's men continued to treat black prisoners as slaves. Some captives were made to bury the dead.[110] For Northerners, such actions were just another violation of the unofficial rules of warfare. In the fall of 1864, Lee and Grant corresponded about Confederates using black laborers on fortifications. Lee made no apologies, saying he would work his captives like slaves, or if possible return them to their masters.

He did not want prisoners killed for inciting insurrection, but he did not believe them equal to white soldiers either. Lee said he would only pull black Federals from his fortifications provided if it could be shown that they were not slaves.[111]

Roughly 200,000 black men would serve in the Union military, but in late 1864 and into 1865, they were still a new feature of war for most Confederates. Southern troops were not impressed by what they saw. At the December 1864 battle of Nashville, John Smith Kendall of the Army of Tennessee admired the bravery of a black flag-bearer, but his valor was conspicuous because those around him fled. After the man was hit, Kendall felt a "sudden compassion." With a sympathy rare among those who fought black troops, he concluded, "He was a big, fine-looking chap. It seemed a pity."[112] That same month, the Virginia infantryman James Thomas Perry saw black soldiers in action. His reaction was typical among Southern troops. "Got my first view of 'cuffee,'" he wrote. They "seemed the blackest of all black animals I ever beheld. They were pretty impudent, flaunting their newspapers in our faces for exchange! Strict orders were issued against firing else several of them would have gone to keep John Brown company in the 'Happy Land of Canaan.'" In contrast to these harsh statements, Perry became wistful when he heard them singing. It reminded him of the "good old 'husking' days in the happy past."[113] Thus was the racial mindset of the Confederate soldier, mixing anger with paternalistic longing and sentimentality for the old days when slaves worked in the fields and "knew their place." Perhaps it was the fact that it was Christmas Eve that made Perry so moody, angry at being in the army and that black soldiers were fighting against him. He was no doubt eager to be home, where he could enjoy some semblance of antebellum life. In the eyes of Southern whites, black people were a tolerable, even desirable, presence as long as Confederates could maintain the "proper" relation between the races.

The massacres of black troops by Confederates soldiers were a predictable outcome of battle between proslavery Rebel troops and their African American enemy. Also at fault was the Davis administration's ambivalent stance toward the capture of African American soldiers. Rebels did not put to death all the black soldiers and white officers they captured, but Confederate armies treated African American units with much greater severity than they treated white ones. Time and again, the war tested the limits of Southern white paternalism, and events showed that Confederates treated black soldiers as slaves and property, not wayward "children." A battle in which "no quarter" was given was one of the most horrific aspects of the Confederacy's efforts to become a slaveholding republic. But within Confederate lines, African Americans were becoming a more valuable commodity than ever, and in time, some would begin to think that they were ready to join the fight for secession.

· 7 ·

FREE TO FIGHT
THE CONFEDERATE ARMY AND THE USE OF SLAVES AS SOLDIERS

The presence of 200,000 African Americans in the United States army and navy, combined with the vast number of slaves who escaped their masters, underscored black people's desire to help the Union crush the Confederacy. It also showed how the United States was adept at forging an alliance, albeit troubled at times, between black soldiers and their mostly white officers.[1] However, as the war turned against the Confederacy in 1863, some white Southerners began thinking it wise to enlist their black population of military age. In 1864 and 1865, the Southern armies engaged in an intense debate about how Confederates could further employ slaves as a tool of the military. The Confederate government finally authorized the use of black troops, but only reluctantly. In March 1865, it passed a weak black enlistment bill, which proved far too late to help the Rebel armies, especially in the West. Nor did the bill fundamentally alter the master-slave relationship in the South, as it did not promise freedom to African Americans who served. Instead, it gave masters the power to decide whether or not their slaves could join the army. Slaves only were free to fight.

The Confederacy's black enlistment bill was a creature of the white South's reluctance to alter the institution of slavery fundamentally. Even supporters of black enlistment—who did not see using black troops as incompatible with slavery—argued from a white-supremacist perspective that viewed Southern blacks as racial inferiors. The debate over enlistment in the South was not a moral one concerning a slave's right to be free. Confederates were not arguing from the abolitionist perspective. Instead, they supported or denounced the idea of black Confederate soldiers using the complex, often contradictory, tenets of the proslavery argument. To some proslavery Southerners, enlisting blacks might have seemed radical, but in fact it mostly was a token effort by a slaveholding nation that had run out of options. The Confederacy only debated freeing its slaves when it became obvious that the North would soon free them anyway. Yet, even when they voted to arm African Americans, Confederates still believed they could give slaves guns without having to liberate most of them.

The historian Bruce Levine has argued in his work on the black enlistment debate that the Army of Northern Virginia "played a pivotal political role in reorienting popular opinion" in support of the bill. However, historians have differed over to what extent the Confederacy's arming of slaves was a revolutionary measure. Some argue that the enlistment debate revealed that white Southerners were prepared to make a radical break concerning slavery. The historian Emory Thomas has written, "The fact was that the Confederacy was prepared to let slavery perish and to fight on! For what? The new nation and its war had achieved a dynamic of their own—a dynamic which overshadowed principles and poses." Other scholars have been more critical of the Confederacy's support for enlisting blacks. In his work on the Army of Northern Virginia, Joseph Glatthaar has noted, "For the most part, soldiers in Lee's army endorsed the concept [of black enlistment]." Chandra Manning, however, challenges the idea that most troops—let alone a majority in Lee's army—supported black enlistment.[2]

In this chapter, and to a greater degree than Levine or Manning, I examine Confederate soldiers' views of black enlistment to show how Rebels who supported the controversial measure were not abolitionists, but fatalists: men willing to take limited measures to arm the slaves because they saw no other way to overcome the Confederacy's manpower shortages and its difficulties in maintaining racial control. In reality, the enlistment debate was not about freeing Southern blacks from bondage, but another permutation of proslavery thinking. Throughout their history, white Southerners had never believed that they could keep all Southern blacks enslaved. As the war turned against the South, they envisioned black enlistment as a way of freeing a portion of their slaves while keeping most in bondage.

Some historians have noted how support for black enlistment did not necessarily undermine Confederates' proslavery notions. Paul Escott has written, "It is not surprising that some of the strongest support for arming the slaves came from [diehard] soldiers, who knew at first hand how desperately the army needed more troops." Yet Escott also concludes that the debate on arming blacks "revealed the limits of white Southerners' creative imaginations, crippled by racism and the desire to retain the benefits and privileges of slaveholding."[3] Given the conflicted nature of the Confederate soldiers' racial mindset by 1865—wanting to maintain slavery while conceding the military necessity of arming slaves—the Rebel army's debate concerning black enlistment provides an ironic end to a war effort riddled with contradictions.

By 1865, some Confederates were prepared to take advantage of unused resources among the black population. The Confederacy could have conscripted tens of thousands of free blacks, but it did not. The army even turned away some who volunteered. In September 1861, Jonathan Devereux, a Louisiana militia officer, refused help from the "colored" guards. He thanked them for their willingness to help and was "assured that they will be equally ready upon a more important occasion."[4] In March 1862, Louisiana governor Thomas Overton Moore called upon the free black population of the state, especially in New Orleans, to defend their homes, property, and "southern rights" from the Federals.[5] The Confederacy briefly enlisted some free blacks to fight, but after the Union seized New Orleans, the Native Guards, a unit consisting of black troops, switched their allegiance. It is no wonder they did. They identified more with the politics of the Union than with a Confederacy that was fighting to keep millions of black people enslaved.[6]

For most of the war, Confederate soldiers could not imagine black men fighting alongside them. One Rebel remembered that, early in the conflict, a *New York Herald* article had mistakenly written of "black" troops attacking Union men. Confederates reading the story had a good laugh. Their unwashed appearance, the result of powder and grime on their faces, apparently made the reporter think that the men were "Negroes."[7] Confederate humor aside, for white Southerners, the presence of black soldiers would have signified an unacceptable move toward racial equality. As the Virginia cavalryman George Hundley recalled in his account of the battle of Manassas, one slave wanted to leave his job as a cook, grab a musket, and fight the Yankees. "Much to my regret," Hundley remembered, an officer stopped the man. To let him fight, the officer explained, would have made the slave equal to the white man. Hundley thought it ironic: blacks did not fight for the South but they later made laws for it during Reconstruction.[8] What Hundley did not understand was that African Americans were fighting for a different South than he was. Even so, his words suggest that the Confederacy lost an opportunity to let blacks enlist.

Advocates of black enlistment had few supporters until the Southern reverses of late 1864, but that does not mean all Confederate soldiers were inflexible on the idea of recruiting slaves. Men such as Alabama Col. William C. Oates and Virginia Gen. Richard Ewell toyed with the idea of enlisting slaves as early as 1862. Neither Oates nor Ewell, however, went public with their ideas.[9] In August 1863, Robert Kean, a soldier turned War Department employee, probably reflected most Confederates' views at the time when he said that "the enlistment of our slaves is a barbarity which no people . . . could tolerate on the principle, the use of savages, which . . . the Declaration of Independence recorded as infamous."[10]

The issue, however, would not go away. "This is one of the weightiest questions that has been brought forth since the beginning of this revolution," said soldier Thomas J. Key in December 1863, concerning black enlistment in the Confederacy. "It will make or ruin the South."[11] By the end of 1863, most Rebel soldiers did not want black Confederate troops helping them, but some men were convinced that the South would face defeat if it did not adopt drastic measures. Lt. Caleb Hobson of the Fifty-First North Carolina wrote in December 1863 that he hoped Congress would put the South's "fine negroes" into the army. He was unenthusiastic about such a plan, but he believed the Confederacy had no choice given its numerical disadvantage. Enlisting black men, he reasoned, was the only way the South could maintain parity in the prisoner exchange.[12] His ideas reflected the state of the war effort, not an ideological commitment to emancipation and black equality. But his views foreshadowed Confederates' willingness to save slavery by using slaves in combat roles.

Patrick Cleburne, from the sun-baked Mississippi Delta town of Helena, Arkansas, was the first Confederate general to advocate the enlistment of black troops formally, and at the peril of his career. Cleburne was no abolitionist. Born in Ireland before moving to America, where he practiced law, he owned no slaves when the war broke out. Yet Cleburne, had he lived, would have married into a slaveholding family.[13] And his friend and fellow Helena native, Gen. Thomas C. Hindman, was a slaveholder and Arkansas' most outspoken Fire-Eater. In early 1864, Cleburne submitted a plan for using slaves as soldiers in the Confederate army. His superiors never seriously considered adopting the measure. A close reading of Cleburne's proposal reveals the cautious nature of its "emancipation" policies, but other generals could not accept placing slaves in the ranks in early 1864. Such reluctance would permeate the enlistment debate into late 1864 and 1865.

In January 1864, Cleburne did not have a sanguine view of the war effort. His army, the Army of Tennessee, had recently suffered a serious defeat at the battle of Chattanooga, where Cleburne earned the nickname

"Stonewall of the West" for holding off Union columns long enough to prevent a complete disaster. It was another in a long string of frustrations and defeats for the western armies. It was little wonder Cleburne saw the military situation in the West as far more critical than in Virginia, where Lee's forces by 1864 were in the same relative position as they were in 1862. Concerning the Army of Tennessee's reverses, Cleburne did not blame specific individuals, but he believed the Confederacy suffered from a lack of imagination and initiative at the higher levels. One way to take greater initiative was by addressing the "Negro question."

Cleburne believed enlisting blacks would benefit the South by greatly increasing the size of Confederate forces. Even more important, the army could better serve as a tool for racial control. Slaves would spy no more for the Federals, Cleburne believed, and white Southerners' fears of insurrection would end. To some extent, Cleburne hoped the presence of black soldiers would instill Confederate nationalism in the slave population. But before that could happen, enlisting "Negroes" would keep slaves under the care and discipline of white men.

Cleburne was convinced that the time had come for an extreme measure. Slavery had helped the Confederacy earlier in the conflict, but now he believed it a liability. By 1864, he noted, the North had 100,000 black men in its armies, and Europe had failed to ally with the Confederacy because of antislavery propaganda. The South, then, must strike at slavery. Cleburne argued that freeing the slaves might help the cause, but to free some and give them muskets would prove better. His plan might even lead to European recognition. At the very least, black men could perform tasks that whites were doing in the army, such as cooking, nursing, and driving wagons.[14]

True to the Revolutionary tradition, Cleburne believed Confederates must take drastic measures in order to avoid "subjugation." In addition to putting blacks into the army, he believed the Confederacy should revise its substitution and exemption laws. As did Jefferson Davis, Cleburne put independence before maintaining slavery. Employing blacks as soldiers was a sacrifice Confederates must make to avoid becoming slaves themselves. If the North were to win—and it seemed likely, given the way the war was going—it would turn the South into a school for Yankee ways. Slaves, Cleburne wrote, were already a "secret police" for Northern forces.[15] And the Confederacy wasted resources by using white men to guard slaveholding areas. Servants and laborers who needed heavy supervision were of little value to Confederates, but they were invaluable to the Yankees. Better to free some slaves, Cleburne thought, than let them fall into enemy hands. He wanted to remove all the "vulnerability," "embarrassment," and "weakness" that resulted from slavery.[16]

Cleburne's proposal, as drastic as it may have seemed to other Confederates, was a military, not a moral measure. It did not express revulsion at the peculiar institution. Cleburne wanted to free the slaves in order to fill the Confederate ranks, not because he thought human bondage was wrong. To him, it simply made good military sense. The enlistment of blacks, he said, would "enable us to take the offensive, move forward, and forage on the enemy."[17] In 1864, a year that saw the worst fighting of the war, Cleburne wanted blacks to help the Confederates bring the battle to the North. He did not want emancipation: he wanted to reform slavery, not end it. He suggested that the Confederacy first make some changes in the institution, including legalizing slave marriages and eradicating the slave trade. Cleburne, who paid lip service to decrying Northern fanaticism—as exemplified by John Brown and Henry Ward Beecher—was not an abolitionist.[18] He did not want the Confederacy to free its slaves overnight. He instead wanted a Southern brand of abolition: liberate the slaves without them being truly free.

Cleburne's views had Jeffersonian overtones. He claimed that white Southerners, who understood blacks, were best at controlling them, and he wanted freedom upon "reasonable terms, and within such reasonable time as will prepare both races for the change." At the earliest, emancipation would not come until after the war. "Satisfy the negro that if he faithfully adheres to our standard during the war he shall receive his freedom and that of his race," he wrote. Most slaves would remain on the farm and plantation, while others would do the fighting. "Leave some of the skill at home and take some of the muscle to fight with," he asserted. Could slaves fight? Cleburne had to reach back to ancient times for an example, but he looked to those who had fought under the Spartans as proof that they could.[19]

Whether large numbers of black Southerners would have enthusiastically fought for the Confederacy is debatable. Nevertheless, despite the obvious devotion many of them showed for the Union, not all black Southerners responded to the war in the same way. The historian William Freehling thinks Southern blacks would have fought well, but he also thinks black disloyalty contributed much to the South's defeat. Even so, he argues, blacks would have embraced military service had white Southerners given them the chance.[20] While in the trenches at Kennesaw Mountain in 1864, the Alabama soldier Wallace Comer reported that his servant, Burrell, wanted to borrow a gun, saying "he wanted to kill one yankee before the war ended."[21] Some blacks did shoot at Union troops during the war—one historian has examined the presence of African American sharpshooters on the Confederate side.[22] But even if some slaves hated the Yankees, or used guns against them, that did not make them soldiers. Only governments can make men soldiers. In wartime, the vast majority of black Southerners remained enslaved, and those who served in the army did so as body servants and menial laborers. To say that African Americans were unenthusiastic about fighting for the South is not to negate their value as soldiers, but to acknowledge their strong support for a Union fighting to free them and their loved ones.

Whether or not black men would have fought well for the Confederacy, Patrick Cleburne believed that abolition would come about if the South lost the war. Therefore, white Southerners had to maintain control over their institutions, which meant striking at their strongest and weakest: slavery. In Cleburne's eyes, slavery was strong in what it had done for the South for generations, but weak in what it was doing now. Politicians might have been worried about the legality of his plan, but Cleburne said emancipation was constitutional, for slaves were allowed to act in the service of their state. He was convinced the slaves could make good soldiers, and he was willing to lead them himself.

Cleburne's scheme did not advocate immediate emancipation, but it proved faster than most white Southerners wanted to go on the slavery issue. His superiors in the Army of Tennessee, some planters, were divided over whether to implement his plan. Generals William J. Hardee and Joseph E. Johnston gave slight approval to it. Others were appalled at the idea of arming slaves, and their vehement opposition won out. For them, Cleburne's ideas were antithetical to the Confederate cause. On 14 January 1864, Gen. Patton Anderson—a Tennessean and veteran of the battles of Shiloh, Murfreesboro, and Chickamauga—wrote to Bishop Polk saying he believed Cleburne's plan "monstrous." If the Confederacy enacted the measure, he thought every man would desert the army. The military, then, must reject Cleburne's ideas for the sake of morale. Before Anderson left for Florida to be with his family, he urged Polk to quash the controversial proposal. He said Polk was a man of "clear head, ripe judgment, and pure patriotism," suggesting Cleburne and his supporters lacked such qualities.[23]

Commanders in the Army of Tennessee were determined to kill Cleburne's measure before common soldiers or civilians heard of the plan. Yet the Georgia general William T. Walker, a favorite of Johnston's who would die at the battle of Atlanta, was so incensed that he wanted the president to know about it. Walker believed enlisting blacks "would ruin the efficacy of our Army and involve our cause in ruin and disgrace."[24] No doubt he assumed that Davis, who was later in the forefront of supporting black enlistment, would express equal revulsion at the proposal.

Cleburne's superiors, including Joseph E. Johnston and Jefferson Davis, had no intention of reprimanding him, but once his ideas became known, the general became very nervous about his future. He hoped that if the army court-martialed him, he could enlist in his old regiment, the Fifteenth Arkansas. The Davis administration would not support enlisting slaves in early 1864, but it did not censure Cleburne. Even so, his plan was controversial enough to sink his chances for promotion. Sadly for Cleburne, he would die at the November 1864 battle of Franklin, a few months before the Confederacy passed legislation allowing African Americans to serve in the Rebel army as soldiers.

By late January 1864, Secretary of War James Seddon decided that men in the Army of Tennessee were not to speak of Cleburne's proposal again. It proved too divisive. Secretary Seddon also made it clear to Joseph E. Johnston that he spoke for Jefferson Davis.[25] Johnston in turn wrote to eight of his generals, including William Hardee and Cleburne, to say that enlisting blacks was impossible. He then reassured the secretary of war that the subject was dead. Cleburne's proposal, he said, had made no "impression" in the army.[26]

Influential Confederates were shocked at the idea that they could not win the war without the help of black troops. The Confederacy rejected Cleburne's plan, but the idea would not go away. In January 1864, Col. A. S. Colyar, a Tennessee member of the Confederate Congress, rejected Cleburne's dour view of the war effort and the need to arm slaves, a proposition he said would overwhelm Cleburne in "ruin."[27] Colyar nevertheless believed that the general's ideas had validity. Colyar did not think freed slaves wanted to fight for the South, but he saw that the Confederacy was headed toward a "crisis" that gave rise to surprising new strategies. Freeing some slaves might make blacks easier to control and give them an incentive to remain as laborers in the South.[28]

At the time he issued it, Cleburne's proposal had more symbolic than military importance. After Cleburne's death and Lee's surrender, some veterans re-fighting the war in print asserted that they had always been hopeful about blacks' fighting abilities. William J. Hardee, who had supported the plan in 1864, believed that the Confederacy had recruited blacks only when "it was too late."[29] In his memoirs, John Bell Hood—who ordered the charge at Franklin, Tennessee, that killed Cleburne—said the Arkansas general had the "boldness and the wisdom" to propose arming the slaves. Had the Confederacy adopted his plan, Hood believed, it would have gained its independence. In September 1864, however, Hood had vowed to William T. Sherman that it was better to "die a thousand deaths than submit to live under you or your Government and your negro allies." In his memoirs, Hood apparently took a different view toward the usefulness of black Southerners.[30]

In their postwar writings, few Confederate veterans thought of Cleburne when they considered where the war had gone wrong. They focused instead on the Battle of Gettysburg and various command decisions. Hood and others at least dwelled on what slaves might have done to stave off Confederate defeat. In 1912, Berkeley Minor, formerly a private in the Stonewall Brigade, argued along the lines of Hood: had Robert E. Lee urged the enlistment of blacks in 1863, the Confederacy would have triumphed. Minor called Lee a "Moses" who could have led Southerners out of the "wilderness." The description was ironic, considering Moses fought to liberate his people from bondage, rather than fight, as Lee did, to keep others enslaved. General Lee eventually supported black emancipation, but Minor thought it too late. Why did the Confederacy wait too long? "We were over-confident," he noted, thinking "we could win against any odds."[31]

It was easy after 1865 to imagine how the South's fortunes could have gone differently. Some believed Stonewall Jackson would have whipped the Yankees at Gettysburg, and others thought Cleburne's proposal would have swelled muster rolls, enabling black and white Confederates to march side by side to victory. Irving Buck, however, who served in the Army of the Tennessee, was not a revisionist. He knew why Southerners hesitated to enlist slaves. "The slave holders were very sensitive," he wrote in 1903, and "totally unprepared to consider such a radical measure."[32] During the war, some Confederates had called on fellow Southerners to rethink the usefulness of slavery. In March 1864, William McPheeters, a surgeon serving in the far western Confederacy, believed in the need for gradual emancipation. "We are fighting not for slavery, but for the right of self government," he concluded.[33] But in early 1864, white Southerners could not take drastic steps toward emancipation, and their hesitancy to move against the institution in any fundamental way had remained consistent since America's founding.

Wartime was the last chance Southerners had to save slavery, and even early in 1865 they resisted reform, which they believed would hasten the miseries of emancipation. Resistance to change was not only ideologically grounded, it also had an element of defiance—or perhaps more accurately, spitefulness. For many Confederate soldiers, to acquiesce to emancipation was to concede defeat. Even into 1865, many refused to accept an impending Federal victory.[34] In essence, they thought freeing the slaves would show that the North had been right about Southern "institutions" all along. In December 1863, one soldier best summarized such views. For him, Confederates wanted independence and were willing to "sacrifice everything" to obtain it. Everything, that is, except slavery, an institution Confederates saw as a "wise one and sanctioned by God."[35]

Because many white Southerners believed that blacks were untrustworthy, Cleburne's desire to give slaves rifles and training proved controversial. Others saw in his measure an implicit insult to white manhood. For Confederates, the use of slaves as soldiers meant white men could not win the war themselves. Even late into the struggle, they wanted the war to remain a white man's fight. "Many of us felt that if we could not win without the negroes, we could not win with them," the Virginia cavalryman Mason Ellzey remembered. Nor did he see how the Confederacy could have overcome the logistical problems inherent in arming and feeding thousands of black troops while whites were starving. "Impressed by these views the vote of the Army was against it," Ellzey concluded.[36]

Cleburne believed that the South could have put 300,000 black men under arms, but even the Union did not enlist that many African Americans during the war. That the Confederacy could have enrolled such a number, black or white, would have been a considerable achievement in 1864 or 1865. Furthermore, service in the army would have stripped slaves from other work projects, which were often as important as the fighting. A civilian from Richmond, Dr. Alexander T. B. Merritt sarcastically wrote of Davis's enlistment plan in January 1865. For one thing, he thought black troops would turn against their masters. Nor did he have high hopes about the Confederacy's logistical capabilities. "Two hundred thousand laborers taken from our fields," he lamented, "where they are absolutely needed, & placed in the army which we now cannot feed 200,000 fewer workers & 200,000 more eaters."[37] Estimates of the number of blacks the Confederacy could have enlisted are pure guesswork. Cleburne and others would have been pleased to see a fraction of 300,000 enrolled, and whether implementing Cleburne's measure would have changed the war in any significant way is impossible to assess. As with the impressment controversy, the question of how to use slaves in the army always conflicted with Confederate manpower shortages. Proslavery and states' rights ideology aside, masters would have proven resistant to the army taking their valuable human property. Enrolling hundreds of thousands of slaves would have put even greater stress on the finances of an anxious and exhausted master class.

In January 1864, most Confederates did not think the military situation as dire as Cleburne described it. But in the course of the year, as military challenges mounted, they moved closer to arming blacks. In February, the Congress authorized the use of free and enslaved black workers as teamsters and cooks in the army. The military had been using black laborers since the war's beginning, but now the Confederacy could draft up to 20,000 more black men to perform various duties. In February 1864, the South had stopped short of an outright draft of black men, but now slaves had a more explicit role in the war effort. That October, after months of slaughter in Virginia coupled with losses to disease and desertion, Thomas J. Goree, a member of Longstreet's staff, worried about the lack of new soldiers. And, by then, many of Lee's men had seen black Union troops in combat. Goree wanted slaves to fill as many positions as possible, and if necessary, they should be put in uniform—to "fight negro with negro," as he put it. He believed black people had more reason to fight for the South than for the North, and it was better for the Confederacy to emancipate its slaves than endure subjugation at the hands of the Federals.[38] By November, the South had suffered the loss of Atlanta and the Shenandoah Valley. Amid its triumphs, the North reelected Abraham Lincoln, who Confederates knew would vigorously prosecute the war as long as he remained in office.

With Lincoln's reelection in November 1864, the Confederacy faced prospects of defeat more real than ever. To some, slavery seemed no longer viable, though that did not make it unimportant or undesirable. In fact, the debate regarding black enlistment underscored how crucial slavery still was to Confederates. On 7 November 1864, Jefferson Davis gave a message to Congress suggesting that the South needed to make changes concerning slavery. Davis noted that the February Conscription Act had not led to the creation of a black labor corps. In response, he believed the government should put 40,000, rather than 20,000, blacks into the army, and he considered whether Confederates should reward their good service with emancipation.[39]

Davis did not discuss putting blacks into uniform, and thus he presented no challenge to the racial or military status quo. He believed the Confederacy should enlist blacks only when the white population was overwhelmed. Yet, arguably, that had already happened. Regarding slavery, a metaphor familiar to Southerners again proved true: citizens could not tear down the old meetinghouse until a new one was built on the same spot. They obviously could not build the new one as long as the old one stood. In other words, the Confederacy would emancipate its slaves only when the North had already done so. Had the South wanted to use black troops, it should have recruited them at least as early as the United States had. But in 1862 and 1863, when black troops were entering the Union army, the Confederacy was too busy denouncing the Emancipation Proclamation, or dismissing its impact, to consider arming the slaves.

Davis's November message reflected the feelings of Rebels still resistant to Confederate emancipation. Having suffered a painful wound during a recent visit to Camp Lee, J. A. Merritt wrote from Richmond to his uncle about Davis's proposal. "I am sorry to see that the sentiment for putting negroes in the army is gaining strength." He was afraid that the idea would "gain ground until congress may think it a military necisty." Robert Kean, likewise, did not support freeing any slaves. He was skeptical of those who urged emancipation, saying "in our Congress the suggestion of the employment of negroes as soldiers finds little favor except with that portion who represent imaginary constituencies." It was easy, he thought, for weak politicians to institute powerful measures.[40]

Even as General Sherman marched virtually unopposed through Georgia and Lee's heavily outnumbered men suffered at Petersburg, Confederates were reluctant to enlist black troops. For every white Southerner who supported the idea, there seemed to be one who did not. And those that did support the idea favored the use of blacks in non-combat roles only. "Jeff Davis recommends the calling out of Forty Thousand able-bodied negroes for teamsters," said Marion Fitzpatrick, serving in the Army of Northern Virginia, in mid-November. It was a measure, he added, that he "heartily support[ed]." Another soldier, however, was less enthusiastic. Concerning Davis's speech, he found reason for "dissatisfaction" in the idea of blacks possibly becoming soldiers, which he hoped "may never occur."[41]

Others could see the end of slavery coming, but they were fatalists, not abolitionists. "There will be many changes in the country in its people and its institutions," Capt. E. John Ellis predicted in December. "Slavery I think will be abolished," he believed, "and I for one won't care a particle." Yet, the previous year he had evinced strong opposition to emancipation. The Union, he wrote then, had "placed arms in the hands of our slaves.... We owe them only hatred!"[42] What had caused such a change in Ellis? By December 1864, he must have seen the difficulty the South would face in its upcoming campaigns. He thought it would be better for the Confederates to determine slavery's future than to have the Federals do it for them. Southerners hated abolitionists, but perhaps their own brand of emancipation might prove tolerable.

As the end of the war loomed, it became easier for Confederates to accept any measure to stave off defeat. One soldier spoke of his comrades' desire that the army enlist between 200,000 and 500,000 blacks. "I can but question the expediency of such a move," he said in December 1864. "Of the propriety," he added, "I have no doubt." Supporters of the enlistment of blacks, he noted, included Robert E. Lee and the Richmond papers.[43] The staff officer Richard Washington Corbin, who had lived most of his life in Paris, was also supportive, albeit cautiously. Confederate defeats, not moral reconsideration, he noted, had necessitated the arming of the slaves. "I still say and think that the negro's happiest condition is slavery," he asserted, but Corbin also thought slaves would fight for their homes. Using them skillfully, he believed, would turn the war against the North, which would liberate the slaves if the Confederacy did not. When freed, he said, the black man's "thriftlessness and indolence" would overshadow "his better qualities, and will destroy his usefulness." When given muskets, however, he thought slaves would make good troops. He was no abolitionist, but Corbin was willing to sacrifice slavery in order to save the Confederacy.[44]

Confederate soldiers who supported black enlistment usually qualified their statements. One South Carolina infantry officer, writing from Tupelo, Mississippi, on 17 January, was not enthusiastic about giving arms to slaves. He was "totally opposed to it, except as a last resort." He thought it only slightly better than subjugation, if at all. He worried about the measure causing demoralization, and wanted authorities to handle the issue with "great discretion." He also wanted the army to assure that distinctions were kept between white and black troops, with "high privileges" given to whites. Even so, he thought the Confederacy could turn blacks into good troops. And he hoped adopting drastic measures would make the Confederacy look better internationally, as a nation fighting for independence, not slavery. Mostly, however, he feared black enlistment would threaten the political equality between the races and would doom the Confederacy within two years.[45]

The enlistment of slaves, ironically, became the last great hope for the Confederacy. By late January 1865, the United States had passed the Thirteenth Amendment, but white Southerners carried on as if they had control over the pace of emancipation. Generals such as Beauregard, Longstreet, and James Patton Anderson opposed the enlistment of blacks, but the idea had supporters among John B. Gordon, Judah P. Benjamin, and Jefferson Davis.[46] Henry Watkins Allen, governor of Confederate-held Louisiana and a former general, also supported the measure, as did the *Richmond Enquirer, Lynchburg Virginian,* and *Mobile Register.*[47] In January 1865, the Alabama officer John W. Inzer wrote in his prison diary about some Richmond papers advocating emancipation. He agreed with them. Slavery, he believed, "must fall, and the sooner, the better for us."[48]

By January 1865, no soldier in the Confederacy had more influence than Robert E. Lee on the subject of arming the slaves. In a letter to Congressman Andrew Hunter, Lee gave his support to enlisting blacks. He believed the master-slave relationship was the best that existed between the races, but events had weakened it. Given the disparity in numbers between the Union and Confederacy, now was the time for the South to take control of emancipation. Otherwise, white Southerners would become slaves to the Yankees. Lee phrased his support for black enlistment in the language of white supremacy. "Long habits of obedience and subordination," he wrote, "coupled with the moral influence which in our country the white man possesses over the black, furnish an excellent foundation for that discipline which is the best guaranty of military efficiency." In other words, white men were used to giving orders, and blacks were used to taking them. As Confederates had sought throughout the war, but never really achieved, Lee wanted to win over the "fidelity" of black people. To do this, he believed the Confederacy should free the families of black soldiers who fought honorably. If not, men forced to fight as slaves would desert to the enemy. Lee believed the difference between gradual or immediate emancipation schemes were "immaterial." The Confederacy must do something quickly or the North would liberate the slaves anyway.[49]

In February 1865, Lee became the general-in-chief of the Confederate army, and he used his enormous influence to win support for black enlistment, a measure he thought "not only expedient, but necessary." Were the army not to use slaves, the Federal army would continue to do so. The South had exhausted its manpower pool, and Lee did not want to impose any more "suffering" upon his people. A slave, he concluded, "under proper circumstances, will make an efficient soldier," as they had "all the physical qualifications" necessary. In addition, he said, "their habits of obedience constitute a good foundation for discipline." Lee, in accordance with Jefferson Davis, wanted to liberate black men who served. Military service, he thought, proved more important than one's status as a free man or slave, and the army should get whatever men it needed to carry on the war effort. Lee believed it was better that a Southerner, whatever his color, serve his country rather than endure Yankee rule. Lee, however, was not prepared to undermine the master class. Rather than conscript all black men of military age, he thought it best to have slaves enter the army with their masters' permission. He also sought the cooperation of slaveholders, not only in giving up their slaves, but in preparing them for combat. He believed conscription would not bring in the "best class" of the black community, nor did he care to have the government control enlistment. Lee wanted to leave the matter, as much as possible, to the conscience of the people and the states.[50]

The process would take time, which Lee believed the Confederacy did not have. Thus he saw no point in waiting. "It will probably be impossible," he said to Jefferson Davis, "to get a large force of this kind in condition to be of service during the present campaign, but I think no time should be lost in trying to collect all we can."[51] It was good politics. Lee proposed enlisting blacks without immediately emancipating slaves, and he wanted the states and individual slaveholders to initiate recruitment. If all went well, the Confederacy might please everyone.

Lee's words shed light on the South's conflicted, even paradoxical, perception of black people. As the North Carolina diarist Catherine Edmondston quipped, "Gen Lee knows more of getting an army in the field than he does of Cuffee."[52] For Edmondston and many other white Southerners, African Americans were reliable workers but they could not make good soldiers. For critics of black enlistment, there was more to fighting and dying than simply taking orders. The enlistment debate revealed that white Southerners could argue for or against black recruitment by using the same tenets of the proslavery argument. The views of Confederates like Edmondston were shared by Robert Kean, who thought black enlistment unacceptable. "How emancipation is to aid in carrying on the war is to me incomprehensible," he complained. "It would strike down at a blow the whole productive power of the country, introduce a thousand domestic questions of amazing intricacy and difficulty, and tear the vitals of society."[53]

Some whites thought the army should not put blacks into uniform because they might revolt, though such fears were alleviated somewhat by the belief in the "loyal darkie." Richard Taylor wrote after the war that Confederate soldiers' "wives and little ones remained safe at home, surrounded by thousands of faithful slaves, who worked quietly in the fields." In Taylor's view, the serenity of the home front proved that masters were kind and slaves contented. Blacks would have fought for the Confederacy, he argued, because they loved their white families as well as their homeland.⁵⁴ Taylor, as did many of his comrades, did not think white Southerners waged war for slavery, and since they did not, he believed blacks would fight well alongside them. His words were written in the light of the emerging Lost Cause, which portrayed slaves as loyal and Confederate troops as unconcerned with maintaining slavery. The wartime reality was much different.

Nevertheless, there was considerable wartime support among prominent Confederates for the enlistment of blacks. In January 1865, John Tyler Jr., a congressman who accompanied Lee's staff during the Overland campaign, wrote to Sterling Price about the practicality of enlisting blacks. Robert E. Lee was a hard man to refuse, and from a constitutional point of view, Tyler believed the Confederacy should back him. The enlistment of slaves into the army was a radical measure, but the possible use of slaves as soldiers had precedent. Commanders had already impressed black workers, and thousands more served the armies in other ways as workers. As did President Davis and General Lee, Tyler could imagine a Confederacy without slavery. "The time has come," he wrote, "to decide our fate, and everything should be done and surrendered to the cause." Davis or Lee might have written those words, and in a precise summation of Southern political thinking, Tyler added, "Life, property, and honor are all lost by submission as fully as by subjugation."⁵⁵ Tyler's was a Jefferson Davis–like appeal to the idea that independence trumped the politics of slavery.

As Confederates debated, Grant and Sherman continued to wreak havoc on the Southern armies and the civilians who supported them. By 1865, the Confederacy's military and diplomatic situation had grown ever worse. In January, in secret, the Davis administration sent the Louisiana planter and politician Duncan Kenner to Europe in a last effort to win foreign recognition for the Confederacy on the condition of emancipation. The mission failed. That same month, the Federals captured Wilmington, North Carolina, a lifeline for supplying Lee's besieged army. In a further diplomatic effort in February, Confederate officials met with Lincoln and Secretary Seward at a conference at Hampton Roads, Virginia, to discuss a possible ceasefire. The North and South were unable to negotiate a peace. The war continued.⁵⁶

At Hampton Roads, the Davis government proved unwilling to emancipate the slaves or stop the war, though they were more flexible on the former than the latter. Some Confederate minds were changing along with the administration. In January, Chaplain Charles Quintard spoke with citizens about the enlistment of black troops. One man said he had all his wealth in slaves but he would emancipate them if it would bring about independence.[57] The Louisiana soldier Felix Poché was against the idea of abolishing slavery, but he felt it preferable to reunion with the "vile Yankees."[58] That same month, Kirby Smith wrote to John Slidell, who was living out the war in Paris, to say that the situation in his theater of combat had "reached a crisis." He believed 95 percent of planters in his district favored gradual emancipation predicated on Southern independence. But in the wake of the Confederacy's rejection of the peace terms offered at Hampton Roads, the South Carolina colonel Irvine Walker thought the only negotiators that mattered were "the sword and the bayonet." Battlefield victories, he believed, were the best way of assuring the survival of "our own domestic laws and institutions." As had been the case for almost four years, the survival of slavery would depend on Confederate military power.[59]

By early 1865, the Confederacy only had one major fighting force left, the Army of Northern Virginia. In Lee's army, the troops hotly debated the subject of black enlistment, yet among soldiers and commanders no consensus existed. Many troops found the idea of serving alongside blacks repellant. In January 1865, the Alabama infantryman Grant Taylor heard that his officers supported the controversial measure, but he could not bear the idea of fighting with the "stinking things," and he believed his men agreed. They would go home instead. "To think we have been fighting four years to prevent the slaves from being freed," he lamented. Now he and his men would have to "turn round and free them to enable us to carry on the war. The thing is outrageous." In his view, the Confederacy should surrender. The cause was already lost. For Taylor, it was a blow to a white man's pride to think he needed the help of "the nigger" to save his country.[60]

Men such as Taylor had a visceral reaction to the idea of black enlistment that was grounded in proslavery thinking. White Southerners feared any movement toward racial equality, even if the Confederacy did not emancipate slaves as a condition of service. To give blacks a powerful and dramatic way to serve the cause broke down a barrier that had existed between the races for centuries. Southern whites needed such barriers. Otherwise, opponents of black enlistment believed, their army would become too much like the dreaded Northern army and radical measures would turn the Southern social world upside down.

Unlike Taylor, other soldiers were more fatalistic. "I will stay," vowed the Georgia soldier J. H. Jenkins, "until the war ends or they kill me." He had no delusions as to where the war effort was going. "I think the best thing we can do is to go back into the Union," he said. "The Negroes are certain to be set free."[61] Jenkins acknowledged that further fighting by Confederates would be for an institution that was now doomed. But some Confederates had no desire to see black people enlisted, regardless of their nation's military prospects. The only shelter or property slaves had, wrote Col. Thomas Munford of the Second Virginia Cavalry in February 1865, was "obtained by indiscriminate plunder and murder."[62] Such words did not bode well for black enlistment.

Proslavery thinking made it difficult for many Confederates to trust that African Americans could effectively serve as soldiers. In February 1865, the Mississippi soldier William Pitt Chambers wrote of some "*bloody* resolutions," in Congress, among them the proposed bill for putting slaves into uniform.[63] Many troops were content to let their nation go the way of human bondage. Richard Maury—once a colonel in the Twenty-Fourth Virginia, who was wounded early in the war and living out the conflict in Richmond—ably summarized the views of the bill's opponents. In late February 1865, he said that the possibility of slaves entering the army was a "*bitter pill*" to swallow. He found emancipation in any form unacceptable. The next day, he wrote of the men in the Fifteenth Alabama, who in a letter published in the *Richmond Enquirer* supported Robert E. Lee's decision to enlist blacks. Maury understood that whatever Lee wanted he should get, but added, "Dont free the negroes."[64]

For generations, some white Southerners had advocated plans for gradual emancipation. In his *Notes on the State of Virginia,* Thomas Jefferson had argued for freeing the slaves eventually (even though his arguments were made alongside statements that emphasized black inferiority), and some Virginia women, among others, supported the colonization of the slaves back to Africa.[65] But by the nineteenth century, manumissions had become very rare and it was extremely dangerous for a Southerner to voice abolitionist sentiments. For generations, the South had lived on the edge of a slippery slope: to allow greater freedom for blacks inevitably led to abolition. In the early 1830s, the Nat Turner Revolt had prompted calls in Virginia for gradual emancipation, but Virginia and the South had instead cracked down, making manumission more difficult and passing stricter laws against slaves learning to read, write, and buy their freedom. Fears of insurrection also prompted laws to keep blacks from owning guns, assembling without a white person present, or even owning a fife and drum, which whites worried slaves would use to call others to arms and kill their white masters.[66]

Even as the Confederacy crumbled, such attitudes persisted. In white Southern minds, when discussing gradual emancipation the key word had always been "gradual." In February 1865, W. W. Heartsill, who served in a Texas regiment, suggested that emancipation would take thirty-five years.[67] In one of the many ironies of the war, had slavery ended around 1900, such a result would have been identical to Lincoln's wartime plan for ending slavery by the end of the century.[68] For Confederates, gradual emancipation schemes were ploys to buy more time for a collapsing nation. They had come far in considering enacting emancipation themselves, but they hoped, as they always had, that it would happen in the future, most likely after they had died, when their descendants could take on the burdens of abolition. Emancipation might come, but few white people wanted it to happen soon.

The enlistment debate revealed that much had changed between the issuance of the Emancipation Proclamation in 1863 and the final year of the war 1865. However, it was military events, not doubts about the morality or desirability of human bondage, that led Confederates to adopt new ways of thinking about slavery. "I think Congress will put two hundred thousand negroes in the field," wrote one soldier to his father." He conceded, "Genl Lee has called for that number and Congress will be certain to give him whatever he asks for."[69] In late February 1865, men in a South Carolina regiment gave their reluctant support to enlisting blacks even though they believed there was no "military necessity" for the measure. Their belief that no "necessity" existed suggests that they were fighting in some other war. They refused to see where the war effort was going, choosing to believe that help from slaves was not essential.[70] Their half-hearted acquiescence probably was as effusive as white Southerners could be when discussing enrolling slaves into the army.

In order to train black troops, white Southerners were prepared to fall back on the orthodoxies of the master-slave relationship as a tool for discipline. In February 1865, the Virginia soldier Daniel Abernethy wrote of "elections today on the negro question whether they will [raise] them in the army or not." Abernethy said that the black troops would be put in brigades and regiments "to them selvs," and that the army would "apointe white ofesers over them which I think well." As in the Northern army, where nearly all the commissioned officers were white, Confederates were not ready to let black men command troops. Some soldiers in Abernethy's unit said "thay wonte stay under such circumstances," and he himself said, "I am tyrde of this war." As Abernethy and others made clear, the Confederate army would continue to be a "white man's army," whether or not black soldiers served in its ranks.[71]

Confederates saw that giving black men rifles and maintaining white supremacy were not incompatible. After all, throughout the history of slavery, masters had given slaves weapons to hunt and kill predators, despite Southern laws against blacks possessing guns. Such practices were done out of convenience and did not undermine the greater edifice of slavery. White Southerners only gave blacks those freedoms they thought would be unthreatening. In wartime, the possibility of slaves getting weapons always raised the specter of race war, but Confederates hoped blacks could fight well so long as they were under their control. The Mississippian R. C. Beckett wrote of an elaborate plan—supported in a similar form by Robert E. Lee—whereby the army would enroll one black soldier for every white one, and the former would become the latter's "own individual property." White soldier-overseers would train these new troops, who were to be cared for by their "temporary masters." Black troops would perform not only military labor, but also washing and cooking. When it came time for battle, they would fight alongside whites and would, Beckett believed, "fight better than those of the enemy." Impending defeat had made some Confederates use their imaginations about how to crush the Yankees. For most Confederates, black people and slaves were still synonymous, and whites needed to treat them that way.[72]

On 15 March, the Forty-Ninth Georgia of the Army of Northern Virginia petitioned the government in favor of black enlistment. The regiment believed white Southerners should take radical measures to achieve their independence. The Georgians remembered that as younger men they had toiled alongside slaves in the field and at the same workbench. They had known black people and were convinced they understood them; thus, whites were not betraying the cause by allowing slaves to fight. The Forty-Ninth Georgia sought the maximum number of black troops that Congress had considered enlisting, and to quicken the process, they believed slaves should serve with their former masters or men who knew them.[73]

The possibility of using black troops in the Confederate army gave some of Lee's troops inflated hopes for future success. In mid-February 1865, Pvt. Joseph Shaner believed that if slaves joined the fight, "we will whail out the Yanks." He said that two-thirds of the black workers at a Richmond hospital had offered to volunteer, and he thought such men would fight "first rate."[74] That same month, the Sixth Virginia Regiment supported enlisting slaves, saying blacks would add strength to "our thinned, though determined ranks."[75] Capt. Samuel J. C. Moore, a Virginia planter and staff officer to Jubal Early, regretted that slaves would enter the army, fearing it would "inevitably lead to emancipation." But he deferred to General Lee's judgment. Like Lee, he believed that blacks would make good soldiers, and for him there was no contradiction in freeing slaves and continuing the struggle. "We entered this war," he wrote, "not to perpetuate slavery, but to maintain our own right to govern ourselves."[76] In his mind, the fact that white Southerners were hesitant to free their slaves did not mean that they wanted to keep that right above all others. In March 1865, when the Alabama infantryman Joseph D. Stapp heard that the army would soon muster 300,000 blacks, he said that anything would be better than "subjugation."[77]

As it turned out, Confederates accepted the Union's conditions for emancipation rather than let the war go on, but they had little choice in the matter. Nevertheless, with General Lee's support for enlisting blacks, others followed. On 13 March 1865, the Confederacy made it official: slaves and free blacks could serve as soldiers. President Davis called up 300,000 men, who would receive the same rations, clothing, and compensation as white soldiers.[78]

Despite its seemingly revolutionary nature, the enlistment act was quite conservative. Col. William C. Oates, who noted the bill's flaws, said after the war that the problem with it lay in its wording, which gave too much power to slaveholders. The fifth section said that the bill did not "authorize a change in the relation which the said slaves shall bear toward their owners, except by consent of the owners and of the State in which they may reside." Not only did it not give the Confederacy power to conscript black troops, it did not grant them freedom before they served. Any black soldier who did not desert to the enemy, Oates concluded, would have been an idiot. John B. Gordon concurred. The problem with the law, as he saw it, was that it did not offer freedom as a condition of service.[79]

As Oates and Gordon noted, the decision to enlist blacks raised legal problems. One impediment was Southern state law. In the antebellum period, states had passed measures against slaves possessing guns, fifes, and drums—measures unfriendly toward blacks who would soon be marching to the beat of drums with muskets in hand. Nor had antebellum laws been kind toward freed slaves. Virginia law said that, once liberated, blacks had to leave the state. If the Confederacy wanted to be consistent with Virginia state law, slaves freed to fight could not remain in Virginia to do it.

Congress's black enlistment act evaded such problems by not giving black soldiers their freedom. But before the law went into effect, Jefferson Davis—aware of the problems such a measure would have caused—included a provision saying blacks would not have to fight as slaves. President Davis, as the historian Robert Durden has noted, "bootlegged freedom" into the enlistment bill.[80] The Confederacy's measure, however, still contained enormous loopholes. For one, the Confederate armies could not simply conscript slaves as they had white soldiers. Nor could they impress them as they did with black menial laborers. The Southern military instead had to rely on slaves volunteering, based on the consent of the slave's master.

Confederates, however, decided to rely on black volunteers not simply because of political calculations. The fact was that by early 1865, conscription had become unworkable. With Federal armies marching at will through most of the Confederacy, Rebel officials lacked the strength they had possessed earlier in the war to draft men. On 7 March 1865, the Confederacy dismantled its Conscript Bureau.

On 24 March, Robert E. Lee asked Jefferson Davis to call upon Governor William "Extra Billy" Smith of Virginia, formerly a general in Lee's army, for the "whole number of negroes, slave and free, between the ages of eighteen and forty-five, for services as soldiers."[81] The machinery of war was in motion to recruit black volunteers into the army. Unfortunately for Lee, other forces were also working against him. The day after he wrote Governor Smith, his army suffered a crushing defeat at Fort Stedman. Lee's defeat there made it much more difficult for his army to break Grant's grip on Petersburg and join forces with Joseph E. Johnston in North Carolina. The impending collapse of the Army of Northern Virginia did not bode well for black enlistment. Recruiting took time, and Lee did not have it.

Regardless of whether or not black soldiers could help Lee's army, there was no shortage of white men applying for commissions to lead the "colored" troops. In the trenches at Chaffin's Bluff, Virginia, William S. Basinger, a Georgia major, said he wanted to command a black regiment because of "preference and duty." He thought raising black Confederates would "shorten the war by half," and he was "quite ready to shew my faith by my works, regardless of the clamors of the discontented." Robert E. Lee was cautious, telling James Longstreet that the army should select men with "influence & connections" for the job. Lee's eldest son, George Washington Custis Lee, who certainly had such connections, wrote to a comrade about the creation of a division of black troops. Custis Lee could not promise the major a place in such a paper force.[82]

Requests to lead black troops perhaps had more to do with hope for a promotion or a desire to evade combat than with any eagerness to lead African Americans into battle. On the one hand, men were tolerant enough to serve with black soldiers. Officers would live with them and drill them, and they would bear the responsibility for how their "colored" troops fared in battle. On the other hand, some Confederates knew that there was little chance they would serve in combat with black troops before the war ended. In late March 1865, General Longstreet wrote of a "growing evil ... in the shape of applications to raise negro companies." Men were volunteering, he believed, only to get a furlough.[83] Longstreet wanted as many men kept in the ranks as possible. He had concerns about officers going home to take months, perhaps a full year, to raise the required black regiments.

The possibility of African Americans serving in the Confederate army did not lessen some white men's skepticism of black soldiers' abilities. In early March, the army surgeon Abner McGarrity wrote of the "dangerous experiment" of enlisting black troops. He feared that they would join the army only to run away. He clearly did not believe they would make good soldiers, but neither did he have confidence in Southerners in general. They were "not the same [as] they were four years ago," he lamented. For him, a few slaves in the army did not change the status of the black race very much. After talking about the enlistment bill, he asked those at home for a servant.[84] Robert Kean had similar feelings. He believed the enlistment of blacks was a "colossal blunder" that upset race relations and would weaken the war effort. "The enemy will probably get four recruits under it to our one," he feared. For Kean, an enslaved black man was the only loyal black man.[85] The North Carolina soldier James Albright said the passage of the black enlistment bill signified "our downfall as a nation." A Georgian in Mahone's division heard of the bill, but he was not effusive in his support. "This will undoubtedly greatly increase our effective force," he noted, "but I think this bill unconstitutional and violently antagonistical to the principles for which we are fighting." He did not expand on what those principles were, but one can assume he meant keeping African Americans in a subordinate position to whites. Nevertheless, and despite his opposition to the bill's politics, he said, "As an act of necessity I cheerfully acquiesce."[86]

In late March, several companies of black troops were mustered in

Richmond. John B. Jones, an employee of the War Department, wrote of the "ridiculous" sight of them, but Marion Hill Fitzpatrick, a sergeant from Georgia, was less mortified. After seeing two companies of black soldiers, he said, "I hope it will work well."[87] Col. Richard Maury probably best reflected white Southerners' mixed reaction to seeing black soldiers in Richmond, where they marched past crowds that mostly consisted of other African Americans. Maury wrote that enlistment efforts went on "bravely" and that he was eager to see the new troops pass through the streets, noting that they looked "quite military." But despite their "military" appearance, Maury was disheartened. "I hate the idea of . . . Cuffee and Sambo [having to serve] very much," he said, "and confound it all if the miserable men at home would only do their duty." Had white men defended the South, as he thought they should have, "we would never have had to resort to [black men's] aid." For Maury, the rise of the black Confederate soldier signified the failure of white manhood. Strong words coming from a soldier who sat out most of the war in Richmond. Nevertheless, he thought that if whites had answered the call, white Confederates never would have considered emancipation. Black soldiers, he regretted, would "become a too common sight to all of us."[88]

As defeat loomed, some slaves fled, others were recaptured, and still others were on their way to becoming Confederate troops. As one would expect, the news of enlisting blacks took some time to reach soldiers outside Virginia. Nevertheless, Joseph E. Johnston, in trouble against Sherman's forces in North Carolina, sought black Confederate soldiers who could serve as "substitutes for extra duty and detailed men." A few days later, the staff officer Eustace Surget, writing from Meridian, Mississippi, said that he had no objection to black troops joining the army, but he also said he did not have enough arms to give them at such short notice. He would enlist blacks as soon as possible, provided masters were willing. On 7 April, a soldier in Texas heard that the government was about to emancipate the slaves, and he heard that Robert E. Lee was foremost behind the measure. By then, however, Lee's army was on the brink of collapse.[89]

The war might have gone on much longer had the number of blacks enrolled in the Confederate army been equal to the number fighting for the North, but by the spring of 1865, there was not enough time for black Confederate soldiers to make a difference. Earlier in the war, the North had hurried to place some of its black units into combat, but it had given them ample supplies, which is what had enabled its black troops to take part in Northern offensives. By the spring of 1865, when the Confederates were finally ready to field black troops, the Confederacy was in a much different position. Black Confederate troops would not have the advantages in supply, maneuver, and morale of their Union counterparts. Using black troops, however, was more than a matter of equipping, feeding, and training them.

The Union had emancipated the slaves partly as a war measure, partly as a moral act. There was no moral equivalent, however, in the Confederacy's desire to emancipate its slaves. For Southern whites, a black man should not obtain his freedom without fighting for it. The Confederacy's desire for black enlistees, then, was hardly a radical measure, given the context in which it occurred. By March 1865, the rebellion was tottering. Most Confederates resented the freeing of any slaves or their use as troops, and the Southern army did not have the time or resources to arm and train the few black soldiers who could have joined the Rebel ranks. Even had the Confederacy enlisted the 300,000 black troops that Cleburne dreamed of, and that Davis called up, that number would have represented merely a fraction of those blacks who were still enslaved. And the only slaves the Confederacy was willing to free were men whose masters allowed them to serve.

It is unlikely that black men would have fought as enthusiastically for the Confederacy as they did for the Union. The Federal government did not keep its soldiers' families enslaved, nor did it force blacks to serve alongside slaveholders or take commands from others in the master class. Racial tensions within the Confederate military would have only compounded the morale problems inherent in an army that could not by the spring of 1865 win decisive victories against the enemy.

The war ended before Confederates could worry much about the consequences of arming black troops. On 9 April 1865, Lee's army surrendered. Johnston's forces followed a few weeks later; and in June, the Confederates in Texas laid down their arms. The conflict ended at the point where the Confederates had at least been willing to enlist slaves as soldiers, but their opposition to such a measure had delayed any meaningful action to make that a reality. The war changed the South far more than it did white people's attitudes toward slavery and race. And after the war, thousands of white men returned home with military experience they would use in paramilitary actions against African Americans, scalawags, and carpetbaggers. After 1865, the Confederate spirit remained strong in the South. Even the proslavery argument would not die.

· 8 ·

RELICS OF THE ANTEBELLUM ERA
CONFEDERATE SOLDIERS AND THE
POSTWAR WORLD

After fighting four years in a conflict that took at least 620,000 lives, Confederate soldiers returned home to communities impoverished and scarred by war. Southern men had seen more than 260,000 comrades die, and the Federal army had done untold damage to homes and farms. Emancipation, furthermore, liquidated billions in Confederate wealth.[1] The war dramatically changed Southern race relations, and in April 1865, with the Confederacy defeated and the slaves freed, the U.S. government began Reconstruction in earnest.[2] Confederates were forced to accept abolition, they very thing they had fought so hard to prevent. Yet, in the face of a Northern political and military presence in the South, resourceful and ruthless former Confederates realized that white supremacy did not depend upon slavery. Had Reconstruction never occurred, they would have restored a "white man's government" in the Southern states even sooner. After 1865, slave patrols no longer existed, but the black codes and the Ku Klux Klan tried to reestablish what whites believed was the "proper" order among the races.

The continued struggle for a "white man's government" took on new forms, from violent anti-Republican riots, to the intimidation of black voters, to assassinations and murder, to widespread Democratic voting fraud, to the reconfiguration of proslavery ideology into a defense of Jim Crow laws and black disfranchisement. "Redemption" would take years, but after Lee's surrender, ex-Confederates continued their war against Northerners' and African Americans' attempts at establishing greater social, economic, and legal equality in the South. Veterans' postwar views provide not only an epilogue to the story of wartime race relations, they also provide further insight into why Confederates acted as they did during the war.[3]

The passage of the Thirteenth Amendment did not immediately free the slaves in the Confederacy. And before the Army of Northern Virginia capitulated at Appomattox, Southern soldiers tried to keep slavery intact. In January 1865, the Louisianan David Pierson heard of Congress's plan to free the slaves in return for European recognition. In response, men apparently were moving their slaves to western Texas in order to sell them for gold. Pierson wished he could have done the same.[4] The war had not ended, and men had not put an end to their efforts to make money from slavery.

As 1865 began, millions of black people remained in bondage. Confederates who vowed to fight on continued to believe in the institution of slavery and the idea that Union victory meant subjugation for white Southerners. Capt. Robert E. Park of the Twelfth Alabama, who was suffering in a Northern prison, railed against the United States, denouncing the "blatant Abolitionists" who "would scarcely be convinced of the truth of a negro slave's fidelity to his master." Northerners, he believed, were "totally ignorant of the real status of the divine institution of slavery."[5]

"Divine" or not, slavery was crumbling. Some Confederate troops' concerns for their slaves made for pathetic letters. "You asked after the servts," wrote the Louisianan James Stubbs to his father in January 1865. "Eliza is still very ill & I would not be surprised if she never recovers." A slave's illness and possible death was not unusual, but Stubbs probably would not have been as pessimistic six months before. Things had worsened for everyone, he noted, "since our recent national reverses." After he returned home, Stubbs gave $20 to the care of his slaves. It was all he could spare. He considered hiring his servants out, but in January 1865, he noted, hires were not getting a third of their asking price.[6]

Stubbs's mastery over his chattels was weakening, but soldiers had not expected abolition to improve the lot of black people. Capt. Thomas W. Patton resigned his commission in August 1864 to attend to matters at home. In January 1865, writing to his mother from Alabama, he said, "All of the negroes here seem to be better contented than I ever found them." Even so, he saw that slavery was near its end, for which he believed "the negroes are most to be pitied."[7] The impending end of slavery filled African Americans with hope, but Southern whites were far less sanguine.

Some Confederates were defiant to the point of being delusional. Writing from Shreveport, the capital of Confederate-held Louisiana, Hugh Montgomery believed that the Confederacy might still obtain European recognition. Montgomery believed he was not fighting for human bondage, but in his dream of an independent nation, he thought slavery would be a "privilige" for seventy-five more years. No one can know how long slavery would have continued had the Confederacy been victorious, but in 1865 Montgomery claimed that slavery would only die out after several generations had passed, even if slavery would "never be what it has been."[8]

In early 1865, with impending defeat, Southern troops, as they had throughout the war, wrote of unruly and disobedient slaves.[9] In contrast to previous years, Confederates could do little to keep blacks in chains for much longer. Lee's men did not have the offensive power they had possessed even a year before. The weaker the Confederate army became, the weaker became the institution of slavery. Alfred Bell, a provost marshal in the Deep South—which by then had no Confederate army to speak of—noted how his wife, living in North Carolina, was "dissatisfied with you[r] Negroes." North Carolina had avoided the destruction wrought in Virginia, Georgia, and South Carolina, but masters, especially along the coast, faced problems with slaves. Early in the war, the Federal invasion of the coast had led slaveholders to move their chattels to the mountainous areas. And in 1865, the United States' seizure of Wilmington closed the Confederacy to the outside world. For Alfred Bell, moving slaves into the North Carolina interior no longer seemed viable. After the war, he hoped his family might find better luck in Texas, which had become a refuge for white Southerners.[10]

The Confederacy's continued efforts to assert racial control represented an attempt to do too much with too little. In March 1865, Gen. Birkett Davenport Fry wrote that a few Yankees were in Charleston and Savannah, but that they had wrought much damage. The "negroes everywhere within their reach have become much demoralized," Fry lamented. Large numbers had gone over to the enemy, and he had had to send cavalry to prevent further escapes.[11] Edward Armstrong, in camp in Greensboro, North Carolina, complained, "Our cook went home last week but I dont expect he will come back again."[12] By 1865, the Confederacy had little hope of further large-scale, organized resistance to the U.S. forces. Even when Federal troops evacuated from occupied areas of the South, the spirit of abolition remained. Col. Christopher Tompkins saw that in 1865, many Virginia slaves "were slow to realize the fact that they were free." But once they did, they rushed to Richmond for new opportunities. "Never was change accomplished so silently," Tompkins wrote.[13]

White Southerners were much slower than African Americans to accept the new reality. In late April 1865, even after General Lee had surrendered, the Texan Junius N. Bragg thought Confederates could keep the Federals busy for a while longer. Fighting, he was convinced, would prove better than surrender, Yankee domination, and black equality.[14] Men worried that the Union would wreak vengeance on the defeated South, a fear that might have kept many in the ranks. On 22 April, Capt. Samuel Foster, a veteran of the Army of Tennessee, wrote that Joseph E. Johnston—who had not yet surrendered to Sherman—could not make any peace terms "but submission reunion free negroes &c, and we have been fighting too long for that." The Confederates had fought for four years to overthrow what they saw as Abraham Lincoln's brand of despotism, which they believed would put Southern men and women at the feet of Northern masters and freed slaves. A few weeks before emancipation came to Texas, Gen. John B. Magruder warned his troops that they must not become "a slave to Yankee power."[15]

With the surrender of the Army of Northern Virginia, the best Southern fighting force was no more. Less than a week later, the assassination of Abraham Lincoln left the task of rebuilding the South to Andrew Johnson, a Tennessee Democrat who hated planters and secessionists but who put the interest of Southern whites before those of the freed slaves. Former Rebels, however, initially did not think Johnson would treat the defeated Confederates lightly. They wrongly thought that Johnson was a radical Republican (he had been elected vice president as a Union Party candidate and had said at the time that treason would be "made odious"). Fearing the worst, Samuel T. Foster believed Johnson would have "all the prominent men concerned [in the Confederacy] put to death, and the rest banished or made slaves."[16] Carter M. Louthan, a Virginian who served the last year of the war in a Northern prison, vowed never to "cease to use my influence to depose all such men as Andrew Johnson and his Party."[17]

President Johnson did not live up to his harsh rhetoric, however. His peace terms, founded on the principle of state "self-Reconstruction" and white supremacy, were generous to the ex-Rebels, so much so that Mississippi and South Carolina passed restrictive black codes while the U.S. Congress was out of session. Rather than punish prominent former Confederates, Johnson pardoned most of them. But in the spring of 1865, the former Confederates did not know the course that Reconstruction would take. As grounded as Johnson's peace plan was on the notion of "white man's government," his conservative policies were only apparent in hindsight. Before then, Confederates worried that Northerners would put them at a social, political, and economic level below black people.[18]

At first, it seemed, former Confederates, at least publicly, were willing to reconcile quickly with the North. Soldiers as different in their background and wartime service as M. Jeff Thompson and Robert E. Lee believed that the best way to confront defeat was to tend to one's business and avoid political debates. Thompson, the partisan "Swamp Fox of the Confederacy," who had been active in the Western Theater, waged war longer than many Confederates, but he was conciliatory, albeit crude, when discussing the postwar world. "If anybody says nigger to you, swear you never knew nor saw one in your life. We have talked about niggers for forty years and have been out-talked. We have fought four years for the nigger and have been damned badly whipped.... The Yankees have won the nigger and will do what they please with him and you have no say in the matter."[19]

Robert E. Lee would not have put things as Thompson did, but his and Thompson's views about confronting the new era were similar. At Appomattox, Lee asked his troops to go home and make good citizens. When called before Congress in 1866 to testify on the state of the South during Reconstruction, Lee said that black men were "as capable of acquiring knowledge as the white man is." Yet he cautiously added that they "like their ease and comfort" and "look more to the present-time than to the future."[20] Since the North had settled the issue of secession and slavery through force, Lee thought it better to say little about race rather than agitate old issues. Lee, as did Thompson, believed one bloody conflict was enough. Southern white men should accept defeat and emancipation, not re-fight old battles. Wise soldiers should carry on the tradition from Cincinnatus to Washington of quietly returning to the farm once the fighting ended.

Some Confederates noted that they had quickly embraced emancipation. The Virginian Carter M. Louthan, writing to a Northern relative in July 1865, said that he had not fought for slavery, and when it came to the institution's demise, he asserted, "I am heartily glad of it." Instead, Louthan said, he had fought for "personal independence." The fact that Louthan was writing to a Northern correspondent most likely made him downplay his commitment to slavery. Even if he claimed not to have defended the institution, the facts suggest otherwise. His father had been a large slaveholder; and in 1861, Carter had gone to war thinking, "Death is preferable to the ignominious chains of a servile Black Republican bondage." After Lincoln issued the Emancipation Proclamation, he had derisively called the president the "King of Abolitionists." Louthan's postwar words were an example of veterans' attempts, which would continue for generations, to purge slavery from the Confederate history books. They would repeatedly say that the South had had no commitment to slavery, or at best only a tenuous one. Even if Louthan rejected the idea that he had fought for slavery, he was too bitter about his wartime imprisonment to have anything good to say about the Union. Nor could he hide his fears about Reconstruction. "The Radical Party now demands that the Negro should be permitted the right of the franchise," he said. Somewhat ominously, he asserted, "The people of each State will settle that for themselves."[21]

Carter Louthan might have equivocated about slavery when writing to a Northern reader, but others were less circumspect. For them, the North had defeated the Confederacy and freed the slaves, but that did not make holding onto slavery ignoble or invalidate the idea that white democracy must prevail. In August 1865, William Lindsay Brandon, a planter who had lost a leg at Malvern Hill and fought with Longstreet at Chickamauga, wrote, "I am as fully persuaded to-day as ever [that slavery] was the true status of the negro."[22] White Southerners bowed to superior military power, but for them, that did not invalidate their cause or render it immoral.

Most Southern whites managed the best they could in the new world that the war had created. Some decided to flee to South America, where they could escape U.S. law, avoid radical Republicans, and find new economic opportunities. Since they could not or would not go north, and with travel to Europe beyond most men's means, the option to go south made sense to them. In South America, some hoped they might find their El Dorado. It was not a new idea. Such dreams had swirled in Southerners' heads in the antebellum period too. Slavery expansionists and filibusters had once hoped to seize Cuba or Nicaragua and mold those places in the South's image. Southerners also wanted to open new lands to slavery. During the Civil War, Southern forces had invaded New Mexico, where, according to one officer, they hoped to find "plenty of room for the extension of slavery which would greatly strengthen the Confederate States."[23] Such dreams went unfulfilled, but some former Confederates chose to live south of the South after Lee's surrender. Generals Sterling Price, Jubal Early, and Joseph O. Shelby settled in Mexico. As Shelby put it, "We are the last of our race. Let us be the best as well." Shelby had been a slaveholder who hoped Emperor Maximilian would allow Mexico to become a haven for former Confederates. Mexico had no slaves, but its economic and political instability, not to mention the warm climate and opportunities for agriculture, gave some men hope of setting up their own fiefdoms. The War for Texas Independence, after all, had shown how little respect white settlers had for Mexican law.[24]

Veterans seeking a better life in South America were exceptional, and perhaps even more than a bit eccentric. But they underscored white Southerners' rejection of the political, racial, and economic environment that existed during Reconstruction. "The Southern States can now no longer compete," wrote one pessimistic veteran in May 1865. He had no doubts about the economic effect the war had had on the once proud slave states. "*Free* Negro labor is the most perfect hallucination that ever entered the brain of the Fanatic," he complained. He planned to settle along the Brazilian Amazon, where he could use slaves to grow cotton, thus recreating the antebellum world in microcosm.[25] For optimistic souls who had dreams of migrating there, slavery still existed in Brazil, and its government would not ban it until 1888. With its sweltering climate, agrarian economy, vast uncultivated lands, and large black population, it gave hope to ex-Confederates searching for a new means to mastery.

Almost as soon as the Confederacy surrendered, Southern veterans embraced a sentimental view of the antebellum era as a place of glistening cotton fields and happy, smiling "darkies." Not long after Lee's surrender, the Tennessee soldier Bromfield Ridley wrote of how he missed the "old times, no more corn shuckin' songs, no more pattin' Judas, no more plaintiff negro melodies, big camp meetin's over yonder soon to go. Old Aunt Dinah and Uncle Tom will only be heard of in the past." Yet, if one wanted to hear black people's songs, one still could, even if the meaning of such tunes had changed. Ridley wrote of one song, "Kingdom Coming" (alternatively known as "The Year of Jubilo"), which contained the lines:

> Massa run, aha!
> Darky stay, oho!
> It must be now dat de kingdom's comin'
> In de year of Jubilo.[26]

Black hymns frequently spoke of suffering on earth but hoped for better things in the afterlife.[27] With emancipation, it seemed that the "Year of Jubilo" had indeed come. Whether former slaves would find equality in an emancipated South was another matter.

The war had brought about radical change, but Southern whites preferred writing of African Americans who had remained loyal to their former masters. The Kentuckian Albert Kirwan remembered a black woman who defended the family silver from "*poo* white trash" bushwhackers.[28] In Confederate eyes, such incidents epitomized black people's devotion to their white "family." The Yankees, they believed, could not destroy the love black people had for their former owners. The Tennessee cavalryman John E. Fisher, who had ridden with Forrest and Wheeler, likewise had a rosy notion of postwar race relations, saying relationships between masters and the freedmen were "cordial."[29] On the long road home from the army, the Louisiana captain E. John Ellis met a black man who still considered himself in the military and insisted on wearing "his Confederate gray."[30] Events in postwar Louisiana would reach horrific levels of racial violence, but in the eyes of Ellis and other former Confederates, black people were perpetually faithful.

In the narratives of faithful slaves, upon returning home, men who had marched with Lee or Johnston until the bitter end were reunited with "uncles" and "mammies," who might break out a bottle of whiskey in celebration and who seemed as happy to see them as their white families were. Reunion stories reflected former Rebels' attempt to underscore instances in which the freed people supposedly put white people's interests ahead of their own. One soldier recalled returning to children crying for bread. In the face of such misery, a sympathetic servant asked the family to sell him in order to help out the family. Despite the fact that the man was no longer a slave, he said that he would work hard and "never claim his freedom."[31]

Letters and diaries from the Reconstruction era speak of much greater racial tensions. The war had ended with white Southerners engaged in an intense debate concerning the enlistment of black troops into the Confederate army. The Confederacy, however, never enrolled African Americans in large numbers. Black men in Federal uniforms were a far more common sight. After their surrender, Confederates could not, as they had at Fort Pillow and the Crater, do much about black troops. "Richmond garrisoned by negroes," wrote one soldier in April 1865. "A very gloomy time for Rebels."[32] In May 1865, Tench Tilghman, a Marylander who went to Florida in the last days of the war, wrote of being "subjected to a trial such as I had hoped never to have been called on to endure"—namely, his surrender to black troops who stripped officers of their pistols and then escorted them into town. Along the way, other black soldiers insulted the white prisoners. Tilghman was fatalistic about his humiliation. "It is of no use," he wrote. "The whole country lies prostrate & it is but little use to kick unaided against the breaks."[33] A soldier in North Carolina suffered a similar experience. Black soldiers, he said, were angered not only at the sight of Confederate prisoners, but at the death of President Lincoln. Another Confederate complained that he did not like having to show a pass to "jet black negro soldiers."[34]

Some defeated Confederates were not passive in the face of such taunts. As they saw it, they had surrendered, but they were still white men who deserved respect from men they thought were their racial inferiors. Surrounded by black troops, one soldier sarcastically remarked that someone should give him a candle, for it was so dark that he could not see. Another said that if he were to have such a gang of blacks, he would put them to better use—as workers. The Federals responded with cries of "bottom rail on top."[35]

The movement of the "bottom rail" toward the top signified an enormous economic shift in the South. Masters soon reclaimed their lands, but most could not reclaim the wealth they had enjoyed before the war. Emancipation liquidated the investment Southern whites had made in human flesh. Men such as Robert E. Lee and Nathan Bedford Forrest struggled to earn a living. Lee and his family had lost "Arlington" and its two hundred slaves, and Forrest could no longer make money from slave trading. Far less prominent Confederates also worried about surviving. In January 1866, Pvt. Ludwig Lehmann, a German American who had moved to Texas before the war, believed emancipation would cause a "great upheaval in our agriculture." Black workers had left their former masters, and he warned that, "without any schooling, their emancipation came too suddenly." According to him, blacks only worked when they wanted to, and farmers in Texas were "apprehensive." He hoped German workers would flock to his state, for he had little faith in African Americans making good.[36]

Slaves no longer, black people had greater freedom than ever before, and in the view of ex-Confederate soldiers, they avoided doing anything productive. In July 1864, Milton Leverett, who was from a Lowcountry South Carolina planter family, had written about the injustice of the army exposing slaves working on fortifications in Georgia to shelling. "Poor wretches," he said, "they see a dreadful time of it, are worked very hard.... I feel very sorry for them." By February 1866, he was less sympathetic. He tried to "drum up negroes all about" to work, but had no luck. "They are such disgusting slow procrastinating wretches," he moaned, who "put off and put off and promise and promise until it will be too late to do anything." Exasperated, he considered free labor "the most difficult task the world has ever seen." The North had great success with it, but many Southerners, who lamented the loss of slavery's comforts, did not want to emulate the Yankees. In their eyes, blacks were now too difficult to manage. Former Confederates wanted a reliable labor source that would not challenge white supremacy.[37]

William Judson Brown, formerly a Confederate officer, was bothered by black people wandering the South in idleness. In December 1865, he complained to a relative, "With as many negroes as are strolling around the country and in our cities doing nothing, it is a shame that persons situated as you all are cannot get help." White people, whether or not they were slaveholders, recognized that blacks were reliable and productive workers. Had they not been, whites—regardless of their paternalistic posturing or desire for racial control—would not have kept slavery for so long. Slavery was the engine of Southern capitalism. After the war, however, white employers wanted African Americans to take on traditional and menial jobs as field workers and house servants. "If you do not get negro help I will try & get you a good white woman," said Brown. But, he continued, "I never did like white servants. They soon get above themselves."[38]

In the Old South, masters believed conscientious care for their workers made for contented slaves. But in the eyes of the Mississippian Frank Montgomery, writing decades after the war, emancipation had ruined the slaveholder's Utopia. In his memoirs, he complained that whites at the turn of the century had to deal with a new breed of black people who quickly filled jails and insane asylums. These criminals and unfortunates apparently were not made up of former slaves—who were, in Confederate lore, inherently loyal—but were their sons and daughters, who had not enjoyed the supposedly civilizing aspects of human bondage. Murder and madness had been rare before the war, Montgomery asserted, but by the latter part of the century they were rampant. What Montgomery, now a judge, found most disturbing were the crimes committed among blacks themselves. One of his former slaves descended into morphine addiction and killed himself after being convicted of murder.[39]

Montgomery's words only tell part of the story. The historian Edward Ayers has shown that the end of slavery did not result in a sharp increase in black crime. Instead, after an initial sharp increase in crime, the number of Southerners sent to prison remained stable and then actually declined. Then, by the mid-1870s, prison populations once again surged. One cannot attribute the rise in the number of black prisoners in the late nineteenth century to a more-debased African American population. It was instead the result of the greater enforcement of laws by the Southern white population, which had a free hand to deal with its "Negro problem" after Reconstruction ended.[40]

As Frank Montgomery's words suggest, however, veterans believed in the Old South notion that white people needed to save blacks from themselves. Unchecked freedom, former soldiers warned, might lead to the eradication of the black race. In June 1865, the Georgian George Mercer believed that the fate of the "unhappy Negro" would prove similar to that of Native Americans: annihilation.[41] White Southerners had long believed that slavery assured black survival. In the white mind, since Native Americans, who had never been slaves in large numbers, had served no purpose in the South, they had been put on the path to removal and extermination. Now that blacks were no longer slaves, they too might "go the way of the Indian."

Southern white fears were unfounded. According to the highly flawed 1870 census, the black population stagnated during the 1860s, but the general trend in the latter decades of the nineteenth century was toward increase. Roughly 4.4 million black people lived in the United States in 1860; in 1900, there were over 8 million.[42] African Americans were hardly "going the way of the Indian." Not only did they grow considerably in numbers, during Reconstruction, unlike Native Americans, they seized considerable political power and civil rights.

Black people believed that the social, political, and economic gains of Reconstruction were long overdue, but former Confederate soldiers branded the period as one of "African domination." They wrote impassioned, purple passages about the horrors of the postwar years. "As a fit climax to . . . Yankee hatred, malice, revenge, and cruelty practiced during the war," the Virginia veteran W. H. Morgan wrote in the early 1900s, "the North bound the prostrate South on the rock of negro domination, while the vultures . . . preyed upon its vitals." Nor did Morgan believe that such abuses had ended with Reconstruction. At the turn of the century, he noted, "Many at the North are still growling and snarling, threatening reduction of representation in Congress, howling about negro disfranchisement, and the separation of the races in schools and public conveyances."[43] For Confederate veterans, Republicans—New Englanders foremost among them—had duped the ignorant blacks with false promises, raising their hopes that equality could exist in the South. Northern meddling, as the veterans saw it, had upset the "natural" balance between the races and led to subsequent bloodshed. For former soldiers, the killing would not have been necessary had the North left the South alone.[44]

Pvt. Robert M. Howard was a Houston County, Georgia, native who joined a South Carolina regiment during the war. In his reminiscences, he wrote plainly in verse about Reconstruction. "This is the white man's government/no nigger to its sway/our white flag . . . all who meet shall obey."[45] In the face of what they saw as a threatening and debased "Negro-Yankee" alliance, former Confederates believed that they must restore all-white governments in the South. Otherwise, they worried, black people would run amok. Confederate troops had feared such things during the war, but they could not serve at the front and in their communities at the same time. When they returned home, however, they worked to undermine Northern policies through brute force.[46]

The Virginia infantryman James Huffman complained of a tyrannical "Negro rule" that would have endured had the Klan not saved the South. The Klan's aim, said the Tennessean Marcus Toney, "was a laudable one." He went on to assert that "blacks who behaved themselves had the best of friends in the Kuklux Klan. I never heard of but two deeds of violence [done] in our midst." The Klan "never burnt negroes," wrote the South Carolina cavalryman U. R. Brooks, but according to him, white people in Delaware and Illinois did.[47]

Ex-Confederates were correct in saying Northerners were not immune to racism and racial violence, but nothing Northerners did compared to the unprecedented number of racial murders that took place in the South during Reconstruction. The violence varied according to state, but postwar carnage was the worst in regions with the highest black populations. In terms of bloodletting, Deep South states such as Louisiana and South Carolina fared worse than Virginia or North Carolina, but even in the Upper South states of Arkansas and Tennessee, blacks along the Mississippi River were especially vulnerable to white retribution. In September 1868, in the wake of Klan violence and political assassinations, a Yankee officer turned Arkansas planter and congressman, Logan H. Roots, was told that when it came to former Confederates in his state, after a "recess of three years . . . they now desire a harvest of bloodshed." In many parts of the South, there had been no "recess," and the Ku Klux Klan that emerged after the war was only one manifestation of white Southerners' seeking to overturn Republican gains. The massacre at Colfax, Louisiana, in 1873, where dozens of African Americans were killed by non-Klansmen eager to eliminate the elected Republican government there, showed how extreme whites' efforts were to crush black civil rights.[48]

Nevertheless, it was the Klan membership that consisted of the most prominent former Confederates of any paramilitary group. It is not surprising that Nathan Bedford Forrest, conqueror of Fort Pillow and a former slave trader, became the first "Grand Wizard" of the Klan. Forrest's actual role in the Klan has been the subject of long debate, but he was the perfect man to lead it. Unlike other Confederate luminaries, such as John B. Gordon, who also served in the Klan, Forrest did not succeed in postwar politics, nor did he prosper under the new free labor system. But

Forrest was a valuable symbol of white resistance to radical Reconstruction. Nicknamed "The Wizard of the Saddle," he had the ideal qualifications for becoming "Grand Wizard." The Klan was created in his home state of Tennessee, which had experienced some of the bloodiest battles of the Civil War. Forrest—quick and cunning, violent and intimidating, seemingly invincible and staunchly independent—was a man that Klansmen wanted to emulate. Much like Forrest, the Klan struck quickly and hard and disappeared afterward.[49]

Regardless of who made up groups such as the Klan and the Knights of the White Camellia, these organizations continued the racial violence that flared during the war. In his memoirs, the veteran Charles S. Powell boasted that his home community, Johnston County, North Carolina, was among the first to "resist the Carpet-Bagger innovation and the Freedman's Bureau atrocities and marched with the great 'Ku Klux Klan' that forced or[d]er throughout the Country. She also donned the 'Red Shirt' and contributed to the disfranchisement of the vexation negro suffrage question." For Powell and many others who believed in a "white man's government," radical Reconstruction was a destructive force. The decade after the war, Powell asserted, was a "hell" that brought "dark days" on the white South.[50]

In fact, nothing approaching an African American dictatorship took place in North Carolina. In 1868, for example, only 14 of the 122 delegates to the state constitutional convention were black.[51] Throughout Reconstruction, only one Southern state, South Carolina, had a majority black legislature. Louisiana had a black governor, P. B. S. Pinchback, but he served only briefly, after the impeachment of his predecessor. When it came to "Negro domination," white Southerners were exaggerating the political power blacks had in the postwar period, thus justifying the violence they believed necessary to overthrow Reconstruction. The Southern state legislatures were operated by white-black coalition governments, not a mythical dictatorship of uneducated and corrupt former slaves. Yet, compared to the antebellum period, for former Confederates, Reconstruction seemed a radical solution to the problem of white rule in the South.[52]

White supremacy took on many forms after the Confederacy's defeat. The Ku Klux Klan had thousands of supporters, but one could find a milder advocacy for a "white man's government" in the powerful Lost Cause. Composed of many former Rebels, who made speeches, erected monuments, and penned recollections of the war that lauded the Confederacy, Lost Cause organizations thrived in the late nineteenth century. The Sons of Confederate Veterans was founded in 1889, the United

Daughters of the Confederacy in 1894. One could also read about the war from a pro-Confederate perspective in the *Southern Historical Society Papers* (established in 1876) or the *Confederate Veteran* (begun in 1894). With such literature came the assumption, tacit or otherwise, that antebellum race relations had been preferable to those that existed after 1865.[53]

Chief among Lost Cause boosters was Jubal Early, who defended not only the Confederacy, but white supremacy. An ill-fated general, Early lauded Robert E. Lee—the man who relieved him of command in 1865—at every opportunity. Early hated James Longstreet, who dared to criticize Lee in print and who became a Republican during Reconstruction. Unlike Longstreet, who fought anti-Republican forces in New Orleans in 1874, Early did not defend the rights of black Southerners.[54] In his 1867 memoirs, Early said that God had stamped black people "with a different colour and an inferior physical and mental organization." Amalgamation, he believed, went against divine will, but keeping the races separate was also, he felt, based in human logic and experience. "Reason, common sense, true humanity to the black, as well as the safety of the white race," he noted, "required that the inferior race should be kept in a state of subordination." Early was not just an apologist for racial hierarchy, he also defended slavery, saying it had not only improved the physical and moral health of the slaves, but had made them as "happy and contented as any [people] in the world, if not more so." Despite the arguments he made for slavery's advantages, Early insisted that he had not fought for the institution in wartime.[55]

White Southerners needed not just leaders like Early to rally around, but an ideology. Just as their choice of Confederate leaders to head paramilitary groups drew on slaveholding former officers, their racial worldview also focused on the Old South. Veterans used antebellum rhetoric to justify the continued violence and oppression of black people. After Reconstruction ended, the South saw the rise of legal segregation, lynching, and disfranchisement. Furthermore, to solidify the victory of a "white man's government," former soldiers initiated a belated defense of the peculiar institution, making a proslavery argument without slavery.[56]

With the end of Reconstruction came a "New South" creed that promoted urbanization and industrialization on a more Northern model. Birmingham, Alabama, would become the "Pittsburgh of the South," and Richmond, Virginia, had the nation's first trolley car line. Many of those living in the New South were too busy constructing textile mills, drinking Coca-Cola, and smoking Durham cigarettes to care much about the Lost

Cause. However, white Southerners' racial attitudes in the New South drew on Old South ways of thinking. Segregation and Jim Crow laws were something new. Yet only the means, not the ends, of white supremacy had changed. The proslavery argument contained much that segregationists and other late-nineteenth-century white supremacists could use. One need only look to the past, former Confederate soldiers saw, to see the necessity of racial control. Their postwar defense of slavery was not original, but it did have a point: the men wanted to show that Southerners had not been wrong in keeping the peculiar institution for so long.

After Lee's surrender, former Confederates had a New South to compare to the Old. Fears of what slaves would do if freed were hypothetical until emancipation took effect. After the freeing of the slaves, however, former Confederate soldiers believed that their worst fears had become reality: once-docile blacks had become a threatening presence in the South. Veterans made perfunctory claims that emancipation was needed medicine. Typical were the words of W. W. Blackford, a former cavalryman in the Army of Northern Virginia, who made a half-hearted apology for slavery. "I am heartily glad that slavery is gone on my children's account," he began, "because I think they are better without them." His words became less apologetic when he stressed the economic and moral advantages of human bondage. When time removed the "fog of fanaticism," he noted, the world would see that "never before were labor and capital brought together under circumstances more advantageous to the development of the laborer—nor was there ever a greater blessing bestowed on the negro race." Otherwise, Blackford asserted, slaves would have been left in "heathenism and barbarism."[57]

Blackford and others made arguments familiar to those who had absorbed the proslavery ideology: slavery provided the best foundation for the relationship between white and black people; the United States Constitution sanctioned it; slaves were well treated and contented; human bondage had civilized blacks; freed slaves were a menace; the institution of slavery did not originate in the South but was rather a Northern invention; and white Southerners had only followed a traditional way of life in holding onto slavery.

Some men's words revealed a Jeffersonian lament over human bondage. "As an institution of human government [slavery was] wrong, no right-thinking man can deny," said Thomas D. Duncan, formerly a Mississippi cavalryman. "It is regrettable," he noted, "that the world ... will never understand the true relation between the master and the slave of the Old South."[58] The "true" relationship, he believed, was a benign one.

As was often the case with Thomas Jefferson, men's racial thinking was not consistent. "Extinction of slavery was expected by all and regretted by none," wrote Richard Taylor. Yet, at the same time, he was bitter toward the United States for bringing about abolition. "Humanitarians shuddered with horror and wept with grief for the imaginary woes of Africans," he wrote. In Taylor's eyes, in succumbing to a love for black Southerners they did not understand, Northerners had betrayed their fellow whites. For him, men of similar skin color should have showed solidarity.[59]

For veterans, slavery might have been an economic and political liability, but it was not a sin. It was an "inheritance from their forefathers [and] by no means an unmitigated evil," said one.[60] When it came to guilt for slavery, Southerners did not feel it.[61] During the war, some had sought to reform slavery, but most only wanted to do so late in the conflict, if at all, when melancholy Confederates calculated the price slavery had exacted on the South. Few had considered eradicating chattel bondage in the boom times. When it came to slavery, Confederate veterans need not retract anything. "The 'sin of slavery,' they never felt," wrote the former general John Tyler Morgan in 1878. "If this is moral obliquity," he said, "[Southerners] are still blind."[62]

Morgan, an antebellum lawyer who had been raised in Tennessee and later Alabama, was elected to the Alabama secession convention, where he voted for disunion. During the war, he headed the Fifth Alabama, which served in Virginia. In 1862, not having seen much action in the East, Morgan returned home. There, he raised a new force, the Fifty-First Alabama Partisan Rangers, which defended citizens and railroads in the northern part of his state. Morgan served briefly under Forrest's command and later took part in the Chickamauga, Knoxville, and Atlanta campaigns. After the war, he lauded the heroes of the Lost Cause, reputedly was a Grand Dragon of the Ku Klux Klan, and was elected and then reelected as a six-term U.S. Senator from Alabama, an office he held until his death in 1907. As senator, Morgan was a strong advocate of the New South creed, which promoted economic expansion, white supremacy, and black disfranchisement. "We did not enslave [black people]," he wrote in 1878. "If their enslavement was a sin, it is not at our door."[63]

After the war, Henry Kyd Douglas believed slavery had been a "curse to the people of the Middle States." Douglas's Virginia was one of those Middle States, but if he claimed slavery was a curse, he spent more time pointing out Northerners' hypocrisy on the race issue than denouncing Southerners for keeping slavery so long. Douglas supposedly harbored no resentment toward abolitionists, but his assessment of Northerners was sarcastic. "I had determined never to own [a slave]," he wrote. "Whether I would have followed the example of shrewd New Englanders . . . by selling my slaves for a valuable consideration before I became an abolitionist, I will not pretend to say."[64] Northerners had made their fortunes from the peculiar institution, the ex-Confederates argued, and when Southerners defended the right to own slaves, the North had betrayed its white neighbors in "Dixie." Determined Southerners eventually rose from the ashes of war, veterans reassured themselves, by reasserting white supremacy and achieving reconciliation with the white North.[65] Still, they harbored resentment against what the North had done to the "righteous" South.

James Henry Hammond and George Fitzhugh had made names for themselves as slavery apologists, but Confederate veterans who defended slavery were an anachronism. Hammond and Fitzhugh's postwar proslavery views were of little interest to anyone outside the South. Northerners had reason to listen to the Fitzhughs and Hammonds of the 1850s, but not to their late-nineteenth-century imitators. "Pitchfork" Ben Tillman and James K. Vardaman were the new race baiters with whom Americans had to contend. Former Confederates nevertheless continued to raise issues they believed were embarrassing to a North that thought itself more progressive on racial issues. In many ways, their indictment was as relevant in the late nineteenth and early twentieth century as it had been decades earlier.

Veterans believed that if the South had wanted black people kept down, the North did not want them at all. In their view, some Northern states—even that stronghold of abolitionism, Massachusetts—had made it clear how undesirable blacks were in their anti-miscegenation laws. The former Rebels also highlighted New England's role in the African slave trade.[66] Nor were the Midwestern states immune to criticism. As Col. Thomas Smith and Leigh Robinson—former soldiers who collaborated on an address to Marylanders—pointed out, in the 1850s Lincoln's Illinois had made it a crime for black people to enter the state. The North, former Confederates argued, was not free of racists or of men who had profited from slavery. As Smith and Robinson wrote, "An old maxim tells us: 'the receiver is as bad as the thief.'"[67] In veterans' eyes, had Northern merchants felt guilty about making money from slavery, they might have given their fortunes back, but they never did. By the early 1800s, the North had abolished slavery within its borders, but veterans underscored how the region was no friend to African Americans. Ex-Confederate soldiers might have carried their indictment further. They could have said how few Americans were abolitionists at any time, and even most of them did not want black people to become the legal and social equals of whites. Yet to have done so would have undermined their reasons for going to war. In 1861, Southerners feared that there were abolitionists everywhere, ready to invade the South and free the slaves.

Confederates rejected Northerners' belief that they were more moral than the South. The emancipation of the slaves, they insisted, whether in the Revolutionary or Civil War era, hinged on Northerners' practical rather than ethical considerations. Col. Edward McCrady, a South Carolinian who had suffered a serious wound at Second Manassas, said the North could afford to let slavery go after the Revolution because there were few black people there (though this was certainly not the case in New York City, which had a slave population to rival that of Charleston). As veterans reasoned, the North's abolition of the institution within its borders, and implicitly later in the South, was not a great sacrifice. "If our Northern brethren had been earnest in freeing these people," McCrady said to a crowd of South Carolina veterans, "they would all have been as philanthropic and disinterested as Vermont with her *seventeen* slaves, and would have emancipated their negroes as suddenly and more immediately than Mr. Lincoln did ours by his famous proclamation."[68] In McCrady's view, it was no great sacrifice to free slaves in Vermont, where few blacks lived, and he reminded his listeners that the North had benefited financially from slavery as much as the South.

The former Confederates' critique of Northern racism had a point, but it could not absolve the South of the immorality of human bondage. After the Revolution, all the Northern states either abolished slavery immediately or gradually. And none of the Northwestern states ever had slavery. Abolitionism certainly faced great opposition in the North. William Lloyd Garrison, for example, was attacked by an anti-abolitionist mob in the 1830s. But the South could claim no meaningful abolitionist movement around that time. Slavery was thriving by the outbreak of the Civil War, but it was an institution whose defenders were becoming frantic over the ever growing Northern critique by abolitionists and free labor Republicans. By April 1861, most states in the Union did not have slavery, and no new slave states had been added since Texas in 1845 (whereas six free states had been admitted in that time). The Confederacy was not only fighting against anti-slavery Northerners, it was fighting against historical trends.

After the war, Confederate veterans clung to the proslavery argument, claiming that free labor proved much more brutal than slavery. The Old

South, as they saw it, had been devoid of exploitation. Slaves had little reason to complain. In 1911, aging soldiers could read in *Confederate Veteran* an article that asserted that some masters had been cruel, but they were "the exception and not the rule."[69] Southerners believed they had invested too much money in the system for masters to treat slaves badly. Masters, slavery apologists noted, provided food, shelter, and medical attention for their servants. Abuses did exist, veterans believed, but no institution was devoid of suffering. Free society's hands, in contrast, were not free of blood. In the antebellum period, men such as John C. Calhoun had lambasted Northern society by arguing that the South's peculiar institution was far more benign than free labor. And extremists such as George Fitzhugh argued that the best form of labor was slave labor, which meant that white people could possibly become slaves, too.

By the turn of the twentieth century, Southerners not only denounced anti-black feeling in the North, they also criticized U.S. colonialism and racism abroad. The North denounced the South for lynching, but as Charles Landon Carter Minor—a former staff officer with Gen. Sam Jones and author of *The Real Lincoln,* which was highly critical of the "Great Emancipator"—noted in highly overblown fashion that U.S. actions against Filipino insurgents were "without a parallel in history."[70] If one measured race relations purely by the body count it exacted, Southern state governments *could* say that they were less racist than the United States was in its brutal conduct overseas. The United States killed far more Filipinos than the South lynched black people in the same period.[71] Yet Southerners who employed such logic missed the point: whatever the United States did in the Philippines did not give moral sanction to Jim Crow and lynching in the South.

The U.S. brand of imperialism had its Southern critics, but in fact the Spanish American War had great support in the South. The Southern military academies rushed to put officers in the ranks, and as the historian David Blight has written, "Southern support for the war and expansion became an overwhelming force by which reunion trumped appeals for racial justice, no matter how eloquently made." The war might have exposed American racism, as Charles Minor noted, but the United States' imperial ambitions, Blight asserts, "gave promoters of Jim Crow in the South a freer hand than ever in fashioning a segregated social system."[72]

By the turn of the twentieth century, Southerners had adopted the attitude of Rudyard Kipling, who famously wrote of the "white man's burden." Former Confederate soldiers believed they had a duty to civilize blacks. Thirty-five years after General Forrest had stormed Fort

Pillow, one veteran, who had not fought there, was asked about the infamous battle. He said, "According to present standards, the garrison should doubtless have been kindly treated on strictly racial grounds—the Negro being peculiarly the white man's burden—although as Sepoys, Indians, Egyptians or Malays they would have been disposed of promptly enough."[73] When it came to African Americans, white Southerners believed that they must tame what they saw as a primitive race of people. In their eyes, Anglo-Saxons were the civilizers of the world, the makers of laws, the builders of empires, and the maintainers of order.[74] Southerners had inherited a political, legal, and economic tradition that depended on white supremacy, and the antebellum period, they claimed, had been one of black people's uplift. Gen. Bradley Johnson, a Marylander who served in the Army of Northern Virginia, said slavery "is the organization of labor in all primitive societies." He did not dwell on whether the South was "primitive," but he believed slavery had benefited blacks by exposing them to Western culture.[75]

Winthrop Jordan has called Europeans' decision to enslave Africans as "unthinking."[76] For Col. Thomas Smith and Leigh Robinson, it was a *thinking* decision. "Let us use the idle sinews of the east to develop the idle fertilities of the west," they wrote in their summation of the intentions of early American slaveholders. "Out of two refractory negations make one intelligent affirmative; thus supplying a reason for existence to two continents, otherwise having none." In other words, the African had been defined by the labor he did in the New World. And in veterans' minds, Europeans had done blacks a favor by enslaving them. Christianity saved them from hell and slave labor rescued them from idleness. America became a "huge employment agency for the idle hands and idle acres of two worlds," Smith and Robinson wrote. Here was the Protestant work ethic in its starkest form: men should work whether they wanted to or not. The New World, therefore, became a factory for black idlers. From Africa came the "heathen raw material," which white men used profitably in America.[77]

Former soldiers saw that in America, black people had adopted many aspects of Anglo-Saxon civilization as their own. They did so, the veterans asserted, because of the poverty of African culture. As Anthony Michael Keiley, a Confederate veteran and once mayor of Richmond, asserted, for four hundred years black people had "undisputed possession of a continent," but they had "not left a trace on the page of history." Whereas other countries had produced "miracles of human achievement," in Africa, there was "only a dreary blank." "In all these teeming centuries *they* have stood still," Keiley continued, pointing out that they had "written no book, painted no picture, carved no statue, built no temple, established no laws, launched no ships, developed no language, achieved no invention."[78] It would be fruitless to correct such assumptions about African history. What is more important is that Confederate veterans worked hard, long after slavery, to justify human bondage.

As the twentieth century dawned, perceptions of the black character still fascinated the white Southern mind. Whites claimed to understand African Americans, but oddly, they often referred to them as "aliens," implying that black Southerners were not or should not be citizens.[79] The passage of the Fourteenth Amendment made that a moot point, but former Confederates made sure that white Southerners eradicated the power that the civil rights amendments gave to African Americans. Southerners, whose ancestors had forced black people to the shores of America against their will, knew that they could not return them to slavery or to their ancestral homeland. And since they could not, their answer to the so-called "Negro problem" was to keep black people at the margins of society, as menial laborers and little else. That meant whites must keep blacks literally and figuratively at a distance.

It was not under slavery, but in the 1880s and 1890s—which one historian has called the "nadir" of American race relations—that whites established a segregated society.[80] In a "progressive" era, white Southerners saw Jim Crow laws as the best means of assuring white supremacy in the South. William Campbell Preston Breckinridge (not to be confused with his cousin John C. Breckinridge) was a Baltimore-born man who moved to Kentucky before the war and served with John Hunt Morgan. Later, Kentuckians elected Breckinridge to Congress. In 1892, he asserted that white Southerners had no choice in the matter of separating the races. They "did not intend that [blacks] should be our enemies," he said. "We did not intend to be barbarous or cruel; and yet we knew that their domination meant ruin and disaster, and that we could not leave the country any more than we could export them."[81] The postwar era showed that America's problem was not just slavery, but race; and for former Confederate soldiers, their transition from proslavery men to segregationists was an easy one. In their eyes, white Southerners had the same problem as before, "the Negro." Just as they were convinced slavery had been the best condition for blacks, so too was segregation. Until whites could somehow send black people back to Africa, or otherwise literally make it a "white man's country," Confederate veterans believed they must cope with blacks as best they could. They thought their way was the best way, and that Northerners were arrogant and hypocritical when they thought they knew better.

Black people had always given shape to white Southern politics, and Confederate veterans used them as a metaphor for their own intellectual purposes. The proslavery argument had never been a fixed one, but one susceptible to political, economic, and social change. In the first years of the nation, men like Thomas Jefferson had argued that slavery should end gradually. By the 1820s, the peculiar institution became one without flaws, one free of guilt—it was as good as any institution could be. Confederates soldiers had grown up in this new environment of slavery as a "positive good." After the war, they modified that argument into a new but familiar creed. The Civil War eradicated slavery, but not white supremacy, racial violence, and paternalistic attitudes. By 1900, former Confederates still thought theirs was a "white man's country."

In the nineteenth century, white Southerners created a racial worldview that contained paradoxical tenets: blacks were lazy, but they formed the foundation of a social and economic "mud sill" class; slaves were "savages," but they rarely revolted and were malleable to discipline; they were not intelligent enough to rise above being field hands, but they were clever enough to make laws that subjugated the South during Reconstruction. Black people were faithful hiders of silverware, yet they were prone to resistance and running away. They were both human and property, beloved family members and "aliens," Africans and Americans, heathens and Christians. That Southern whites described black people in such terms would cause problems well beyond Lee's surrender at Appomattox. Racial politics survived the Civil War with a few variations on old themes. After the conflict, Confederate veterans certainly lived in a different world, but the "Negro problem" gave them a familiar subject upon which to create a New South.

Conclusion
"REPUBLICS HAVE PROVERBIALLY SHORT MEMORIES"

This work has shown the proslavery nature of the Confederate army and the Rebel military's attempts to protect the peculiar institution from various threats. The war might have ended at the Battle of Bull Run, and slavery might have lasted indefinitely. But it did not, and the bloodier the war became, the greater were the North's efforts to crush slavery. Confederates had to fight many battles—not only against the Union army; this was a war between whites and whites, whites and blacks, and, to some extent, it was a conflict among black people as well. But slavery finally ended in the South as a result of external, not internal, reasons. Southern whites did not want slavery to die. Instead, the United States military killed it. Had Lincoln been another James Buchanan and never used force against the secessionists, the Confederacy not only would have kept slavery within its borders, it might have extended it into what is now the western United States, South America, or the Caribbean.

In hindsight, it is easy to see how the peculiar institution undermined the Confederate cause. Hundreds of thousands of slaves fled their masters, and many joined the Union army, where they killed, wounded, and captured Southern whites who were fighting to keep them in bondage. Enslaved women and children could not enlist in the military, but the loss of their labor proved severe to Southern slaveholders. The loss of field workers meant crops were not planted or harvested; the loss of domestics meant tables were left uncleared, food uncooked, and white families went without nurses. The escape to Yankee lines of slave artisans and carpenters meant that houses were not built or repaired. Slaves who remained under their masters' control helped the Union cause through work slowdowns and stoppages, the sabotaging of equipment, and other forms of resistance. Some even plotted slave revolts. The slaves gave Confederates much to worry about, and their resistance elicited violent responses from secessionists and the armies that protected them.

Slavery also served as a valuable propaganda tool for the United States. What began as a war to bring the South back into the Union—though President Lincoln never considered the seceded states legally out of the Union—became a war for re-union *and* emancipation. Antislavery feeling in Europe (the British had abolished slavery in its colonies in the 1830s, and Russia freed its serfs in 1861) undermined the Confederacy's attempts to gain diplomatic recognition there. Had the Confederacy obtained the financial and political support it needed from Europe, the war might have gone very differently.

It is possible to argue that the Confederacy was doomed because it was a slaveholding nation fighting a more industrialized and more populous United States that did not need slavery. But as David Potter has warned, hindsight is "the historian's chief asset and his main liability."[1] We know that the Civil War ended in the destruction of the Confederacy. What is important to understand is that Confederates believed they could win the war, despite the long odds they faced. Northern victory and the abolition of slavery were not inevitable. The war's outcome ultimately depended on thousands of choices, choices that had dramatic consequences.

Despite the many ways slavery worked against the Confederacy, it also helped it. In 1861, the South had the largest slave population in history. When Lee surrendered in 1865, most Southern blacks were still in bondage. True, many enslaved people had fled their masters, but far more had remained at home, willingly or not, where they grew the crops and performed the countless tasks that sustained the Rebel armies. Slaves worked in Confederate factories and as teamsters, acted as spies and scouts, and served alongside their masters in the camps, where they tended horses, cooked, cleaned, and performed odd jobs. Thousands of impressed slaves repaired Confederate roads, dug trenches, and filled sandbags. Slave labor was essential to the Confederate military.

The Confederacy also used slavery to its advantage as a propaganda tool. In 1861, Vice President Alexander Stephens argued that slavery would provide the foundation for the new, independent South. The institution of slavery served to unite white Southerners against the forces of abolitionism. Despite the problem of desertion within the Confederate army and angry cries of "rich man's war, poor man's fight," the vast majority of Southern white males of military age served in the Confederate military for a significant amount of time. Many complained about the daily miseries of army life, but they were convinced that their defeat would

CONCLUSION

mean the freeing of the slaves, which would let loose horrible forces on the white South. Even Confederates from non-slaveholding families had been raised in a proslavery environment—or at very least were antiabolitionist. Southern whites, regardless of their views of slavery as an institution, believed in the natural inferiority of blacks and the need for racial control.

Confederates, who thought they were fighting a second American Revolution, never believed that slavery would hurt them diplomatically. For them, what mattered most were events on the battlefield. In late 1862, Confederate generals and their armies—like Benedict Arnold and Horatio Gates before them—moved northward, trying to win their Saratoga. Beyond conquering more slave territory for the Rebellion, it was hoped that Bragg's invasion of Kentucky and Lee's foray into Maryland would spur Democratic antiwar feeling in the North and convince Europeans that the Confederacy was a viable military power.

Nor did the Union's numerical advantage assure victory. Had Lincoln not won reelection—which he believed was unlikely as late as August 1864—Confederates indeed might have won the war. Neither was it the case that the South failure to gain diplomatic recognition was a result of its slaveholding status. When the American Revolution began, all the colonies fighting the English had slaves. Even after the Revolution, none of the Southern states abolished slavery, and Northern slavery would survive well into the nineteenth century. When the Civil War began in 1861, it was not at all a certainty that slavery would be extinguished with the end of hostilities.

Confederates could have kept slavery longer by staying in the Union—or by accepting one of Lincoln's plans to emancipate the slaves gradually and with compensation. However, as David Potter has written, historians of the secession movement have suffered from being "too rational." The secessionists, Potter has noted, "were operating in an atmosphere of extreme excitement, in which gusts of emotion constantly swept the floor as well as the galleries."[2] Confederate troops were thus swept up in the excitement born of the South's reactionary political climate.

In the Jacksonian period, the South had expanded democracy for white males. But the South's political point of view—as expressed by John C. Calhoun, the Fire-Eaters, and proslavery Supreme Court justices—was always a defensive one. Unlike the case of the American Revolution, the Confederacy did not produce an ideology on a par with the principles of "life, liberty, and the pursuit of happiness." Theirs was a backward-looking revolution. World opinion was moving in the direction of liberating slaves, but the Confederacy was militantly opposed to any interference with its "institutions." Fears of tyranny and oppression at Lincoln's hand might seem irrational to us, but they were the product of an anti-abolitionist feeling that drove the South to a fever pitch.

Yet even after it became clear that the Confederacy would not conquer the border states, would not gain an alliance with Britain or France, and would not even be able to sustain the yeomen–planter unity that had been a hallmark of slavery, the Confederates kept fighting. Southern whites were convinced that their defeat and the ensuing emancipation of the slaves would unleash upon them everything they feared: black-on-white rape, the forced equality between the races, and the end of white political supremacy in the South. A man did not have to own slaves to realize that Northern victory would radically change the Southern social fabric. Yet, despite their anxieties about slave rebellion and resistance, Confederate troops continued to believe in the righteousness of slavery and the loyalty of most slaves to their white "families," not to mention the institution's economic rewards.

Despite the long odds they faced, Southerners fought hard against the better-equipped and supplied Yankees for four bloody years. At several points, the South even seemed to be winning the war. Those fighting in Virginia especially became skilled at crushing Northern hopes of subduing the rebellion. Lee's two invasions into Union territory gave Southerners the chance to bring the war to the enemy. The fact that Confederate soldiers captured black people while in Pennsylvania in 1863 shows that they were not content to take a defensive posture toward slavery.

The enlistment of thousands of African Americans into the Union army should have given Confederates cause for alarm. Black troops added 180,000 men to the Northern ranks, and "colored" units' desire to fight for their freedom proved to be a powerful motivator. But Confederates did not believe that blacks could make good soldiers. They had begun the war claiming, with hyperbole, that one Rebel could whip ten Yankees. In 1861, they might also have said—had blacks then been fighting—that one Confederate was worth any number of "Negro" soldiers. That turned out to be not true either. African Americans scored victories at Milliken's Bend, Fort Pocahontas, Mobile, and elsewhere. In contrast, the Confederates could claim victories against black forces at Battery Wagner, Plymouth, Fort Pillow, the Crater, and Saltville. Still, Confederates never acknowledged the importance African Americans played in bringing about their ultimate defeat.

When it came to enlisting blacks, Confederates found themselves in

CONCLUSION

a conundrum: the recruitment of African Americans became acceptable only as a last-ditch effort, but once the rebellion was in that last ditch, it lacked the ability to use blacks effectively as soldiers. Confederates were much more comfortable using "Negroes" as body servants and impressed laborers. To suggest that slaves might make good soldiers offended Southern white sensibilities. Eventually, the Confederacy passed a black enlistment bill that would not fundamentally undermine slavery. The bill would allow blacks who took up arms to gain their freedom, but it did not apply to their families. And because the Confederacy had abandoned conscription by that point, masters still controlled the fate of their chattels.

The black enlistment debate showed that racial control was as important to white Southerners as the Confederacy itself—in many ways, more so. After the war, Reconstruction would show that the former Rebels were as determined to keep blacks as subservient as they had been before the war. Once white Southerners felt that they had freed themselves from "Negro domination," many veterans, using the old proslavery rhetoric, defended the establishment of Jim Crow laws and other means of racial oppression. The window of opportunity for civil rights for the former slaves did not remain open long in the South. It was not until the civil rights movement of the mid-twentieth century—what C. Vann Woodward has called the nation's "Second Reconstruction"—that African Americans regained much of what they had lost after the "Redemption" of the South in the 1870s.

Slavery proved to be tenacious in the South, not because whites adhered to an unchanging and rigid view of human bondage, but because proslavery ideology—indeed, slavery itself—proved so malleable. Confederates were generous paternalists one minute, heartless family-separating capitalists the next. There were many types of masters, many types of slaves, and many ways in which the former sought to dominate the latter. It was slavery's flexibility that made the antebellum South so prosperous and allowed Confederate armies to remain in the field for four years. The Southern plantation was the engine of Southern prosperity. But the plantation myth has also created misguided notions about the Civil War era. Just as there were many Souths, there were many types of slavery—industrial and agricultural, rural and urban, plantation and small farm. Some masters bought slaves, others inherited them, while still others hired them and hired them out. The average slaveholder (who was not a planter) did not own the average slave (who lived on a plantation). Slavery was a staple of life in the Lowcountry and in the Upcountry, in the production of tobacco, of cotton, of wheat, of sugar, and of rice. The Confederates who defended slavery were defending it in all its different forms.

Despite the obvious importance of slavery to the Confederacy, postwar writings about the "War Between the States" quickly pushed race to the margins of Southern memory, or erased it entirely. "Republics have proverbially short memories," Frederick Douglass lamented before a Rochester audience shortly after Robert E. Lee's surrender. "Only the other day," he said to the cheering crowd, "it seemed as if this nation were in danger of losing a just appreciation of the awful crimes of this rebellion. We were manifesting almost as much gratitude to Gen. Lee for surrendering as to Gen. Grant for compelling him to surrender!" Douglass worried that Lee seemed to be "about the most popular man in America" despite the rebellion's legacy of "treason and slavery."[3] For Douglass, the North's adulation of Robert E. Lee betrayed the cause for which so many black and white Northerners had fought. He was not about to forget the bondage that he and millions of other African Americans had endured at the hands of Southern masters. But Douglass did not speak for all Americans. He certainly did not speak for the former Confederates. As David Blight has written, Robert E. Lee "represented one kind of soldier—those who simply wished to forget as much and as fast as possible, some for their personal peace, others because it served the political ends of reconciliation."[4]

Americans' proverbially short memories were apparent in Confederate veterans' writings about the war. Former soldiers were fond of saying that they had not fought for what one of them called the "narrow question of perpetuating negro slavery." Others agreed.[5] They claimed that slaveholders made up only a small minority of Southerners. And if most people never owned slaves, they reasoned, why would they have fought for such a right? One veteran quoted a man who said that only one of every eighty-nine Southerners had been of the master class. When it came to the Confederate army, others estimated that non-slaveholding soldiers represented up to two-thirds, or even four-fifths, of the total number of soldiers who fought.[6]

These veterans were correct in noting that most Southerners and indeed most Confederates soldiers were not slaveholders. But the low number of slaveholders in the Confederacy did not mean that most men did not have stake in its survival. This book has shown that the pro-slavery ideology was entrenched in the minds of Southern whites of all classes—privates and officers, planters as well as yeomen. After the war, the former Confederates declared that they had fought for friends, family,

CONCLUSION

and comrades—all of which seemed nobler and less provocative than having fought for the peculiar institution. If they spoke of having fought for states' rights or Southern independence, they often failed to acknowledge exactly whose "rights" they were fighting for or why independence was necessary.

To erase the defense of slavery from the Confederate mission made the defense of secession not only disingenuous, but absurd. Some former Confederates *did* argue that slavery had an important role in causing the war. The boosters of the Lost Cause mythology may have then muted their voices, but that did not mean that all Southerners dismissed slavery's importance in the Confederate cause. Richard Taylor said that slavery was a sticky subject that worked by "ingeniously attaching itself to exciting questions of the day." However sticky the subject, he believed it was not the most important one. What, then, of Alexander Stephens, who said the Confederacy's cornerstone rested on a foundation of slavery and white supremacy? Taylor thought Stephens was playing politics, seizing an opportunity early in the war to align himself with the proslavery interests. Taylor nevertheless included "property" among the "principles and rights" that led men to defend the Confederacy.[7] "Property" could include many things, but for Southerners, their most valuable possessions were their four million slaves, worth billions of dollars.

Other veterans also addressed slavery's importance to the Confederacy. George Washington Cable, the author of *Old Creole Days* and *The Silent South,* did not ignore the importance of race and race-mixing in Southern culture. Because of his openness in discussing miscegenation in southern Louisiana, he became an outcast, living his final years in Massachusetts. But despite his later, more liberal views, in 1861 Cable had believed in "Union, Slavery, and a White Man's Government." He eventually concluded that the war had wasted hundreds of thousands of lives, and despite his best efforts, he found constitutional or biblical arguments for keeping slavery unconvincing. Nevertheless, in 1861 he had enlisted to keep slavery intact, and even after the war, he expressed no love for the "multitudinous, unclean, stupid, ugly, ignorant, and insolent" former slaves.[8] Cable's conservatism weakened over time, but in 1861 he differed little from his Confederate comrades concerning the "proper" role of black people in the South.

The Georgian John B. Gordon understood that one could not discuss the Confederacy without addressing slavery and race. He was unapologetic about his support of slavery and white supremacy. After serving in the Army of Northern Virginia, Gordon became a member of the Ku

Klux Klan. He later served in the U.S. Senate, where he advocated fiscal conservatism and white supremacy in the post-Reconstruction South. He did not embrace the Lost Cause's view of the war's origins. "Slavery was undoubtedly the immediate fomenting cause of the woeful American conflict," he asserted, though he qualified his statement by saying that "slavery was far from being the sole cause."[9]

Col. William C. Oates, famous for his assault on Little Round Top at the Battle of Gettysburg, wrote that "disputation and contention about slavery in Congress and among the people was the provoking and immediate cause of secession and war!" Oates dismissed the idea that slavery was the reason most men had fought.[10] Yet Oates could not explain why it was that non-slaveholding soldiers would fight for a slaveholding republic. Perhaps the Virginia partisan Col. John Singleton Mosby had the answer. "It was perfectly logical to fight for slavery," he wrote in his memoirs, "if it was right to own slaves."[11] Mosby, a postwar Republican and United States diplomat, hated the Lost Cause culture with its reunions, speeches, and veterans' attempts to erase slavery from Civil War history. In 1907, Mosby responded to a speech by Judge George L. Christian of the United Confederate Veterans in which Christian denied that Southerners deserved the blame for slavery or the war. Mosby sarcastically wrote that Christian would have others believe that "the Virginia people were the abolitionists & the Northern people were pro-slavery," and he mocked Christian's attempts to argue that slavery was a "patriarchal" institution. So were polygamy and circumcision, Mosby quipped. Mosby was unapologetic about his Confederate past, but for reasons different from men like Christian. "A soldier fights for his country—right or wrong," Mosby wrote, and "he is not responsible for the political merits of the cause he fights in."[12]

Mosby's strong words about the slavery debate revealed that decades after Lee's surrender, Southerners still grappled with the war's legacy. Unfortunately, the idea that the Confederacy had not fought for slavery was kept alive from one generation to another. "These men, our fathers, fought not for personal advantage; not, as some historians avow, to preserve slavery," claimed the Sons of Confederate Veterans in 1923.[13] The Sons, in turn, passed down this myth to their sons. Many Americans still believe it.

NOTES

ABBREVIATIONS

DU   Duke University Special Collections, Durham, North Carolina

LSU   Hill Memorial Library, Louisiana State University, Baton Rouge

LVA   Library of Virginia, Richmond

MOC   Eleanor S. Brockenbrough Library, The Museum of the Confederacy, Richmond, Virginia

OR   U.S. War Department, *The War of the Rebellion: A Compilation of the Official Records of the Union and Confederate Armies*

SHC   Southern Historical Collection, University of North Carolina, Chapel Hill

UALR   UALR Center for Arkansas History and Culture, Arkansas Studies Institute, Little Rock

VHS   Virginia Historical Society, Richmond

INTRODUCTION

1. James Paul Verdery to sister, 31 July 1864, Eugene Verdery Papers, DU. Throughout, I quote soldiers as they wrote, only using "[sic]" when ambiguity threatens.

2. The previously accepted figure of 620,000 battle deaths has recently been challenged by historians (see Hacker, "A Census-Based Count of the Civil War Dead").

3. On guilt over slavery, see Hattaway, Jones, and Beringer, *Why the South Lost the Civil War*, 336–97.

4. Wiley, *The Life of Johnny Reb*, 10.

5. Glatthaar, "The 'New' Civil War History."

6. J. I. Robertson, *Soldiers Blue and Gray*, 9.

7. R. Mitchell, *Civil War Soldiers*, 4–5.

8. Roland, *Reflections on Lee*, 109–10.

9. McPherson, *For Cause and Comrades*, 91.

10. Power, *Lee's Miserables*, 302.

11. Berry, *All That Makes a Man*, 188.

12. Manning, *What This Cruel War Was Over*, 32 (first quotation); Phillips, *Diehard Rebels*, 4 (second quotation).

13. Glatthaar, *General Lee's Army,* 176; Sheehan-Dean, *Why Confederates Fought,* 34; Noe, *Reluctant Rebels,* 10. See also Laskin, "Good Old Rebels," 45–94.

14. Exceptions include Mohr, *On the Threshold of Freedom;* Levine, *Confederate Emancipation;* E. L. Jordan, *Black Confederates and Afro-Yankees in Civil War Virginia;* and Robinson, *Bitter Fruits of Bondage.*

15. Peter Coclanis once waggishly wrote that some historians employ a Woody Hayes–like methodology of "three anecdotes and a cloud of (documentary) dust" (Coclanis, "Thirty-Six Views of Mount Morgan," 360). Coclanis was referencing Woody Hayes, the legendary football coach at Ohio State University who once said that his coaching style involved "three yards and a cloud of dust."

16. McPherson, *For Cause and Comrades,* 110. Other Civil War historians have employed larger sample sizes. Joseph Glatthaar's research for *General Lee's Army* was based on the writings of 1,000 men; Aaron Sheehan-Dean's *Why Confederates Fought* used a sample size of 993; Elisabeth Laskin's "Good Old Rebels," 647; Chandra Manning's *What This Cruel War Was Over,* 477; and Kenneth Noe's *Reluctant Rebels,* 320.

17. See Escott, *"What Shall We Do with the Negro?"*

1. "THE QUESTION OF SLAVERY"

1. W. W. Freehling, *Prelude to Civil War;* Sinha, *The Counterrevolution of Slavery;* Ford, *Origins of Southern Radicalism.*

2. William Grimball to sister, 20 November 1860, John B. Grimball Papers, DU.

3. John L. Agurs to cousin, 24 December 1860, Eglantine Agours Letters, DU.

4. W. C. Davis, *Look Away!,* 55–84.

5. W. H. King, *No Pardons to Ask, Nor Apologies to Make,* 2.

6. Entry for 10 March 1861, in Mays, "Sketches from the Journal of a Confederate Soldier," 41.

7. Bonner, *Mastering America,* 233.

8. Glatthaar, *General Lee's Army,* 19–20; C. E. Brooks, "The Social and Cultural Dynamics of Soldiering in Hood's Texas Brigade."

9. Ferdinand Boesel to unknown recipient, 17 July 1862, in Jordan-Bychkov, Brannum, and Hood, "Boesel Letters," 465.

10. William Crow to brother and sister, 4 April 1861, in Crow, *When I Think of Home,* 8.

11. William H. Baxter to uncle, 17 April 1861, Thomas Baxter Papers, DU.

12. Janney, *Burying the Dead but Not the Past,* 206.

13. E. L. Jordan, *Black Confederates and Afro-Yankees in Civil War Virginia,* 5–23.

14. H. A. Wise, *Seven Decades of the Union,* 249–50 (quotation). On Wise's role in secession, see N. D. Lankford, *Cry Havoc!,* 50–51.

15. Henry Constantine Wayne to Jeb Stuart, 12 April 1861, James Ewell Brown Stuart Papers, VHS.

16. Entry for 2 February 1861, in Apperson, *Repairing the "March of Mars,"* 34.

17. Henry K. Ramsey to Mary Thomas Tyler, 7 February 1861, Louthan Family Papers, VHS.

18. John Preston Sheffey to Miss Josie, 23 March 1861, in Sheffey, *Soldier of Southwestern Virginia*, 15.

19. Charles Trueheart to sister, 1 March 1861, in Trueheart and Trueheart, *Rebel Brothers*, 21.

20. Carter McKim Louthan to Ella Brown Louthan, 13 November 1860 (first quotation); Carter to Ella, 21 January 1861 (second quotation); Carter to Ella, 17 April 1861 (third quotation); all in Louthan Family Papers, VHS.

21. Janney, *Burying the Dead but Not the Past*, 206.

22. John Pegram to Nancy, 22 March 1862, Confederate States of America: Archives, Army Miscellany, Prison Papers (Letters, Etc.), 1861–1865, DU; John R. Lowrey to mother, 28 April 1861, John Robert Lowrey Papers, SHC.

23. On the events of 1861, see Thompson, "An Address to the Citizens of the State of Missouri"; and for his views on Ruffin, see "Reminiscences of M. Jeff Thompson," M. Jeff Thompson Papers, SHC. On Ruffin, see Walther, *The Fire-Eaters*, 257.

24. Thompson, "Address to the Citizens of the State of Missouri," M. Jeff Thompson Papers, SHC.

25. D. E. Reynolds, *Texas Terror*; Mohr, *On the Threshold of Freedom*, 3–67.

26. Frank Voss to mother, 3 March 1861, in Schoeberlein and Brethauer, "Letters of a Maryland Confederate," 350.

27. W. D. Jordan, *Tumult and Silence at Second Creek*.

28. William H. Ker to sister, 27 October 1861 (first quotation), and William H. Ker to sister, 7 November 1861 (second quotation), John Ker and Family Papers, LSU.

29. Robinson, "In the Shadow of Old John Brown."

30. John David Workman to Mary C. Wright, 2 June 1861, Wright-Boyd Family Papers, LSU; J. Clark to cousin, 16 August 1861, Confederate States of America: Archives, Army Miscellany, Officers & Soldiers' Miscellany Letters, 1861, DU.

31. Charles Liebermann to Frances Lenora Davis Liebermann, 23 August 1861, Liebermann Family Papers, VHS.

32. Thomas [last name torn] to mother, 10 May 1861, Confederate States of America: Archives, Army Miscellany, Officers & Soldiers' Miscellany Letters, 1861, DU.

33. John J. Good to wife, 1 September 1861, in Good, *Cannon Smoke*, 63–64.

34. Faust, *James Henry Hammond and the Old South*; Woodward, Introduction to *Cannibals All!*

35. Fletcher, *Rebel Private Front and Rear*, 1–2, 153–54; R. E. Lee Jr., *Recollections and Letters of General Robert E. Lee*, 231.

36. Richard Maury to Beverly Munford, 1 June 1907, Beverly Bland Munford Papers, VHS.

37. Gibbons, *The Recollections of an Old Confederate Soldier*, 19–20.

38. Noll, *The Civil War as a Theological Crisis*, 33–36.

39. James Sinclair to John W. Ellis, 4 May 1861, in Ellis, *Papers*, 2:716.

40. Everett, *Chaplain Davis and Hood's Texas Brigade*, 55–56.

41. John Wightman to John C. Pemberton, 2 May 1862, *OR*, 1:14:489–90. Citations to the Official Records of the Union and Confederate Armies are notated by Series: Volume (part no. in parentheses, if applicable): and page number(s). Thus,

here, the notation indicates Series 1, Volume 14, and pages 489–90. Subsequent citations to the *OR* will follow this notation.

42. Elliott, "Extract from a Sermon Preached by Bishop Elliott" (microfilm), Troy E. Middleton Library, Louisiana State University, Baton Rouge.

43. William Cowper Nelson to mother, 29 October 1862, in W. C. Nelson, *The Hour of Our Nation's Agony*, 102.

44. Gibbons, *The Recollections of an Old Confederate Soldier*, 20. See also Johnston, "Civil War Reminiscences," 71.

45. Cater, *As It Was*, 173.

46. Huffman, *Ups and Downs of a Confederate Soldier*, 105.

47. Wood, *Doctor to the Front*, 173.

48. Edward Dorr Tracy to wife, 14 May 1861, Edward Dorr Tracy Letters, SHC.

49. T. H. Williams, *P. G. T. Beauregard*, 168.

50. J. J. Wilson to John N. Wilson, 6 August 1861, in R. G. Evans, *The 16th Mississippi Infantry*, 12.

51. *New York Times*, 19 August 1894, 21. Donald Bridgman Sanger's Longstreet biography cites this article but omits the part concerning the right to slavery (see Sanger, *James Longstreet*, 1:17).

52. The United States army had 950 staff and line officers in 1860, and 395 of them were from slaveholding states. Among Southerners, 213 joined the Confederate army. Despite some well-known examples of U.S. officers who went over to the Confederacy, such as Robert E. Lee and James Longstreet, the vast majority remained loyal to the Union (see Escott, *Military Necessity*, 3).

53. Longstreet's Proclamation, 17 June 1862, *OR*, 1:11(3):605–6 (emphasis added).

54. See Thomas Cobb to wife, 4 May 1861, in Cobb, "Extracts from Letters to His Wife," 287; Cater, *As It Was*, 58–60; and William Eustace Trahern, William Eustace Trahern Memoir, pp. 15–16, VHS.

55. Roderick McMillan to sister, 31 May 1861, Alexander McMillan Papers, DU.

56. C. B. Rouss, "To the Brave Soldiers of the South," Confederate States of America: Archives, Army Miscellany, Officers & Soldiers' Letters, 1861, DU. This piece originally appeared in the *Winchester (Va.) Times*, 5 July 1861.

57. Hundley, *Prison Echoes of the Great Rebellion*, 234–35.

58. Cobb, "Letter . . . to the People of Georgia," in Wakelyn, *Southern Pamphlets on Secession*, 92.

59. See William Grimball to sister, 20 November 1860, John B. Grimball Papers, DU; and entry for 31 December 1861, in Patterson, *Yankee Rebel*, 11.

60. On Republican ideology, see Foner, *Free Soil, Free Labor, Free Men*.

61. E. John Ellis to mother, 29 April 1862, E. P. Ellis and Family Papers, LSU. On white Southern fear of "isms," see Hobson, *Tell about the South*, 68.

62. A. P. Crawford, *Twilight at Monticello*, 102.

63. Entry for 25 May 1863, in Braudaway, "A Texan Records the Civil War Siege of Vicksburg, Mississippi," 110.

64. Henry Wise to wife, 3 November 1862, Henry Alexander Wise Papers, VHS (quotation). On interracial sex in the South, see Jordan, *White Man's Burden*, 69–86.

65. See J. G. Penn to mother, 11 August 1861, Green W. Penn Papers, DU; and Simon P. Wingard to Maria, 9 February 1862, Simon P. Wingard Papers, DU.

66. H. Montgomery, *Howell Cobb's Confederate Career,* 70.

67. McPherson, *Ordeal by Fire,* 2:356–57. Citing the historian Ella Lonn, McPherson notes that 9–10 percent of Rebel troops were foreign-born, in comparison with the 7.5 percent of Southern white males of military age who were foreign-born. In the Northern army, 26 percent of soldiers were foreign-born, compared with the 31 percent of foreign-born white males of military age in the Union states.

68. Jimerson, *The Private Civil War,* 127–28.

69. Houghton and Houghton, *Two Boys in the Civil War and After,* 191.

70. McCarthy, *Detailed Minutiae of Soldier Life,* 7.

71. See McWhiney and Jamieson, *Attack and Die;* and R. D. Watson, *Yeoman versus Cavalier.*

72. Alex Spence to "Dear Tommy," 11 May 1861, in Spence and Spence, *Getting Used to Being Shot At,* 6 (emphasis in original).

73. Augustus Henry Mathers to wife, 7 January 1862, in Doty, "The Civil War Letters of Augustus Henry Mathers," 113–14.

74. "Proclamation to the People of Central and North Missouri," 26 November 1861, *OR,* 1:8:697.

75. See Peter W. Hairston to "darling Fanny," 9 June 1861, in Trout, *With Pen and Saber,* 9; James Madison Brannock to wife, 16 April 1862, James Madison Brannock Papers, VHS; and James C. Bates to sister, 16 June 1862, in Bates, *A Texas Cavalry Officer's Civil War,* 133–34.

76. Ted Barclay to sister, 3 March 1862, in Barclay, *Ted Barclay,* 56–57.

77. Lafayette McLaws to wife, 16 November 1862, in McLaws, *A Soldier's General,* 159.

78. Isaac Hall to wife and children, 13 June 1862, in McGinty, Hall, and Hall, "The Human Side of War," 76.

79. Richard W. Simpson to aunt, 20 September 1861, in Simpson and Simpson, *"Far, Far From Home,"* 72.

80. See James Stubbs to brother, 16 November 1862, Jefferson Stubbs Family Papers, LSU.

81. Royster, *Revolutionary People at War,* 33.

82. The Virginia Fire-Eater Edmund Ruffin was one of them. He used his last diary entry to declare his hatred for the "Yankee race" (see entry for 18 June 1865, in Ruffin, *Diary,* 3:949).

83. Thomas Goree to Mary Frances Goree Kittrell, 18 February 1862, in Goree, *Longstreet's Aide,* 76. The complete sentence from Jefferson and Dickinson's document reads: "We will, in defiance of every hazard, with unabating firmness and perseverance, employ for the preservation of our liberties; being, with one mind, resolved to die freemen rather than live slaves."

84. Will to Elizabeth McKee, September 1861, in McKee, *Letters,* 32.

85. See Cobb, "Letter . . . to the People of Georgia," in Wakelyn, *Southern Pamphlets on Secession,* 89.

2. Planters and Yeomen, Officers and Privates

1. See Ambrose, "Yeomen Discontent in the Confederacy"; Smallwood, "Disaffection in Confederate Texas"; Bond, *Political Culture in the Nineteenth-Century*

South, 89; Escott, *After Secession,* 94–134; Hahn, *Roots of Southern Populism,* 86–133; Harris, *Plain Folk and Gentry in a Slave Society;* Kruman, *Parties and Politics in North Carolina,* 241–70; C. C. Bolton, *Poor Whites of the Antebellum South;* and Ash, "Poor Whites in the Occupied South," 59.

2. Gallagher, *The Confederate War,* 18.

3. See Cooper, *Liberty and Slavery;* and Thornton, *Politics and Power in a Slave Society,* xxi (quotation). See also Howe, *What Hath God Wrought.*

4. Wright, *Political Economy of the Cotton South,* 39 (quotation), 52–55; Harris, *Plain Folk and Gentry in a Slave Society,* 85; Fogel and Engerman, *Time on the Cross,* 250.

5. Fredrickson, *The Black Image in the White Mind,* 61.

6. Pessen, "The Egalitarian Myth and the American Social Reality," 989–1034.

7. See Wayne, "An Old South Morality Play," 842; M. Crawford, "Political Society in a Southern Mountain Community," 375; Shade, "Society and Politics in Antebellum Virginia's Southside," 6; and R. B. Campbell, "Planters and Plain Folk," 369–98.

8. Olsen, "Historians and the Extent of Slave Ownership in the Southern United States," 401–17.

9. McCurry, *Masters of Small Worlds,* 33, 242–43; Wetherington, *Plain Folk's Fight,* 47; Beringer, "A Profile of the Members of the Confederate Congress," 518–41.

10. McCurry, *Masters of Small Worlds,* 92–129, 112 (quotation).

11. Wetherington, *Plain Folk's Fight,* 2.

12. Frank, *With Ballot and Bayonet,* 3.

13. Diary entry for 2 August 1861, in Hubbs, *Voices from Company D,* 31.

14. Hundley, *Social Relations in Our Southern States,* 191–222.

15. Ibid., 200.

16. De Bow, "The Interest in Slavery of the Southern Non-Slaveholder," 171.

17. McCaslin, *Lee in the Shadow of Washington.* Lee spent most of his antebellum life in the army, but for several years in the 1850s he tried to improve his wife's Arlington plantation.

18. David Jackson Logan to wife, 21 June 1863, in D. J. Logan, "A Rising Star of Promise," 102.

19. Thomas Green to mother, 19 February 1865, Green W. Penn Papers, DU.

20. Rudolf C. Coreth to family, 13 November 1861, in Goyne, *Lone Star and Double Eagle,* 23.

21. Charles Liebermann to Frances Davis Lenora Liebermann, 11 December 1861 and 12 January 1862, Liebermann Family Papers, VHS.

22. D. P. Gibson to Mary B. Cotton, 6 June 1861, in Laurence, "Letters from a North Louisiana Tiger," 131.

23. See Wynne, *A Hard Trip,* 21; and Wallenstein, "Rich Man's War, Rich Man's Fight," 22–23.

24. See J. B. Paxton, "Fighting for Independence and Slavery."

25. Felix Guilford to parents, 10 January 1862, William Henry Tripp and Araminta Guilford Tripp Papers, SHC (first quotation); entry for late September 1863, in Cannon, *Inside of Rebeldom,* 142 (second quotation).

26. On a soldier's face being made as "black as a negro," see John J. Jefcoat to wife, 19 December 1862, John J. Jefcoat Correspondence, DU; on Confederates' lack of money, see U. G. Owen to wife, 16 July 1864, in E. L. Mitchell and U. G. Owen,

"Letters of a Confederate Surgeon," 171; on one soldier's lament that a comrade would steal a "quarter off" of "a dead nigger's eyes," see Grant Taylor to wife and children, 10 January 1864, in G. Taylor and M. J. S. Taylor, *This Cruel War,* 214; on a "rising" that made one man's lip swell "as thick as a Negroes," see E. P. Petty to wife, 26 October 1863, in Petty, *Journey to Pleasant Hill,* 271; and on battlefield corpses, see H. Montgomery, *Howell Cobb's Confederate Career,* 69.

27. James Michael Barr to wife, 30 December 1863, in Barr, *Let Us Meet in Heaven,* 171.

28. William Rufus Barlow to parents, 24 August 1862, William Rufus Barlow Letters, MOC.

29. Alford Smith to mother, 1 September 1862, Confederate States of America: Archives, Army Miscellany, Officers & Soldiers' Miscellany Letters, 1861, DU (first quotation); Ira Yeldell Traweek to Minerva Direnda Traweek Loomis, 1 February 1863, Minerva Direnda Traweek Loomis Papers, VHS (second quotation). See also J. H. Stone to wife, 3 November 1862, Baughn Family Collection, MOC.

30. Frank L. Richardson to father, 4 September 1861, Frank Liddell Richardson Papers, SHC.

31. Frank L. Richardson to mother, 8 October 1862, ibid.

32. Frank L. Richardson to Bethia C. Richardson, 6 August 1864 , ibid.

33. John Barrett Pendleton to wife, 22 May 1861, Pendleton Family Papers, VHS.

34. S. B. Gulledge to mother, 18 June 1861, in Pettigrew, *Letters to Lauretta,* 161.

35. Miller W. Francis to mother, 31 August 1861, in Pate, *When This Evil War Is Over,* 47.

36. See Edwin H. Fay to wife, 2 August 1862, in Fay and Fay, *"This Infernal War,"* 127; and Thomas R. Lightfoot to cousin, 29 May 1861, in Burnett, "Letters of Three Lightfoot Brothers," 389.

37. Clement Anselm Evans to wife, 29 November 1861, in C. A. Evans, *Intrepid Warrior,* 93.

38. See Edwin H. Fay to wife, 5 May 1862, in Fay and Fay, *"This Infernal War,"* 45.

39. Entry for 17 November 1861, William T. Kinzer Diary, VHS.

40. See Entry for 30 October 1861, in Silver, "Robert A. Moore," 289–90.

41. Entries for 1 August 1861 and 18 August 1861, in Hubbs, *Voices from Company D,* 30, 36.

42. Charles Batchelor to Albert Batchelor, August 1861, Albert A. Batchelor Papers, LSU.

43. William T. Casey to mother, 5 June 1862, William Thomas Casey Papers, VHS.

44. Smith, *The Anson Guards,* 195; Edwin H. Fay to wife, 21 April 1862, in Fay and Fay, *"This Infernal War,"* 39 (quotation).

45. Allen and Bohannon, *Campaigning with "Old Stonewall,"* 20.

46. Weitz, "Drill, Training, and the Combat Performance of the Civil War Soldier."

47. Entry for 23 July 1861, in Hubbs, *Voices from Company D,* 24.

48. Watkins, *Company Aytch,* 33–34. In August 1862, the Confederate army banned flogging, but shooting remained the preferred method of execution for desertion and other serious crimes.

49. Entry for 24 September 1861, in Hubbs, *Voices from Company D,* 52.

50. Entry for 30 January 1862, in R. Watson, *Southern Service on Land & Sea,* 21.

51. John S. Foster to sister, 19 August 1861, James Foster Family Correspondence, LSU.

52. Thomas, *The Confederate Nation,* 153.

53. Charles Liebermann to Frances Lenora Davis Liebermann, 25 April 1862, Liebermann Family Papers, VHS.

54. Joseph E. Brown to Howell Cobb, 8 May 1862, in Gienapp, *The Civil War and Reconstruction,* 131.

55. Augustus Pitt Adamson to sister, 22 June 1862, in Abell and Gecik, *Sojourns of a Patriot,* 74.

56. See A. B. Moore, *Conscription and Conflict in the Confederacy;* Tatum, *Disloyalty in the Confederacy;* and Robinson, *Bitter Fruits of Bondage.*

57. Entry for 19 April 1862, G. H. Tichenor Diaries, LSU.

58. James L. Reid to wife, 7 March 1862, James L. Reid Letters, DU (first quotation); Ras Stirman to sister, 16 May 1862, in Carr, *In Fine Spirits,* 39 (second quotation); E. John Ellis to sister, 29 July 1862 (third quotation), E. P. Ellis and Family Papers, LSU.

59. Lewis Warlick to Cornelia McGrimsey, 3 June 1862, in McGrimsey and Warlick, *My Dearest Friend,* 87.

60. See Wyatt-Brown, *Honor and Violence in the Old South;* and Wyatt-Brown, *The Shaping of Southern Culture,* 203–54.

61. Peter Dekle to wife, 16 May 1862 (first and second quotations), and Dekle to wife, 16 July 1862 (third quotation), in Mahon, "Peter Dekle's Letters," 12–14.

62. William H. Tripp to wife, 12 May 1862, William H. Tripp and Araminta Guilford Tripp Papers, SHC.

63. See Richard C. Gatlin to Lawrence Branch, 18 February 1862, *OR,* 1:51(2): 474–75.

64. John G. Shorter to Jefferson Davis, 22 October 1862, *OR,* 1:52(2):380.

65. See Weitz, *Higher Duty,* 159; and R. B. Todd to John L. Lewis, 10 March 1862, *OR,* 1:6:851–52.

66. William J. Houston to John W. Ellis, 5 May 1861, in Ellis, *Papers,* 2:720.

67. Roderick McMillan to sister, 12 June 1861, Alexander McMillan Papers, DU.

68. Robinson, *Bitter Fruits of Bondage,* 38–57.

69. See Weitz, *More Damning than Slaughter,* esp. 86–116.

70. *Atlanta Southern Confederacy,* 30 October 1862, in Gienapp, *The Civil War and Reconstruction,* 133–34. Most newspapers supported the "Twenty Slave Law" (see Silver, "Propaganda in the Confederacy," 502).

71. Heber Bennett to wife, 23 October 1862, Bennett Family Papers, LSU.

72. John A. Harris to "Dear Becky and children," 14 February 1863, John Achilles Harris Letters, LSU.

73. Arthur W. Hyatt Papers, vol. 3: 1865–1895, LSU.

74. D. H. Hill's General Orders No. 8, Department of North Carolina, 24 April 1863, *OR,* 1:51(2):694.

75. Daniel Ruggles to B. S. Ewell, 10 August 1863, *OR,* 1:24(3):1053.

76. See Caleb Bond Hobson to Nathan B. Dozier, 12 December 1863, in W. H. A. Speer, *Voices from Cemetery Hill,* 182.

77. Scarborough, *The Overseer,* 10, 139–40.
78. Watkins, *Company Aytch,* 31–33.
79. Sheehan-Dean, *Why Confederates Fought,* 3.
80. Pope Barrow to father, 9 October 1862, in Coulter, *Lost Generation,* 78.
81. William H. Grimball to father, 1 October 1863, John B. Grimball Papers, DU.
82. David Jackson Logan to the *Yorkville Enquirer,* 12 November 1863, in D. J. Logan, *"A Rising Star of Promise,"* 127.
83. See Marrs, "Desertion and Loyalty in the South Carolina Infantry"; and Gallagher, *The Confederate War,* 32.
84. See Dotson, "'Grave and Scandalous Evil Infected to Your People,'" 393.
85. Van Buskirk, *Rebel at Large,* 87.
86. Walker, *Great Things Are Expected of Us,* xv.
87. Bevier, *History of the First and Second Missouri Confederate Brigades,* 294.
88. Entry for 19 September 1863, in W. R. Montgomery, *Georgia Sharpshooter,* 26.
89. James Stubbs to sister, 29 June 1862, Jefferson Stubbs Family Papers, LSU.
90. Sacher, "The Loyal Draft Dodger?"
91. Joseph T. Scott to the *Daily Columbus (Ga.) Enquirer,* 31 December 1863, in A. W. Jones, "A Georgia Confederate Soldier Visits Montgomery, Alabama," 112.
92. See Thomas, *The Confederate Nation,* 260–61; W. C. Davis, *Look Away!,* 238; and A. B. Moore, *Conscription and Conflict in the Confederacy,* 308.
93. Contrary to the Lost Cause notion that Lee had far fewer men than usual at the start of the 1865 campaign season, William Marvel makes the case that postwar Confederates drastically undercounted Lee's forces by March 1865 (see Marvel, *Lee's Last Retreat,* 201–6).

3. THE GREATEST OF MASTERS

1. Majewski, *Modernizing a Slave Economy,* 146.
2. R. Taylor, *Destruction and Reconstruction,* 147.
3. Marshall, *An Aide-De-Camp of Lee,* 65.
4. *Montgomery Advertiser,* 6 November 1861, in Gienapp, *The Civil War and Reconstruction,* 197. On the relative size of Confederate armies, see McPherson, *Ordeal by Fire,* 2:190.
5. See Mohr, *On the Threshold of Freedom,* 120–89.
6. Ayers, *In the Presence of Mine Enemies,* 371.
7. E. John Ellis to mother, 11 March 1862, E. P. Ellis and Family Papers, LSU.
8. James M. Holloway to wife, 9 April 1863, James M. Holloway Papers, VHS.
9. See Martinez, "For the Defense of the State"; Spraggins, "Mobilization of Negro Labor"; Quarles, *The Negro in the Civil War,* 272–76; W. C. Davis, *Look Away!,* 149–50; Thomas, *The Confederate Nation,* 236; B. H. Nelson, "Confederate Slave Impressment Legislation"; Trexler, "Opposition of Planters"; Brewer, *The Confederate Negro;* Wiley, *The Life of Johnny Reb,* 328–29; and Wiley, *Southern Negroes,* 110–33.
10. Berlin et al., *The Destruction of Slavery,* 664.
11. See Scarborough, *Masters of the Big House,* 337. For a contrary opinion, see Lebergott, "Why the South Lost."
12. Entry for 16 June 1862, in Chesnut, *A Diary from Dixie,* 252.
13. See Osthaus, "The Work Ethic of the Plain Folk."

14. Entry for 8 July 1863, in Green, *Johnny Green of the Orphan Brigade*, 80.

15. Robert H. Miller to William Miller, 26 June 1861, Robert H. Miller Letters, 1861, LSU.

16. Stone, *Wandering to Glory*, 163.

17. Report of P. G. T. Beauregard, 24 September 1862, *OR*, 1:14:612; A. D. Banks to Joseph E. Johnston, 5 May 1863, *OR*, 1:23(2):817; William A. Tesh to father, 23 May 1862, William A. Tesh Letters, DU; Corsan, *Two Months in the Confederate States*, 77.

18. Diary entry for 19 January 1861, in Lane, *The Times that Prove People's Principles*, 16.

19. Roderick McMillan to brother, 25 April 1861, Alexander McMillan Papers, DU.

20. William H. Grimball to father, 27 January 1862, John B. Grimball Papers, DU.

21. Jeremy Francis Gilmer to W. W. Mackall, 7 December 1861, *OR*, 1:52(2):233; Jeremy Francis Gilmer to Isham Harris, 11 December 1861, *OR*, 1:7:757.

22. Isham Harris to Albert Sidney Johnston, 31 December 1861, *OR*, 1:7:811.

23. John Magruder to R. S. Garnett, 25 May 1861, *OR*, 1:2:878.

24. G. B. Cosby to Charles A. Crump, 28 July 1861, *OR*, 1:2:1007.

25. John Lee Holt to wife, 29 August 1861, in J. L. Holt, *I Wrote You Word*, 12.

26. John B. Magruder to Samuel Cooper, 30 January 1862, *OR*, 1:51(2):457.

27. R. H. Chilton to John B. Magruder, 15 February 1862, *OR*, 1:51(2):472–73.

28. John Tyler and Hill Carter to James Seddon, 26 August 1861, *OR*, 1:4:636.

29. Entry for 19 November 1862, James Calvin Marcom Diary, DU.

30. John B. Magruder to Robert E. Lee, 8 April 1862, *OR*, 1:11(3):430–31; D. H. Hill to Joseph E. Johnston, 26 April 1862, *OR*, 1:11(3):465.

31. John C. Pemberton to Isaac Hayne, 22 March 1862, *OR*, 1:6:415–16.

32. Augustus P. Adamson to parents, 14 April 1862, in Abell and Gecik, *Sojourns of a Patriot*, 45.

33. W. R. Boggs to J. R. Waddy, 29 May 1862, *OR*, 1:14:546 (quotation); J. R. Waddy to Hugh Mercer, 11 June 1862, *OR*, 1:14:557; John C. Pemberton to Alfred Holt Colquitt, 14 June 1862, *OR*, 1:14:565; John C. Pemberton to James Chesnut, 26 July 1862, *OR*, 1:14:589.

34. Entry for 9 June 1862, in Chesnut, *The Private Mary Chesnut*, 373.

35. William T. Withers to John Perkins et al., 28 February 1862, *OR*, 1:52(2):278–79.

36. H. Montgomery, *Howell Cobb's Confederate Career*, 65.

37. Howell Cobb to G. W. Randolph, 5 August 1862, *OR*, 4:2:35.

38. P. G. T. Beauregard to D. B. Harris, 21 April 1862, *OR*, 1:10(2):430–31.

39. Special Orders 65, issued 6 October 1862, in Bailey, *In the Saddle with the Texans*, 59.

40. Entry for 10 August 1862, in Edmondston, *Journal of a Secesh Lady*, 233.

41. Francis Gilmer to James Seddon, 9 February 1863, *OR*, 1:51(2):679.

42. Entry for 19 August 1862, in Lane, *The Times that Prove People's Principles*, 68. On a Georgia slaveholder's complaint, see Joseph M. White to George Randolph, 8 September 1862, in Berlin et al., *The Destruction of Slavery*, 699–700.

43. P. G. T. Beauregard to Francis W. Pickens, 8 November 1862, *OR,* 1:14:672.
44. Circular issued by Thomas Jordan, 17 February 1863, *OR,* 1:14:782.
45. Leonidas L. Polk to Zebulon Vance, 23 March 1863, in Vance, *Papers,* 2:95.
46. Gustavus Smith to Robert E. Lee, 26 November 1862, *OR,* 1:18:787. Smith was prone to complaining. Robert E. Lee finally relieved him of command in June 1862 for bickering with Jefferson Davis, and Smith resigned in February 1863 because he felt other commanders were unfairly promoted ahead of him. Nevertheless, he later served in Georgia.
47. Gideon Pillow to Planters of Lauderdale, Lawrence, and Franklin Counties, 6 March 1863, *OR,* 4:2:421.
48. Francis Pickens to P. G. T. Beauregard, 5 November 1862, *OR,* 1:14:667–68.
49. P. G. T. Beauregard to Hugh Mercer, 24 March 1863, *OR,* 1:14:842.
50. See Berlin, *Slaves without Masters;* and Ely, *Israel on the Appomattox.*
51. See E. R. Ingram, *In View of the Great Want of Labor,* v–vii.
52. Robert E. Lee to James Seddon, 25 March 1863, *OR,* 1:25(2):683–84.
53. E. R. Ingram, *In View of the Great Want of Labor,* vii.
54. Francis Parker to William P. Miles, 23 November 1863, *OR,* 4:2:978–79.
55. Statement of C. L. Goodwin, 31 March 1863, William Massie Papers, DU.
56. T. N. Waul to John C. Pemberton, 27 April 1863, *OR,* 1:24(3):795–96.
57. L. H. Minor to Secretary G. W. Randolph, 2 May 1862, in Berlin et al., *The Destruction of Slavery,* 698–99.
58. James H. Evans Petition, 1865, James H. Evans Papers, VHS.
59. Rachel Jefcoat to John J. Jefcoat, 3 June 1862, John J. Jefcoat Correspondence, DU.
60. William H. Echols to D. B. Harris, 11 June 1863, *OR,* 1:14:972.
61. Charles H. Dimmock to Henry T. Clark, 19 September 1861, in Yearns and Barrett, *North Carolina Civil War Documentary,* 253–54.
62. Caleb G. Forshey to Lemuel Conner, 27 November 1863, Lemuel Parker Conner Family Papers, LSU.
63. D. B. Harris to Thomas Jordan, 11 June 1863, *OR,* 1:14:971–72.
64. David Harris to Thomas Jordan, 5 December 1863, *OR,* 1:28(2):533–34.
65. Hugh Mercer to James Seddon, 21 July 1863, *OR,* 1:28(2):215–16.
66. William Alexander Smith to Zebulon Vance, 3 January 1863, in Vance, *Papers,* 2:4.
67. James Seddon to Zebulon Vance, 4 February 1863, *OR,* 4:2:385–86; Zebulon Vance to James Seddon, 12 February 1863, *OR,* 4:2:393–94.
68. Zebulon Vance to James Seddon, 28 April 1863, *OR,* 1:18:1027–28; Zebulon Vance to William Whiting, 26 May 1863, in Vance, *Papers,* 2:174–75; William Whiting to D. H. Hill, 8 June 1863, *OR,* 1:27(3):870.
69. William H. Baxter to Matilda, 5 August 1862, Thomas Baxter Papers, DU.
70. H. E. Merritt to father, 20 November 1862, William H. E. Merritt Papers, DU.
71. Giles Underhill to Verey[?], 8 December 1862, Ranson Lee Papers, DU; Inscoe and McKinney, *The Heart of Confederate Appalachia,* 209.
72. V. Sulakowski to Edmund P. Turner, 30 April 1863, *OR,* 1:15:1063–64.
73. David Jackson Logan to wife, 26 November 1863, in D. J. Logan, *"A Rising Star of Promise,"* 130.

74. Charles Russell to H. C. McNeill, 4 May 1863, *OR*, 1:15:1072.

75. W. C. Bibb to James Seddon, 23 July 1863, in Berlin et al., *The Destruction of Slavery*, 704–05.

76. Entry for 22 August 1863, William Gordon McCabe Diary, McCabe Family Papers, VHS. I was able to review this document through the courtesy of the Society of the Cincinnati in the State of Virginia and the Society of the Cincinnati in the State of Georgia.

77. Entry for 6 July 1863, James C. Marcom Diary, DU.

78. A. P. Hayne to Jefferson Davis, 8 August 1863, in Berlin et al., *The Destruction of Slavery*, 695–96.

79. Jonathan Watson to Samuel Cooper, 4 August 1863, *OR*, 1:24(3):1044.

80. William Neblett to wife, 5 October 1863, in Neblett, *A Rebel Wife in Texas*, 163.

81. Samuel W. Melton to James Seddon, 11 November 1863, *OR*, 4:2:946.

82. James Bates to sister, 16 July 1864 [includes entry for 22 July], in Bates, *A Texas Cavalry Officer's Civil War*, 310.

83. See J. Y. Dashiell to John B. Magruder, 4 June 1863, *OR*, 1:26(2):36.

84. S. S. Anderson to John B. Magruder, 26 June 1863, *OR*, 1:26(2):85–86.

85. Stephen Yancey ["By order of Maj. Gen. J. Bankhead Magruder"] to the "Planters of Texas," 4 July 1863, *OR*, 1:26(2):103.

86. A. G. Dickinson to John B. Cary, 6 April 1897 (quotation), Cary Family Papers, VHS; Edmund P. Turner to W. R. Scurry, 29 July 1863, *OR*, 1:26(2):125–26; S. Hart's Indorsement, 4 August 1863, *OR*, 1:26(2):155; John B. Magruder to W. R. Boggs, 1 September 1863, *OR*, 1:26(2):195–96.

87. Entry for 16 August 1863, in Kean, *Inside the Confederate Government*, 96.

88. Kirby Smith to Richard Taylor, 10 September 1863, *OR*, 1:26(2):216–18.

89. Magruder's Indorsement No. 2, 9 October 1863, *OR*, 1:26(2):269.

90. General Orders No. 138, 24 October 1863, *OR*, 4:2:897–98.

91. William H. Grimball to father, 3 January 1863, John B. Grimball Papers, DU.

92. Rudolf C. Coreth to family, 9 December 1863, in Goyne, *Lone Star and Double Eagle*, 113.

93. Von Sheliha to Thomas H. Watts, 13 December 1863, *OR*, 1:26(2):501–4.

94. Parrish, *Richard Taylor*, 254–55; Richard Taylor to John G. Walker, 3 February 1864, *OR*, 1:34(2):939 (quotation). The story of the trans-Mississippi region largely is the story of officers in disagreement over grand strategy (see Parrish, *Richard Taylor*, 287).

95. William Smith to citizens of Lunenburg, 16 February 1864, Local Government Records Collection, Lunenburg County Court Records, LVA.

96. James H. Beard to wife, 2 April 1864, in Joiner, *Little to Eat and Thin Mud to Drink*, 130; Alfred C. Weeks to James A. Peebles, 7 May 1864, Hunter Family Papers, VHS.

97. Leonidas Polk to Thomas McKinney Jack, 28 January 1864, *OR*, 1:32(2):629; Leonidas Polk to Thomas Hill Watts, 28 January 1864, *OR*, 1:32(2):629–30.

98. Escott, *After Secession*, 207.

99. Charles Anderson to James Chalmers, 4 August 1864, *OR*, 1:39(2):752–53; James Chalmers to H. C. Davis, 5 August 1864, *OR*, 1:39(2):757.

100. Benjamin Farinholt to the citizens of Charlotte and Halifax, 4 July 1864, in Wessells, *In Bold Measure*, 92–93.

101. Entry for 7 May 1864, in S. T. Foster, *One of Cleburne's Command,* 71; Nisbet, *Four Years on the Firing Line,* 169; Eugene Verdery to sister, 4 July 1864, Eugene Verdery Papers, DU.

102. Report of P. G. T. Beauregard, 18 September 1864, *OR,* 1:28(1):70.

103. Sam Jones to R. S. Ripley, 23 June 1864, *OR,* 1:35(2):537; Sam Jones to M. L. Bonham, 29 June 1864, *OR,* 1:35(2):542–43 (quotation).

104. Robert E. Lee to Jefferson Davis, 2 September 1864, *OR,* 1:42(2):1228 (quotation); Robert E. Lee to James Seddon, 17 September 1864, *OR,* 1:42(2):1256; Robert E. Lee to James Seddon, 20 September 1864, *OR,* 1:42(2):1260–61; Special Orders No. 224, 21 September 1864, *OR,* 1:42(2):1268.

105. James Seddon to Robert E. Lee, 22 September 1864, *OR,* 1:42(2):1269 (first quotation); Robert E. Lee to James Seddon, 4 October 1864, *OR,* 1:42(3):1134 (second quotation); James Seddon to Robert E. Lee, 5 October 1864, *OR,* 1:42(3):1135.

106. Robert E. Lee to James Seddon, 11 December 1864, *OR,* 1:42.3:1267; James Longstreet to Robert E. Lee, 27 December 1864, *OR,* 1:42(3):1324.

107. Nathan Bedford Forrest to Richard Taylor, 12 October 1864, *OR,* 1:39(3): 815–17.

108. John B. Magruder to Robert Johnson, 5 November 1864, *OR,* 1:41(4):1030.

109. Circular No. 3 by Richard D. Screven, office commandant for Mississippi, 17 February 1865, *OR,* 1:49(1):1019.

110. General Orders No. 99, 3 March 1865, *OR,* 1:49(1):1025.

111. Samuel Lockett to E. Surget, 13 March 1865, *OR,* 1:49(1):1055; R. L. Gibson to Dabney Maury, 5 April, 1865, *OR,* 1:49(2):1204.

4. "SEND ME THE NEGRO BOY"

1. Scott, *Lee and Jackson's Bloody Twelfth,* xx; Faust, *This Republic of Suffering,* 90.

2. Glatthaar, *General Lee's Army,* 304.

3. Ruffin Thomson to father, 20 June 1862, Ruffin Thomson Papers, SHC.

4. Eugene Verdery to sister, 2 April 1863, Eugene Verdery Papers, DU; Alex Spence to sister, 7 March 1864, in Spence and Spence, *Getting Used to Being Shot At,* 92.

5. S. A. M. to son, August 1861, Confederate States of America: Archives, Army Miscellany, Officers and Soldiers' Letters, 1861, DU (quotation). On one slave's enthusiasm for the cause, see Tally Simpson to sister, 12 October 1861, in Simpson and Simpson, *"Far, Far from Home,"* 76.

6. On coffee, see Edward Burruss to sisters, 29 December 1862, John C. Burruss Family Papers, LSU; on biscuits, see S. F. Tenney to Miss Alice, 18 January 1862, in Duffee "War Letters of S. F. Tenney," 279; on a dry blanket, see James Griffith to wife, 13 April 1862, in McArthur and Burton, *"A Gentleman and an Officer,"* 196.

7. William H. Grimball to father, 27 September 1862, John B. Grimball Papers, DU.

8. Robert W. Banks to sister, 12 October 1862, in Osborn, "The Civil War Letters of Robert W. Banks," 147.

9. See E. L. Jordan, *Black Confederates and Afro-Yankees in Civil War Virginia,* 185–200; Wiley, *Southern Negroes,* 134–45.

10. R. Taylor, *Destruction and Reconstruction*, 68–69.

11. Harry Lewis to mother, 15 November 1863, Harry Lewis Letters, SHC.

12. See Charles M. Watts to Dr. Morris, 19 October 1864, Moore Family Papers, VHS; William G. Morton to sister, 26 December 1862, William Goodridge Morton Papers, VHS.

13. James Jackson Davis to wife, 7 August 1862, James Jackson Davis Papers, DU; W. B. G. Andrews to father, 20 December 1864, William B. G. Andrews Papers, DU; William A. Penn to mother, 27 October 1864, Alexander McMillan Papers, DU.

14. See Martin, *Divided Mastery;* and Dew, *Bond of Iron.*

15. On paying a slave for sending off a letter, see Frank Adams to mother, n.d., Israel Adams Family Papers, LSU; on selling apples, see Paca, "'Tim's Black Book,'" 457; on a wakeup call, see entry for 12 May 1863, in Trout, *With Pen and Saber,* 201–2; on a barbershop, see F. E. Daniel, *Recollections of a Rebel Surgeon,* 131.

16. Little and Maxwell, *A History of Lumsden's Battery,* 60–61.

17. George Briggs to unknown, 17 June 1862, George Briggs Papers, DU.

18. Thomas Toon to brother, 4 December 1862, Thomas Toon Letter, DU.

19. Joseph Shields to mother, 15 February 1863, Joseph D. Shields Papers, LSU (first quotation); Theophilus to Harriet Perry, 23 May 1863, in Perry and Perry, *Widows by the Thousand,* 134 (second quotation).

20. See McArthur and Burton, "*A Gentleman and an Officer,*" 29; Albert B. Fall to mother, 6 January 1862, "Civil War Letters of Albert B. Fall," 156.

21. James Stubbs to sister, 28 October 1862, Jefferson Stubbs Family Papers, LSU.

22. Entry for 1 October 1861, in Silver, "Robert A. Moore," 279.

23. R. Taylor, *Destruction and Reconstruction,* 68. On foragers, see also Baylor, "The Army Negro."

24. Edwin H. Fay to wife, 27 May 1862 and 5 February 1865, in Fay and Fay, "*This Infernal War,*" 63, 422; entry for 31 May 1862, in "Diary of Reverend J. G. Law," 25; Quince Stanford to brother, 19 August 1862, in Mathis, *In the Land of the Living,* 31; Spencer Glasgow Welch to wife, 1 September 1863, in Welch, *A Confederate Surgeon's Letters to His Wife,* 76–77.

25. See S. R. Nelson and C. Sheriff, *A People at War,* 131.

26. Powell, "War Tales," p. 33, Charles S. Powell Memoirs, DU.

27. Tally Simpson to sister, 24 September 1862, in Simpson and Simpson, "*Far, Far from Home,*" 146–47. On theft in the Confederate army, see Glatthaar, *General Lee's Army,* 176–80.

28. Entry for 15 January 1862, Robert A. Means Diary, Ferneyhough Family Papers, VHS.

29. Silas, *Civil War Reminiscences,* 79.

30. On Washington's slaves, see P. D. Morgan, *Slave Counterpoint,* 356; on slaves stealing horses and sweetcakes, see Robert W. Parker to wife, 22 January 1862 and 19 January 1864, in R. W. Parker, *Lee's Last Casualty,* 62, 128; on slave beating, see also entry for 13 May 1863, in Fremantle, *Diary,* 74.

31. James L. Reid to wife, 30 [August?] 1861, James L. Reid Papers, DU.

32. General Orders No. 28, issued 4 March 1864, *OR,* 4.3:186; R. S. Ewell et al., to Gen. S. Cooper, 19 March 1864, in Ramseur, *Bravest of the Brave,* 204–5.

33. Stephen Dodson Ramseur to sister, 17 October 1853, in Ramseur, *Bravest of the Brave,* 10; Ramseur to "Dear Dave," 8 November 1856, ibid., 43; Ramseur to brother, 28 January 1864, ibid., 196; William A. Graham Jr. to father, 26 April 1864, in W. A. Graham, *Papers,* 6:77. See also Clayton Coleman to wife, 7 April 1864, Clayton Coleman Letters, MOC.

34. Wallace Comer to mother, 20 May 1864, Comer Family Papers, SHC.

35. See, e.g., Chapman, *Ten Months in the "Orphan Brigade,"* 65; and J. W. Jones, "Reminiscences of the Army of Northern Virginia," 86.

36. William B. G. Andrews to family, 11 September 1864, William B. G. Andrews Papers, DU.

37. Lewis Grimball to father, 1 October 1863, and William Grimball to father, 2 April 1863, John B. Grimball Papers, DU.

38. James Francis Preston to Charles [otherwise unidentified], 28 August 1861, James Francis Preston Letter, LVA.

39. James L. Reid to wife, 31 December 1861, James L. Reid Letters, DU. On the ubiquity of slave hiring, see Martin, *Divided Mastery,* 8.

40. Caleb S. McCurdy to brother, 6 March 1863, and to J. M. McCurdy, 20 December 1863, Caleb S. McCurdy Papers, DU.

41. W. A. Jefcoat to John J. Jefcoat, 4 January 1864, John J. Jefcoat Correspondence, DU (first quotation); William D. Smith to Bettie Smith, 28 August 1864, William D. Smith Papers, DU (second quotation).

42. Lewis Warlick to Cornelia McGimsey, 13 September 1864, in McGimsey and Warlick, *My Dearest Friend,* 181.

43. Edwin A. Penick to wife, 16 March 1862, Edwin Anderson Penick Papers, VHS; Alfred J. Flournoy Jr. to wife, 22 May 1861, Alfred Flournoy Family Papers, LSU (quotation). On sending "love," see also John Fain to mother, 16 August 1861, Archibald E. Henderson Papers, DU; and William Cocke to parents, 20 May 1862, Cocke Family Papers, VHS.

44. Ruffin H. Thomson to father, 4 December 1862, Ruffin Thomson Papers, SHC.

45. Von Borcke, *Memoirs of the Confederate War for Independence,* 2:188.

46. G. S. West to William S. Carter, 17 December 1862, William S. Carter Papers, DU.

47. Charles C. Jones Jr. to Rev. George Howe, 19 March 1863, in C. C. Jones, *The Children of Pride,* 359; Faust, *James Henry Hammond and the Old South,* 378.

48. Boykin, *A Memorial Volume of the Hon. Howell Cobb of Georgia,* 47.

49. Kolchin, *American Slavery,* 126.

50. Fred Fleet to father, 20 February 1863, in Fleet, *Green Mount,* 207.

51. Jerome B. Yates to Mrs. Obedience Yates and Marie Yates Swanson, 14 August 1863, in R. G. Evans, *The 16th Mississippi Infantry,* 194; James Ward Stuart to Laura Stuart, 13 April 1864, in C. C. Reynolds, *Letters to Laura,* 27.

52. John R. Lowrey to mother, 22 July 1862, John Robert Lowrey Papers, SHC; John Lane Stuart to mother, 29 August 1862, John Lane Stuart Papers, DU.

53. Guil [otherwise unidentified] to mother, 29 August 1862, Confederate States of America: Archives, Army Miscellany, Officers and Soldiers Miscellany Letters, 1861, DU.

54. William Dorsey Pender to wife, 25 September 1862, in Pender, *The General to His Lady,* 177.

55. William Nelson to wife, 24 November 1862, William T. Nelson Papers, VHS.

56. Grant Taylor to wife and children, 11 December 1862, in G. Taylor and M. J. S. Taylor, *This Cruel War,* 133 (first quotation); Grant Taylor to wife and children, 22 April 1863, ibid., 177 (second quotation).

57. William R. Carter to father, 11 October 1861, William R. Carter Letter, LVA.

58. See Banasik, *Missouri Brothers in Gray,* 80–81; General Clement Evans to wife, 11 December 1863, in C. A. Evans, *Intrepid Warrior,* 292; and Evans to wife, 23 December 1864, ibid., 528.

59. Edwin H. Fay to wife, 24 January 1863, in Fay and Fay, "*This Infernal War,*" 217.

60. W. Johnson, *Soul by Soul,* 7; Kolchin, *American Slavery,* 126.

61. William Alexander Thom to brother, 26 April 1863, in Thom, "*My Dear Brother,*" 93.

62. William B. Pettit to wife, 9 April 1863, in Pettit, *Civil War Letters,* 101.

63. James Barrow to father, 23 December 1863, in Coulter, *Lost Generation,* 88–89.

64. Arthur Grimball to mother, 18 March 1863 (first quotation), and Berkley Grimball to father, 26 March 1863 (second quotation), John B. Grimball Papers, DU.

65. R. H. Brooks to wife, 7 April 1863, in R. H. Brooks, *Keep All My Letters,* 77.

66. See, e.g., Brannon, "True Story of the Old South," 45.

67. Toney, *The Privations of a Private,* 12.

68. See Martin, *Divided Mastery,* 8.

69. Albert Sidney Johnston to daughter, 4 January 1860, in Shaw, "Albert Sidney Johnston in Texas," 317. Johnston is referring to a quotation from Edward Moore's 1753 play *The Gamester*. The quotation has also sometimes been attributed to Dr. Samuel Johnson.

70. Cooper, "Cotton Crisis," 381–91; R. B. Campbell and R. G. Lowe, "Some Economic Aspects of Antebellum Texas Agriculture," 353–78.

71. Simon P. Wingard to wife, 18 July 1862, Simon P. Wingard Papers, DU.

72. Tadman, *Speculators and Slaves,* 44; Wiley, *Southern Negroes,* 97; Trexler, "Values of Slaves in Missouri," 74.

73. On prices in 1861, see E. L. Jordan, *Black Confederates and Afro-Yankees in Civil War Virginia,* 5; on New Orleans, see Eaton, *The Civilization of the Old South;* on Charleston, see David Jackson Logan to wife, 30 August 1863, and Logan to wife, 26 November 1863, in D. J. Logan, "*A Rising Star of Promise,*" 115, 129; on prices in Richmond, see Martinez, "The Slave Market in Civil War Virginia."

74. Entry for 29 April 1863, in Fremantle, *Diary,* 48.

75. John J. Good to wife, 6 December 1861, in Good, *Cannon Smoke,* 142–43.

76. Milton Leverett to mother, 8 April 1862, in F. W. Taylor, C. T. Matthews, and J. T. Power, *The Leverett Letters,* 115–16.

77. See Malinda to Grant Taylor, 8 May 1862, in G. Taylor and M. J. S. Taylor, *This Cruel War,* 15; G. W. Bolton to father, 18 December 1862, in G. W. Bolton, "*In Defense of My Country,*" 21; and G. M. McDowell to father, 27 November 1862, George M. McDowell Letter, VHS.

78. Charles C. Jones Jr. to father, 16 October 1862, in C. C. Jones, *The Children of Pride,* 303–6.

79. William H. Grimball to mother, 29 May 1863, John B. Grimball Papers, DU.

80. Stubbs to brother, 16 November 1862, Jefferson Stubbs Family Papers, LSU.

81. Archibald Bolling to Mr. Armistead, 3 January 1863, Armistead and Blanton Family Papers, VHS.

82. E. P. Petty to wife, 3 December 1862, and E. P. Petty to wife, May 1863, in Petty, *Journey to Pleasant Hill*, 104, 213. On Arkansas' ruin and the subsequent effect on Texas, see diary entry for 24 November [1862?], in Shaw, "A Texas Ranger Company at the Battle of Arkansas Post," 275; on planters' 1863 flight to Texas, see entries for 2 May, 7 May, and 10 May, in Fremantle, *Diary*, 56, 63–65, 68; and on Texas's importance as a new slavery frontier, see R. B. Campbell, *An Empire for Slavery*.

83. William D. Howard to father, 14 January 1859, Howard Family Papers, SHC.

84. Frank L. Richardson to father, 30 March 1862, Frank Lidell Richardson Papers, SHC; on safety in Texas, Elizabeth to William Neblett, 26 April 1863, in Neblett, *A Rebel Wife in Texas*, 97; on "demoralized" black troops, see William to Eleanor Nugent, 25 September 1863, in Nugent and Nugent, *My Dear Nellie*, 136.

85. Roland, *The Confederacy*, 126.

86. John Magruder to Philip N. Luckett, 10 September 1863, *OR*, 1:26(2):220.

87. Jonathan Lewis to mother, 12 January 1863, and Jonathan Lewis to mother, 21 July 1863, Harry Lewis Letters, SHC.

88. Edwin H. Fay to wife, 24 January 1863, in Fay and Fay, *"This Infernal War,"* 217.

89. Harriet Perry to Theophilus Perry, 8 February 1863, in Perry and Perry, *Widows by the Thousand*, 94.

90. Letter of 20 April 1863, in E. F. Paxton, *Memoir and Memorials*, 98.

91. William Wakefield Garner to wife, 18 August 1863, in McBrien and Garner, "Letters of an Arkansas Confederate Soldier," 182.

92. James M. Simpson to wife, 16 July 1863, Allen and Simpson Family Papers, SHC.

93. Alexander Faulkner Fewell to brother, 2 February 1863, in Fewell, *"Dear Martha ...,"* 102; James C. Francis to father, 27 March 1863, in Pate, *When this Evil War Is Over*, 121.

94. Theophilus to Harriet Perry, 20 June 1863, in Perry and Perry, *Widows by the Thousand*, 143.

95. John W. Reese to wife, 27 February 1863, John W. Reese Papers, DU.

96. Theophilus to Harriet Perry, 8 March 1863, in Perry and Perry, *Widows by the Thousand*, 110; will dated 13 November 1863, ibid., 167.

97. John S. Lewis to Mrs. Nancy Lewis, 31 July 1863, in R. G. Evans, *The 16th Mississippi Infantry*, 187; Jerome B. Yates to Mrs. Obedience Yates, 21 August 1863, ibid., 197.

98. J. O. Shelby to J. F. Belton, June 13, 1864, *OR*, 1:34(4):670.

99. David Jackson Logan to wife, 30 August 1863 (first quotation), and Logan to the *Yorkville Enquirer*, 1 September 1863 (second quotation), in D. J. Logan, *"A Rising Star of Promise,"* 115, 118.

100. Burdekin and Weidenmier, "Inflation Is Always and Everywhere a Monetary Phenomenon," 1621–30.

101. Robert C. Gilliam to wife, 20 February 1864, in Hudson and Gilliam, "From Paraclifta to Marks' Mill," 289.

102. James Anderson to "Dear Mary" [late February or early March 1864], in J. Anderson, "A Captured Confederate Officer," 65.

103. Glatthaar, *General Lee's Army*, 313–14.

104. James Paul Verdery to sister, 14 October 1864, Eugene Verdery Papers, DU.

105. Thomas Jackson Strayhorn to sister, 7 August 1864, in Wagstaff and Strayhorn, "Letters of Thomas Jackson Strayhorn," 327.

106. Clement Evans to wife, 3 October 1864, in C. A. Evans, *Intrepid Warrior*, 463.

107. Samuel Wiley to Eliza DeWitt Wiley, 26 November 1864, in Bird and Bird, *The Granite Farm Letters*, 215.

108. Spencer Barnes to sister, 1 November 1864, Spencer Barnes Letters, MOC.

109. Hugh W. Montgomery to A. W. Hyatt, 24 January 1865, Arthur W. Hyatt Papers, vol. 2, LSU.

110. Edwin Fay to wife, 2 March and 13 March 1865 (quotation), in Fay and Fay, *"This Infernal War,"* 424, 435.

111. U. G. Owen to wife, 1 April 1865, in E. L. Mitchell and U. G. Owen, "Letters of a Confederate Surgeon," 180.

5. "We Crushed Their Freedom"

1. H. H. Manigault to J. B. Grimball, 14 July 1863, and Lewis Grimball to J. B. Grimball, 30 August 1863, John B. Grimball Papers, DU.

2. See Gallagher, *The Confederate War*, 47; and Ash, *Middle Tennessee Society Transformed*.

3. See Genovese, *From Rebellion to Revolution*.

4. "Honor for the Old-Time Negro," 410.

5. Dinkins, "The Negroes as Slaves," 67.

6. "Typical of the Old South," 202.

7. Gordon, *Reminiscences of the Civil War*, 383.

8. Baylor, "The Army Negro," 365.

9. J. P. Austin, *The Blue and the Gray*, 208.

10. Dinkins, "The Negroes as Slaves," 62–63; Keiley, *In Vinculis*, 82–83.

11. Glenn, "Defence of Petersburg," 20.

12. On the slave named Box, see Mosgrove, "General Morgan's Last Raid," 120; on slaves cheering as Confederates charged across a bridge, see R. Taylor, *Destruction and Reconstruction*, 269; on hiding food, see E. A. Moore, *The Story of a Cannoneer under Stonewall Jackson*, 225; on hiding jewelry and silver, see Col. T. Smith and L. Robinson, "Brilliant Eulogy on General W. H. Payne," 332; on hiding silver, see "Fidelity of Negro War Servants," 384; on hiding a regiment's pay, see "Faithful Albert Peete (Bate)," 293; on two slaves carrying a wounded soldier to safety, see Brooke, "Autobiography of St. George Tucker Brooke Written for His Children," p. 51, VHS; on a slave carrying a soldier, see Dinkins, *Personal Recollections and Experiences in the Confederate Army*, 53–54, and also W. H. Morgan, *Personal Reminiscences of the War*, 167–68; on a black girl informant, see Pierrepont, *Reuben Vaughan Kidd*, 371.

13. Oates, *War between the Union and the Confederacy*, 155.

14. Franklin and Schweninger, *Runaway Slaves*, 282.

15. See Guelzo, *Lincoln's Emancipation Proclamation*, 309–10. Joseph T. Glat-

thaar puts the number of black escapees between 500,000 and 700,000 (see Boritt, *Why the Confederacy Lost,* 142). The editors at the Freedom and Southern Society Project have written, "At least 500,000 slaves gained freedom during the conflict" (see Hahn et al., *Freedom,* 3).

16. See Litwack, "Many Thousands Gone"; Jimerson, *The Private Civil War,* 50–85; Wish, "Slave Disloyalty under the Confederacy"; W. W. Freehling, *The South vs. the South,* 85–114; D. Williams, "'The Faithful Slave' Is About Played Out,'" 83–104; Wiley, *Southern Negroes,* 63–84; and E. L. Jordan, *Black Confederates and Afro-Yankees in Civil War Virginia,* 216–31.

17. Mohr, *On the Threshold of Freedom,* 77.

18. Thomas J. Goree to mother, 23 June 1861, in Goree, *Longstreet's Aide,* 18 (quotation). On the shotgun-wielding slave, see Jerome Yates to mother, 20 August 1861, in R. G. Evans, *The 16th Mississippi Infantry,* 17.

19. See Daniel Ruggles to R. S. Garnett, 8 May 1861, *OR,* 1:2:820; Ben McCulloch to S. Cooper, 19 November 1861, *OR,* 1:3:742–43; John J. Good to wife, 21 November 1861, in Good, *Cannon Smoke,* 128–29.

20. Clement Anselm Evans to wife, 13 November 1861, in C. A. Evans, *Intrepid Warrior,* 78.

21. Grimsley, *The Hard Hand of War,* 49.

22. William H. Tripp to wife, 20 May 1862, William H. Tripp and Araminta Guilford Tripp Papers, SHC.

23. Entry for 13 November 1861, in Lane, *The Times that Prove People's Principles,* 42. On the Sea Islands and Port Royal experiment, see Rose, *Rehearsal for Reconstruction.*

24. John C. Edrington to mother, 1 May 1862, in Edrington, "Letters of John C. Edrington," 1020.

25. Samuel Burney to wife, 7 January 1862, in Burney and Shepherd, *A Southern Soldier's Letters Home,* 98.

26. Bonner, *Mastering America,* 4.

27. Milton Leverett to mother, 7 February 1862, in F. W. Taylor, C. T. Matthews, and J. T. Power, *The Leverett Letters,* 112.

28. John Hall to Effie Hall, 26 April 1862, in Richard and Richard, *The Defense of Vicksburg,* 22.

29. James Bates to William Bramlette, May 1862, in Bates, *A Texas Cavalry Officer's Civil War,* 123; Frederic Leverett to father, 25 August 1862, in F. W. Taylor, C. T. Matthews, and J. T. Power, *The Leverett Letters,* 169; letter of 4 June 1862, in Stokes, *Saddle Soldiers,* 89.

30. Entry for 16 May 1862, in Drummond, *A Confederate Yankee,* 54.

31. James C. Bates to sister, 16 June 1862, in Bates, *A Texas Cavalry Officer's Civil War,* 134.

32. See Albert Davidson to father, 8 September 1861, in Turner and Davidson, "Lieutenant Albert Davidson," 59; D. P. Gibson to Mary B. Cotton, 6 June 1861, in Laurence, "Letters from a North Louisiana Tiger," 131; and entry for 17 September 1862, in Porter, "War Diary," 302.

33. Donald, *Lincoln,* 362–63.

34. Entry for 8 August 1862, in Sheeran, *Confederate Chaplain,* 2–3.

35. Edwin H. Fay to wife, 2 August 1862, in Fay and Fay, *"This Infernal War,"* 129.

36. Gideon Pillow to Jefferson Davis, 28 July 1862, *OR,* 1:52(2):332.

37. Dr. M. F. T. Evans to sister, 30 April 1861, in M. F. T. Evans, "Dr. Evans and the War (1861–1865)," 159.

38. Entry for 15 September 1862, in Haynes, *The Field Diary of a Confederate,* 19–20. In early 1862, another soldier was optimistic about secessionist feeling among Marylanders, but he said the army should remain on the defensive (see James M. Holloway to wife, 3 March 1862, James M. Holloway Papers, VHS).

39. Account of 17 September 1862, in Turner and Davidson, "Captain Greenlee Davidson," 206.

40. Undated entry, in Thom, *"My Dear Brother,"* 60.

41. Henry A. Wise to wife, 6 October 1862, Wise Family Papers, VHS; W. Watson, *Life in the Confederate Army,* 432.

42. See Gammage, *The Camp, the Bivouac, and the Battle Field,* 102.

43. See J. S. Wise, *The End of an Era,* 74.

44. Sorrel, *Recollections of a Confederate Staff Officer,* 1.

45. See James C. Bates to William Bramlette, November [?] 1862, in Bates, *A Texas Cavalry Officer's Civil War,* 207; and John Welsh to mother and wife, 26 January 1863, in Bean, "A House Divided," 410.

46. Daniel C. Govan to wife, 28 October 1861, Daniel Chevilette Govan Papers, SHC; Thomas K. Archbell to William H. Tripp, 18 October 1861, William Henry Tripp and Araminta Guilford Tripp Papers, SHC.

47. Buckner to the "Freemen of Kentucky," 24 September 1862, *OR,* 1:52(2):359–61.

48. Humphrey Marshall to George Randolph, 5 November 1862, *OR,* 1:20(2):390.

49. Robert E. Lee to Jefferson Davis, 2 October 1862, *OR,* 1:19(2):644.

50. See Manning, *What This Cruel War Was Over,* 81–111; and McPherson, *For Cause and Comrades,* 117–30.

51. D. P. Gibson to Mary B. Cotton, 1 February 1863, in Laurence, "Letters from a North Louisiana Tiger," 144 (first quotation); entry for 30 January 1863, James Calvin Marcom Diary, DU (second quotation).

52. McPherson, *Ordeal by Fire,* 2:457.

53. E. John Ellis to Tabitha Ellis, 12 December 1862 (first quotation), and E. John Ellis to parents, 18 March 1863 (second quotation), E. P. Ellis and Family Papers, LSU.

54. John S. Foster to brother, 9 August 1862, and John S. Foster to father, 20 February 1863, James Foster Family Correspondence, LSU.

55. See Lorimer, "The Role of Anti-Slavery Sentiment in English Reactions to the American Civil War."

56. Ruffin Thomson to father, 26 February 1863, Ruffin Thomson Papers, SHC.

57. Roger Q. Mills to wife, 5 November 1862, Heiskell Civil War Collection, UALR.

58. Edwin Taliaferro to mother, 4 January 1863, Taliaferro Family Papers, VHS.

59. Entry for 7 January 1863, in J. B. Jones, *A Rebel War Clerk's Diary,* 148.

60. E. John Ellis to sister, 29 October 1862, E. P. Ellis and Family Papers, LSU.

61. Dunaway, *Reminiscences of a Rebel,* 78–79.

62. Hubbard, *Notes of a Private,* 166.

63. Undated entry, pp. 32–33, Virgil Murphey Diary, SHC.

64. G. M. Foster, "The Limitations of Federal Healthcare for Freedmen," 356–57.

65. Silas, *Civil War Reminiscences,* 123. On one slave becoming a prostitute, see Nisbet, *Four Years on the Firing Line,* 148–49.

66. John to Gaillard Foster, 18 April 1863, James Foster and Family Correspondence, LSU.

67. See Sparkman, "Riding with Chrisman," 50–51; and Christ, *Civil War Arkansas, 1863,* 139, 145–96.

68. T. B. Lamar to William H. Jackson, 8 August 1863, *OR,* 1:24(3):1049.

69. Entry for 25 May 1862, in W. L. Wilson, *A Borderland Confederate,* 17.

70. T. Alexander, "A Regular Slave Hunt," 82–89; entry for 23 June 1863, James W. Albright Diary and Reminiscences, SHC.

71. See George W. Beale to mother, 13 July 1863, in Beale, "A Soldier's Account of the Gettysburg Campaign," 322; and dispatch for 27 June 1863, in P. W. Alexander, *Writing and Fighting the Confederate War,* 156. On the taking of Virginia slaves, see Nisbet, *Four Years on the Firing Line,* 121. According to Mark Neely, black people were not "sold into slavery," but sent to Virginia prisons (see Neely, *Southern Rights,* 139–40).

72. Thomas Fanning Wood to parents, 29 June 1863, in Wood, *Doctor to the Front,* 102.

73. Spencer Glasgow Welch to wife, 28 June 1863, in Welch, *A Confederate Surgeon's Letters to His Wife,* 58 (quotation). On slaves' plundering in Pennsylvania, see Owen, *In Camp and Battle with the Washington Artillery of New Orleans,* 242; and William Dorsey Pender to wife, 28 June 1863, in Pender, *The General to His Lady,* 254–55.

74. Report of William Stokes, 16 September 1863, *OR,* 1:28(1):730.

75. R. H. Williams, *With the Border Ruffians,* 232–33.

76. F. A. Montgomery, *Reminiscences of a Mississippian in Peace and War,* 71.

77. Entry for 5 July 1863, in Braudaway, "A Texan Records the Civil War Siege of Vicksburg, Mississippi," 125.

78. William Nugent to Eleanor Nugent, 27 August 1863, in Nugent and Nugent, *My Dear Nellie,* 129.

79. William H. Grimball to father, 10 June 1863, John B. Grimball Papers, DU.

80. E. John Ellis to sister, 15 November 1863, E. P. Ellis and Family Papers, LSU.

81. William Nugent to wife, 7 September 1863, in Bettersworth and Silver, *Mississippi in the Confederacy,* 354.

82. William Grimball to father, 22 November 1863; Arthur Grimball to father, 7 May 1864; Peyton G. Bowman to J. B. Grimball, 20 May 1864, John B. Grimball Papers, DU.

83. Thomas W. Francis to James C. Francis, 1 January 1864, in Pate, *When This Evil War Is Over,* 164.

84. See entry for 14 April 1864, in Barber, *Holding the Line,* 177.

85. Pierrepont, *Rueben Vaughan Kidd,* 343.

86. See H. C. Monell to Richard Taylor, 13 February 1864, *OR,* 1:34(2):966; Stephen D. Lee to T. M. Jack, 13 March 1864, *OR,* 1:32(3):620; and the entry for July 31, 1864, in Heartsill, *Fourteen Hundred and 91 Days in the Confederate Army,* 211.

87. Entry for winter 1863–64, in Mays, "Sketches from the Journal of a Confederate Soldier," 115.

88. Reuben Allen Pierson to William H. Pierson, 22 March 1864, in Cutrer and Parrish, *Brothers in Gray,* 228.

89. Azariah Denny to father, 29 April 1864, in Jackson et al., *Surry County Soldiers in the Civil War,* 328.

90. Jerome Yates to Tom O. Davis, 18 January 1864, in R. G. Evans, *The 16th Mississippi Infantry,* 233–34.

91. Fred A. Brode to F. B. Josephine Trinchard, 26 July 1864, Fred A. Brode Letters, MOC.

92. Entry for 10 July 1864, in Park, "Diary," 379.

93. William T. Casey to mother, 28 June 1864, William Thomas Casey Papers, VHS.

94. See the diary entry for 13 September 1864 (quotation); and Fred Fleet to father, 21 May 1862; in Fleet, *Green Mount,* 338, 126–27.

95. Park, "Twelfth Alabama Infantry," 286.

96. John Hampden Chamberlayne to mother, 29 October 1864, in Chamberlayne, *Ham Chamberlayne,* 288.

97. James Bates to sister, entry for 20 July 1864 in letter dated 16 July 1864, in Bates, *A Texas Cavalry Officer's Civil War,* 310.

98. See the entry for 21 November 1864, in Green, *Johnny Green of the Orphan Brigade,* 174; W. W. Parker, "How I Kept House in Camp," 325; and Dinkins, "The Negroes as Slaves," 66–67.

99. Cannon, *Inside of Rebeldom,* 42–43.

100. John Bell Hood to William T. Sherman, 12 September 1864, *OR,* 1:39(2):422. On Confederates' stiffening of their resolve, see J. Campbell, *When Sherman Marched North from the Sea.*

101. William W. Ward to James B. Hale, 15 October 1864, in Ward, *"For the Sake of My Country,"* 145.

102. Entry for 26 June 1864, in Hundley, *Prison Echoes,* 81–82; James C. Bates to William Bramlette, 13 October 1864, in Bates, *A Texas Cavalry Officer's Civil War,* 325–26. On Lincoln's election, see William to Eleanor Nugent, 10 September 1864, in Nugent and Nugent, *My Dear Nellie,* 203.

103. Samuel Wiley to mother, 26 November 1864, in Bird and Bird, *The Granite Farm Letters,* 214.

104. George Stedman to William T. Harris, 9 November 1864, in Leidecker, "Beyond the Strife," 197.

105. Fred Fleet to father, 9 December 1864, in Fleet, *Green Mount,* 349. The desire to reopen the African slave trade did not die in 1807, the last year that slave imports were legally allowed in the United States, but continued among some antebellum Southerners, especially South Carolinians (see Sinha, *The Counterrevolution of Slavery,* 125–52).

106. Vorenberg, "'Deformed Child,'" 256.

107. William Poague to mother, 11 February 1865, in Poague, *Gunner with Stonewall,* 148.

108. Willie Milling to brother, 20 May 1865, D. Y. Milling Correspondence, LSU.

6. On Battlefields and in Prisons

1. See Isaac Affleck to Mr. and Mrs. Affleck, 25 March 1863, in Wooster, "With the Confederate Cavalry in the West," 10; and Harden Perkins Cochrane to sister, 18 July 1863, in Cochrane, "Letters," 278.

2. Henry Semple to wife, 27 March 1863, Henry C. Semple Papers, SHC.

3. U. R. Brooks, *Butler and His Cavalry in the War of Secession*, 363–64.

4. Winston to Octavia Stephens, 16 March 1863, in Hodges and Kerber, "'Rogues and Black Hearted Scamps,'" 82.

5. Hundley, *Prison Echoes*, 40–41.

6. See Urwin, *Black Flag Over Dixie*; and Burkhardt, *Confederate Rage, Yankee Wrath*.

7. See Frank, *With Ballot and Bayonet*, 142–64; Grimsley, *The Hard Hand of War*; and Royster, *The Destructive War*.

8. On Butler, see Keiley, *In Vinculis*, 36–37, 45; and E. W. Tazewell to J. Pembroke Thom, 6 January 1863, in Thom, "*My Dear Brother*," 77.

9. Grimsley, *The Hard Hand of War*, 67–95.

10. J. B. Slade to Jeremiah Slade, 9 August 1862, William Slade Papers, DU.

11. John Letcher to George Randolph, 28 July 1862, *OR*, 2:4:829.

12. General Orders No. 60, 21 August 1862, *OR*, 1:14:599.

13. Henry Orr to parents, 21 August 1862, in J. Q. Anderson, *Campaigning with Parsons' Texas Cavalry Brigade*, 62–63.

14. Jonathan R. F. Tattnall to S. Croom, 8 November 1862, in Berlin et al., *The Black Military Experience*, 570–71; John W. Forney to Jonathan Tattnall, 11 November 1862, ibid., 571.

15. Hugh Mercer to Thomas Jordan, 14 November 1862, to P. G. T. Beauregard [first indorsement], 17 November 1862, and to James A. Seddon [second indorsement], 17 November 1862, *OR*, 2:4:945–46.

16. James Seddon to P. G. T. Beauregard, 30 November 1862, *OR*, 2:4:954.

17. Jefferson Davis's proclamation, 23 December 1862, *OR*, 1:15:907–8.

18. S. R. Nelson and C. Sheriff, *A People at War*, 135.

19. Jefferson Davis's proclamation, 23 December 1862, *OR*, 1:15:907–8.

20. Entry for 15 February 1863, in Kean, *Inside the Confederate Government*, 40.

21. Cleland K. Huger Jr., to D. E. Huger Smith, 20 January 1863, in D. E. H. Smith, A. R. H. Smith, and A. R. Childs, *Mason Smith Family Letters*, 33.

22. David Hunter to Jefferson Davis, 23 April 1863, in Berlin et al., *The Black Military Experience*, 573.

23. Sanders, *While in the Hands of the Enemy*, 146–62.

24. See "Order of Retaliation," 30 July 1863, in *Collected Works of Abraham Lincoln*, 7:357; and Glatthaar, *Forged in Battle*, 201.

25. Christopher Memminger to Edward G. Palmer, 27 July 1863, in Towles, *A World Turned Upside Down*, 371–72.

26. James Seddon to [Milledge L. Bonham?], 25 August 1863, in J. Davis, *Papers*, 9:355.

27. *Charleston Mercury*, 10 August 1863, 2 (Jefferson Davis quotation); entry for 3 August 1863, James W. Albright Diary, SHC.

28. Memorandum for Stephen D. Lee, 31 August 1863, *OR*, 1:30(4):573.

29. James Seddon to Kirby Smith, 12 August 1863, *OR,* 1:22(2):965.

30. Frederic Percival Leverett to mother, 17 June 1863, in F. W. Taylor, C. T. Matthews, and J. T. Power, *The Leverett Letters,* 223.

31. Entry for 4 June 1863, in Porter, "War Diary," 311; Winston to Octavia Stephens, 16 March 1863, in Hodges and Kerber, "'Rogues and Black Hearted Scamps,'" 81–82.

32. Clement Anselm Evans to wife, 4 July 1863, in C. A. Evans, *Intrepid Warrior,* 222.

33. N. A. Davis, *Chaplain Davis and Hood's Texas Brigade,* 72.

34. Entry for 18 January 1863, in J. B. Jones, *A Rebel War Clerk's Diary,* 152–53.

35. Early, *Memoir of the Last Year of the War for Independence,* 290–91.

36. Walter Taylor to sister, 1 August 1863, in W. H. Taylor, *Lee's Adjutant,* 65.

37. M. Jeff Thompson to William Pierson, 1 October 1863, and M. Jeff Thompson to George D. Prentice, 2 October 1863, M. Jeff Thompson Papers, SHC.

38. O'Brien, *Things Grew Beautifully Worse,* 25–26.

39. See Fitzgerald, "Another Kind of Glory," 244; and Stamp, "Ten Months Experience in Northern Prisons," 490–95. On Point Lookout, see Huffman, *Ups and Downs of a Confederate Soldier,* 91–92.

40. S. R. Nelson, *Iron Confederacies,* 109–10.

41. W. H. Morgan, *Personal Reminiscences of the War of 1861–5,* 237.

42. Entry for 30 January 1865, in Barnhill, "The Diary of Samuel Beckett Boyd," 35.

43. Entries for 28 February 1864 and 2 July 1864, in Inzer, *The Diary of a Confederate Soldier,* 65, 86.

44. Entry for 9 December 1864, in Park, "Diary," 233 (first quotation); Keiley, *In Vinculis,* 47 (second quotation). Mason's "Challenge" might refer to a toy locomotive produced in the 1860s having black-and-white lithograph paper coverings. Mason was a prominent locomotive manufacturer in the 1850s and '60s. The toy trains Keiley might be referring to included "Union," "America," "U.S. Grant," and "Challenge" (see E. P. Alexander, *The Collector's Book of the Locomotive*).

45. Reuter, *The Mulatto in the United States,* 247.

46. E. John Ellis Memoir, p. 51, E. John Ellis Diary, LSU.

47. Marvel, *Andersonville,* ix; L. R. Speer, *Portals to Hell,* 151–54, 187–93, 259–66, 285; Gillispie, *Andersonvilles of the North,* 178–89.

48. M. Jeff Thompson, "Reminiscences," M. Jeff Thompson Papers, SHC.

49. Entry for 23 May 1864, in Leon, *Diary of a Tar Heel Confederate,* 64.

50. Traywick, "Prison Life at Point Lookout," 433; Loehr, "Point Lookout," 118 (quotation).

51. Entry for 1–29 April 1864, in Malone, *Whipt 'em Everytime,* 100–101; entry for 12 June 1864, in Leon, *Diary of a Tar Heel Confederate,* 66. On "Potts," see Keiley, "Prison-Pens North," 337; on a shooting at Fort Delaware, see Swann, *Excerpts from Swann's "Prison Life at Fort Delaware,"* 128.

52. William H. Laird to W. A. Crafts, 19 April 1864, in Beitzell, *Point Lookout,* 35–36.

53. Bowden, "Some of My Experiences as a Confederate Soldier," pp. 20–21, John Malachi Bowden Papers, DU.

54. Diary entry for 12 April 1864, in Malone, *Whipt 'em Everytime,* 101.

55. Edwin Young to Board of Commissioners, 23 March 1864, in Beitzell, *Point Lookout,* 33.

56. Robert E. Lee to Jefferson Davis, 26 June 1864, *OR,* 1:37(1):767.

57. Tap, *Over Lincoln's Shoulder,* 187–92.

58. Statement of Jerry Stewart, 30 April 1864, *OR,* 1:32(1):537–38 (first quotation); report by "Memphis," 18 April 1864, in Nieman, *The Day of Jubilee.*

59. See Brooksher, "Betwixt Wind and Water," in Greenberg and Waugh, *The Price of Freedom,* 1:287–97; Castel, "The Fort Pillow Massacre: A Fresh Examination of the Evidence"; and Cimprich, "The Fort Pillow Massacre: Assessing the Evidence."

60. Grant, *Personal Memoirs,* 395 (first quotation); report by "Memphis," 18 April 1864, in Nieman, *The Day of Jubilee,* 69 (second quotation).

61. Dinkins, *Personal Recollections,* 155.

62. Rodgers, "Battle of Jenkin's Ferry," Robert M. Rodgers Papers, DU.

63. Handerson, *Yankee in Gray,* 73.

64. See Forrest's battle at Johnsonville, Tennessee, in Dinkins, *Personal Recollections,* 207–8.

65. Clayton Coleman to wife, 24 April 1864, Clayton Coleman Letters, MOC.

66. On Arkansas, see Avera, "Extracts from the Memoirs of William Avera," 107.

67. See, e.g., Joel Griffin to George Pickett, 15 December 1863, *OR,* 1:29(2):872–73.

68. Cash, *The Mind of the South,* 117–18. On black-on-white rape, Cash says, "If the actual danger was small, it was nevertheless the most natural thing in the world for the South to see it as very great, to believe in it, fully and in all honesty, as a menace requiring the most desperate measures if it was to be held off."

69. John J. Jefcoat to wife, 6 July 1864, John J. Jefcoat Papers, DU.

70. Entry for 23 September 1864, in Key and Campbell, *Two Soldiers,* 138–39.

71. McPherson, *Ordeal by Fire,* 2:426–28; E. L. Jordan, *Black Confederates and Afro-Yankees in Civil War Virginia,* 276–78.

72. William Nelson Pendleton to [wife?], 2 August 1864, in S. P. Lee, *Memoirs of William Nelson Pendleton,* 360.

73. Daniel Abernethy to parents, 7 August 1864, Daniel Abernethy Letters, DU; entry for 30 July 1864, James Thomas Perry Diary, VHS (original held by the Fredericksburg and Spotsylvania National Military Park); Scott, "Memoir of Service in the Confederate Army," pp. 26–27, Alfred Lewis Scott Memoir, VHS.

74. McCabe, *The Defense of Petersburg,* 38 (first quotation); Andrew Sydnor Barksdale to sister, 1 August 1864, Andrew Sydnor Barksdale Letters, MOC (second quotation).

75. R. A. Barrier to father, 6 August 1864, in Barrier, *Dear Father,* 60.

76. Entry for 30 July 1864, James Thomas Perry Diary, VHS.

77. Scott, "Memoir of Service in the Confederate Army," pp. 26–27, Alfred Lewis Scott Memoir, VHS.

78. Stewart, "The Charge of the Crater," 80.

79. Suderow, "The Battle of the Crater," 219–24.

80. Haskell, *Memoirs,* 77.

81. Alva Spencer to "Dearest Maggie," 6 August 1864, in A. B. Speer, *My Dear Friend,* 138.

82. Dunlop, *Lee's Sharpshooters,* 185.

83. Andrew Sydnor Barksdale to sister, 1 August 1864, Andrew Sydnor Barksdale Letters, MOC.

84. Callaway, *The Bloody Links*, 55–56.

85. Kinard, *The Battle of the Crater*, 64.

86. Slotkin, *No Quarter*, 294.

87. Andrew Sydnor Barksdale to sister, 1 August 1864, Andrew Sydnor Barksdale Letters, MOC.

88. Mahone, *The Battle of the Crater*.

89. Scott, "Memoir of Service in the Confederate Army," pp. 26–27, Alfred Lewis Scott Memoir, VHS.

90. Haskell, *Memoirs*, 78–79.

91. Stewart, "The Charge of the Crater," 89.

92. Haskell, *Memoirs*, 77.

93. Bernard, "The Battle of the Crater," 25; Houghton and Houghton, *Two Boys in the Civil War and After*, 133.

94. Haskell, *Memoirs*, 78.

95. Suderow, "The Battle of the Crater," 223; B. K. O'Brien, *Things Grew Beautifully Worse*, 41 (quotation); Featherston, "Graphic Account of the Battle of the Crater," 367.

96. William Pegram to "My dear Jenny," 1 August 1864, Pegram-Johnson-McIntosh Papers, VHS (first quotation); Robert D. Graham to Susan Washington Graham, 6 June 1863, in W. A. Graham, *Papers*, 5:500–501 (second quotation).

97. Ralph C. Reynolds to "Dear Bettie," 3 August 1864, in Johnston and Williams, *Hard Times*, 2:198.

98. Entry for 6 August 1864, in Hundley, *Prison Echoes*, 110.

99. D. Holt, *A Mississippi Rebel in the Army of Northern Virginia*, 289.

100. Sorrel, *Recollections of a Confederate Staff Officer*, 227; Stone, *Wandering to Glory*, 196.

101. Edmund F. Stone to Samuel Marion Stone, 7 December 1864, Edmund F. Stone Letter, VHS.

102. Dunlop, *Lee's Sharpshooters*, 162, 184.

103. C. W. Trueheart to brother, 28 August 1864, in Trueheart and Trueheart, *Rebel Brothers*, 115.

104. See Faust, *This Republic of Suffering*.

105. C. W. Trueheart to brother, 28 August 1864, in Trueheart and Trueheart, *Rebel Brothers*, 116; Stewart, "The Charge of the Crater," 86.

106. Haskell, *Memoirs*, 78.

107. C. W. Trueheart to brother, 28 August 1864, in Trueheart and Trueheart, *Rebel Brothers*, 115.

108. Edgar Smithwick to mother, 9 August 1864, Edgar Smithwick Papers, DU (first quotation); C. W. Trueheart to brother, 28 August 1864, in Trueheart and Trueheart, *Rebel Brothers*, 115 (second quotation); entry for 30 July 1864, in Walters, *Norfolk Blues*, 138 (third quotation).

109. Rufus King Felder to unknown, 18 September 1864, in Chicoine and Felder, "'. . . Willing Never To Go in Another Fight,'" 590.

110. Phillips, "Reminiscences," James Eldred Phillips Reminiscences, VHS.

111. Ulysses S. Grant to Robert E. Lee, 2 October 1864, in Grant, *Papers*, 12:258;

Robert E. Lee to Ulysses S. Grant, 3 October 1864, ibid., 12:263; Robert E. Lee to Ulysses S. Grant, 19 October 1864, ibid., 12:323–27.

112. Kendall, "Recollections of a Confederate Officer," 1210.

113. Entry for 24 December 1864, James Thomas Perry Diary, VHS. The song *Happy Land of Canaan,* written by William A. Wray, concerns John Brown's raid on Harpers Ferry. Its second verse, composed in dialect, says, "At Harper's Ferry section/They had an insurrection/Ole Brown thought de niggers would sustain him/But ole Governor Wise/Put de spectacles on his eyes/And sent him to de happy land of Canaan."

7. FREE TO FIGHT

1. Glatthaar, *Forged in Battle.*
2. Levine, *Confederate Emancipation,* 113; Thomas, *The Confederacy as Revolutionary Experience,* 131; Glatthaar, *General Lee's Army,* 453; Manning, *What This Cruel War Was Over,* 208.
3. Escott, "What Shall We Do with the Negro?" 194 (first quotation), 197 (second quotation); see also Escott, *After Secession,* 226–55. On Confederate soldiers supporting black enlistment more out of necessity than choice, see Power, *Lee's Miserables,* 251–55.
4. Jonathan Devereux to J. L. Lewis, 29 September 1861, *OR,* 4:1:625.
5. General Orders No. 426, Headquarters of Louisiana Militia, 24 March 1862, *OR,* 4:1:1020.
6. Hollandsworth, *The Louisiana Native Guards.*
7. N. A. Davis, *Chaplain Davis and Hood's Texas Brigade,* 62.
8. George Hundley, "Beginning and the Ending: Reminiscences of the First and Last Days of War," George Jefferson Hundley Reminiscences, VHS. Hundley identified himself as a general, but neither Ezra Warner's *Generals in Gray* nor Bruce Allardice's *More Generals in Gray* identify him as such.
9. Oates, *War between the Union and the Confederacy,* 496–505; Richard to Elizabeth Ewell, 20 July 1862, in Ewell, *The Making of a Soldier,* 113.
10. Entry for 13 August 1863, in Kean, *Inside the Confederate Government,* 92.
11. Diary entry for 28 December 1863, in Key and Campbell, *Two Soldiers,* 17–18.
12. Caleb Hobson to B. Dozier, 12 December 1863, in W. H. A. Speer, *Voices from Cemetery Hill,* 182.
13. At the time of his death in November 1864 at Franklin, Tennessee, Cleburne was engaged to Mobile native Susan Tarleton, whose father, George W. Tarleton, owned twenty-two slaves according to the 1860 census.
14. Cleburne's proposal, 2 January 1864, *OR,* 1:52(2):586–91.
15. Ibid., 1:52.2:587.
16. Ibid., 1:52.2:590.
17. Ibid.
18. Ibid., 1:52.2:589.
19. Ibid., 1:52.2:591.
20. W. W. Freehling, *The South vs. the South,* 195.
21. Wallace Comer to mother, 14 June 1864, Comer Family Papers, SHC.

22. Yee, "The Black Confederate Sharpshooter."

23. Patton Anderson to Leonidas Polk, 14 January 1864, *OR,* 1:51(2):598–99.

24. William H. Walker to Jefferson Davis, 12 January 1864, *OR,* 1:52(2):595.

25. Johnston's circular, 31 January 1864, *OR,* 1:52(2):608; Johnston's letter to James Seddon, 2 February 1864, ibid., 608–9.

26. Joseph E. Johnston to James Seddon, 2 February 1864, in Ridley, *Battles and Sketches of the Army of Tennessee,* 293.

27. Colyar to Albert S. Marks, 30 January 1864, in Buck and Cleburne, *Cleburne and His Command,* 49.

28. J. P. Young, who served in Forrest's cavalry, said few men had supported the enlistment of blacks. Still, he thought it had little to do with why Cleburne—considered the "Stonewall Jackson of the West"—was not promoted to lieutenant general (see ibid., 53).

29. Hardee, "Biographical Sketch of Major-General Patrick R. Cleburne," 157.

30. Hood, *Advance and Retreat,* 296; John Bell Hood to William T. Sherman, 12 September 1864, *OR,* 1:39(2):419–22.

31. Berkeley Minor, "If Lee Could Have Stood at the Helm," *Richmond Times-Dispatch,* 15 January 1912.

32. Buck, "Negroes in Our Army," 215–16.

33. Entry for 6 March 1864, in McPheeters, *I Acted from Principle,* 116.

34. Gallagher, *The Confederate War,* 162–64; Rable, "Despair, Hope, and Delusion"; Phillips, *Diehard Rebels,* 147–77.

35. Entry for 30 December 1863, in Key and Campbell, *Two Soldiers,* 19.

36. Ellzey, "The Cause We Lost and the Land We Love," pp. 64–65, Mason Graham Ellzey Memoir, VHS.

37. Alexander T. B. Merritt to brother, 17 January 1865, William H. E. Merritt Papers, DU.

38. Thomas J. Goree to sister, 21 October 1864, in Goree, *Longstreet's Aide,* 137.

39. Entry for 7 November 1864, Crenshaw, "Diary," 228.

40. J. A. Merritt to uncle, 9 November 1864, William H. E. Merritt Papers, DU; entry for 20 November 1864, in Kean, *Inside the Confederate Government,* 177.

41. Marion Hill Fitzpatrick to wife, 11 November 1864, in Fitzpatrick, *Letters to Amanda,* 185; entry for 8 November 1864, in Walters, *Norfolk Blues,* 172.

42. E. John Ellis to father, 27 December 1864 (first quotation), and E. John Ellis to mother, 26 June 1863 (second quotation), E. P. Ellis and Family Papers, LSU.

43. C. W. Trueheart to father, 31 December 1864, in Trueheart and Trueheart, *Rebel Brothers,* 135. On St. John Liddell's support for emancipation, see Liddell, *Liddell's Record,* 192.

44. Richard W. Corbin to mother, 29 December 1864, in Corbin, *Letters of a Confederate Officer,* 89–90.

45. C. Irvine Walker to unknown, 17 January 1865, in Walker, *Great Things Are Expected of Us,* 164–65.

46. Mohr, *On the Threshold of Freedom,* 278; Wesley, "The Employment of Negroes as Soldiers in the Confederate Army," 248.

47. Durden, *The Gray and the Black,* 74–142.

48. Entry for 8 January 1865, in Inzer, *The Diary of a Confederate Soldier,* 119.

49. Robert E. Lee to Andrew Hunter, 11 January 1865, *OR,* 4:3:1012–13.

50. Robert E. Lee to Andrew Barksdale, 18 February 1865 [copy], St. Paul's Church Vestry Book, VHS (original held by the Vestry of St. Paul's Church, Richmond, Va.).

51. Robert E. Lee to Jefferson Davis, 10 March 1865, in R. E. Lee, *Wartime Papers*, 914.

52. Entry for 30 December 1864, in Edmondston, *"Journal of a Secesh Lady,"* 651.

53. Entry for 1 January 1865, in Kean, *Inside the Confederate Government*, 183–84.

54. R. Taylor, *Destruction and Reconstruction*, 257.

55. John Tyler to Sterling Price, 23 January 1865, *OR,* 1:48(1):1342.

56. Durden, *The Gray and the Black*, 143–86.

57. Entry for 26 January 1865, in Quintard, *Doctor Quintard, Chaplain C.S.A. and Second Bishop of Tennessee*, 222.

58. Entry for 22 January 1865, in Poché, *A Louisiana Confederate*, 208.

59. E. Kirby Smith to John Slidell, 9 January 1865, *OR,* 1:48(1):1319–20; C. Irvine Walker to unknown, 8 February 1865 in Walker, *Great Things Are Expected of Us,* 168.

60. Grant Taylor to wife and children, 11 January 1865, in G. Taylor and M. J. S. Taylor, *This Cruel War,* 323 (quotation); see also Benjamin Freeman to family, 15 March 1865, in Freeman, *Confederate Letters,* 61.

61. J. H. Jenkins to wife, 21 January 1865, in Lane, *"Dear Mother,"* 341.

62. Munford, "Resolution of Col. Thomas Munford."

63. Entry for 19 February 1865, in Chambers, "My Journal," 362.

64. Entries for 20 and 21 February 1865, Richard Lancelot Maury Diary, VHS.

65. Varon, "Evangelical Womanhood and the Politics of the African Colonization Movement in Virginia."

66. A. G. Freehling, *Drift toward Dissolution;* Masur, *1831,* 48–62.

67. Entry for 16 February 1865, in Heartsill, *Fourteen Hundred and 91 Days in the Confederate Army,* 230.

68. Donald, *Lincoln,* 396.

69. William B. G. Andrews to father, 21 February 1865, William B. G. Andrews Papers, DU.

70. Report issued 23 February 1865, in Berlin et al., *The Black Military Experience,* 299.

71. Daniel Abernethy to parents, 16 February 1865, Daniel Abernethy Letters, DU.

72. Beckett, "A Sketch of the Career of Company B," 42 (quotation); see also Grant Taylor to wife and children, 11 January 1865, in G. Taylor and M. J. S. Taylor, *This Cruel War,* 322–23. On Lee's support for a similar plan, see Power, *Lee's Miserables,* 267.

73. 49th Georgia Regiment to Walter Taylor, 15 March 1865, *OR,* 1:46(2):1316.

74. Joseph F. Shaner to sister, 15 February 1865, Joseph F. Shaner Papers, VHS.

75. "Resolution of the Sixth Virginia Regiment," 15 February 1865, in Berlin et al., *The Black Military Experience,* 297. See also A. A. Louther to Walter Taylor, 14 February 1865, ibid., 296.

76. Samuel J. C. Moore to Randolph Kownslar, 22 February 1865, Thornton Tayloe Perry Papers, VHS.

77. Joseph D. Stapp to mother, 4 March 1865, Joseph D. Stapp Letters, VHS; see also entry for 17 February 1865, in Hubbs, *Voices from Company D,* 354–55.

78. Bell Smith to Jefferson Davis, 16 March 1865, *OR,* 1:46(3):1315; General Orders No. 14, 23 March 1865, *OR,* 4:3:1161.

79. Oates, *The War between the Union and the Confederacy,* 501 (quotation), 502; Gordon, *Reminiscences of the Civil War,* 382.

80. Durden, *The Gray and the Black,* 268.

81. Robert E. Lee to Jefferson Davis, 24 March 1865, *OR,* 1:46(3):1339.

82. William S. Basinger to mother, 23 February 1865, William Starr Basinger Papers, SHC (first quotation); Robert E. Lee to James Longstreet, 28 March 1865, John Walter Fairfax Papers, VHS (second quotation). On men applying for a commission, see George Washington Custis Lee to G. Carter, 14 March 1865, Carter Family Papers, VHS.

83. James Longstreet to Walter Taylor, 25 March 1865, in Longstreet, *From Manassas to Appomattox,* 651; see also, James Longstreet to Walter Taylor, 30 March 1865, *OR,* 1:46(3):1367.

84. Abner McGarrity to wife, 6 March 1865, in Burnett, "Letters of a Confederate Surgeon," 62 (quotation); A. E. McGarrity to wife, 11 March 1865, ibid., 64.

85. Entry for 23 March 1863, in Kean, *Inside the Confederate Government,* 204.

86. Entry for 16 March 1865, James W. Albright Diary and Reminiscences, DU; Alva Benjamin Spencer to "Dearest Maggie," 24 March 1865, in A. B. Speer, *My Dear Friend,* 197.

87. Entry for 23 March 1865, in J. B. Jones, *A Rebel War Clerk's Diary,* 522; Marion Hill Fitzpatrick to wife, 27 March 1865, in Fitzpatrick, *Letters to Amanda,* 205–6.

88. Entry for 23 March 1865, Richard Lancelot Maury Diary, VHS.

89. Joseph E. Johnston to Robert E. Lee, 1 April 1865, *OR,* 1:47(3):737; E. Surget to William Lyon, 4 April 1865, *OR,* 1:49(2):1199; George to Martha Ingram, 7 April 1865, in G. W. Ingram and M. Ingram, *Civil War Letters,* 79.

8. Relics of the Antebellum Era

1. Andreano, *The Economic Impact of the American Civil War,* 81; Gunderson, "Origin of the American Civil War," 917; Huston, *Calculating the Value of the Union,* 24–66.

2. The Union had begun the process in 1863 with Lincoln's "10 Percent Plan" for admitting states back into the Union, though areas such as southern Louisiana, western Tennessee, and the Sea Islands of Georgia and South Carolina, were already under Federal control by then.

3. Carter, *When the War Was Over;* Lemann, *Redemption;* Perman, *The Road to Redemption;* Budiansky, *The Bloody Shirt.*

4. David Pierson to William H. Pierson, 11 January 1865, in Cutrer and Parrish, *Brothers in Gray,* 222.

5. Entry for 19 March 1865, in Park, "Diary," 126–27.

6. Stubbs to father, 21 January 1865, Jefferson Stubbs Family Papers, LSU.

7. Thomas W. Patton to mother, 6 January 1865, in Watford, *The Civil War in North Carolina,* 189.

8. Hugh W. Montgomery to A. W. Hyatt, 24 January 1865, Arthur W. Hyatt Papers, vol. 2, LSU.

9. See Joseph Wheeler to L. McClaws, 21 January 1865, *OR,* 1:47(2):1034–35; and William T. Poague to mother, 21 February 1865, in Poague, *Gunner with Stonewall,* 150.

10. Alfred Bell to wife, 31 January 1865, in Watford, *The Civil War in North Carolina,* 192.

11. B. D. Fry to J. M. Otey, 12 March 1865, *OR,* 1:47(2):1383–84.

12. Edward Armstrong to cousin, 22 March 1865, Edward H. Armstrong Letters, MOC.

13. Memorandum for 7 April 1865, in Rachal, "The Occupation of Richmond, April 1865," 192–93.

14. Junius N. Bragg to wife, 23 April 1865, in Bragg, *Letters of a Confederate Surgeon,* 272.

15. Diary entry for 22 April 1865, in S. T. Foster, *One of Cleburne's Command,* 166. Magruder is quoted in L. C. Daniel, *Confederate Scrap-Book,* 4.

16. Johnson is quoted in Foner, *Reconstruction,* 177. Concerning Foster's worries, see the entry for 26 April 1865, in S. T. Foster, *One of Cleburne's Command,* 168.

17. Carter M. Louthan to Virginia Shaffer, 16 July 1865, Louthan Family Papers, VHS.

18. Carter, *When the War Was Over;* McKitrick, *Andrew Johnson and Reconstruction.*

19. Monaghan, *Swamp Fox of the Confederacy,* 105.

20. Thomas, *Robert E. Lee,* 382.

21. Carter M. Louthan to Virginia Shaffer, 16 July 1865 (first quotation); Carter M. Louthan to Ella Louthan, 25 June 1861 (second quotation); Carter M. Louthan to Berta Shaffer, 10 April 1863 (third quotation); Carter M. Louthan to Virginia Shaffer, 16 July 1865 (fourth quotation); all in Louthan Family Papers, VHS.

22. J. D. Smith, *An Old Creed for the New South,* 33.

23. Josephy, *Civil War in the American West,* 18. On Mexico, see Bonner, *Mastering America,* 306.

24. Shelby is quoted in Shalhope, "Race, Class, Slavery, and the Antebellum Southern Mind," 568. On Confederates in South America, see Hill, "Confederate Exodus to Latin America."

25. Henry M. Price to Sir Frederic Bruce, 24 May 1865, in Merli, "Alternative to Appomattox," 217.

26. Entry for 5 June 1865, in Ridley, *Battles and Sketches of the Army of Tennessee,* 481.

27. See Raboteau, *Slave Religion.*

28. Green, *Johnny Green of the Orphan Brigade,* 202–3 (quotation). On black loyalty to the family, see James A. Graham to father, 30 May 1865, in W. A. Graham, *Papers,* 216.

29. Fisher, "Life on the Common Level," 307 (quotation). On good relations between whites and blacks, see Breckinridge, "What the Ex-Confederate Has Done in Peace," 231.

30. Diary entry for 1 July 1865, E. John Ellis Memoir, p. 38, E. John Ellis Diary, LSU.

31. R. Campbell, *Lone Star Confederate*, 91; Bevier, *History of the First and Second Missouri*, 472; Houghton and Houghton, *Two Boys in the Civil War and After*, 153 (quotation).

32. Entry for 5 April 1865, in Peyton, *Eyewitness to War in Virginia*, 198.

33. Entry for 26 May 1865, in Tilghman and Hanna, "Confederate Baggage and Treasure Train Ends Its Flight in Florida," 177.

34. Collins, *Chapters from the Unwritten History of the War between the States*, 305–6; memorandum for 13 April 1865, in Rachal, "The Occupation of Richmond," 195 (quotation).

35. Diary entry for 17 May 1865, in S. T. Foster, *One of Cleburne's Command*, 177–78.

36. Ludwig Lehmann to brother-in-law, January 1866, in Kamphoefner and Helbich, *Germans in the Civil War*, 473.

37. Milton Leverett to mother, 23 July 1864 (first quotation), and Milton Leverett to mother, 3 February 1866 (second and third quotations), in F. W. Taylor, C. T. Matthews, and J. T. Power, *The Leverett Letters*, 345, 402–3. See also Nisbet, *Four Years on the Firing Line*, 240–41; and General Wigfall to son, 21 September 1868, in Wallace, "Confederate Exiles in London," 146.

38. William Brown to Lucy Snyder, 6 December 1865, Louthan Family Papers, VHS.

39. F. A. Montgomery, *Reminiscences of a Mississippian in Peace and War*, 21, 113.

40. Ayers, *Vengeance and Justice*, 169.

41. Entry for 11 June 1865, in Lane, *The Times that Prove People's Principles*, 254.

42. Davie, *Negroes in American Society*, 231.

43. W. H. Morgan, *Personal Reminiscences of the War of 1861–5*, 272.

44. Dunaway, *Reminiscences of a Rebel*, 129–30; Duncan, *Recollections*, 200; Dooley, *John Dooley, Confederate Soldier*, 205; Cater, *As It Was*, 218–19.

45. Howard, *Reminiscences*, 183.

46. Gillette, *Retreat from Reconstruction*; Zuczek, *State of Rebellion*; T. C. Holt, *Black over White*.

47. Huffman, *Ups and Downs of a Confederate Soldier*, 107 (first quotation); Toney, *The Privations of a Private*, 124–25 (second and third quotations); U. R. Brooks, *Stories of the Confederacy*, 351 (fourth quotation).

48. James Carson to Logan H. Roots, 14 September 1868, Logan H. Roots Papers, UALR; Lemann, *Redemption*.

49. Forrest's role in the Klan has been debated. At the height of Klan activity in the Reconstruction era, a congressional committee asked Forrest to testify concerning his involvement. Forrest, as ever, proved elusive and did not incriminate himself. In the 1930s, however, the conservative Tennessee historian Stanley Horn wrote that Forrest was "beyond any reasonable doubt, the [first] Grand Wizard of the Invisible Empire" (see Horn, *Invisible Empire*, 325 ; see also Hurst, *Nathan Bedford Forrest*, 259–356). Whether or not one can prove beyond all doubt that Forrest participated in the Klan, his own background and personal politics were in harmony with the Klan.

50. Powell, "Memoirs," p. 8 (first quotation) and p. 27 (second quotation), Charles S.

Powell Memoirs, DU. On the Klan in North Carolina, see S. R. Nelson, *Iron Confederacies,* 99–100, 108–14.

51. Hume and Gough, *Blacks, Carpetbaggers, and Scalawags,* 141.
52. Foner, *Reconstruction,* 346–411.
53. See G. M. Foster, *Ghosts of the Confederacy.*
54. Budiansky, *The Bloody Shirt,* 157–62.
55. Early, *Memoir of the Last Year of the War for Independence,* viii.
56. J. D. Smith, *An Old Creed for the New South,* 17–67.
57. Blackford, *War Years with Jeb Stuart,* 12–13.
58. Duncan, *Recollections,* 172.
59. R. Taylor, *Destruction and Reconstruction,* 288–89.
60. Handerson, *Yankee in Gray,* 28.
61. G. M. Foster, "Guilt over Slavery."
62. J. T. Morgan, "Address," 15.
63. W. C. Davis and J. Hoffman, *The Confederate General,* 4:190–91; Fry, *John Tyler Morgan and the Search for Southern Autonomy;* J. T. Morgan, "Address," 25.
64. Douglas, *I Rode with Stonewall,* 15.
65. Blight, *Race and Reunion.*
66. Former Confederates were correct about Northern racism. Massachusetts, for example, had an anti-miscegenation law, but repealed it in 1843 after hearing abolitionist complaints. Southerners were also correct that New England, because of its large maritime shipping industry, had played an important role in the international slave trade.
67. Col. T. Smith and L. Robinson, "Brilliant Eulogy on General W. H. Payne," 319–21. On Sherman's and Lincoln's racial views, see A. H. Lankford's editorial, "Hypocrisy of the 'Elson History'"; and Col. T. Smith and L. Robinson, "Brilliant Eulogy of General W. H. Payne," 314 (quotation).
68. McCrady, "Address," 250 (emphasis in original).
69. Burress, "Civilization of Negroes in the South."
70. Minor, "The Old System of Slavery," 127.
71. The 1890s was the worst decade for African American victims of lynching (see Tolnay and Beck, *Festival of Violence*). Whatever the number per year, it was far less than the tens of thousands of Filipinos killed during the Spanish-American War (see Karnow, *In Our Image,* 12).
72. Lindgren, "Apostasy of a Southern Anti-Imperialist," 151–78. On Southern military academies, see Andrew, *Long Gray Lines,* 105–14; on Southern support and racism, see Blight, *Race and Reunion,* 352 (quotation).
73. John Cussons to Kate Mason Rowland, 30 June 1899, Kate Mason Rowland Papers, VHS.
74. Breckinridge, "What the Ex-Confederate Has Done in Peace," 230.
75. "Heroic and Patriotic Marylanders."
76. W. D. Jordan, *The White Man's Burden,* 26.
77. Col. T. Smith and L. Robinson, "Brilliant Eulogy on General W. H. Payne," 310–11.
78. Keiley, *In Vinculis,* 210–11.
79. Houghton and Houghton, *Two Boys in the Civil War and After,* 56; see also Wyeth, *With Sabre and Scalpel,* 320.

80. R. W. Logan, *The Negro in American Life and Thought*.
81. Breckinridge, "What the Ex-Confederate Has Done in Peace," 231.

CONCLUSION

1. Potter, *The Impending Crisis*, 145.
2. Ibid., 414.
3. Speech of 15 April 1865, in Douglass, *Papers*, 4:76.
4. Blight, *Race and Reunion*, 149.
5. W. Jones, *Under the Stars and Bars*, v. See also Booth, *Maryland Boy in Lee's Army*, 6; W. A. Smith, *The Anson Guards*, 2; Howard, *Reminiscences*, 79; and W. Watson, *Life in the Confederate Army*, 44.
6. William C. Oates put the percentage of non-slaveholders who fought for the Confederacy at two-thirds (Oates, *The War between the Union and the Confederacy*, 497); two veterans of the war put the number at four-fifths (Houghton and Houghton, *Two Boys in the Civil War and After*, 191). Randolph McKim put the number at 10 percent (see McKim, *A Soldier's Recollections*, 22); and a North Carolinian claimed that only 2 percent of the men owned slaves (see Shotwell, *Papers*, 1:21).
7. R. Taylor, *Destruction and Reconstruction*, 4 (first quotation), 27 (second quotation).
8. E. Wilson, *Patriotic Gore*, 551–52.
9. Gordon, *Reminiscences of the Civil War*, 19.
10. Oates, *The War between the Union and the Confederacy*, 495–96 (quotation), 498.
11. Mosby, *Memoirs*, 20.
12. John Singleton Mosby to Samuel F. Chapman, 4 June 1907, in Mosby, *Take Sides with the Truth*, 73–75. Christian's speech is in "Report of the History Committee of the U.C.V.," in McGuire and Christian, *The Confederate Cause and Conduct in the War between the States*, 176–81.
13. Hayden, "Report of the Commander, R. E. Lee Camp, No. 1, S.C.V.," 12.

Bibliography

Archival Sources

Duke University Special Collections, Durham, North Carolina [DU]

Daniel Abernethy Papers
Eglantine Agours Letters
William B. G. Andrews Papers
Thomas Baxter Papers
John Malachi Bowden Papers
George Briggs Papers
William S. Carter Papers
Confederate States of America: Archives, Army Miscellany, Officers & Soldiers' Miscellaneous Letters, 1861
Confederate States of America: Archives, Army Miscellany, Prison Papers (Letters, Etc.), 1861–1865
James Jackson Davis Papers
John B. Grimball Papers
Archibald E. Henderson Papers
John J. Jefcoat Correspondence
Ranson Lee Papers
James Calvin Marcom Diary
William Massie Papers
Caleb McCurdy Papers
Alexander McMillan Papers
William H. E. Merritt Papers
Green W. Penn Papers
Charles S. Powell Memoirs
John W. Reese Papers
James L. Reid Letters
Robert M. Rodgers Papers
William Slade Papers
William D. Smith Papers
Edgar Smithwick Papers
John Lane Stuart Papers
William A. Tesh Letters
Thomas Toon Letter

BIBLIOGRAPHY

Eugene Verdery Papers
Simon P. Wingard Papers

*Eleanor S. Brockenbrough Library,
The Museum of the Confederacy, Richmond, Virginia [MOC]*

Edward H. Armstrong Letters
Andrew Sydnor Barksdale Letters
William Rufus Barlow Letters
Spencer Barnes Letters
Baughman Family Collection
Fred A. Brode Letters
Clayton Coleman Letters

Hill Memorial Library, Louisiana State University, Baton Rouge [LSU]

Israel Adams Family Papers
Albert A. Batchelor Papers
Bennett Family Papers
John C. Burruss Family Papers
Lemuel Parker Conner Family Papers
E. John Ellis Diary
E. P. Ellis and Family Papers
Alfred Flournoy Family Papers
James Foster Family Correspondence
John Achilles Harris Letters
Arthur W. Hyatt Papers
John Ker and Family Papers
Robert H. Miller Letters
D. Y. Milling Correspondence
Joseph D. Shields Papers
Jefferson Stubbs Family Papers
G. H. Tichenor Diaries
Wright-Boyd Family Papers

Library of Virginia, Richmond [LVA]

William R. Carter Letter
Local Government Records Collection, Lunenburg County Court Records
James Francis Preston Letter

Southern Historical Collection, University of North Carolina, Chapel Hill [SHC]

Allen and Simpson Family Papers
James W. Albright Diary and Reminiscences
William Starr Basinger Papers
Comer Family Papers
Daniel Chevilette Govan Papers
Howard Family Papers
Harry Lewis Letters
Virgil Murphey Diary

BIBLIOGRAPHY

John Robert Lowrey Papers
Frank Liddell Richardson Papers
Henry C. Semple Papers
M. Jeff Thompson Papers
Ruffin Thomson Papers
Edward Dorr Tracy Letters
William Henry Tripp and Araminta Guilford Tripp Papers

*UALR Center for Arkansas History and Culture,
Arkansas Studies Institute, Little Rock [UALR]*

Heiskell Civil War Collection
Logan H. Roots Papers

Virginia Historical Society, Richmond [VHS]

Armistead and Blanton Family Papers
James Madison Brannock Papers
St. George Tucker Brooke Autobiography
Carter Family Papers
Cary Family Papers
William Thomas Casey Papers
Chisholm Family Papers
Cocke Family Papers
Mason Graham Ellzey Memoir
James H. Evans Papers
John Walter Fairfax Papers
Ferneyhough Family Papers
James M. Holloway Papers
George Jefferson Hundley Reminiscences
Hunter Family Papers
William T. Kinzer Diary
Liebermann Family Papers
Minerva Direnda Traweek Loomis Papers
Louthan Family Papers
Majette Family Papers
Richard Lancelot Maury Diary
McCabe Family Papers
George M. McDowell Papers
Moore Family Papers
William Goodridge Morton Papers
Beverley Bland Munford Papers
William T. Nelson Papers
Pegram-Johnson-McIntosh Papers
Pendleton Family Papers
Edwin Anderson Penick Papers
James Thomas Perry Diary
Thornton Tayloe Perry Papers
James E. Phillips Reminiscences

BIBLIOGRAPHY

Kate Mason Rowland Papers
Alfred Lewis Scott Memoir
Joseph F. Shaner Letters
J. E. Shuman Letter
St. Paul's Church Vestry Book
Joseph D. Stapp Letters
Edmund Fitzgerald Stone Letter
James Ewell Brown Stuart Papers
Taliaferro Family Papers
William Eustace Trahern Memoir
Henry Alexander Wise Papers

Published Sources

Abell, Richard Bender, and Fay Adamson Gecik, eds. *Sojourns of a Patriot: The Field and Prison Papers of an Unreconstructed Confederate.* Murfreesboro, Tenn.: Southern Heritage Press, 1998.

Alexander, Edwin P. *The Collector's Book of the Locomotive.* New York: C. N. Potter, 1966.

Alexander, Peter Wellington. *Writing and Fighting the Confederate War: The Letters of Peter Wellington Alexander, Confederate War Correspondent.* Edited by William B. Styple. Kearney, N.J.: Belle Grove, 2002.

Alexander, Ted. "A Regular Slave Hunt: The Army of Northern Virginia and Black Civilians in the Gettysburg Campaign." *North and South,* September 2001, 82–89.

Allardice, Bruce. *More Generals in Gray.* Baton Rouge: Louisiana State University Press, 1995.

Allen, Randall, and Keith S. Bohannon, eds. *Campaigning with "Old Stonewall": Confederate Captain Ujanirtus Allen's Letters to His Wife.* Baton Rouge: Louisiana State University Press, 1998.

Ambrose, Stephen E. "Yeomen Discontent in the Confederacy." *Civil War History* 8 (June 1962): 259–68.

Anderson, James. "A Captured Confederate Officer: Nine Letters from Captain James Anderson to His Family," edited by George M. Anderson, S.J. *Maryland Historical Magazine* 76 (March 1981): 62–69.

Anderson, John Q., ed. *Campaigning with Parsons' Texas Cavalry Brigade, CSA: The War Journals and Letters of the Four Orr Brothers, 12th Texas Cavalry Regiment.* Hillsboro, Texas: Hill Junior College Press, 1967.

Andreano, Ralph L., ed. *The Economic Impact of the Civil War.* Cambridge, Mass.: Schenkman, 1962.

Andrew, Rod. *Long Gray Lines: The Southern Military School Tradition, 1839–1915.* Chapel Hill: University of North Carolina Press, 2001.

Apperson, John Samuel. *Repairing the "March of Mars": The Civil War Diaries of John Samuel Apperson, Hospital Steward in the Stonewall Brigade, 1861–1865.* Edited by John Herbert Roper. Macon, Ga.: Mercer University Press, 2001.

Ash, Stephen V. *Middle Tennessee Society Transformed, 1860–1870: War and Peace in the Upper South.* Baton Rouge: Louisiana State University Press, 1988.

———. "Poor Whites in the Occupied South." *Journal of Southern History* 57 (February 1991): 39–62.
Austin, J. Luke. *General John Bratton: Sumter to Appomattox in Letters to His Wife.* Sewanee, Tenn.: Proctor's Hall Press, 2003.
Austin, J. P. *The Blue and the Gray: Sketches of a Portion of the Unwritten History of the Great American Civil War.* Atlanta: Franklin, 1899.
Avera, William. "Extracts from the Memoirs of William Avera," edited by Henry Cathey. *Arkansas Historical Quarterly* 22 (Summer 1963): 99–116.
Ayers, Edward L. *In the Presence of Mine Enemies: War in the Heart of America, 1859–1863.* New York: W. W. Norton, 2003.
———. *Vengeance and Justice: Crime and Punishment in the 19th-Century American South.* New York: Oxford University Press, 1984.
Ayers, Edward L., Gary W. Gallagher, and Andrew J. Torget, eds. *Crucible of the Civil War: Virginia from Secession to Commemoration.* Charlottesville: University of Virginia Press, 2006.
Bailey, Anne J., ed. *In the Saddle with the Texans: Day-by-Day with Parsons's Cavalry Brigade, 1861–1865.* Abilene, Texas: McWhiney Foundation Press, 2004.
Banasik, Michael E., ed. *Missouri Brothers in Gray: The Reminiscences and Letters of William J. Bull and John P. Bull.* Unwritten Chapters of the Civil War West of the River, vol. 1. Iowa City, Iowa: Camp Pope Bookshop, 1998.
Barber, Flavel C. *Holding the Line: The Third Tennessee Infantry, 1861–1864.* Edited by Robert H. Ferrell. Kent, Ohio: Kent State University Press, 1994.
Barclay, Ted. *Ted Barclay, Liberty Hall Volunteers: Letters from the Stonewall Brigade, 1861–1864.* Edited by Charles W. Turner. Natural Bridge Station, Va.: Rockbridge Pub. Co., 1992.
Barnhill, A. Virgil, Jr. "The Diary of Samuel Beckett Boyd: January 1, 1865–April 3, 1865." *Tennessee Ancestors,* April 1995, 29–43.
Barr, James Michael. *Let Us Meet in Heaven: The Civil War Letters of James Michael Barr, 5th South Carolina Cavalry.* Edited by Thomas D. Mays. Abilene, Tex.: McWhiney Foundation Press, 2001.
Barrier, Rufus Alexander. *Dear Father: Confederate Letters Never Before Published.* Edited by Beverly Barrier Troxler and Billy Dawn Barrier Auciello. Margate, Fla.: B. B. Troxler; No. Billerica, Mass.: B. D. B. Auciello, 1989.
Bates, James C. *A Texas Cavalry Officer's Civil War: The Diary and Letters of James C. Bates.* Edited by Richard Lowe. Baton Rouge: Louisiana State University Press, 1999.
Baylor, George. "The Army Negro." *Southern Historical Society Papers* 31 (1903): 365–69.
Beale, George W. "A Soldier's Account of the Gettysburg Campaign: Letter from George W. Beale." *Southern Historical Society Papers* 11 (1883): 320–27.
Bean, W. G. "A House Divided: The Civil War Letters of a Virginia Family." *Virginia Magazine of History and Biography* 59 (October 1951): 397–422.
———. "The Valley Campaign of 1862 as Revealed in Letters of Sandie Pendleton." *Virginia Magazine of History and Biography* 78 (July 1970): 326–64.
Beckett, R. C. "A Sketch of the Career of Company B, Armistead's Cavalry Regiment." *Publications of the Mississippi Historical Society,* no. 8 (1904): 33–50.

BIBLIOGRAPHY

Beitzell, Edwin W. *Point Lookout Prison Camp for Confederates.* Abell, Md.: E. W. Beitzell, 1972.

Beringer, Richard E. "A Profile of the Members of the Confederate Congress." *Journal of Southern History* 33 (November 1967): 518–41.

Beringer, Richard E., Herman Hattaway, and Archer Jones. *Why the South Lost the Civil War.* Athens: University of Georgia Press, 1986.

Berlin, Ira. *Slaves without Masters: The Free Negro in the Antebellum South.* New York: Pantheon, 1975.

Berlin, Ira, et al., eds. *The Destruction of Slavery.* Freedom: A Documentary History of Emancipation, 1861–1867, ser. 1, vol. 1. New York: Cambridge University Press, 1982.

———. *The Black Military Experience.* Freedom: A Documentary History of Emancipation, 1861–1867, ser. 2. New York: Cambridge University Press, 1985.

Bernard, George S. "The Battle of the Crater." *Southern Historical Society Papers* 18 (1890): 3–38.

Berry, Stephen W., II. *All that Makes a Man: Love and Ambition in the Civil War South.* New York: Oxford University Press, 2003.

Bettersworth, John K., and James W. Silver, eds. *Mississippi in the Confederacy: As They Saw It.* Baton Rouge: Published for the Mississippi Dept. of Archives and History, Jackson, by Louisiana State University Press, 1961.

Bevier, R. S. *History of the First and Second Missouri Confederate Brigades, 1861–1865 and from Wakusa to Appomattox, a Military Anagraph.* St. Louis: Bryan, Brand and Co., 1879.

Bird, Edgeworth, and Sallie Bird. *The Granite Farm Letters: The Civil War Correspondence of Edgeworth & Sallie Bird.* Edited by John Rozier. Athens: University of Georgia Press, 1988.

Blackford, W. W. *War Years with Jeb Stuart.* 1945. Reprint, Baton Rouge: Louisiana State University Press, 1993.

Blair, William. *Virginia's Private War: Feeding Body and Soul in the Confederacy, 1861–1865.* New York: Oxford University Press, 1998.

Blight, David. *Race and Reunion: The Civil War in American Memory.* Cambridge, Mass.: Belknap Press of Harvard University Press, 2001.

Bolton, Charles C. *Poor Whites of the Antebellum South: Tenants and Laborers in Central North Carolina and Northeast Mississippi.* Durham, N.C.: Duke University Press, 1993.

Bolton, George Washington. *"In Defense of My Country": The Letters of a Shiloh Confederate Soldier, Sergeant George Washington Bolton, and His Union Parish Volunteers (1861–1864).* Edited by Sue Lyles Eakin and Morgan Peoples. Bernice, La.: Published for the Corney Creek Festival, 1983.

Bond, Bradley. *Political Culture in the Nineteenth-Century South: Mississippi, 1830–1890.* Baton Rouge: Louisiana State University Press, 1995.

Bonner, Robert E. *Mastering America: Southern Slaveholders and the Crisis of American Nationhood.* New York: Cambridge University Press, 2009.

Booth, George Wilson. *A Maryland Boy in Lee's Army.* Lincoln: University of Nebraska Press, 2000.

Boritt, Gabor, ed. *Why the Confederacy Lost.* New York: Oxford University Press, 1992.

Boykin, Samuel. *A Memorial Volume of the Hon. Howell Cobb of Georgia.* Philadelphia: J. B. Lippincott, 1870.

Bragg, Julius Newport. *Letters of a Confederate Surgeon, 1861–65.* Edited by Mrs. T. J. Gaughan. Camden, Ark.: n.p., 1960.

Brannon, C. H. "A True Story of the Old South: Notes from a Confederate Diary." *Register of the Kentucky Historical Society* 37 (January 1939): 40–53.

Braudaway, Douglas Lee. "A Texan Records the Civil War Siege of Vicksburg, Mississippi: The Journal of Maj. Maurice Kavanaugh Simons, 1863." *Southwestern Historical Quarterly* 105 (July 2001): 93–134.

Breckinridge, John C. "What the Ex-Confederate Has Done in Peace." *Southern Historical Society Papers* 20 (1892): 225–37.

Brewer, James H. *The Confederate Negro: Virginia's Craftsmen and Military Laborers.* Durham, N.C.: Duke University Press, 1969.

Brooks, Charles E. "The Social and Cultural Dynamics of Soldiering in Hood's Texas Brigade." *Journal of Southern History* 67 (September 2001): 535–72.

Brooks, Richard Henry. *Keep All My Letters: The Civil War Letters of Richard Henry Brooks, 51st Georgia Infantry.* Edited by Katherine S. Holland. Macon: Mercer University Press, 2003.

Brooks, U. R. *Butler and His Cavalry in the War of Secession, 1861–1865.* Columbia, S.C.: State Company, 1909.

———. *Stories of the Confederacy.* Columbia, S.C.: State Company, 1912.

Buck, Irving A. "Negroes in Our Army." *Southern Historical Society Papers* 31 (1903): 215–28.

Buck, Irving A., and Pat Cleburne. *Cleburne and His Command.* ("Stonewall Jackson of the West" by Thomas Robson Hay). Jackson, Tenn.: McCowat-Mercer Press, 1959.

Budiansky, Stephen. *The Bloody Shirt: Terror after Appomattox.* New York: Viking, 2008.

Burdekin, Richard C. K., and Marc D. Weidenmier. "Inflation Is Always and Everywhere a Monetary Phenomenon." *American Economic Review* 91 (December 2001): 1621–30.

Burkhardt, George S. *Confederate Rage, Yankee Wrath: No Quarter in the Civil War.* Carbondale: Southern Illinois University Press, 2006.

Burnett, Edmund Cody. "Letters of a Confederate Surgeon: Dr. Abner Embry McGarity, 1862–1865." Pt. 4. *Georgia Historical Quarterly* 30 (March 1946): 35–70.

———. "Letters of Three Lightfoot Brothers, 1861–1864." Pt. 1. *Georgia Historical Quarterly* 25 (December 1941): 371–99.

Burney, Samuel A., and Sarah Elizabeth Shepherd. *A Southern Soldier's Letters Home: The Civil War Letters of Samuel Burney, Army of Northern Virginia.* Edited by Nat Turner. Macon, Ga.: Mercer University Press, 2002.

Burress, L. R. "Civilization of Negroes in the South." *Confederate Veteran* 19 (May 1911): 229.

Butler, Lindley S., and Alan D. Watson, eds. *The North Carolina Experience: An Interpretive and Documentary History.* Chapel Hill: University of North Carolina Press, 1984.

Callaway, Felix Richard. *The Bloody Links.* [Shreveport?, La.: n.p., 1907?].

Campbell, Jacqueline. *When Sherman Marched North from the Sea: Resistance on the Confederate Home Front*. Chapel Hill: University of North Carolina Press, 2003.

Campbell, Randolph B. *An Empire for Slavery: The Peculiar Institution in Texas, 1821–1865*. Baton Rouge: Louisiana State University Press, 1989.

———. "Planters and Plain Folk: Harrison County, Texas, as a Test Case, 1850–1860." *Journal of Southern History* 40 (August 1974): 369–98.

Campbell, Randolph B., and Richard G. Lowe. "Some Economic Aspects of Antebellum Texas Agriculture." *Southwestern Historical Quarterly* 82 (April 1979): 351–78.

Campbell, Robert. *Lone Star Confederate: A Gallant and Good Soldier of the 5th Texas Infantry*. Edited by George Skoch and Mark W. Perkins. College Station: Texas A & M University Press, 2003.

Cannon, J. P. *Inside of Rebeldom: The Daily Life of a Private in the Confederate Army*. Washington, D.C.: National Tribune, 1900.

Carr, Pat. *In Fine Spirits: The Civil War Letters of Ras Stirman with Historical Comments*. Fayetteville, Ark.: Washington County Historical Society, 1986.

Carter, Dan. *When the War Was Over: The Failure of Self-Reconstruction in the South, 1865–1867*. Baton Rouge: Louisiana State University Press, 1985.

Cash, Wilbur J. *The Mind of the South*. New York: Vintage, 1941.

Castel, Albert. "The Fort Pillow Massacre: A Fresh Examination of the Evidence." *Civil War History* 4 (March 1958): 37–50.

Cater, Douglas John. *As It Was: Reminiscences of a Soldier of the Third Texas Cavalry and the Nineteenth Louisiana Infantry*. Introduction by T. Michael Parrish. Austin: State House Press, 1990.

Chamberlayne, John Hampden. *Ham Chamberlayne—Virginian: Letters and Papers of an Artillery Officer in the War for Southern Independence*. Edited by C. G. Chamberlayne. Richmond, Va.: Dietz, 1932.

Chambers, William Pitt. "My Journal: The Story of a Soldier's Life Told by Himself." *Publications of the Mississippi Historical Society* 5 (1925): 227–386.

Chapman, Conrad Wise. *Ten Months in the "Orphan Brigade": Conrad Wise Chapman's Civil War Memoir*. Edited by Ben L. Bassham. Kent, Ohio: Kent State University Press, 1999.

Chesnut, Mary Boykin Miller. *A Diary from Dixie*. Edited by Ben Ames Williams. Boston: Houghton Mifflin, 1950.

———. *The Private Mary Chesnut: The Unpublished Diaries*. Edited by C. Vann Woodward and Elisabeth Muhlenfeld. New York: Oxford University Press, 1984.

Chicoine, Stephen, and Rufus King Felder. "'. . . Willing Never To Go in Another Fight': The Civil War Correspondence of Rufus King Felder of Chappell Hill." *Southwestern Historical Quarterly* 106 (April 2003): 574–97.

Christ, Mark K. *Civil War Arkansas, 1863: The Battle for a State*. Norman: University of Oklahoma Press, 2010.

Cimprich, John. "The Fort Pillow Massacre: Assessing the Evidence." In *Black Soldiers in Blue: African American Troops in the Civil War Era*, edited by John David Smith, 150–68. Chapel Hill: University of North Carolina Press, 2002.

Clark, James Lemuel. *Civil War Recollections of James Lemuel Clark*. Edited by L. D. Clark. College Station: Texas A&M University Press, 1984.

Clavin, Matthew J. *Toussaint Louverture and the American Civil War: The Promise and Peril of a Second Haitian Revolution*. Philadelphia: University of Pennsylvania Press, 2010.

Cobb, Thomas R. "Extracts from Letters to his Wife, February 3, 1861–December 10, 1862." *Southern Historical Society Papers* 28 (1900): 280–301.

Cochrane, Harden Perkins. "The Letters of Harden Perkins Cochrane, 1862–1864." Arranged by Harriet Fitts Ryan. Pts. 3, 5. *Alabama Review* 8 (April 1955): 143–52; 8 (October 1955): 277–90.

Coclanis, Peter A. "Thirty-Six Views of Mount Morgan: *Slave Counterpoint* in Context." *South Carolina Historical Magazine* 100 (October 1999): 355–67.

Collins, R. M. *Chapters from the Unwritten History of the War between the States*. St. Louis: Nixon-Jones, 1893.

Connor, Forrest P., and Robert H. Miller. "Letters of Lieutenant Robert H. Miller to His Family, 1861–1862." *Virginia Magazine of History and Biography* 70 (January 1962): 62–91.

Cooper, William J. "The Cotton Crisis: Another Look." *Agricultural History* 49 (April 1975): 381–91.

———. *Liberty and Slavery: Southern Politics to 1860*. Columbia: University of South Carolina Press, 2000.

Corbin, Richard W. *Letters of a Confederate Officer to His Family in Europe during the Last Year of the War of Secession*. Paris, France: Neal, 1913.

Corsan, W. C. *Two Months in the Confederate States: An Englishman's Travels through the South*. Edited with an introduction by Benjamin H. Trask. 1863. Reprint, Baton Rouge: Louisiana State University Press, 1996.

Coulter, E. Merton. *Lost Generation: The Life and Death of James Barrow, C.S.A.* Confederate Centennial Studies, no. 1. Tuscaloosa, Ala.: Confederate Publishing Co., 1956.

Crawford, Alan Pell. *Twilight at Monticello: The Final Years of Thomas Jefferson*. New York: Random House, 2008.

Crawford, Martin. "Political Society in a Southern Mountain Community: Ashe County, North Carolina, 1850–1861." *Journal of Southern History* 55 (August 1989): 373–90.

Crenshaw, Edward. "Diary of Edward Crenshaw of the Confederate States Army." *Alabama Historical Quarterly* 2 (Fall 1940): 365–85.

Crow, William Harrison. *When I Think of Home: The Civil War Letters of William Harrison "Tip" Crow*. Researched and compiled by DeWayne R. Welborn. Decorah, Iowa: Anundsen Publishing, 1996.

Cutrer, Thomas W., and T. Michael Parrish, eds. *Brothers in Gray: The Civil War Letters of the Pierson Family*. Baton Rouge: Louisiana State University Press, 1997.

Dame, William Meade. *From the Rapidan to Richmond*. Baltimore: Green-Lucas, 1920.

Daniel, F. E. *Recollections of a Rebel Surgeon*. Chicago: Clinic, 1901.

Daniel, Lizzie Cary. *Confederate Scrap-Book*. Richmond, Va.: J. L. Hill, 1893.

Davie, Maurice R. *Negroes in American Society*. New York: Whittlesey House, 1949.

Davis, Jefferson. *The Papers of Jefferson Davis*. Edited by Lynda L. Crist, Mary Seaton Dix, and Kenneth H. Williams. 12 vols. to date. Baton Rouge: Louisiana State University Press, 1971–.

BIBLIOGRAPHY

Davis, Nicholas A. *Chaplain Davis and Hood's Texas Brigade.* Edited by Donald E. Everett. 1962. Reprint, Baton Rouge: Louisiana State University Press, 1999.

Davis, William C. *Look Away! A History of the Confederate States of America.* New York: Free Press, 2002.

Davis, William C., and Julie Hoffman, eds. *The Confederate General.* 6 vols. Harrisburg, Pa.: National Historical Society, 1991.

De Bow, J. D. B. "The Interest in Slavery of the Southern Non-Slaveholder." In *Slavery Defended: The Views of the Old South,* edited by Eric L. McKitrick, 169–77. Englewood Cliffs, N.J.: Spectrum, 1963.

Dew, Charles B. *Bond of Iron: Master and Slave at Buffalo Forge.* New York: W. W. Norton, 1995.

Dickinson, Henry C. *Diary of Capt. Henry C. Dickinson, C.S.A.: Morris Island, 1864–1865.* Denver: Press of the Williamson-Haffner Co., 1967.

Dinkins, James. "The Negroes as Slaves." *Southern Historical Society Papers* 35 (1907): 60–68.

Dixon, William Daniel. *Personal Recollections and Experiences in the Confederate Army.* Cincinnati: Robert Clarke Co. Press, 1897.

Donald, David. *Lincoln.* New York: Simon and Schuster, 1995.

Dooley, John. *John Dooley, Confederate Soldier: His War Journal.* Edited by Joseph T. Durkin. Washington, D.C.: Georgetown University Press, 1945.

Dotson, Rand. "'The Grave and Scandalous Evil Infected to Your People': The Erosion of Confederate Loyalty in Floyd County, Virginia." *Virginia Magazine of History and Biography* 108 (October 2000): 393–434.

Doty, Franklin A., ed. "The Civil War Letters of Augustus Henry Mathers, Assistant Surgeon, Fourth Florida Regiment, C.S.A." *Florida Historical Quarterly* 36 (October 1957): 94–124.

Douglas, Henry Kyd. *I Rode with Stonewall.* 1940. Reprint, St. Simons Island, Ga.: Mockingbird Books, 1961.

Douglass, Frederick. *The Frederick Douglass Papers. Series One, Speeches, Debates, and Interviews.* Vol. 4, *1864–80,* edited by John W. Blassingame and John R. McKivigan. New Haven: Yale University Press, 1991.

Drummond, Edward William. *A Confederate Yankee: The Journal of Edward William Drummond, a Confederate Soldier from Maine.* Edited by Roger S. Durham. Knoxville: University of Tennessee Press, 2004.

Duffee, E. B., Jr., ed. "War Letters of S. F. Tenney, A Soldier of the Third Georgia Regiment." *Georgia Historical Quarterly* 57 (Summer 1973): 277–95.

Dunaway, Wayland Fuller. *Reminiscences of a Rebel.* New York: Neale, 1913.

Duncan, Thomas D. *Recollections of Thomas D. Duncan: A Confederate Soldier.* Nashville: McQuiddy Printing, 1922.

Dunlop, W. S. *Lee's Sharpshooters or the Forefront of Battle.* Little Rock: Tunnah and Pittard, 1899.

Durden, Robert F. *The Gray and the Black: The Confederate Debate on Emancipation.* 1972. Reprint, Baton Rouge: Louisiana State University Press, 2000.

Early, Jubal A. *A Memoir of the Last Year of the War for Independence, in the Confederate States of America.* Lynchburg, Va.: Charles W. Button, 1867.

Eaton, Clement. *The Civilization of the Old South.* Lexington: University of Kentucky Press, 1968.

BIBLIOGRAPHY

Edmondston, Catherine Devereux. *"Journal of a Secesh Lady": The Diary of Catherine Ann Devereux Edmondston, 1860–1866.* Edited by Beth G. Crabtree and James W. Patton. Raleigh: Division of Archives and History, Department of Cultural Resources, 1979.

Edrington, John C. "Letters of John C. Edrington." *Northern Neck of Virginia Historical Magazine* (1961): 1019–22.

Elliott, Stephen. "Extract from a Sermon Preached by Bishop Elliott, on the 18th September, Containing a Tribute to the Privates of the Confederate Army." [Savannah?, Ga.: n.p., 1862].

Ellis, John Willis. *The Papers of John Willis Ellis.* Vol. 2, *1860–1861.* Edited by Noble J. Tolbert. Raleigh: State Department of Archives and History, 1964.

Ely, Melvin Patrick. *Israel on the Appomattox: A Southern Experiment in Black Freedom from the 1790s through the Civil War.* New York: Alfred A. Knopf, 2004.

Escott, Paul D. *After Secession: Jefferson Davis and the Failure of Confederate Nationalism.* Baton Rouge: Louisiana State University Press, 1978.

———. *Military Necessity: Civil-Military Relations in the Confederacy.* Westport, Conn.: Greenwood, 2006.

———. *"What Shall We Do with the Negro?": Lincoln, White Racism, and Civil War America.* Charlottesville: University of Virginia Press, 2009.

Evans, Clement Anselm. *Intrepid Warrior, Clement Anselm Evans, Confederate General from Georgia: Life, Letters, and Diaries of the War Years.* Compiled and edited by Robert Grier Stephens. Dayton, Ohio: Morningside, 1992.

Evans, M. F. T. "Dr. Evans and the War (1861–1865)." *Tyler's Historical and Genealogical Magazine* 3 (1922; reprinted, 1967): 157–63.

Evans, Robert G., comp. and ed. *The 16th Mississippi Infantry: Civil War Letters and Reminiscences.* Jackson: University Press of Mississippi, 2002.

Ewell, Richard Stoddard, ed. *The Making of a Soldier: Letters of General R. S. Ewell.* Arranged and edited by Percy Gatling Hamlin. Richmond, Va.: Whittet and Shepperson, 1935.

"Faithful Albert Peete (Bate)" (obituary). *Confederate Veteran* 20 (June 1912): 293.

Fall, Albert B. "Civil War Letters of Albert B. Fall: Gunner for the Confederacy." *Register of the Kentucky Historical Society* 59 (April 1961): 150–68.

Faust, Drew Gilpin. *James Henry Hammond and the Old South: A Design for Mastery.* Baton Rouge: Louisiana State University Press, 1982.

———. *This Republic of Suffering: Death and the American Civil War.* New York: Alfred A. Knopf, 2008.

Fay, Edwin H., and Lucy E. Fay. *"This Infernal War": The Confederate Letters of Sgt. Edwin H. Fay.* Edited by Bell Irvin Wiley. Austin: University of Texas Press, 1958.

Featherston, John C. "Graphic Account of the Battle of the Crater." *Southern Historical Society Papers* 33 (1905): 358–74.

Fewell, Alexander Faulkner. *"Dear Martha . . . ": The Confederate War Letters of a South Carolina Soldier Alexander Faulkner Fewell.* Edited by Robert Harley Mackintosh, Jr. [Columbia?, S.C.]: Mackintosh, 1976.

"Fidelity of Negro War Servants." *Confederate Veteran* 5 (July 1897): 384.

Fisher, John E. "Life on the Common Level: Inheritance, Conflict, and Instruction." *Tennessee Historical Quarterly* 26 (Fall 1967): 304–22.

Fitzgerald, Michael. "Another Kind of Glory: Black Participation and Its Consequences in the Campaign for Confederate Mobile." *Alabama Review* 54 (October 2001): 243–75.

Fitzpatrick, Marion Hill. *Letters to Amanda: The Civil War Letters of Marion Hill Fitzpatrick, Army of Northern Virginia*. Edited by Jeffrey C. Lowe and Sam Hodges. Macon, Ga.: Mercer University Press, 1998.

Fleet, Benjamin Robert. *Green Mount: A Virginia Plantation Family during the Civil War*. Edited by Betsy Fleet and John D. P. Fuller. Lexington: University of Kentucky Press, 1962.

Fletcher, William A. *Rebel Private, Front and Rear: Memoirs of a Confederate Soldier*. 1908. Reprint, New York: Dutton, 1995.

Fogel, Robert William, and Stanley L. Engerman. *Time on the Cross: The Economics of American Negro Slavery*. 1974. Reprint, New York: W. W. Norton, 1989.

Foner, Eric. *Free Soil, Free Labor, Free Men: The Ideology of the Republican Party before the Civil War*. New York: Oxford University Press, 1970.

———. *Reconstruction: America's Unfinished Revolution, 1863–1877*. New York: Harper and Row, 1988.

Ford, Lacy K. *Origins of Southern Radicalism: The South Carolina Upcountry, 1800–1860*. New York: Oxford University Press, 1988.

Foster, Gaines M. *Ghosts of the Confederacy: Defeat, the Lost Cause, and the Emergence of the New South*. New York: Oxford University Press, 1987.

———. "Guilt over Slavery: A Historiographical Analysis." *Journal of Southern History* 56 (November 1990): 665–94.

———. "The Limitations of Federal Health Care for Freedmen, 1862–1868." *Journal of Southern History* 48 (August 1982): 349–72.

Foster, Samuel T. *One of Cleburne's Command: The Civil War Reminiscences and Diary of Capt. Samuel T. Foster, Granbury's Texas Brigade, CSA*. Edited by Norman D. Brown. Austin: University of Texas Press, 1980.

Frank, Joseph Allan. *With Ballot and Bayonet: The Political Socialization of American Civil War Soldiers*. Athens: University of Georgia Press, 1998.

Franklin, John Hope, and Loren Schweninger. *Runaway Slaves: Rebels on the Plantation*. New York: Oxford University Press, 1999.

Fredrickson, George M. *The Black Image in the White Mind: The Debate on Afro-American Character and Destiny, 1817–1914*. New York: Harper and Row, 1971.

Freehling, Alison Goodyear. *Drift toward Dissolution: The Virginia Slavery Debate of 1831–32*. Baton Rouge: Louisiana State University Press, 1982.

Freehling, William W. *Prelude to Civil War: The Nullification Controversy in South Carolina, 1816–1836*. New York: Oxford University Press, 1965.

———. *The South vs. the South: How Anti-Confederate Southerners Shaped the Course of the Civil War*. New York: Oxford University Press, 2001.

Freeman, Benjamin H. *The Confederate Letters of Benjamin H. Freeman*. Edited by Stuart T. Wright. Hicksville, N.Y.: Exposition Press, 1974.

Fremantle, Sir James Arthur Lyon. *The Fremantle Diary: Being the Journal of Lieutenant Colonel James Arthur Lyon Fremantle, Coldstream Guards on His Three Months in the Southern States*. Editing and commentary by Walter Lord. Boston: Little, Brown, 1954.

BIBLIOGRAPHY

Fry, Joseph A. *John Tyler Morgan and the Search for Confederate Autonomy.* Knoxville: University of Tennessee Press, 1992.

Gallagher, Gary. *The Confederate War.* Cambridge, Mass.: Harvard University Press, 1997.

Gammage, W. L. *The Camp, the Bivouac, and the Battle Field: Being a History of the Fourth Arkansas Regiment, from Its First Organization Down to the Present Day.* Little Rock: Arkansas Southern Press, 1958.

Genovese, Eugene. *From Rebellion to Revolution: Afro-American Slave Revolts in the Making of the Modern World.* Baton Rouge: Louisiana State University Press, 1979.

Gibbons, A. R. *The Recollections of an Old Confederate Soldier.* Shelbyville, Mo.: Herald Print, [1914?].

Gienapp, William E., ed. *The Civil War and Reconstruction: A Documentary Collection.* New York: W. W. Norton, 2001.

Gillette, William. *Retreat from Reconstruction, 1869–1879.* Baton Rouge: Louisiana State University Press, 1979.

Gillispie, James Massie. *Andersonvilles of the North: The Myths and Realities of Northern Treatment of Civil War Confederate Prisoners.* Denton: University of North Texas Press, 2008.

Glatthaar, Joseph T. *Forged in Battle: The Civil War Alliance of Black Soldiers and White Officers.* Baton Rouge: Louisiana State University Press, 2000.

———. *General Lee's Army: From Victory to Collapse.* New York: Free Press, 2008.

———. "The 'New' Civil War History: An Overview." *Pennsylvania Magazine of History and Biography* 95 (July 1991): 339–69.

Glenn, John F. "Defence of Petersburg." *Southern Historical Society Papers* 35 (1907): 1–24.

Good, John J. *Cannon Smoke: The Letters of Captain John J. Good, Good-Douglas Texas Battery, CSA.* Compiled and edited by Lester Newton Fitzhugh. Hillsboro, Tex.: Hill Junior College Press, 1971.

Gordon, John B. *Reminiscences of the Civil War.* New York: Charles Scribner's Sons, 1903.

Goree, Thomas J. *Longstreet's Aide: The Civil War Letters of Major Thomas J. Goree.* Edited by Thomas W. Cutrer. Charlottesville: University Press of Virginia, 1995.

Goyne, Minetta Altgelt. *Lone Star and Double Eagle: Civil War Letters of a German-Texas Family.* Fort Worth: Texas Christian University Press, 1982.

Graham, James Augustus. *The James A. Graham Papers, 1861–1884.* Edited by H. M. Wagstaff. James Sprunt Historical Studies, vol. 20, no. 2. Chapel Hill: University of North Carolina Press, 1928.

Graham, William Alexander. *The Papers of William Alexander Graham.* Edited by Max R. Williams and J. G. de Roulhac Hamilton. 8 vols. Raleigh, N.C.: State Department of Archives and History, 1957–.

Grant, Ulysses S. *Personal Memoirs of U. S. Grant.* 1885–86. Reprint, New York: Barnes and Noble Books, 2003.

———. *The Papers of Ulysses S. Grant.* Vol. 12, *August 16–November 15, 1864.* Edited by John Y. Simon. Carbondale: Southern Illinois University Press, 1984.

Green, Johnny. *Johnny Green of the Orphan Brigade: The Journal of a Confederate Soldier.* Edited by A. D. Kirwan. Lexington: University of Kentucky Press, 1956.

Greenberg, Martin H., and Charles G. Waugh, eds. *The Price of Freedom: Slavery and the Civil War.* 2 vols. Nashville: Cumberland House, 2000.

Grimsley, Mark. *The Hard Hand of War: Union Military Policy toward Southern Civilians, 1861–1865.* New York: Cambridge University Press, 1995.

Grimsley, Mark, and Brooks D. Simpson. *The Collapse of the Confederacy.* Lincoln: University of Nebraska Press, 2001.

Guelzo, Allen C. *Lincoln's Emancipation Proclamation: The End of Slavery in America.* New York: Simon and Schuster, 2004.

Gunderson, Gerald. "Origin of the American Civil War." *Journal of Economic History* 34 (December 1974): 915–50.

Hacker, J. David. "A Census-Based Count of the Civil War Dead." *Civil War History* 57 (December 2011): 307–48.

Hahn, Steven. *Roots of Southern Populism: Yeomen Farmers and the Transformation of the Georgia Upcountry, 1850–1890.* New York: Oxford University Press, 1983.

Hahn, Steven, Steven F. Miller, Susan E. O'Donovan, John C. Rodrigue, and Leslie S. Rowlan, eds. *Freedom: A Documentary History of Emancipation, 1861–1867: Land and Labor.* Chapel Hill: University of North Carolina Press, 2008.

Handerson, Henry E. *Yankee in Gray.* Pittsburgh: Press of Western Reserve University, 1962.

Hardee, W. J. "Biographical Sketch of Major-General Patrick R. Cleburne." *Southern Historical Society Papers* 31 (1903): 151–63.

Harris, J. William. *Plain Folk and Gentry in a Slave Society: White Liberty and Black Slavery in Augusta's Hinterlands.* 1985. Reprint, Baton Rouge: Louisiana State University Press, 1998.

Haskell, John Cheves. *The Haskell Memoirs.* Edited by Gilbert E. Govan and James W. Livingood. New York: G. P. Putnam's Sons, 1960.

Hayden, Horace E., Jr. "Report of the Commander, R. E. Lee Camp, No. 1, S.C.V." *Stars and Bars* (May 1923): 11–13.

Haynes, Draughton Stith. *The Field Diary of a Confederate Soldier while Serving in the Army of Northern Virginia.* Darien, Ga.: Ashantilly Press, 1963.

Heartsill, W. W. *Fourteen Hundred and 91 Days in the Confederate Army: A Journal Kept by W. W. Heartsill for Four Years, One Month, and One Day. Or, Camp Life, Day by Day, of the W. P. Lane Rangers from April 19, 1861, to May 20, 1865.* Edited by Bell Irvin Wiley. Jackson, Tenn.: McCowat-Mercer Press, 1954.

"Heroic and Patriotic Marylanders." *Confederate Veteran* 2 (September 1894): 260.

Hill, Lawrence F. "The Confederate Exodus to Latin America." Parts 1, 2, and 3. *Southwestern Historical Quarterly* 39 (October 1935): 100–34; 39 (January 1936): 161–99; 39 (April 1936): 309–26.

Hobson, Fred. *Tell about the South: The Southern Rage to Explain.* Baton Rouge: Louisiana State University Press, 1983.

Hodges, Ellen E., Stephen Kerber, Winston Stephens, and Octavia Stephens. "'Rogues and Black Hearted Scamps': Civil War Letters of Winston and Octavia Stephens, 1862–63." *Florida Historical Quarterly* 57 (July 1978): 54–82.

BIBLIOGRAPHY

Hollandsworth, James G. *The Louisiana Native Guards: The Black Military Experience during the Civil War.* Baton Rouge: Louisiana State University Press, 1995.

Holt, Daniel. *A Mississippi Rebel in the Army of Northern Virginia: The Civil War Memoirs of Private Daniel Holt.* Edited by Thomas D. Cockrell and Michael B. Ballard. Baton Rouge: Louisiana State University Press, 1995.

Holt, John Lee. *I Wrote You Word: The Poignant Letters of Private Holt.* Edited by James A Mumper; compiled by M. Ellen Bailey, Mary Andrews Dalby. Lynchburg, Va.: H. E. Howard, 1993.

Holt, Thomas C. *Black over White: Negro Political Leadership in South Carolina during Reconstruction.* Urbana: University of Illinois Press, 1977.

"Honor for the Old-Time Negro." *Confederate Veteran* 20 (September 1912): 410.

Hood, John Bell. *Advance and Retreat: Personal Experiences in the United States and Confederate States Armies.* New Orleans: Published for the Hood Orphan Memorial Fund, 1880.

Horn, Stanley F. *Invisible Empire: The Story of the Ku Klux Klan, 1866–1871.* Boston: Houghton Mifflin, 1939.

Houghton, W. R., and M. B. Houghton. *Two Boys in the Civil War and After.* Montgomery, Ala.: Paragon Press, 1912.

Howard, Robert M. *Reminiscences.* Columbus, Ga.: Gilbert Printing, 1912.

Howe, Daniel Walker. *What Hath God Wrought: The Transformation of America, 1815–1848.* New York: Oxford University Press, 2007.

Hubbard, John Milton. *Notes of a Private, Company E, 7th Tennessee Regiment, Forrest's Cavalry Corps, C.S.A.* St. Louis: Nixon-Jones, 1911.

Hubbs, G. Ward, ed. *Voices from Company D: Diaries by the Greensboro Guards, Fifth Alabama Infantry Regiment, Army of Northern Virginia.* Athens: University of Georgia Press, 2003.

Hudson, James J., and Robert C. Gilliam. "From Paraclifta to Marks' Mill: The Civil War Correspondence of Lieutenant Robert C. Gilliam." *Arkansas Historical Quarterly* 17 (Autumn 1958): 272–302.

Huffman, James. *Ups and Downs of a Confederate Soldier.* New York: W. E. Rudge's Sons, 1940.

Hume, Richard L., and Jerry B. Gough. *Blacks, Carpetbaggers, and Scalawags: The Constitutional Conventions of Radical Reconstruction.* Baton Rouge: Louisiana State University Press, 2008.

Hundley, Daniel R. *Social Relations in Our Southern States.* Edited by William J. Cooper. Baton Rouge: Louisiana State University Press, 1979. Reprint of the 1860 edition published by H. B. Price, New York.

———. *Prison Echoes of the Great Rebellion.* New York: S. W. Green, Printer, 1874.

Hurst, Jack. *Nathan Bedford Forrest: A Biography.* New York: Vintage, 1993.

Huston, James L. *Calculating the Cost of the Union: Slavery, Property Rights, and the Economic Origins of the Civil War.* Chapel Hill: University of North Carolina Press, 2003.

Ingram, E. Renée. *In View of the Great Want of Labor: A Legislative History of African American Conscription in the Confederacy.* Westminster, Md.: Willowbend Books, 1999.

Ingram, George W., and Martha Ingram. *Civil War Letters of George W. and Martha F. Ingram, 1861–1865. Compiled by Henry L. Ingram. College Station: Texas A & M University Press, 1973.

Inscoe, John, and Gordon McKinney. *The Heart of Confederate Appalachia: Western North Carolina in the Civil War.* Chapel Hill: University of North Carolina Press, 2000.

Inzer, John Washington. *The Diary of a Confederate Soldier: John Washington Inzer, 1834–1928.* Edited by Mattie Lou Teague Crow. Huntsville, Ala.: Strode, 1977.

Jackson, Hester Bartlett, ed., et al. *Surry County Soldiers in the Civil War.* Charlotte, N.C.: Delmar, 1992.

Janney, Caroline E. *Burying the Dead but Not the Past: Ladies' Memorial Associations and the Lost Cause.* Chapel Hill: University of North Carolina Press, 2008.

Jimerson, Randall C. *The Private Civil War: Popular Thought during the Sectional Conflict.* Baton Rouge: Louisiana State University Press, 1988.

Johnston, John. "The Civil War Reminiscences of John Johnston, 1861–1865 (Part I)," edited by William T. Alderson. *Tennessee Historical Quarterly* 13 (March 1954): 65–82.

Johnson, Walter. *Soul by Soul: Life inside the Antebellum Slave Market.* Cambridge, Mass.: Harvard University Press, 1999.

Johnston, Jane Echols, and Brenda Lynn Williams, comps. and eds. *Hard Times, 1861–1865: A Collection of Confederate Letters, Court Minutes, Soldier Records, and Local Lore from Craig County, Virginia.* 3 vols. [New Castle, Va.?]: J. E. Johnston; [Newport, Va.?]: B. L. Williams, 1986–[1990].

Joiner, Gary D., ed. *Little to Eat and Thin Mud to Drink: Letters, Diaries, and Memoirs from the Red River Campaigns, 1863–1864.* Knoxville: University of Tennessee Press, 2007.

Jones, Allen W. "A Georgia Confederate Soldier Visits Montgomery, Alabama." *Alabama Historical Quarterly* 25 (Spring/Summer 1963): 99–113.

Jones, Charles Colcock. *The Children of Pride: A True Story of Georgia and the Civil War.* Edited by Robert Manson Myers. New Haven, Conn.: Yale University Press, 1984.

Jones, J. William. "Reminiscences of the Army of Northern Virginia." *Southern Historical Society Papers* 10 (1882): 81–90.

Jones, John B. *A Rebel War Clerk's Diary.* Condensed, edited, and annotated by Earl Schenck Miers. New York: Sagamore Press, 1958.

Jones, Washington. *Under the Stars and Bars: A History of the Surry Light Artillery.* 1909. Reprint, Marietta, Ga.: Morningside, 1975.

Jordan, Ervin L., Jr. *Black Confederates and Afro-Yankees in Civil War Virginia.* Charlottesville: University Press of Virginia, 1995.

Jordan, Winthrop D. *Tumult and Silence at Second Creek: An Inquiry into a Civil War Slave Conspiracy.* Baton Rouge: Louisiana State University Press, 1993.

———. *The White Man's Burden: Historical Origins of Racism in the United States.* New York: Oxford University Press, 1974.

Jordan-Bychkov, Terry G., Allen R. Brannum, and Paula K. Hood, eds. "The Boesel Letters: Two Texas Germans in Sibley's Brigade." Translated by Irma Ohlendorf Schwarz. *Southwestern Historical Quarterly* 102 (April 1999): 457–86.

Josephy, Alvin M. *The Civil War in the American West.* New York: Alfred A. Knopf, 1991.

Kamphoefner, Walter D., and Wolfgang Helbich, eds. *Germans in the Civil War: The Letters They Wrote Home.* Translated by Susan Carter Vogel. Chapel Hill: University of North Carolina Press, 2006.

Karnow, Stanley. *In Our Image: America's Empire in the Philippines.* New York: Random House, 1989.

Kean, Robert Garlick Hill. *Inside the Confederate Government: The Diary of Robert Garlick Hill Kean, Head of the Bureau of War.* Edited by Edward Younger. New York: Oxford University Press, 1957.

Keiley, A. M. *In Vinculis; or, the Prisoner of War.* New York: Blelock and Co., 1866.

———. "Prison-Pens North." *Southern Historical Society Papers* 18 (1890): 333–40.

Kendall, John Smith. "Recollections of a Confederate Officer." *Louisiana Historical Quarterly* 29 (October 1946): 1041–1228.

Key, Thomas J., and Campbell, Robert J. *Two Soldiers: The Campaign Diaries of Thomas J. Key, CSA, December 7, 1863–May 17, 1865, and Robert J. Campbell, U.S.A., January 1, 1864–July 21, 1864.* Edited by Wirt Armistead Cate. Chapel Hill: University of North Carolina Press, 1938.

Kinard, Jeff. *The Battle of the Crater.* Fort Worth, Texas: Ryan Place Publishers, 1995.

King, Spencer B., Jr., ed. *Rebel Lawyer: Letters of Theodorick W. Montfort.* Athens: University of Georgia Press, 1965.

King, William Henry. *No Pardons to Ask, Nor Apologies to Make: The Journal of William Henry King, Gray's 28th Louisiana Infantry Regiment.* Edited by Gary D. Joiner, Marilyn S. Joiner, and Clifton D. Cardin. Knoxville: University of Tennessee Press, 2006.

Kolchin, Peter. *American Slavery, 1619–1877.* Rev. ed. New York: Hill and Wang, 2003.

Kruman, Marc W. *Parties and Politics in North Carolina, 1836–1865.* Baton Rouge: Louisiana State University Press, 1993.

Lane, Mills, ed. *"Dear Mother: Don't grieve about me. If I get killed, I'll only be dead": Letters from Georgia Soldiers in the Civil War.* Savannah, Ga.: Beehive Press, 1990.

———. *The Times That Prove People's Principles: Civil War in Georgia.* Savannah, Ga.: Beehive Press, 1993.

Lankford, A. H. "Hypocrisy of the 'Elson History'" (editorial). *Confederate Veteran* 20 (March 1912): 103.

Lankford, Nelson D. *Cry Havoc! The Crooked Road to Civil War, 1861.* New York: Viking, 2007.

Laskin, Elisabeth L. "Good Old Rebels: Soldiering in the Army of Northern Virginia, 1862–1865." PhD diss., Harvard University, 2003.

Laurence, Debra Nance, ed. "Letters from a North Louisiana Tiger." *North Louisiana Historical Association Journal* 10 (Fall 1979): 130–47.

Law, J. G. "Diary of Reverend J. G. Law." *Southern Historical Society Papers* 12 (1884): 538–43.

Lebergott, Stanley. "Why the South Lost: Commercial Purpose in the Confederacy, 1861–1865." *Journal of American History* 70 (June 1983): 58–74.

Lee, Robert E. *The Wartime Papers of Robert E. Lee.* Edited by Clifford Dowdey and Louis H. Manarin. Boston: Little, Brown, 1961.

BIBLIOGRAPHY

Lee, Robert E., Jr. *Recollections and Letters of General Robert E. Lee.* Garden City, N.Y.: Garden City, 1924.

Lee, Susan Pendleton. *Memoirs of William Nelson Pendleton, D.D., Rector of Latimer Parish, Lexington, Virginia; Brigadier-General C.S.A.; Chief of Artillery, Army of Northern Virginia.* Philadelphia: J. B. Lippincott Co., 1893.

Leidecker, Kurt F. "Beyond the Strife." *Register of the Kentucky Historical Society* 47 (April 1949): 186–243.

Lemann, Nicholas. *Redemption: The Last Battle of the Civil War.* New York: Farrar, Straus and Giroux, 2006.

Leon, L. *Diary of a Tar Heel Confederate Soldier.* Charlotte, N.C.: Stone, 1913.

Levine, Bruce. *Confederate Emancipation: Southern Plans to Free and Arm Slaves during the Civil War.* New York: Oxford University Press, 2006.

Liddell, St. John Richardson. *Liddell's Record.* Edited by Nathaniel Cheairs Hughes. Baton Rouge: Louisiana State University Press, 1997.

Lincoln, Abraham. *The Collected Works of Abraham Lincoln.* 8 vols. Edited by Roy P. Basler. New Brunswick, N.J.: Rutgers University Press, 1953–55.

Linderman, Gerald. *Embattled Courage: The Experience of Combat in the American Civil War.* New York: Free Press, 1987.

Lindgren, James. "Apostasy of a Southern Anti-Imperialist: Bryan, the Spanish-American War, and Business Expansion." *Southern Studies* 2 (Summer 1991): 151–78.

Little, George, and George Maxwell. *A History of Lumsden's Battery, CSA.* Tuscaloosa, Ala.: R. E. Rhodes Chapter, United Daughters of the Confederacy, 1905(?).

Litwack, Leon F. "Many Thousands Gone: Black Southerners and the Confederacy." In *The Old South in the Crucible of War: Essays,* edited by Harry P. Owens and John J. Cooke, 47–63. Jackson: University Press of Mississippi, 1993.

Loehr, Charles T. "Point Lookout." *Southern Historical Society Papers* 18 (1890): 113–20.

Logan, David Jackson. *"A Rising Star of Promise": The Civil War Odyssey of David Jackson Logan, 17th South Carolina Volunteers, 1861–1864.* Edited by Samuel N. Thomas, Jr., and Jason H. Silverman. Campbell, Calif.: Savas Pub. Co., 1998.

Logan, Rayford W. *The Negro in American Life and Thought: The Nadir, 1877–1901.* New York: Dial Press, 1954.

Longstreet, James. *From Manassas to Appomattox: Memoirs of the Civil War in America.* Philadelphia: J. B. Lippincott, 1896.

Lorimer, Douglas A. "The Role of Anti-Slavery Sentiment in English Reactions to the American Civil War." *Historical Journal* 19 (June 1976): 405–20.

Mahon, John K. "Peter Dekle's Letters." *Civil War History* 4 (March 1958): 11–22.

Mahone, William. *The Battle of the Crater.* Petersburg, Va.: Franklin Press, 1864.

Majewski, John D. *Modernizing a Slave Economy: The Economic Vision of the Confederate Nation.* Chapel Hill: University of North Carolina Press, 2009.

Malone, Bartlett Yancey. *Whipt 'em Everytime: The Diary of Bartlett Yancey Malone.* Edited by William Whatley Pierson, Jr. Jackson, Tenn.: McCowat-Mercer Press, 1960.

Manning, Chandra. *What This Cruel War Was Over: Soldiers, Slavery, and the Civil War.* New York: Alfred A. Knopf, 2007.

Marrs, Aaron W. "Desertion and Loyalty in the South Carolina Infantry, 1861–1865." *Civil War History* 50 (March 2004): 47–65.

Marshall, Charles. *An Aide-De-Camp of Lee: Being the Papers of Colonel Charles Marshall, Sometime Aid-de-Camp, Military Secretary, and Assistant Adjutant General on the Staff of Robert E. Lee, 1862–1865.* Edited by Frederick Maurice. Boston: Little, Brown, 1927.

Martin, Jonathan Martin. *Divided Mastery: Slave Hiring in the American South.* Cambridge, Mass.: Harvard University Press, 2004.

Martinez, Jaime Amanda. "For the Defense of the State: Slave Impressment in Confederate Virginia and North Carolina." PhD diss., University of Virginia, 2008.

———. "The Slave Market in Civil War Virginia." In *Crucible of the Civil War: Virginia from Secession to Commemoration,* edited by Edward L. Ayers, Gary W. Gallagher, and Andrew J. Torget, 106–35. Charlottesville: University of Virginia Press, 2006.

Marvel, William. *Andersonville: The Last Depot.* Chapel Hill: University of North Carolina Press, 1994.

———. *Lee's Last Retreat: The Flight to Appomattox.* Chapel Hill: University of North Carolina Press, 2002.

Masur, Louis. *1831: Year of Eclipse.* New York: Hill and Wang, 2001.

Mathis, Ray, comp. and ed. *In the Land of the Living: Wartime Letters by Confederates from the Chattahoochee Valley of Alabama and Georgia.* Troy, Ala.: Troy State University Press, 1981.

Mays, Samuel Elias. "Sketches from the Journal of a Confederate Soldier." *Tyler's Historical and Genealogical Quarterly* 5 (July 1923): 30–53; 5 (October 1923): 95–126.

McArthur, Judith N., and Orville Vernon Burton. *"A Gentleman and an Officer": A Military and Social History of James B. Griffin's Civil War.* New York: Oxford University Press, 1996.

McBrien, D. D., and William Wakefield Garner. "Letters of an Arkansas Confederate Soldier." *Arkansas Historical Quarterly* 2 (March 1943): 58–70; 2 (June 1943): 171–84; 2 (September 1943): 268–86.

McCabe, W. Gordon. *The Defense of Petersburg: Address of Capt. W. Gordon McCabe.* Richmond, Va.: G. W. Gary, 1876.

McCarthy, Carlton. *Detailed Minutiae of Soldier Life in the Army of Northern Virginia, 1861–1865.* Richmond, Va.: B. F. Johnson, 1899.

McCaslin, Richard B. *Lee in the Shadow of Washington.* Baton Rouge: Louisiana State University Press, 2001.

McCrady, Colonel Edward, Jr. "Address of Colonel Edward McGrady, Jr." *Southern Historical Society Papers* 16 (1888): 246–61.

McCurry, Stephanie. *Masters of Small Worlds: Yeomen Households, Gender Relations, and the Political Culture of the Antebellum South Carolina Lowcountry.* New York: Oxford University Press, 1995.

McGimsey, Cornelia, and Lewis Warwick. *My Dearest Friend: The Civil War Letters of Cornelia McGimsey and Lewis Warlick.* Edited by Mike Lawing and Carolyn Lawing. Durham, N.C.: Carolina Academic Press, 2000.

McGinty, Garnie W., Isaac Hall, and Mary Hall. "The Human Side of War: Letters

between a Bienville Parish Civil War Soldier and His Wife." *North Louisiana Historical Association Journal* 13 (Spring–Summer 1982): 59–81.
McGuire, Hunter, and George L. Christian. *The Confederate Cause and Conduct in the War between the States.* Richmond, Va.: L. H. Jenkins, 1913.
McKee, Hugh, ed. *The McKee Letters, 1859–1880: Correspondence of a Georgia Farm Family during the Civil War and Reconstruction.* Milledgeville, Ga.: Boyd Pub. Co., 2000.
McKim, Randolph. *A Soldier's Recollections: Leaves from the Diary of a Young Confederate.* New York: Longmans, Green, 1911.
McKitrick, Eric L. *Andrew Johnson and Reconstruction.* Chicago: University of Chicago Press, 1960.
———, ed. *Slavery Defended: The Views of the Old South.* Englewood Cliffs, N.J.: Spectrum, 1963.
McKivigan, John R., and Mitchell Snay, eds. *Religion and the Antebellum Debate over Slavery.* Athens: University of Georgia Press, 1998.
McLaws, Lafayette. *A Soldier's General: The Civil War Letters of Major General Lafayette McLaws.* Edited by John C. Oeffinger. Chapel Hill: University of North Carolina Press, 2002.
McPheeters, William M. *I Acted from Principle: The Civil War Diary of Dr. William M. McPheeters, Confederate Surgeon in the Trans-Mississippi.* Edited by Cynthia DeHaven Pitcock and Bill J. Gurley. Fayetteville: University of Arkansas Press, 2002.
McPherson, James M. *For Cause and Comrades: Why Men Fought in the Civil War.* New York: Oxford University Press, 1997.
———. *Ordeal by Fire: The Civil War and Reconstruction.* 2 vols. 2nd ed. New York: McGraw-Hill, 1993.
———. *What They Fought For, 1861–1865.* Baton Rouge: Louisiana State University Press, 1994.
McWhiney, Grady, and Perry D. Jamieson. *Attack and Die: Civil War Tactics and the Southern Heritage.* Tuscaloosa: University of Alabama Press, 1982.
Merli, Frank J., ed. "Alternative to Appomattox: A Virginian's Vision of an Anglo-Confederate Colony on the Amazon, May 1865," *Virginia Magazine of History and Biography* 94 (April 1986): 210–19.
Minor, Charles. "The Old System of Slavery." *Southern Historical Society Papers* 30 (1902): 125–29.
Mitchell, Enoch L., and U. G. Owen. "Letters of a Confederate Surgeon in the Army of Tennessee to His Wife." *Tennessee Historical Quarterly* 5 (June 1946): 142–81.
Mitchell, Reid. *Civil War Soldiers.* 1988. Reprint, New York: Penguin, 1997.
Mohr, Clarence L. *On the Threshold of Freedom: Masters and Slaves in Civil War Georgia.* Athens: University of Georgia Press, 1986.
Monaghan, Jay. *Swamp Fox of the Confederacy: The Life and Military Services of M. Jeff Thompson.* Confederate Centennial Studies, 2. Tuscaloosa, Ala.: Confederate Pub. Co., 1956.
Montgomery, Frank A. *Reminiscences of a Mississippian in Peace and War.* Cincinnati: Robert Clarke Company Press, 1901.
Montgomery, Horace. *Howell Cobb's Confederate Career.* Confederate Centennial Studies, 10 Tuscaloosa, Ala.: Confederate Pub. Co., 1959.

BIBLIOGRAPHY

Montgomery, William Rhadamanthus. *Georgia Sharpshooter: The Civil War Diary and Letters of William Rhadamanthus Montgomery, 1839–1906*. Edited by George Montgomery, Jr. Macon: Mercer University Press, 1997.

Moore, Albert Burton. *Conscription and Conflict in the Confederacy*. New York: Macmillan, 1924.

Moore, Edward A. *The Story of a Cannoneer under Stonewall Jackson*. New York: Neale, 1907.

Morgan, John T. "Address of General John T. Morgan." *Southern Historical Society Papers* 5 (1878): 1–33.

Morgan, Philip D. *Slave Counterpoint: Slavery in the Eighteenth Century Chesapeake and Lowcountry*. Chapel Hill: University of North Carolina Press, 1998.

Morgan, W. H. *Personal Reminiscences of the War of 1861–5*. Lynchburg, Va.: J. P. Bell, 1911.

Mosby, John Singleton. *The Memoirs of Colonel John S. Mosby*. Edited by Charles Wells Russell. Bloomington: Indiana University Press, 1959.

———. *Take Sides with the Truth: The Postwar Letters of John Singleton Mosby to Samuel F. Chapman*. Edited by Peter A. Brown. Lexington: University Press of Kentucky, 2007.

Mosgrove, George Dallas. "General Morgan's Last Raid." *Southern Historical Society Papers* 35 (1907): 110–20.

Munford, Thomas. "Resolution of Colonel Thomas Munford, Adopted by the 2nd Virginia Cavalry Regiment, February 28, 1865." *Southern Historical Society Papers* 16 (1888): 355–56.

Myers, Frank M. *The Comanches: A History of Whites' Battalion, Virginia Cavalry*. Marietta, Ga.: Continental Book Co., 1956.

National Park Service. "Soldiers and Sailors Database" (CWSS—Civil War Soldiers and Sailors System). http://www.civilwar.nps.gov/cwss.

Neblett, Elizabeth Scott. *A Rebel Wife in Texas: The Diary and Letters of Elizabeth Scott Neblett, 1852–1864*. Edited by Erika L. Murr. Baton Rouge: Louisiana State University Press, 2001.

Neely, Mark E. *Southern Rights: Political Prisoners and the Myth of Confederate Constitutionalism*. Charlottesville: University Press of Virginia, 1999.

Nelson, Bernard H. "Confederate Slave Impressment Legislation, 1861–1865." *Journal of Negro History* 31 (October 1946): 392–410.

Nelson, Scott Reynolds. *Iron Confederacies: Southern Railways, Klan Violence, and Reconstruction*. Chapel Hill: University of North Carolina Press, 1999.

Nelson, Scott Reynolds, and Carol Sheriff. *A People at War: Civilians and Soldiers in America's Civil War*. New York: Oxford University Press, 2007.

Nelson, William Cowper. *The Hour of Our Nation's Agony: The Civil War Letters of Lt. William Cowper Nelson of Mississippi*. Edited by Jennifer W. Ford. Knoxville: University of Tennessee Press, 2007.

Nieman, Donald G. *The Day of Jubilee: Civil War Experiences of Black Southerners*. New York: Garland, 1994.

Nisbet, James Cooper. *Four Years on the Firing Line*. Edited by Bell Irvin Wiley. Jackson, Tenn.: McCowat-Mercer Press, 1963.

Noe, Kenneth. *Reluctant Rebels: The Confederates Who Joined the Army after 1861*. Chapel Hill: University of North Carolina Press, 2010.

Noll, Mark A. *The Civil War as a Theological Crisis.* Chapel Hill: University of North Carolina Press, 2006.

Nugent, William L., and Eleanor Smith Nugent. *My Dear Nellie: The Civil War Letters of William L. Nugent to Eleanor Smith Nugent.* Edited by William M. Cash and Lucy Somerville Howorth. Jackson: University Press of Mississippi, 1977.

Oates, William C. *The War between the Union and the Confederacy.* New York: Neale, 1905.

O'Brien, John. *Things Grew Beautifully Worse: The Wartime Experiences of Captain John O'Brien, 30th Arkansas Infantry, C.S.A.* Edited by Brian K. Robertson. Little Rock: Butler Center for Arkansas Studies, Central Arkansas Library System, 2000.

Olsen, Otto H. "Historians and the Extent of Slave Ownership in the Southern United States." *Civil War History* 50 (December 2004): 401–17.

Osborn, George C., ed. "The Civil War Letters of Robert W. Banks." *Journal of Mississippi History* 5 (July 1943): 141–54.

———. "Writings of a Confederate Prisoner of War." *Tennessee Historical Quarterly* 10 (March 1951): 74–90, 161–84.

Osthaus, Carl R. "The Work Ethic of the Plain Folk: Labor and Religion in the Old South." *Journal of Southern History* 70 (November 2004): 745–82.

Owen, William Miller. *In Camp and Battle with the Washington Artillery of New Orleans.* 1855. Reprint, Baton Rouge: Louisiana State University Press, 1999.

Paca, Edmund C., ed. "'Tim's Black Book': The Civil War Diary of Edward Tilghman Paca, Jr., CSA." *Maryland Historical Magazine* 89 (Winter 1994): 453–66.

Park, Robert E. "Diary of Captain Robert E. Park." *Southern Historical Society Papers* 3 (1877): 55–61, 123–27, 244–54.

———. "Diary of Captain Robert E. Park, Macon, Georgia: Late Captain Twelfth Alabama Regiment, Confederate States Army." *Southern Historical Society Papers* 1 (1876): 370–86, 430–37.

———. "Diary of Captain Robert E. Park, Twelfth Alabama Regiment." *Southern Historical Society Papers* 2 (1876): 25–30, 172–80, 232–39, 306–15.

———. "The Twelfth Alabama Infantry, Confederate States Army." *Southern Historical Society Papers* 33 (1905): 193–296.

Parker, Robert W. *Lee's Last Casualty: The Life and Letters of Sgt. Robert W. Parker, Second Virginia Cavalry.* Edited by Catherine M. Wright. Knoxville: University of Tennessee Press, 2008.

Parker, W. W. "How I Kept House in Camp." *Southern Historical Society Papers* 23 (1895): 318–28.

Parrish, T. Michael. *Richard Taylor: Soldier Prince of Dixie.* Chapel Hill: University of North Carolina Press, 1992.

Pate, James P., ed. *When This Evil War Is Over: The Correspondence of the Francis Family, 1860–1865.* Tuscaloosa: University of Alabama Press, 2006.

Patterson, Edmund DeWitt. *Yankee Rebel: The Civil War Journal of Edmund DeWitt Patterson.* Edited by John G. Barrett. Chapel Hill: University of North Carolina Press, 1966.

Paxton, Elisha Franklin. *Memoir and Memorials: Elisha Franklin Paxton, Brigadier General, CSA: Composed of His Letters from Camp and Field.* New York: Neale, 1907.

Paxton, James B., Jr. "Fighting for Independence and Slavery: Confederate Perceptions of Their War Experiences." M.A. thesis, Virginia Polytechnic and State University, 1997.
Pender, William Dorsey. *The General to His Lady: The Civil War Letters of William Dorsey Pender to Fanny Pender.* Edited by William W. Hassler. Chapel Hill: University of North Carolina Press, 1962.
Perman, Michael. *The Road to Redemption: Southern Politics, 1869–1879.* Chapel Hill: University of North Carolina Press, 1984.
Perry, Theophilus, and Harriet Perry. *Widows by the Thousand: The Civil War Letters of Theophilus and Harriet Perry, 1862–1864.* Edited by M. Jane Johansson. Fayetteville: University of Arkansas Press, 2000.
Pessen, Edward. "The Egalitarian Myth and the American Social Reality: Wealth, Mobility, and Equality in the 'Era of the Common Man.'" *American Historical Review* 76 (October 1971): 989–1034.
Pettigrew, Elizabeth Blackwell. *Letters to Lauretta, 1849–1863 from Darlinton, SC, and a Confederate Soldier's Camp.* Edited by W. Joseph Bray, Jr., and Jerome J. Hale. Bowie, Md.: Heritage Books, 1993.
Pettit, William Beverley, and Arabella Speairs. *Civil War Letters of Arabella Speairs and William Beverley Pettit of Fluvanna County, Virginia, March 1862–March 1865. Vol. 1, March 1862–February 1864.* Edited by Charles W. Turner. Roanoke: Virginia Lithograph and Graphics, 1988.
Petty, Elijah P. *Journey to Pleasant Hill: The Civil War Letters of Captain Elijah P. Petty, Walker's Texas Division CSA.* Edited by Norman D. Brown. San Antonio: University of Texas, Institute of Texan Cultures, 1982.
Peyton, John William. *Eyewitness to War in Virginia, 1861–1865: The Civil War Diary of John William Peyton.* Edited by Walbrook D. Swank. Shippensburg, Pa.: Burd St. Press, 2003.
Phillips, Jason. *Diehard Rebels: The Confederate Culture of Invincibility.* Athens: University of Georgia Press, 2007.
Pierrepont, Alice V. D. *Reuben Vaughan Kidd: Soldier of the Confederacy.* Petersburg, Va.: Violet Bank, 1947.
Pinnell, Eathan Allen. *Serving with Honor: The Diary of Captain Eathan Allen Pinnell of the Eighth Missouri Infantry (Confederate).* Edited by Michael E. Banasik. Unwritten Chapters of the Civil War West of the River, vol. 3. Iowa City, Iowa: Camp Pope Bookshop, 1999.
Poague, William Thomas. *Gunner with Stonewall: Reminiscences of William Thomas Poague, a Memoir, Written for His Children in 1903.* Edited by Monroe F. Cockrell. Jackson, Tenn.: McCowat-Mercer Press, 1957.
Poché, Felix Pierre. *A Louisiana Confederate: Diary of Felix Pierre Poché.* Edited by Edwin C. Bearss; translated from the French by Eugenie Watson Somdal. Natchitoches, La.: Louisiana Studies Institute, Northwestern State University, 1972.
Porter, William Clendenin, and J. V. Frederick. "War Diary of W. C. Porter." *Arkansas Historical Quarterly* 11 (Winter 1952): 286–314.
Potter, David M. *The Impending Crisis, 1848–1861.* New York: Harper Torchbooks, 1976.
Power, J. Tracy. *Lee's Miserables: Life in the Army of Northern Virginia from the Wilderness to Appomattox.* Chapel Hill: University of North Carolina Press, 1997.

Purdue, Howell, and Elizabeth Purdue. *Pat Cleburne, Confederate General: A Definitive Biography.* Hillsboro, Texas: Hill Jr. College Press, 1973.

Quintard, Charles Todd. *Doctor Quintard, Chaplain, C.S.A. and Second Bishop of Tennessee: The Memoir and Civil War Diary of Charles Todd Quintard.* Edited by Sam Davis Elliott. Baton Rouge: Louisiana State University Press, 2003.

Quarles, Benjamin. *The Negro in the Civil War.* 1953. Reprint, Boston: Little, Brown, 1969.

Rable, George C. "Despair, Hope, and Delusion: The Collapse of Confederate Morale Reexamined." In *The Collapse of the Confederacy,* edited by Mark Grimsley and Brooks D. Simpson, 147–77. Lincoln: University of Nebraska Press, 2001.

Raboteau, Albert J. *Slave Religion: The "Invisible Institution" in the Antebellum South.* New York: Oxford University Press, 1978.

Rachal, William M., ed. "The Occupation of Richmond, April 1865: The Memorandum of Events of Colonel Christopher Q. Tompkins." *Virginia Magazine of History and Biography* 73 (April 1965): 189–98.

Ramseur, Stephen Dodson. *The Bravest of the Brave: The Correspondence of Stephen Dodson Ramseur.* Edited by George G. Kundahl. Chapel Hill: University of North Carolina Press, 2010

Reuter, Edward Byron. *The Mulatto in the United States, including a Study of the Role of Mixed-Blood Races throughout the World.* New York: Negro Universities Press, 1969.

Reynolds, Cathleen Carlson, ed. *Letters to Laura: Civil War Correspondence to Laura Stuart of Wytheville, Virginia, 1863–1865.* Wytheville, Va.: Wytheville County Genealogical and Historical Association, 2004.

Reynolds, Donald E. *Texas Terror: The Slave Insurrection Panic of 1860 and the Secession of the Lower South.* Baton Rouge: Louisiana State University Press, 2007.

Richard, Allan C., Jr., and Mary Margaret Higginbotham Richard, eds. *The Defense of Vicksburg: A Louisiana Chronicle.* College Station: Texas A & M University Press, 2004.

Richardson, Frank L. "War as I Saw It (Part II)." *Louisiana Historical Quarterly* 6 (April 1923): 223–54.

Ridley, Bromfield L. *Battles and Sketches of the Army of Tennessee.* Mexico, Mo.: Missouri Printing and Publishing, 1906.

Robertson, James I., Jr. *Soldiers Blue and Gray.* 1988. Reprint, Columbia: University of South Carolina Press, 1998.

Robinson, Armstead L. *Bitter Fruits of Bondage: The Demise of Slavery and the Collapse of the Confederacy, 1861–1865.* Charlottesville: University of Virginia Press, 2005.

———. "In the Shadow of Old John Brown: Insurrection Anxiety and Confederate Mobilization, 1861–1863." *Journal of Negro History* 65 (Autumn 1980): 279–97.

Roland, Charles. *The Confederacy.* Chicago: University of Chicago Press, 1960.

———. *Reflections on Lee: A Historian's Assessment.* Mechanicsburg, Pa.: Stackpole Books, 1995.

Rose, Willie Lee. *Rehearsal for Reconstruction: The Port Royal Experiment.* Indianapolis: Bobbs-Merrill, 1964.

Royster, Charles. *The Destructive War: William Tecumseh Sherman, Stonewall Jackson, and the Americans.* New York: Vintage, 1991.

———. *A Revolutionary People at War: The Continental Army and the American Character, 1775–1783.* Chapel Hill: University of North Carolina Press, 1979.

Ruffin, Edmund. *The Diary of Edmund Ruffin.* Vol. 3, *A Dream Shattered: June, 1863–June, 1865.* Edited by William K. Scarborough. Baton Rouge: Louisiana State University Press, 1989.

Sacher, John. "The Loyal Draft Dodger?: A Reexamination of Confederate Substitution." *Civil War History* 57 (June 2011): 153–78.

Sanders, Charles W. *While in the Hands of the Enemy: Military Prisons of the Civil War.* Baton Rouge: Louisiana State University Press, 2005.

Sanger, Donald Bridgman. *James Longstreet: I. Soldier.* Baton Rouge: Louisiana State University Press, 1952.

Scarborough, William K. *Masters of the Big House: Elite Slaveholders of the Mid-Nineteenth-Century South.* Baton Rouge: Louisiana State University Press, 2003.

———. *The Overseer: Plantation Management in the Old South.* 1966. Reprint, Athens: University of Georgia Press, 1984.

Schoeberlein, Robert W., and Andrew Brethauer, eds. "Letters of a Maryland Confederate." *Maryland Historical Magazine* 98 (Fall 2003): 345–61.

Scott, Irby Goodwin. *Lee and Jackson's Bloody Twelfth: The Letters of Irby Goodwin Scott, First Lieutenant, Company G, Putnam Light Infantry, Twelfth Georgia Volunteer Infantry.* Edited by Johnnie Perry Pearson. Knoxville: University of Tennessee Press, 2010.

Shade, William G. "Society and Politics in Antebellum Virginia's Southside." *Journal of Southern History* 53 (May 1987): 163–93.

Shalhope, Robert E. "Race, Class, Slavery, and the Antebellum Southern Mind." *Journal of Southern History* 37 (November 1971): 557–74.

Shaw, Arthur Marvin, ed. "Albert Sidney Johnston in Texas: Letters to Relatives in Kentucky, 1847–1860." *Register of the Kentucky Historical Society* 40 (July 1942): 291–317.

———. "A Texas Ranger Company at the Battle of Arkansas Post." *Arkansas Historical Quarterly* 9 (Winter 1950): 270–97.

Sheehan-Dean, Aaron. *Why Confederates Fought: Family and Nation in Civil War Virginia.* Chapel Hill: University of North Carolina Press, 2007.

Sheeran, James B. *Confederate Chaplain: A War Journal of Rev. James B. Sheeran, C.SS.R, 14th Louisiana, C.S.A.* Edited by Joseph T. Durkin. Milwaukee: Bruce, 1960.

Sheffey, John Preston. *Soldier of Southwestern Virginia: The Civil War Letters of Captain John Preston Sheffey.* Edited by James I. Robertson, Jr. Baton Rouge: Louisiana State University Press, 2004.

Shotwell, Randolph Abbott. *The Papers of Randolph Abbott Shotwell: Three Years in Battle and Three in Federal Prisons.* Edited by J. G. de Roulhac Hamilton; with the collaboration of Rebecca Cameron. Vol. 1. Raleigh: North Carolina Historical Commission, 1929.

Silas, Uncle. *The Civil War Reminiscences of Major Silas T. Grisamore, C.S.A.* Edited by Arthur W. Bergeron, Jr. Baton Rouge: Louisiana State University Press, 1993.

Silver, James W. "Propaganda in the Confederacy." *Journal of Southern History* 11 (November 1945): 487–503.

———, ed. "Robert A. Moore: The Diary of a Confederate Soldier." *Louisiana Historical Quarterly* 39 (July 1956): 245–374.

Simpson, R. W., and Taliaferro N. Simpson. *"Far, Far from Home": The Wartime Letters of Dick and Tally Simpson Third South Carolina Volunteers.* Edited by Guy R. Everson and Edward H. Simpson, Jr. New York: Oxford University Press, 1994.

Sinha, Minisha. *The Counterrevolution of Slavery: Politics and Ideology in Antebellum South Carolina.* Chapel Hill: University of North Carolina Press, 2001.

Slotkin, Gerald. *No Quarter: The Battle of the Crater, 1864.* New York: Random House, 2009.

Smallwood, James. "Disaffection in Confederate Texas: The Great Hanging at Gainesville." *Civil War History* 22 (December 1976): 349–60.

Smith, Colonel Thomas, and Leigh Robinson. "Brilliant Eulogy on General W. H. Payne." *Southern Historical Society Papers* 36 (1908): 285–353.

Smith, Daniel E. Huger, Alice R. Huger Smith, and Arney R. Childs, eds. *Mason Smith Family Letters, 1860–1868.* Columbia: University of South Carolina Press, 1950.

Smith, John David. *An Old Creed for the New South: Proslavery Ideology and Historiography, 1861–1918.* Westport, Conn.: Greenwood Press, 1985.

Smith, W. A. *The Anson Guards: Company C, Fourteenth Regiment North Carolina Volunteers, 1861–1865.* Charlotte, N.C.: Stone Publishing, 1914.

Sorrel, G. Moxley. *Recollections of a Confederate Staff Officer.* 1905. Reprint, New York: Bantam Books, 1992.

Sparkman, Lyle, ed. "Riding with Chrisman." *White County Heritage* 30 (1992): 46–52.

Speer, Alva Benjamin. *My Dear Friend: The Civil War Letters of Alva Benjamin Speer, 3rd Georgia Regiment, Company C.* Edited by Clyde G. Wiggins III. Macon, Ga.: Mercer University Press, 2007.

Speer, Lonnie R. *Portals to Hell: Military Prisons of the Civil War.* Mechanicsburg, Pa.: Stackpole Books, 1997.

Speer, William Henry Asbury. *Voices from Cemetery Hill: The Civil War Diary, Reports, and Letters of Colonel William Henry Asbury Speer (1861–1864).* Edited by Allen Paul Speer. Johnson City, Tenn.: Overmountain Press, 1997.

Spence, Alexander E., and Thomas S. Spence. *Getting Used to Being Shot At: The Spence Family Civil War Letters.* Edited by Mark K. Christ. Fayetteville: University of Arkansas Press, 2002.

Spraggins, Tinsley Lee. "Mobilization of Negro Labor for the Department of Virginia and North Carolina, 1861–1865." *North Carolina Historical Review* 24 (1947): 160–97.

Stamp, J. B. "Ten Months Experience in Northern Prisons." *Alabama Historical Quarterly* 18 (Winter 1946): 486–98.

Stewart, William H. "The Charge of the Crater." *Southern Historical Society Papers* 25 (1897): 77–90.

Stokes, William. *Saddle Soldiers: The Civil War Correspondence of General William Stokes of the 4th South Carolina Cavalry.* Edited by Lloyd Halliburton. Orangeburg, S.C.: Sandlapper Pub. Co., 1993.

Stone, DeWitt Boyd, Jr., ed. *Wandering to Glory: Confederate Veterans Remember Evans' Brigade.* Columbia: University of South Carolina Press, 2002.

Suderow, Bryce A. "The Battle of the Crater: The Civil War's Worst Massacre." *Civil War History* 43 (September 1997): 219–24.

Swann, John S. *Excerpts from Swann's "Prison Life at Fort Delaware."* Edited by Elizabeth Cometti. West Virginia History, vol. 2. Charleston, W.Va.: State Dept. of Archives and History, 1941.

Tadman, Michael. *Speculators and Slaves: Masters, Traders, and Slaves in the Old South.* Madison: University of Wisconsin Press, 1989.

Tap, Bruce. *Over Lincoln's Shoulder: The Committee on the Conduct of War.* Lawrence: University Press of Kansas, 1998.

Tatum, Georgia Lee. *Disloyalty in the Confederacy.* Chapel Hill: University of North Carolina Press, 1934.

Taylor, Frances Wallace, Catherine Taylor Matthews, and J. Tracy Power, eds. *The Leverett Letters: Correspondence of a South Carolina Family 1851–1868.* Columbia: University of South Carolina Press, 2000.

Taylor, Grant, and Malinda J. Slaughter Taylor. *This Cruel War: The Civil War Letters of Grant and Malinda Taylor, 1862–1865.* Edited by Ann K. Blomquist and Robert A. Taylor. Macon, Ga.: Mercer University Press, 2000.

Taylor, Richard. *Destruction and Reconstruction: Personal Experiences of the Late War.* 1879. Reprint, New York: Longmans, Green, 1955.

Taylor, Walter Herron. *Lee's Adjutant: The Wartime Letters of Colonel Walter Herron Taylor, 1862–1865.* Edited by R. Lockwood Tower with John S. Belmont. Columbia: University of South Carolina Press, 1995.

Thom, J. Pembroke. *"My Dear Brother": A Confederate Chronicle.* Edited by Catherine Thom Bartlett. Richmond, Va.: Dietz, 1952.

Thomas, Emory M. *The Confederacy as Revolutionary Experience.* 1971. Reprint, Columbia: University of South Carolina Press, 1991.

———. *The Confederate Nation, 1861–1865.* New York: Harper and Row, 1979.

———. *Robert E. Lee: A Biography.* New York: W. W. Norton, 1995.

Thompson, James Thomas, and Aurelia Austin. "A Georgia Boy with 'Stonewall' Jackson: The Letters of James Thomas Thompson." *Virginia Magazine of History and Biography* 70 (July 1962): 314–31.

Thornton, J. Mills. *Politics and Power in a Slave Society: Alabama, 1800–1860.* Baton Rouge: Louisiana State University Press, 1978.

Tilghman, Tench Francis, and A. J. Hanna. "The Confederate Baggage and Treasure Train Ends Its Flight in Florida: A Diary of Tench Francis Tilghman." *Florida Historical Quarterly* 17 (January 1939): 159–80.

Tolnay, Stewart E., and E. M. Beck. *A Festival of Violence: An Analysis of Southern Lynchings, 1882–1930.* Urbana: University of Illinois Press, 1995.

Toney, Marcus B. *The Privations of a Private. The Campaign under Gen. R. E. Lee; the Campaign under Gen. Stonewall Jackson; Bragg's Invasion of Kentucky; the Chickamauga Campaign; the Wilderness Campaign; Prison Life in the North; the Privations of a Citizen; the Ku-Klux Klan; a United Citizenship.* Nashville: Printed for the Author, 1905.

Towles, Louis P., ed. *A World Turned Upside Down: The Palmers of South Santee, 1818–1881.* Columbia: Published by the University of South Carolina Press in

cooperation with the Caroline McKissick Dial South Caroliniana Library Endowment Fund and the South Caroliniana Society, 1996.
Traywick, Rev. J. B. "Prison Life at Point Lookout." *Southern Historical Society Papers* 18 (1890): 431–35.
Trexler, Harrison A. "The Opposition of Planters to the Employment of Slaves as Laborers by the Confederacy." *Mississippi Valley Historical Review* 27 (September 1940): 211–24.
———. "Values of Slaves in Missouri." *Missouri Historical Review* 8 (January 1914): 69–85.
Trout, Robert J., ed. *With Pen and Saber: The Letters and Diaries of J. E. B. Stuart's Staff Officers*. Mechanicsburg, Pa.: Stackpole Books, 1995.
Truehart, Charles William, and Henry Martyn Trueheart. *Rebel Brothers: The Civil War Letters of the Truehearts*. Edited by Edward B. Williams. College Station: Texas A & M University Press, 1995.
Turner, Charles W., ed. *The Allen Family of Amherst County, Virginia: Civil War Letters*. Berryville, Va.: Rockbridge Pub. Co., 1995.
Turner, Charles W., and Albert Davidson. "Lieutenant Albert Davidson—Letters of a Virginia Soldier." *West Virginia History* 39 (October 1977): 49–71.
Turner, Charles W., and Greenlee Davidson. "Captain Greenlee Davidson: Letters of a Virginia Soldier." *Civil War History* 17 (September 1971): 197–221.
"Typical of the Old South." *Confederate Veteran* 20 (May 1912): 202.
United States War Department. *The War of the Rebellion: A Compilation of the Official Records of the Union and Confederate Armies*. 70 vols. in 128. Washington, D.C.: Government Printing Office, 1880–1901.
———. *The War of the Rebellion: A Compilation of the Official Records of the Union and Confederate Armies*. Making of America Website, Cornell University Library. http://digital.library.cornell.edu/m/moawar/waro.html.
Urwin, Gregory, ed. *Black Flag over Dixie: Racial Reprisals and Atrocities in the Civil War*. Carbondale: Southern Illinois University Press, 2004.
Van Buskirk, Philip. *Rebel at Large: The Diary of Confederate Deserter Philip Van Buskirk*. Edited by Barry Richard Burg. Jefferson, N.C.: McFarland and Co., 2009.
Vance, Zebulon Baird. *The Papers of Zebulon Baird Vance*. Vol. 2, *1863*. Edited by Joe A. Mobley. Raleigh: Division of Archives and History, North Carolina Dept. of Cultural Resources, 1995.
Varon, Elizabeth R. "Evangelical Womanhood and the Politics of the African Colonization Movement in Virginia." In *Religion and the Antebellum Debate over Slavery*, edited by John R. McKivigan and Mitchell Snay, 169–95. Athens: University of Georgia Press, 1998.
Von Borcke, Heros. *Memoirs of the Confederate War for Independence*. 2 vols. 1866. Reprint: New York: P. Smith, 1938.
Vorenberg, Michael. "'The Deformed Child': Slavery and the Election of 1864." *Civil War History* 47 (September 2001): 240–57.
Wagstaff, Henry McGilbert, and Thomas Jackson Strayhorn. "Letters of Thomas Jackson Strayhorn." *North Carolina Historical Review* 13 (October 1936): 311–34.
Wakelyn, Jon L., ed. *Southern Pamphlets on Secession: November 1860–April 1861*. Chapel Hill: University of North Carolina Press, 1996.

Walker, Kendrick Anne, ed. "Governor John Gill Shorter: Miscellaneous Papers, 1861–1863." Pt. 2. *Alabama Review* 11 (October 1958): 267–83.

Wallace, Sarah Agnes, ed. "Confederate Exiles in London, 1865–1870." *South Carolina Historical and Genealogical Magazine* 52 (July 1951): 143–53.

Wallenstein, Peter. "Rich Man's War, Rich Man's Fight: Civil War and the Transformation of Public Finance in Georgia." *Journal of Southern History* 50 (February 1984): 15–42.

Walker, C. Irvine. *Great Things Are Expected of Us: The Letters of Col. C. Irvine Walker, 10th South Carolina Infantry, CSA*. Edited by William Lee White and Charles Denny Runion. Knoxville: University of Tennessee Press, 2009.

Walter, Eric. *The Fire-Eaters*. Baton Rouge: Louisiana State University Press, 1992.

Walters, John. *Norfolk Blues: The Civil War Diary of the Norfolk Light Artillery Blues*. Edited and introduced by Kenneth Wiley. Shippensburg, Pa.: Burd Street Press, 1997.

Ward, W. W. *"For the Sake of My Country": The Diary of Col. W. W. Ward, 9th Tennessee Cavalry, Morgan's Brigade, C.S.A.* Edited by R. B. Rosenburg. Murfreesboro, Tenn.: Southern Heritage Press, 1992.

Warner, Ezra. *Generals in Gray: Lives of the Confederate Commanders*. Baton Rouge: Louisiana State University Press, 1959.

Watford, Christopher M., ed. *The Civil War in North Carolina: Soldiers' and Civilians' Letters and Diaries, 1861–1865*. Jefferson, N.C.: McFarland, 2003.

Watkins, Sam. *Company Aytch, or, a Sideshow of the Big Show and Other Sketches*. 1883. Reprint, New York: Plume, 1999.

Watson, Ritchie Devon, Jr. *Yeomen versus Cavalier: The Old Southwest's Fictional Road to Rebellion*. Baton Rouge: Louisiana State University Press, 1993.

Watson, Robert. *Southern Service on Land & Sea: The Wartime Journal of Robert Watson*. Edited by R. Thomas Campbell. Knoxville: University of Tennessee Press, 2002.

Watson, William. *Life in the Confederate Army: Being the Observations and Experiences of an Alien in the South during the American Civil War*. 1887. Reprint, Baton Rouge: Louisiana State University Press, 1995.

Wayne, Michael. "An Old South Morality Play: Reconsidering the Social Underpinnings of the Proslavery Ideology." *Journal of American History* 77 (December 1990): 838–63.

Weitz, Mark A. "Drill, Training, and the Combat Performance of the Civil War Soldier: Dispelling the Myth of the Poor Soldier, Great Fighter." *Journal of Military History* 62 (April 1998): 263–89.

———. *A Higher Duty: Desertion amongst Georgia Troops during the Civil War*. Lincoln: University of Nebraska Press, 2000.

———. *More Damning than Slaughter: Desertion in the Confederate Army*. Lincoln: University of Nebraska Press, 2005.

Welch, Spencer Glasgow. *A Confederate Surgeon's Letters to His Wife*. 1911. Reprint, Marietta, Ga.: Continental Book Co., 1954.

Wesley, Charles H. "The Employment of Negroes as Soldiers in the Confederate Army." *Journal of Negro History* 4 (July 1919): 239–53.

Wessells, D. Thomas, Jr. *In Bold Measure: The Biography of Col. Benjamin Lyons Farinholt, CSA*. Baltimore: PublishAmerica, 2006.

Wetherington, Mark V. *Plain Folk's Fight: The Civil War & Reconstruction in Piney Woods Georgia.* Chapel Hill: University of North Carolina Press, 2005.

Wiley, Bell Irvin. *The Life of Johnny Reb: The Common Soldier of the Confederacy.* 1943. Reprint, Baton Rouge: Louisiana State University Press, 2008.

———. *Southern Negroes, 1861–1865.* 1938. Reprint, New Haven, Conn.: Yale University Press, 1965.

Williams, David. "'The Faithful Slave Is About Played Out": Civil War Slave Resistance in the Lower Chattahoochee Valley." *Alabama Review* 52 (April 1999): 83–104.

Williams, Robert Hamilton. *With the Border Ruffians: Memoirs of the Far West: 1852–1868.* Edited by E. W. Williams. Toronto: Musson Books, 1919.

Williams, T. Harry. *P. G. T. Beauregard: Napoleon in Gray.* 1955. Reprint, Baton Rouge: Louisiana State University Press, 1995.

Wilson, Edmund. *Patriotic Gore: Studies in the Literature of the American Civil War.* 1962. Reprint, New York: W. W. Norton, 1994.

Wilson, William Lyle. *A Borderland Confederate.* Edited by Festus P. Summers. Pittsburgh: University of Pittsburgh Press, 1962.

Wise, Henry A. *Seven Decades of the Union.* Philadelphia: J. B. Lippincott, 1872.

Wise, John S. *The End of an Era.* Boston: Houghton Mifflin and Co., 1900.

Wish, Harvey. "Slave Disloyalty under the Confederacy." *Journal of Negro History* 23 (October 1938): 435–50.

Wood, Thomas Fanning. *Doctor to the Front: The Recollections of Confederate Surgeon Thomas Fanning Wood, 1861–1865.* Edited by Donald B. Koonce. Knoxville: University of Tennessee Press, 2000.

Woodward, C. Vann. Introduction to *Cannibals All! Or, Slaves without Masters*, by George Fitzhugh, vii–xxxviii. 1960. Reprint, Cambridge, Mass.: Belknap Press of Harvard University Press, 2006.

Wooster, Ralph A. "With the Confederate Cavalry in the West: The Civil War Experiences of Isaac Dunbar Affleck." *Southwestern Historical Quarterly* 83 (July 1979): 1–28.

Wright, Gavin. *The Political Economy of the Cotton South: Households, Markets, and Wealth in the Nineteenth Century.* New York: W. W. Norton, 1978.

Wyatt-Brown, Bertram. *Honor and Violence in the Old South.* New York: Oxford University Press, 1986.

———. *The Shaping of Southern Culture: Honor, Grace, and War, 1760s–1880s.* Chapel Hill: University of North Carolina Press, 2001.

Wyeth, John Allan. *With Sabre and Scalpel: The Autobiography of a Soldier and a Surgeon.* New York: Harper & Bros., 1914.

Wynne, Ben. *A Hard Trip: A History of the 15th Mississippi Infantry.* Macon, Ga.: Mercer University Press, 2003.

Yearns, W. Buck, and John G. Barrett, eds. *North Carolina Civil War Documentary.* Chapel Hill: University of North Carolina Press, 1980.

Yee, Gary. "The Black Confederate Sharpshooter." *Military Collector and Historian* 59 (Summer 2007): 144–46.

Zuczek, Richard. *State of Rebellion: Reconstruction in South Carolina.* Columbia: University of South Carolina Press, 1996.

Index

abolitionism, 2, 8, 11, 14–16, 21–24, 26, 61, 88, 113, 121, 124–25, 139, 160, 166–67, 172–73, 181, 195–97, 204
Adams County, Miss., 17
Adamson, Augustus, 61
Adams Run, S.C., 104
Africa, 38, 141, 150, 165, 199–200
African American soldiers: and accounts of assaults on women, 145–46; and the Battle of the Crater, 1, 7–8, 146–52, 187, 206; conduct at Point Lookout, 140–43; enlistment into Confederate army, 7–8, 62, 155–79, 187; enlistment into U.S. army, 111, 130–31, 206; physical description of, 141, 153; and the postwar South, 187–88
Agurs, John L., 12
Alamance County, N.C., 140
Albert (slave), 90
Albright, James, 121, 177
Alfred (slave), 89
Alleck (slave), 93
Allen, Henry Watkins, 168
Allen, Ujanirtus, 42
All That Makes a Man, 5
amalgamation. *See* race-mixing
American Revolution, 29–30, 124, 159, 197, 205
Anderson, James, 101
Anderson, Patton, 161, 167
Anderson, Samuel S., 71
Andrews, William B. G., 89
Andersonville Prison (Camp Sumter), 142–43
Antietam campaign, 6, 26, 41, 50, 111–14
Apperson, John, 14
Armageddon, or the United States in Prophecy (Baldwin), 131

Armstrong, Edward, 182
Army of Mississippi, 110, 114
Army of Northern Virginia: and the Battle of the Crater, 147–52; and black enlistment debate, 8, 156, 171–77; body servants used in, 81, 87; invades Maryland, 1862, 111–14; invades Pennsylvania, 80, 121–22; morale of, 124; and proslavery argument, 5; slave-ownership in, 12–13; surrender of, 179, 181, 183
Army of Tennessee, 8, 76, 81, 103, 153, 158–59, 161–63
Army of the Potomac, 116, 146
Atlanta, Ga., 75, 86, 88, 102, 126, 152, 161, 165, 195
Atlanta Southern Confederacy, 48
Attack and Die (McWhiney and Jamieson), 3
Ayers, Ed, 56, 189

Baldwin, S. D., 131
Banks, Nathaniel P., 71, 98
Barksdale, Andrew S., 147–48
Barnes, Spencer, 103
Barr, James Michael, 38
Barrow, James, 94
Basinger, William S., 176
Batchelor, Albert, 41
Bates, James C., 111, 126–27
Battery Wagner, S.C., 206
Baxter, William H., 13
Baylor, George, 106
Beard, James C., 75
Beaufort, S.C., 109–10
Beauregard, P. G. T., 23, 27, 54, 58, 62–63, 76, 134, 167
Beckett, R. C., 174
Beecher, Henry Ward, 160

INDEX

Bell, Alfred, 182
Benjamin, Judah P., 27, 168
Bennett, Heber, 48
Berry, Stephen, 5
Bibb, W. C., 69
Birmingham, Ala., 193
black codes, 180, 183
Blackford, W. W., 194
Blight, David, 198, 208
body servants. *See* slaves
Boesel, Ferdinand, 13
Bolling, Archibald, 97
border states, 2, 6, 16, 107, 112, 206
Box (slave), 106
Bragg, Braxton, 75, 115, 117, 205
Bragg, Junius N., 182
Brandon, William Lindsay, 185
Brazil, 186
Breckinridge, John C., 200
Breckinridge, William Campbell Preston, 200
Britain. *See* England
Brode, Fred A., 125
Brooks, R. H., 95
Brooks, U. R., 131, 191
Brown, John, 14, 17, 22, 24, 153, 160
Brown, Joseph E., 44, 67
Brown, William Judson, 188–89
Buchanan, James, 203
Buck, Irving, 163
Buckner, Simon Bolivar, 114
Buell, Don Carlos, 109, 114
Bull Run, Battle of. *See* Manassas, Va.
Burney, Samuel, 109
Burnside, Ambrose, 145, 147
Burrell (slave), 88, 160
Butler, Benjamin, 132, 134, 141

Cable, George Washington, 209
Calhoun, John C., 6, 18–19, 34, 198, 205
Callaway, F. R., 148
Camp Caroline, Va., 90
Cannon, J. P., 37
Carter, Charles Landon, 198
Carter, Hill, 60
Carter, James H., 90
Carter, William R., 93
Carter, William S., 90
Casey, William T., 41
Cash, Wilbur, 145
Cater, Douglas John, 22

Chambers, William Pitt, 172
Chancellorsville, Va., 56, 106
Charles (slave), 89
Charles (slave of Robert E. Park), 125
Charleston, S.C., 61, 66–67, 69, 96, 123, 182, 197
Charlottesville, Va., 82
Chattanooga, Tenn., 54, 73, 158
Chesnut, Mary, 61
Chickamauga, 106, 161, 185, 195
Christian, George L., 210
Cincinnatus, 184
Civil War Soldiers (Mitchell), 4
Clark, Henry T., 66
Cleburne, Patrick, 8, 26, 158–64, 179
Cobb, Howell, 30, 44, 61–62, 91
Cold Harbor, Va., 147
Coleman, Clayton, 145
Colfax, La., 191
colonization. *See under* slaves
Columbia, S.C., 96
Colyar, A. S., 162
Combahee River, 122
Comer, Wallace, 88, 160
Confederate Veteran, 105, 193, 198
Confiscation Act, 11, 132
Congress, Confederate: admits Missouri into Confederacy, 112; and Currency Reform Act, 101; Jefferson Davis addresses, 165; and having too much power, 50; and lost slaves, 60; passes draft, April 1862, 44; passes third draft, 1864, 73, 77, 165; passes impressment law, 64–65; planters in, 34; and recruitment of black troops, 166, 172–74; and rumors of freeing slaves, 181
Congress, U.S., 111, 115, 132, 190, 210
conscription, 6, 31, 43–45, 50–55, 57, 67, 73, 77, 80, 165, 169, 175–76, 207
Constitution, Confederate, 12, 14, 62, 128, 135
Constitution, U.S., 12, 14, 20, 25, 194
Cooper, Samuel, 72–73
Corbin, Richard Washington, 167
Coreth, Rudolf, 36, 73
Corinth, Miss., 110
Corsan, W. C., 58
Corwin Amendment, 25
Cosby, George B., 59
Cowin, John Henry, 35, 41–42

Crater, Battle of, 1, 7–8, 126, 146–52, 187, 206
Crow, William, 13
Cuba, 185

Dandy (slave), 85
Darien, Ga., 138
Davis, Jefferson: A. P. Hayne writes to, 69; addresses troops, 136–37; and becoming a dictator, 50; and Confederate policy toward captured African Americans, 134–36, 153; and diplomacy, 170; and enlistment of black Confederate troops, 162, 164–65, 168–70, 176, 179; Gideon Pillow writes to, 112; John G. Shorter writes to, 46; and John J. Pettus, 47; reaction to David Hunter's emancipation order, 133; reaction to Emancipation Proclamation, 134–35; and Robert E. Lee's need for more slaves, 76; and use of black laborers in the Confederate army, 165–66
De Bow, James, 35
De Bow's Review, 16, 35
Declaration of Independence, 158
"Declaration of the Causes and Necessity of Taking up Arms" (1775), 29
Dekle, Peter, 45
Democratic Party, 2, 109, 115, 127, 180, 183, 205
desertion, 50–51, 165, 204
Devereux, Jonathan, 157
Dew, Thomas R., 6, 19
Dick (slave), 109
Dickinson, A. G., 71
Dickinson, John, 29
Diehard Rebels, 5
Dimmock, Charles H., 66
Dinkins, James, 105–6, 144
Douglas, Henry Kyd, 195
Douglass, Frederick, 208
Drummond, Edward W., 111
Dunaway, Wayland, 119
Duncan, Thomas D., 194
Durden, Robert, 176
Durkin, Joseph, 111

Early, Jubal, 87, 125, 139, 175, 185, 193
Edmondston, Catherine, 62, 169
Eliza (slave), 181

Ellen (slave), 102
Elliott, Stephen, 20
Ellis, E. John, 25, 45, 56, 116, 118–19, 123, 141, 166, 187
Ellzey, Mason, 164
Emancipation Proclamation: Confederate reaction to, 113, 117, 134, 166, 184; and fear of slave insurrection, 113–14, 118; Lincoln issues, 6, 104, 108, 113–14, 116, 133, 184; and Northern public opinion, 115–16
Embattled Courage, 3
England, 32, 116–17, 204
Escott, Paul, 156
Evans, Clement A., 40, 66, 102, 108, 138
Evans, James H., 66
Ewell, Richard, 87, 158

Farinholt, Benjamin, 75
Fay, Edwin H., 40, 85, 94, 98, 103
Fewell, Alexander, 99
Fifteenth Alabama Infantry Regiment, 172
Fifty-Fifth Massachusetts Infantry Regiment, 141
Fisher, John E., 187
Fitzhugh, George, 6, 18–19, 196, 198
Fitzpatrick, Marion, 166, 178
Five Forks, 106
Fleet, Fred, 91, 126, 128
Fletcher, William, 19
Floyd County, Va., 51
Foner, Eric, 31
For Cause and Comrades, 4, 7
Forney, John H., 133–34
Forrest, Nathan Bedford: compared to Robert E. Lee, 8, 150; conduct at Fort Pillow, 143–44, 198; gathers slaves in Mississippi, 75; and postwar finances, 188; role in Ku Klux Klan, 191–92; sends slaves to Richard Taylor, 77; and wagon drivers, 78
Fort Brown, Tex., 69
Fort Donelson, Tenn., 43, 58, 61, 109, 112
Fort Fisher, N.C., 109
Fort Gregg, S.C., 69
Fort Henry, Tenn., 43, 58, 61, 109, 112
Fort Jackson, S.C., 61
Fort Mill, S.C., 106
Fort Pillow, Tenn., 7–8, 143–44, 146–48, 187, 191, 198–99, 206

INDEX

Fort Pocahontas. *See* Wilson's Wharf
Fort Pulaski, Ga., 61, 140–41
Fort Stedman, 176
Fort Sumter, 32, 112
Forty-Ninth Georgia Infantry Regiment, 174
Foster, John, 43, 116–17, 120
Foster, Samuel, 183
Fourteenth Amendment, 200
France, 117, 206
Francis, James, 99
Francis, Thomas W., 124
Francis, Miller W., 40
Franklin, John Hope, 107
Franklin, Tenn., 119, 162
Fredericksburg, Va., 50, 90, 117, 145
Fredrickson, George, 33
free blacks, 64–65, 119, 157, 175
Freedom: A Documentary History of Emancipation, 57
Freehling, William, 160
Fremantle, Arthur, 87, 96
Fry, Birkett Davenport, 182

Galveston, Tex., 69
Garner, William W., 98
Garrison, William Lloyd, 21, 23, 197
Garysville, Va., 68
Gatlin, Richard, 46
General Orders No. 3, 108
General Orders No. 28, 87–88
General Orders No. 60, 133
George (slave), 92
Gettysburg, Pa., Battle of, 23, 50, 69, 99, 117, 121, 138, 163, 210
Gibbons, Alfred Ringgold, 19, 22
Gibson, D. P., 37, 116
Gilliam, Robert C., 101
Gilmer, Jeremy Francis, 59, 62
Glatthaar, Joseph, 3, 5, 13, 80, 101, 156
Good, John J., 18, 96
Goodwin, Claudius L., 66
Gordon, John B., 87, 168, 175, 191, 209–10
Goree, Thomas J., 165
Govan, Daniel C., 114
Graham, William A., Jr., 88
Grant, Ulysses S., 60, 74, 76, 117, 124–26, 132, 139, 146, 152, 170, 176, 208
Green, Thomas, 36
Grimball, Arthur, 95, 123

Grimball, Berkley, 95
Grimball, Lewis, 104
Grimball, William H., 11, 25, 50, 59, 73, 82, 89, 96–97, 123
Grisamore, Silas T., 86
Guilford, Felix, 37
Gulledge, S. B., 40

Haiti (St. Domingue), 114, 118
Hall, Isaac, 29
Hall, John, 110
Halleck, Henry, 108
Hammond, James Henry, 18–19, 33–34, 91, 196
Hampton Roads Conference, 128, 170–71
Hampton, Wade, 66
Handerson, Henry, 145
"Happy Land of Canaan," 153
Hardee, William J., 161–62
Harpers Ferry, Va., 14, 22
Harris, David Bullock, 62, 67
Harris, Isham, 59
Harris, John A., 48
Haskell, John Cheves, 149, 151
Hayne, A. P., 69
Heartsill, W. W., 173
Helena, Ark., 120, 158
Hemings, Sally, 25
Henry, Patrick, 29–30, 151
Herrenvolk democracy, 33
Hill, A. P., 77
Hill, D. H., 60, 68
Hindman, Thomas, 158
Hobson, Caleb, 49, 158
Holt, Daniel, 150
Hood, John Bell, 13, 126–27, 162, 163
Houston, Tex., 71
Howard, Robert M., 190
Howard, William D., 97
Hubbard, John Milton, 119
Huffman, James, 22, 191
Huger, Clayton, 135
Hundley, Daniel R., 24, 35, 127, 131–32, 150
Hundley, George, 157
Hunter, Andrew, 168
Hunter, David, 111, 133, 136

immigrants, 26–27
impressment, 2, 8–9, 50, 53, 55–80, 164, 170, 176, 204

278

INDEX

Inscoe, John, 68
Inzer, John Washington, 140, 168
Island No. 10, 43, 58, 109

Jackson, Andrew, 32
Jacksonian Era, 32, 44, 205
Jackson, Stonewall, 15, 54, 121, 163
Jackson, William Hicks, 121
Jamieson, Perry, 3
Jefcoat, John J., 66, 90, 145
Jefferson County, Ala., 18
Jefferson, Thomas, 14, 18, 19, 25, 29, 160, 172, 194, 195, 201
Jenkins, J. H., 172
Jenkins' Ferry, 144–45, 147
Jim (slave), 84
Jim (slave of James H. Carter), 91
Jim Crow, 106, 180, 194, 198, 200, 207
John (slave), 97
Johnson, Andrew, 52, 183
Johnson, Bradley, 199
Johnson's Island, 139
Johnston, Albert Sidney, 43, 59, 95
Johnston, Joseph E., 54, 58, 75–76, 103, 137, 161–62, 176, 178–79, 183
Johnston County, N.C., 192
Joint Committee on the Conduct of War, 143
Jones, Charles C., 91, 96
Jones, John B., 118, 139, 178
Jones, Sam, 76, 198
Jordan, Thomas, 63
Jordan, Winthrop, 199
Juneteenth, 98

Kean, Robert, 71, 135, 158, 166, 169, 177
Keiley, Anthony Michael, 141–42, 199
Kelly's Ford, Va., 90
Kendall, John Smith, 153
Kenner, Duncan, 170
Kennesaw Mountain, Ga., 126, 160
Kentucky, invasion of, 6, 112, 114–15, 205
Ker, William H., 17
Key, Thomas J., 158
Kidd, Reuben Vaughan, 124
"Kingdom Coming" ("Year of Jubilo"), 186
King, William Henry, 12
Kinzer, William, 40
Kipling, Rudyard, 198
Kirwan, Albert, 186
Knights of the White Camilla, 192

Knoxville, Tenn., 195
Kolchin, Peter, 91, 94
Ku Klux Klan, 140, 180, 191–92, 195, 209–10

Lawton, Alexander, 61
Lee, Fitzhugh, 146
Lee, George Washington Custis, 176–77
Lee, Robert E.: attitude towards postwar South, 183–84; compared to Nathan Bedford Forrest, 8, 150; compared to Zachary Taylor, 35; correspondence with U. S. Grant, 152–53; demands more slaves for work at Petersburg, 76–77; and enlisting black Confederate troops, 76, 163, 167–70, 172–76, 178; and entrenching, 57; finances after the Civil War, 188; and free blacks, 65; and George Washington, 36; Gustavus W. Smith complains to, 63; invades Maryland, 41, 50, 112, 115, 205; invades Pennsylvania, 80, 121–22, 138, 206; and Nathan Bedford Forrest, 8; and Point Lookout, 143; and size of his armies, 53–54; surrender of, 179, 182, 185–86, 201, 204, 208, 210; testifies before U.S. Congress, 184; and views on slavery, 4, 19
Lee, Stephen D., 137
Lehmann, Ludwig, 188
Letcher, John, 133
Leverett, Milton, 110, 188
Levi (slave), 92
Levine, Bruce, 156
Lewis, Harry, 83
Liberator, 21
Lieber Code, 135
Liebermann, Charles, 18, 36, 44
Life of Johnny Reb, The (Wiley), 2
Lincoln, Abraham: and abolitionist generals, 109, 111; assassination of, 35, 183, 187; and colonization, 24; Daniel R. Hundley and, 35; Emancipation Proclamation issued by, 111, 113, 115; and estimates of slave runaways, 107; and gradual emancipation, 173; and Hampton Roads Conference, 170; Inaugural Address of, 25; Preliminary Emancipation Proclamation issued by, 133; and *The Real Lincoln,*

INDEX

Lincoln, Abraham (*continued*) 198; reelection of, 102, 125, 127, 165, 205; and retaliation order, 136; and secession crisis, 12, 15, 22, 29–30; and slave unrest, 119; and views on slavery, 24, 128
Linderman, Gerald, 3
Little Rock, Ark., 120
Loehr, Charles T., 142
Logan, David Jackson, 36, 50, 100
London Times, 117
Longstreet, James, 23, 29, 77, 114, 135, 165, 167, 176–77, 185, 193
Lost Cause, 27, 83, 85, 102, 107, 170, 192–95, 209–10
Louisiana Native Guards, 64, 157
Louisville Journal, 139
Louthan, Carter McKim, 15, 183–85
Lowrey, John R., 16, 92
Lunenburg County, Va., 74
Lynchburg Virginian, 168
Lynching, 193, 198

Magruder, John B.: and defending Virginia, 59–60; and Kirby Smith, 72; and movement of slaves into Texas by planters, 77; and Texas, 70–73, 98, 183
Mahone, William, 1, 148, 177
Malachi, John, 142
Malone, Bartlett, 143
Malvern Hill, 185
Manassas, Va.: Battle of, 24, 157, 203; muddiness of, 37; Second Battle of, 112, 197
Manigault, Henry H., 104
Manning, Chandra, 5, 9, 156
Manuel (slave), 134
Marcom, James C., 60, 69
Marshall, Humphrey, 115
Maury, Dabney, 19
Maury, Richard, 19, 172, 178
Mays, Samuel Elias, 12, 124
McCabe, W. Gordon, 147
McCarthy, Carlton, 27
McClellan, George B., 60, 109, 127
McCook, Alexander, 114
McCrady, Edward, 197
McCurdy, Caleb, 89
McCurry, Stephanie, 33–34
McGarrity, Abner, 177

McKee, Will, 30
McKinney, Gordon, 68
McLaws, Lafayette, 29, 118
McMillan, Roderick, 24, 46, 58
McPheeters, William, 163
McPherson, James, 4, 7, 27
McWhiney, Grady, 3
Melton, Samuel W., 70
Memminger, Christopher, 136
Memphis, Tenn., 62, 70, 110, 143
Mercer, George, 190
Mercer, Hugh, 58, 63, 67, 134
Merritt, Alexander T. B., 164
Merritt, J. A., 166
Mexico, 185
Middletown, Md., 113
Miller, Robert H., 57
Milliken's Bend, La., 138, 206
Milling, Willie, 129
Minor, Berkeley, 163
Minor, Charles Landon Carter, 198
Minor, L. H., 66
miscegenation. *See* race-mixing
Mississippi Delta, 46
Mississippi River, 43, 47
Mississippi River Valley, 47, 61, 110
Mitchell, Reid, 4
Mobile, Ala., 58, 73, 75, 78
Mobile Bay, 75, 102, 126
Mobile Register, 168
Molly (slave), 97
Montgomery, Frank, 189
Montgomery, Hugh W., 181–82
Montgomery, James, 138
Montgomery, William R., 53
Montgomery Advertiser, 56
Moore, Samuel J. C., 175
Moore, Thomas Overton, 157
Morgan, John Hunt, 200
Morgan, John Tyler, 195
Morgan, W. H., 190
Mosby, John Singleton, 210
Munford, Thomas, 172
Murfreesboro, Tenn., 54, 117, 161

Nashville, Tenn., 59, 119, 153
Natchez, Miss., 17, 120
Native Americans, 32, 190
Neblett, William H., 70
Nelson, William Cowper, 21
Nelson, William T., 92

INDEX

New Civil War History, 3
New Mexico, 185
New Military History, 4
New Orleans, La., 27, 43, 96, 109, 157, 193
New Social History, 3
New York, N.Y., 197
New York Herald, 157
New York World, 115
Niblett's Bluff, La., 71
Nicaragua, 185
Noe, Kenneth, 5
Notes on the State of Virginia (Jefferson), 172
Nugent, William, 98, 122–23

Oates, William C., 107, 158, 175, 210
O'Brien, John, 140
Old Creole Days, 209
overseers, 43, 48–49, 53, 72–73, 174
Owen, U. G., 103

Park, Robert E., 125–26, 141, 181
Parker, Francis, 65
Parker, Robert W., 87
Parsons, William H., 62
Patton, Thomas W., 181
Paxton, Elisha, 98
Pegram, John, 16
Pegram, William, 150
Pelham, John, 90
Pemberton, John C., 20, 61, 66
Pender, William, 92
Pendleton, John B., 39–40
Penn, William A., 84
Perry, James Thomas, 147, 153
Perry, Theophilus, 98–100
Perryville, Ky., 114
Petersburg, Va., 62, 68, 84, 90, 101–2, 126, 128, 145–46, 148, 151–52, 166, 176
Pettit, William Beverley, 94
Pettus, John J., 47
Petty, E. P., 97
Phillips, Jason, 5
Philippines, 198
Pickens, Francis, 63–64
Pierson, David, 181
Pierson, Reuben Allen, 124–25
Pillow, Gideon, 64, 111–12
Pinchback, P. B. S., 192

planters: Andrew Johnson and, 183; in Georgia, 34; in Louisiana, 73–74; John Magruder and, 77; in Mobile, Ala., 73; in South Carolina, 33–34, 76; in Texas, 70–72, 98; and relationship to yeomen, 206; slaves returned to, 119
Plymouth, N.C., 7, 145, 147, 206
Poague, William, 128
Poché, Felix, 171
Point Lookout Prison (Camp Hoffman), 140–43
Poison Spring, Ark., 144
Polk, Leonidas Bishop, 63, 114, 161
Polk, Leonidas L., 63, 75
Pope, John, 132
Port Hudson, La., 58, 71, 73, 122, 138
Potter, David, 204–5
Powell, Charles S., 86, 192
Power, J. Tracy, 4, 9
Prentice, George D., 139
Press (slave), 81
Preston (slave), 90
Preston, James Francis, 89
Price, Sterling, 28, 170, 185
prison camps, 139–43
proslavery argument, 7, 16, 26, 30, 34, 40, 120, 155, 169, 179–80, 193–94, 197, 201, 208; religious aspects of, 19–21, 131, 150

Quintard, Charles, 171

race-mixing, 25–26, 115, 125, 193, 196, 209
Rachel (slave), 89
racism, 4, 7, 51, 108, 115, 117, 121, 139, 146, 156, 191, 196–98
Rains, Gabriel James, 139
Raleigh, N.C., 69
Ramseur, Stephen, 87–88
Ramsey, Henry K., 14–15
Randolph, George, 115, 133
Randolph, John, 30
Reconstruction, 23, 157, 180, 183–87, 189–93, 207
Real Lincoln, The (Minor), 198
Reese, John W., 99
Reid, James L., 45, 87
Republican Party, 12–13, 15, 23–26, 28, 88, 109, 115–16, 127, 180, 183–85, 190–91, 193, 197

INDEX

Richardson, Frank L., 38–39, 98
Richmond, Va., 13–14, 58–59, 62, 81, 96, 101, 103, 118, 146–47, 152, 167–68, 172, 174, 178, 182, 193, 199
Richmond Enquirer, 168, 172
Ridley, Bromfield, 186
Riley (slave), 94
Ringgold, Ga., 18
Robertson, James I., 3
Robinson, Armstead, 47
Robinson, Leigh, 196, 199
Rodgers, Robert M., 144–45
Roland, Charles, 4
Roots, Logan H., 191
Rosecrans, William, 117
Ruffin, Edmund, 16
Ruggles, Daniel, 49
Russia, 117, 204

Sabine Pass, 71
Saltville, Va., 206
Sam (slave), 85
Savannah, Ga., 58, 61, 63, 67, 82, 102, 108, 134, 182
Schweninger, Loren, 107
Scott, Alfred Lewis, 147, 149
Scott, Irby Goodwin, 80
Sea Islands, 109
Secessionville, S.C., 69
Second Confiscation Act, 132
Seddon, James, 65, 67–68, 77, 134, 136–38, 162
Semple, Henry, 130
Seven Days Battles, 23, 50, 57, 112
Seward, William, 15–16, 107, 170
Shaner, Joseph, 174
Sheehan-Dean, Aaron, 50
Sheffey, John Preston, 15
Shelby, Joseph O., 100, 185
Sheliha, Von, 73
Shenandoah Valley, 102, 127, 165
Sheridan, Phil, 127
Sherman, William T., 75–77, 116, 126–27, 132, 146, 152, 163, 166, 170, 178, 183
Shreveport, La., 181
Silent South, The (Cable), 209
Shiloh, Tenn., Battle of, 43, 54, 95, 110, 161
Shorter, John G., 46
Simpson, James, 99
Simpson, Tally, 86

Sinclair, James, 19
Sixth Virginia Infantry Regiment, 174–75
slaves: as body servants, 80–88, 101; colonization of, 24, 172; death of, 60, 89–90; disciplining of, 91–94; and estimates of wartime runaways, 107; as foragers, 85–86; health of, 66–67; hiring of, 89–90; as informants, 106; and insurrection scares, 16–17, 23, 46–47, 113–14; "loyalty" of, 105–8, 112, 121–22, 169, 206; and "Sambo" stereotype, 88, 151–52; and slave trade, 88, 94–95, 101, 128; and theft, 86–87; used as metaphor for army life, 37–42; value of, 96, 99
Slidell, John, 171
Smith, E. Kirby, 72, 137–38, 171
Smith, Gustavus W., 63
Smith, Ira J., 120
Smith, Thomas, 196, 199
Smith, William A., 67
Smith, William "Extra Billy," 74, 176
Social Relations in Our Southern States (Hundley), 35, 131
Soldiers Blue and Gray (Robertson), 3
Sons of Confederate Veterans, 192, 210
Sorrel, Moxley, 114
Southern Historical Society Papers, 193
Southern Negroes, 1861–1865 (Wiley), 2
Spanish American War, 198
Spanish Fort, 78
Special Orders No. 65, 62
Spence, Alex, 27, 82
Spotsylvania, Va., 147
Stapp, Joseph D., 175
Stedman, George, 128
Stephens, Alexander, 204, 209
Stephens, Winston, 131
Stewart (slave), 118–19
Stewart, William, 147
St. Martin's Parish, La., 17
Stone, Edmund F., 151
Stonewall Brigade, 14–15, 28, 163
Stowe, Harriet Beecher, 21–24
Strayhorn, Thomas, 102
Stuart, James Ward, 92
Stuart, Jeb, 14–15
Stuart, John Lane, 92
Stubbs, James, 53, 85, 97, 181
substitutes, 43–45, 47, 53, 67, 178

INDEX

Suderow, Bryce, 149
Surget, Eustace, 178

Taliaferro, Edwin, 118
Tarboro, N.C., 68
Tattnall, John, 133–34
Taylor, Grant, 93, 171
Taylor, Richard, 56, 74, 77, 83, 169–70, 195, 209
Taylor, Zachary, 35
Thirteenth Amendment, 1, 128, 167, 180
Thomas, Emory, 156
Thomson, Ruffin, 81, 90, 117
Thompson, M. Jeff, 16, 139, 142, 183–84
Tichenor, G. H., 44
Tilghman, Tench, 187
Tillman, Ben, 196
Tompkins, Christopher, 182
Toney, Marcus, 95, 191
Toon, Thomas, 84
Tracy, Edward Dorr, 22
Tredegar Iron Works, 14
Tripp, William H., 45–46, 109
Trueheart, Charles, 15, 151–52
Turner, Nat, 17, 21, 107, 113, 172
"Twenty Slave Law," 2, 6, 47–51
Tyler, John, Jr., 60, 170

Uncle Tom's Cabin, 21, 22, 92
United Confederate Veterans, 210
United Daughters of the Confederacy, 192–93

Van Buskirk, Phillip, 51–52
Vance, Zebulon, 67–68
Vardaman, James K., 196
Verdery, Eugene, 76, 81–82
Verdery, James Paul, 1, 101–2
Vermont, 197
Vesey, Denmark, 17, 34
Vicksburg, Miss., 26, 50, 54, 57–58, 62, 69, 71, 73, 81, 99, 117, 122
Voss, Frank, 17

Walker, Irvine C., 52, 171
Walker, William T., 161–62
War Department, Confederate, 60, 71, 118, 135, 139, 158, 178
Warlick, Lewis, 90
Washington, D.C., 47, 81, 111, 115, 125, 136
Washington, George, 14, 29, 36, 86, 184
Watkins, Sam, 42, 49–50, 52
Watson, Jonathan, 70
Watson, Robert, 42, 49
Watson, William, 113
Wayne, Henry Constantine, 14
Weeks, Alfred, 75
Weitz, Mark, 47
Wesley (slave), 84
Wetherington, Mark, 34
What They Fought For (McPherson), 4
What This Cruel War Was Over (Manning), 5
Wheeler, Joseph, 187
Whiting, William, 68
Wightman, John, 20
Wilderness, 147
Wiley, Bell, 2–4
Wiley, Samuel, 102–3
Williams, Robert Hamilton, 122
Williamsburg, Va., 59
Wilmington, N.C., 16, 58, 68, 170, 182
Wilson's Creek, Mo., 112
Wilson's Wharf (Fort Pocahontas), Va., 146, 206
Wingard, Simon P., 95–96
Wise, Henry A., 14, 26, 91, 113
Withers, William, 61
Wood, Thomas F., 22, 121
Woodward, C. Vann, 18, 207
Workman, John David, 17
Wright (slave), 86
Wright, Gavin, 33

Yates, Jerome, 90–91, 125
yeomen, 31–36, 48, 54, 206, 208
Yorktown, Va., 59–60, 93

A NATION DIVIDED: STUDIES IN THE CIVIL WAR ERA

Neither Ballots nor Bullets: Women Abolitionists and the Civil War
Wendy Hamand Venet

Black Confederates and Afro-Yankees in Civil War Virginia
Ervin L. Jordan Jr.

Longstreet's Aide: The Civil War Letters of Major Thomas J. Goree
Thomas W. Cutrer

Lee's Young Artillerist: William R. J. Pegram
Peter S. Carmichael

*Yankee Correspondence: Civil War Letters between
New England Soldiers and the Homefront*
Nina Silber and Mary Beth Sievens, editors

*Southern Rights: Political Prisoners and the Myth
of Confederate Constitutionalism*
Mark E. Neely Jr.

*Apostles of Disunion: Southern Secession Commissioners
and the Causes of the Civil War*
Charles B. Dew

Exile in Richmond: The Confederate Journal of Henri Garidel
Michael Bedout Chesson and Leslie Jean Roberts, editors

*Ashe County's Civil War: Community and Society
in the Appalachian South*
Martin Crawford

The War Hits Home: The Civil War in Southeastern Virginia
Brian Steel Wills

Lincoln's Tragic Admiral: The Life of Samuel Francis Du Pont
Kevin J. Weddle

A Separate Civil War: Communities in Conflict in the Mountain South
Jonathan Dean Sarris

Civil War Petersburg: Confederate City in the Crucible of War
A. Wilson Greene

*Take Care of the Living: Reconstructing Confederate
Veteran Families in Virginia*
Jeffrey W. McClurken

The Big House after Slavery:
Virginia Plantation Families and Their Postbellum Experiment
Amy Feely Morsman

The Enemy Within: Fears of Corruption in the Civil War North
Michael Thomas Smith

Civil War Talks: Further Reminiscences of
George S. Bernard and His Fellow Veterans
Hampton Newsome, John Horn, and John G. Selby, editors

Worth a Dozen Men: Women and Nursing in the Civil War South
Libra R. Hilde

Reconstructing the Campus: Higher Education
and the American Civil War
Michael David Cohen

Frederick Douglass: A Life in Documents
L. Diane Barnes, editor

Confederate Visions: Nationalism, Symbolism,
and the Imagined South in the Civil War
Ian Binnington

Marching Masters: Slavery, Race, and the
Confederate Army during the Civil War
Colin Edward Woodward

www.ingramcontent.com/pod-product-compliance
Lightning Source LLC
Chambersburg PA
CBHW031800220426
43662CB00007B/475